CARAVAGGIO IN FILM AND LITERATURE
POPULAR CULTURE'S APPROPRIATION OF A BAROQUE GENIUS

LEGENDA

LEGENDA, founded in 1995 by the European Humanities Research Centre of the University of Oxford, is now a joint imprint of the Modern Humanities Research Association and Routledge. Titles range from medieval texts to contemporary cinema and form a widely comparative view of the modern humanities, including works on Arabic, Catalan, English, French, German, Greek, Italian, Portuguese, Russian, Spanish, and Yiddish literature. An Editorial Board of distinguished academic specialists works in collaboration with leading scholarly bodies such as the Society for French Studies, the British Comparative Literature Association and the Association of Hispanists of Great Britain & Ireland.

MHRA

The Modern Humanities Research Association (MHRA) encourages and promotes advanced study and research in the field of the modern humanities, especially modern European languages and literature, including English, and also cinema. It also aims to break down the barriers between scholars working in different disciplines and to maintain the unity of humanistic scholarship in the face of increasing specialization. The Association fulfils this purpose primarily through the publication of journals, bibliographies, monographs and other aids to research.

LONDON AND NEW YORK

Routledge is a global publisher of academic books, journals and online resources in the humanities and social sciences. Founded in 1836, it has published many of the greatest thinkers and scholars of the last hundred years, including Adorno, Einstein, Russell, Popper, Wittgenstein, Jung, Bohm, Hayek, McLuhan, Marcuse and Sartre. Today Routledge is one of the world's leading academic publishers in the Humanities and Social Sciences. It publishes thousands of books and journals each year, serving scholars, instructors, and professional communities worldwide.

www.routledge.com

ITALIAN PERSPECTIVES

Editorial Committee
Professor Simon Gilson, University of Warwick (General Editor)
Dr Francesca Billiani, University of Manchester
Dr Manuele Gragnolati, Somerville College, Oxford
Dr Catherine Keen, University College London
Professor Martin McLaughlin, Magdalen College, Oxford

Founding Editors
Professor Zygmunt Barański and Professor Anna Laura Lepschy

In the light of growing academic interest in Italy and the reorganization of many university courses in Italian along interdisciplinary lines, this book series, founded now continuing under the Legenda imprint, aims to bring together different scholarly perspectives on Italy and its culture. *Italian Perspectives* publishes books and collections of essays on any period of Italian literature, language, history, culture, politics, art, and media, as well as studies which take an interdisciplinary approach and are methodologically innovative.

RECENT TITLES IN THIS SERIES

12. *Speaking Out and Silencing*, ed. by Anna Cento Bull and Adalgisa Giorgio
13. *From Florence to the Heavenly City: The Poetry of Citizenship in Dante*, by Claire E. Honess
14. *Orality and Literacy in Modern Italian Culture*, ed. by Michael Caesar and Marina Spunta
15. *Pastoral Drama in Early Modern Italy: The Making of a New Genre*, by Lisa Sampson
16. *Sweet Thunder: Music and Libretti in 1960s Italy*, by Vivienne Suvini-Hand
17. *Il teatro di Eduardo De Filippo*, by Donatella Fischer
18. *Imagining Terrorism*, ed. by Pierpaolo Antonello and Alan O'Leary
19. *Boccaccio and the Book: Production and Reading in Italy 1340-1520*, by Rhiannon Daniels
20. *Ugo Foscolo and English Culture*, by Sandra Parmegiani
21. *The Printed Media in Fin-de-siècle Italy: Publishers, Writers, and Readers*, ed. by Ann Hallamore Caesar, Gabriella Romani, and Jennifer Burns
22. *Giraffes in the Garden of Italian Literature*, by Deborah Amberson
23. *Remembering Aldo Moro*, ed. by Ruth Glynn and Giancarlo Lombardi
24. *Disrupted Narratives: Illness, Silence and Identity*, by Emma Bond
25. *Dante and Epicurus: A Dualistic Vision of Secular and Spiritual Fulfilment*, by George Corbett
26. *Edoardo Sanguineti: Literature, Ideology and the Avant-Garde*, ed. by Paolo Chirumbolo and John Picchione
27. *The Tradition of the Actor-Author in Italian Theatre*, ed. by Donatella Fischer
28. *Leopardi's Nymphs*, by Fabio A. Camilletti
29. *Gadda and Beckett: Storytelling, Subjectivity and Fracture*, by Katrin Wehling-Giorgi
30. *Caravaggio in Film and Literature*, by Laura Rorato

Managing Editor: Dr Graham Nelson, 41 Wellington Square, Oxford OX1 2JF, UK
www.legendabooks.com

Ottavio Leoni, *Caravaggio* (c. 1621), Florence: Biblioteca Marucelliana

Caravaggio in Film and Literature

Popular Culture's Appropriation of a Baroque Genius

❖

Laura Rorato

LONDON AND NEW YORK

2014

First published 2014 by Modern Humanities Research Association and Routledge

2 Park Square, Milton Park, Abingdon, Oxfordshire OX14 4RN
52 Vanderbilt Avenue, New York, NY 10017

Routledge is an imprint of the Taylor & Francis Group, an informa business

First issued in paperback 2020

Copyright © Modern Humanities Research Association and Taylor & Francis 2014

All rights reserved. No part of this book may be reprinted or reproduced or utilised in any form or by any electronic, mechanical, or other means, now known or hereafter invented, including photocopying and recording, or in any information storage or retrieval system, without permission in writing from the publishers.

Notice:
Product or corporate names may be trademarks or registered trademarks, and are used only for identification and explanation without intent to infringe.

ISBN: 978-1-909662-00-1 (hbk)
ISBN: 978-0-367-59991-1 (pbk)

CONTENTS

Acknowledgements		ix
List of Illustrations		x
Introduction: Michelangelo Merisi da Caravaggio — A Self-Perpetuating Myth		1
1	Caravaggio in Context	15
	The socio-historical context	16
	How does Caravaggio fit in this context? Key events in Merisi's early life	18
	Rome and other key events in Caravaggio's life	19
	Caravaggio's fortune	31
2	Michelangelo Merisi's Lives: The 'Painter as Character' Genre	40
	Caravaggio *pittore maledetto* versus Caravaggio the hero of the poor	42
	The author/painter as character genre	47
	Michelangelo Merisi and his lives: a case study	49
3	Caravaggio, Crime Fiction, and the Noir	69
	Mean Streets: Scorsese and Caravaggio	74
	Margaret Truman: *Murder at the National Gallery*	80
	Neil Griffiths: *Saving Caravaggio*	86
	Forgery and revenge: Fabio Baldassarri's *Il mistero del Caravaggio* and Noel Charney's *The Art Thief*	90
	When truth is stranger than fiction: Jonathan Harr's *The Lost Painting*	97
	Gilda Piersanti's *Jaune Caravage*	101
4	Caravaggio and Homoerotic Concerns	119
	Dominique Fernandez's *Dans la main de l'ange*	120
	Thom Gunn	133
	Caravaggio and Derek Jarman	144
	Samuel M. Steward's *The Caravaggio Shawl*	160
5	Deleuzian Folds: Michael Ondaatje's and Anthony Minghella's Caravaggio	175
	David Caravaggio: an artist in disguise	176
	Key pictorial intertextual references	188
	Conclusion: Caravaggio and the Neo-Baroque — Some Final Considerations	203
	Bibliography	209
	Index	221

*To Heinz, for having followed me all the way
through this long and perilous journey
&
To Ricco who was looking forward
to the publication of this volume*

ACKNOWLEDGEMENTS

Given the nature of this project, I am indebted to a vast number of people and I am grateful to them all, even if they may not be included in this list. However, first and foremost, I would like to express my gratitude to the AHRC for having believed in this project and having made its realization possible. Also, I would like to thank the following friends: Anna Laura and Giulio Lepschy for their constant support, particularly in the initial stages of this work; Mary Heeley for having patiently read all the draft chapters and for her encouraging remarks; Linda Shortt and Claudio Brancaleoni for always being there for me and having put up even with my bleakest moods. Words are not sufficient to express the extent of my gratitude to Heinz Schmidt, which is why I have dedicated the book to him.

My colleagues and friends Jordi Cornella Detrell, Helena Miguelez Carballeira, Simona Storchi, and Adalgisa Giorgio should also be thanked for having looked at various sections of this volume and for their helpful advice. I am very grateful to Lucia Rinaldi for having lent me various books on crime fiction and the noir. Without her help, Chapter 3 would have taken a lot longer to write. I would also like to thank Andrew Hiscock for sharing with me his knowledge of the Renaissance period. Since my French is rather rusty, I am very grateful to Zara Fergyson and Stephanie James for their expert linguistic advice. My parents Anna and Claudio must also be mentioned. For years, they patiently collected even the slightest piece of information on Caravaggio to be published in the Italian press and sent it to me. I could not have had better research assistants.

I would also like to thank all the speakers and the participants at the 2011 conference on Caravaggio which took place in London at the Institute of Germanic and Romance Studies, including my PhD students, who worked extremely hard to make sure the event run smoothly. Finally, I am grateful to Graham Nelson of Legenda for promptly and patiently dealing with all my queries, to Caroline Lynch for replacing me whilst I was on study leave, and last, but certainly not least, Linda Jones of the College of Arts and Humanities at Bangor University for her invaluable help with various technical issues. And, as a caffeine addict, I must not forget to express my gratitude to the staff of Bulkeley's Hotel in Beaumaris for providing me with the best cappuccino in North Wales.

L.R., Bangor, March 2014

LIST OF ILLUSTRATIONS

Frontispiece. Ottavio Leoni, *Caravaggio* (c. 1621), Florence: Biblioteca Marucelliana.
Fig. 1.1. Caravaggio, *Amor Vincit Omnia* (c. 1600), Berlin: Gemäldegalerie.
Fig. 1.2. Caravaggio, *Lute Player* (1595), St Petersburg: Hermitage Museum.
Fig. 1.3. Caravaggio, *Boy Bitten by a Lizard* (1593–94). Reproduced by courtesy of the National Gallery, London.
Fig. 2.1. Caravaggio, *David with the Head of Goliath* (1606–07), Rome: Galleria Borghese.
Fig. 2.2. Caravaggio, *The Incredulity of St Thomas* (1601), Potsdam: Sanssouci Palace (Picture Gallery).
Fig. 3.1. Caravaggio, *Judith Beheading Holofernes* (1598–99), Rome: Galleria Nazionale d'Arte Antica.
Fig. 3.2. Caravaggio, *Bacchus* (1595–96), Flornce: Uffizi Gallery.
Fig. 3.3. Caravaggio, *The Taking of Christ* (c. 1602), Dublin: National Gallery of Ireland.
Fig. 3.4. Caravaggio, *Basket of Fruit* (1596), Milan: Pinacoteca Ambrosiana.
Fig. 3.5. Caravaggio, *The Calling of St Matthew* (1599–1600), Rome: Contarelli Chapel in San Luigi dei Francesi.
Fig. 4.1. Caravaggio, *The Beheading of St John the Baptist* (1608), Malta: Valletta, St John's Cathedral.
Fig. 4.2. Caravaggio, *The Conversion of St Paul* (c. 1600–01), Rome: Odaleschi Collection.
Fig. 4.3. Caravaggio, *The Conversion of St Paul* (c. 1600–01), Rome: Cerasi Chapel in Santa Maria del Popolo.
Fig. 4.4. Caravaggio, *The Raising of Lazarus* (c. 1608–09), Messina: Museo Nazionale.
Fig. 4.5. Caravaggio, *The Sacrifice of Isaac* (c. 1603), Florence: Uffizi Gallery.
Fig. 4.6. Caravaggio, *Medusa* (1597), Florence: Uffizi Gallery.
Fig. 4.7. Caravaggio, *The Martyrdom of St Matthew* (c. 1599–1600), Rome: San Luigi dei Francesi.
Fig. 5.1. Caravaggio, *St Jerome Writing* (c. 1605–06), Rome: Galleria Borghese.
Fig. 5.2. Caravaggio, *Narcissus* (1597–98), Rome: Galleria Nazionale d'Arte Antica.

INTRODUCTION

Michelangelo Merisi da Caravaggio:
A Self-Perpetuating Myth

> Caravaggio is the most renowned Old Master of recent times. More articles, books, exhibitions, films and novels have been devoted to him than to all of his contemporaries combined.
>
> PATRICK HUNT, *Caravaggio*, p. ix

The idea of writing a book about fictional representations of Caravaggio came to me as far back as 2004 when I was writing a paper on art as inauguration in Pino Di Silvestro's novel *La fuga, la sosta* for the Romance Studies Colloquium on the theme of 'Celebration', which took place in Newark, New Jersey. Di Silvestro's book can be considered a 'celebration' of a fragment of Caravaggio's life, namely the few weeks the painter spent in Syracuse, between the beginning of October and the end of November 1608 when, after fleeing Malta, he landed in Sicily and painted his controversial *The Burial of St Lucy*.[1] It was on that occasion that I discovered that Di Silvestro's interest in Caravaggio was part of a much larger worldwide phenomenon. It became very quickly apparent to me that although fictional responses to the painter's life and works have been a fairly regular feature over the centuries, during the second half of the twentieth century, but particularly since the 1980s and even more so during the 2000s, we see a real boom in the interest in Caravaggio outside the world of art history, a trend which is still very much alive today. Despite this wealth of material, it also became clear that there was a gap in the existing Caravaggio scholarship. To date, no real effort has been made to study the impact of the Baroque painter across various artistic genres and in different contexts. Whilst the influence of Caravaggio on contemporary painters and photographers is well documented thanks to the seminal work of Mieke Bal, studies of responses to Caravaggio's life and works in film or literature are rarer and usually tend to focus solely on an individual artist (e.g. Martin Scorsese, Derek Jarman, and Michel Ondaatje). This monograph addresses such a gap in the field of Caravaggio studies. Given this dearth of scholarship, a panoramic overview of the appropriation of Caravaggio by popular culture seemed most fitting. The true extent of the Caravaggio myth can be fully appreciated only by bringing together a series of case studies that include authors and directors from different countries (Canada, France, Great Britain, Italy, Norway, and the United States) and literary and filmic texts belonging to different genres (e.g. fictional biographies/docudramas, crime fiction/ noirs, homoerotic literature/film and postcolonial literature). This approach reveals how the interaction of popular culture with the old master of Baroque painting leads not only to a better understanding of certain aspects of postmodernism and neo-Baroque poetics, but also to a deeper appreciation of Caravaggio's art. As Bal work demonstrated,

> the images [and we could add the texts] of today present us with a 'Caravaggio' who is entirely ours [...] an irreversible *new* Old Master, who changes the Caravaggio we thought we knew as well as the historical illusion that we knew him.[2]

From a methodological point of view, owing to the sheer volume of the existing material across the various genres, it was impossible to offer a comprehensive picture of everything that is available on the market. In order to strike a balance between variety and depth of analysis it was necessary to work with case studies. When selecting the texts and films for the case studies I decided to concentrate mainly on works entirely devoted (or at least containing major references) to Caravaggio or whose references to the Lombard painter had a wider significance in the entire production of that particular artist (as the case of Thom Gunn in Chapter 4 reveals). In terms of genres, I decided to pay particular attention to fictional biographies and detective fiction, not only because most of the fictional works available on the market belong to one of these categories, but also because they raise interesting questions about the aforementioned relationship between the Baroque and neo-Baroque/Postmodernism. Also, according to David Carrier, 'Caravaggio's recent rise to fame is due, in part, to gay politics',[3] and indeed homoerotic fiction and cinema offer some of the most interesting examples of contemporary responses to Caravaggio. Finally, I wanted to include a very different appropriation of Caravaggio in the context of postcolonial studies, which is why I decided to devote an entire chapter to Michael Ondaatje's novels *In the Skin of a Lion* (1987) and *The English Patient* (1992), and to Anthony Minghella's adaptation of the latter. What emerges from this monograph is that, whilst Caravaggio's influence on cinema is undoubtedly significant,[4] it is even more prominent in literature. This is visible in the case studies selected for each of the chapters as they comprise several literary works and only one cinematic example. Compared to writers, directors and filmmakers favour a more oblique engagement with the painter, focusing mainly on his use of light, his corporeality, and the sense of melodrama that we find in many of his paintings.[5] Naturally, this does not mean that Caravaggio's legacy on these artists is less important, but, for the sake of consistency, I decided to use only material containing direct quotations of the Lombard painter, as it is in these examples that the true extent of the Caravaggio myth is revealed. Although there is no shortage of evidence of the impact of Caravaggio on theatre, this falls outside the scope of this work and might be explored in future publications. However, it is worth mentioning that the 400th anniversary of the painter's death was marked by a proliferation of plays and theatrical performances of all kinds, including the experimental work for children and adolescents by the theatre company Le Nuvole in Naples, the *tableaux vivants* of Malatheatre, also based in Naples, and the ballets of the Lyric Dance Company in Florence.[6]

Even though, undoubtedly, the 1951 exhibition in Milan curated by Longhi was instrumental in perpetuating the myth of the Lombard painter, its success and that of other subsequent exhibitions devoted to Caravaggio were not sufficient to justify the sudden explosion of fictional works engaging with his life, or some aspect of his oeuvre, that began in the 1980s and escalated drastically at the beginning of the twenty-first century. This monograph argues that a complex series of circumstances, some relating to the painter's life and works and some transcending it, contributed to Caravaggio's ever-increasing popularity. The first significant wave of fictional interest in Caravaggio which began in the 1980s was partially fostered by the success of the gay liberation movements of the 1970s, but it was not confined to homoerotic literature.[7] The more recent phase, on the other hand, is the result of a renewed interest in realism which characterized the end of the twentieth and the beginning of the twenty-first century, and which, in many cases, as Chapter 2 and Chapter 3 reveal, manifested itself in the revitalization of certain genres, such as biography, historical docudramas, crime fiction, and the noir. However, the single most important overarching factor capable of explaining the current 'Caravaggio mania' is the fascination with neo-Baroque aesthetics that has characterized the twentieth and twenty-first centuries. As argued by Angela Ndalianis, during the last decades of the twentieth century and the beginning of the twenty-first, 'a neo-Baroque logic has taken a deeper root and has been nurtured within a global postmodern context', becoming so ingrained in our culture that it can no longer be reduced to 'mere style or retro-fascination with the Baroque'.[8] Furthermore, when considering the development of neo-Baroque aesthetics, we must not forget the central role played by Baroque painting. With its 'multiple and shifting viewpoints', Baroque painting forced the viewer's gaze to move 'restlessly into and across the surface of (often vast) compositional spaces', transforming the viewing experience into something 'similar to a process of deconstruction' ('Neo-Baroques', p. 270). Also, according to Scrivano, the viewer of a Baroque painting, unable to grasp specific details, is forced to take in everything or nothing and to rely on appearances as if they were some sort of reality,[9] thus anticipating the Postmodern/neo-Baroque topos of the impossibility of distinguishing between appearances and reality.

Regarding Caravaggio, we could argue that, without the twentieth century's renewed interest in the Baroque, his art would never have been fully appreciated and his myth would never have reached its current proportions. Although nowadays associating Caravaggio with the Baroque seems natural, this was not always the case. Given his lifespan (1571–1610), he could be seen as belonging to the Renaissance, but his style of painting differs from those of High Renaissance and Mannerism. Hibbard, in commenting on Caravaggio's *Supper at Emmaus* (1600–1601), explains clearly why this is the case. *Supper at Emmaus* is interesting, he argues, because if on the one hand it shows that Caravaggio had studied the masters of High Renaissance, on the other, the painting 'does not belong with the relatively naïve dramas of the 1590s'.[10] According to Hibbard, the spectator is drawn into the painted religious drama and although this kind of illusionism is also typical of Mannerism, mannerist artists are interested in virtuosity for the sake of it as 'the manner tends to become the meaning, the subject merely a motif' (p. 78). Caravaggio, instead, penetrates 'the picture plane not as an exhibitionist but as a dramatist who seizes our attention in order to illuminate the meaning of the story within the frame' (ibid.). Yet, during the first half of the twentieth century, some art historians (e.g. Marangoni and Berenson) were reluctant to classify Caravaggio as Baroque. Longhi was one of the first scholars to argue against the tendency to interpret Caravaggio as an epilogue of the Renaissance or, even worse, a classic. Longhi was particularly critical of Marangoni's position, which he considered to be misleading. In his review of Marangoni's 1917 article 'Valori mal noti e trascurati della pittura italiana del Seicento in alcuni pittori di "Natura morta"', Longhi argued: 'io non credo si possa parlare sul serio di plasticità e di volume in Caravaggio, se non si vul correre il rischio di crederlo per davvero un quattro o un cinquecentista' [I do not think that we can seriously talk of volume and plasticity in Caravaggio unless we are prepared to run the risk of really mistaking him for an exponent of the Quattrocento or Cinquecento].[11] Apart from Longhi, other major scholars who insisted on the importance of studying Caravaggio in the context of the Baroque were Mahon, Cinotti, and Calvesi. In defence of those who were sceptical about labelling Caravaggio Baroque, we must keep in mind that this term began to be applied to the visual arts only at the end of the eighteenth century, as before that time it had mainly negative connotations and was considered to be 'the superlative form of "bizarre"'.[12] Despite a renewed interest in seventeenth-century art, scholars were initially unwilling to use concepts 'that had no part to play in the highly sophisticated discourse of the period' (Cropper and Dempsey, p. 494).

Interestingly, one of the key arguments used by art historians who see Caravaggio as belonging to the Baroque is his realism. John Rupert Martin, for instance, presents naturalism as one of the essential characteristics of the Baroque. The most useful way of approaching the Baroque, particularly when dealing with representational arts, he argues, is to look at it as 'a succession of phases in an international development'.[13] Martin divides the Baroque into three stages (Early Baroque, High Baroque, and Late Baroque), and in defining the Early Baroque he identifies Italy as its birthplace, Caravaggio as one of its most prominent figures, and naturalism as one of its key features (pp. 28–30). Yet, although most art historians would agree with a definition of Caravaggio as a realist painter, his kind of realism is far from uncontroversial.[14] His realist elements (dirty feet and fingernails, skin conditions, overripe fruit, etc.) in some ways go against the illusionism of verisimilitude that we associate with realist art as Caravaggio does not let us forget that what we are looking at is not a direct reproduction of reality but its representation. Even mythological or supernatural visions are represented through the filter of everyday experience so that, as Cropper notes, 'his angels and cupids, while undoubtedly *veri*, or true to the reality of experience, lack verisimilitude — they do not convince us that they actually are angels and cupids'.[15] In this sense, of course, Caravaggio can be seen as a 'precursor' of postmodernism. His idiosyncratic form of realism and the tendency of many of his works to blur the boundaries between sacred and profane, between inside and outside, and the fact that they resist a single interpretation and challenge fixed notions of identity, make Caravaggio particularly appealing to artists willing to explore the performative element in questions of identity and sexuality and to challenge traditional grand narratives.

Of all the aforementioned characteristics of Caravaggio's realism, the most controversial one was his tendency 'to avoid, or at least to minimize, the presence of the supernatural or the mystical', which was probably the reason why some of his paintings were rejected.[16] Paintings like *Death of the Virgin*, the first *St Matthew*, or the now lost *Resurrection of Christ* were shocking because they stressed 'the uncompromising *earthiness* of the saintly figures' (Varriano, p. 130) and because his models were ordinary people (a prostitute who had drowned in the Tiber, in the case of *Death of the Virgin*) who could be easily recognized by his contemporaries. I would argue that these features contribute to Caravaggio's ever-increasing popularity in the twenty-first century when the philosophical/cultural scene is dominated by debates on the end of postmodernism and a return to stronger forms of realism.[17] In this context, we see a resurfacing of the image of Caravaggio as the hero of the poor or, in other words, the 'populist' image of Caravaggio, which had already been promoted by Longhi in 1951, but which had a much longer tradition. Already during his lifetime, in fact, it became clear that Caravaggio's works had the power to appeal not only to his wealthy patrons and buyers but also to ordinary people. Baglione, for instance, commenting on Caravaggio's *Madonna di Loreto* (1604–05) in his *Le vite de' scultori, pittori et architetti* (1642) claimed:

> In the first chapel on the left in the church of Sant' Agostino, he painted the Madonna of Loreto from life with two pilgrims; one of them has muddy feet and the other wears a soiled and torn cap; and because of this pettiness in the details of a grand painting the public made a great fuss over it. (p. 46)

In 1834, Laviron would express very similar opinions:

> Ses ouvrages fixèrent puissamment l'attention de toutes les classes de la société, et de celles là surtout qui d'ordinaire sont les plus indifférentes au succès d'une oeuvre d'art. En effet il avait trouvé la peinture du peuple, la peinture qui peut être facilement comprise et jugée par tous parce qu'elle donne à chaque chose toute la puissance d'expression qu'elle peut avoir dans la nature, et ne sacrifie jamais rien de la vérité entière des objects.[18]
>
> [His works powerfully attracted the attention of all social classes, particularly of those who are usually indifferent to the success of a work of art. In actual fact, he had discovered popular painting, a style of painting that can be easily understood and judged by everyone, because it bestows upon each single thing the same force of expression it could have in nature, and does not sacrifice any aspect of the whole truth of the objects.]

As we will see, Caravaggio's emphasis on emotions (another distinctive feature of the Baroque) and his ability to appeal to a wide range of people are particularly interesting for those contemporary artists who want to explore new forms of non-ideological engagement but who believe that art can help us make the world a better place.

Other aspects of the Baroque and of Caravaggio's paintings which are to be found in Postmodernism/neo-Baroque are the tendency towards self-reference and a passion for ambiguous and distorted quotations and repetition. Such tools, according to the Italian semiotician Omar Calabrese, allow the artist to use the past creatively, thus renewing it. By playing with various fragments of the past,

Calabrese argues, 'the artist restores ambiguity, density and opaqueness, relating its aspects and signification to the present'.[19] In this way, Calabrese reminds us, modernity can be conceived as 'the concurrence of all epochs and the coexistence of the possible with the real' (p. 182), a view that is particularly relevant to contemporary reappropriations of Caravaggio by popular culture, as the following chapters will show.

Looking at Caravaggio through the Postmodern/neo-Baroque lens enables us to understand more clearly his popularity outside the world of art history. The nature of the works devoted to the Lombard painter confirms the postmodern predilection for meta-biographical narratives, historical docudramas, crime fiction, and the noir. Caravaggio is an ideal figure in this context as some of the darker aspects of his life can be interpreted differently so that they are either signs of his violent temper and pathological personality, or examples of a particular political climate and a reflection of the violence of Renaissance society. In this way Caravaggio 'speaks' to the two strands of postmodernism, the more engaged one promoted by critics with a Marxist background, like Jameson, and the more commercial one that stresses the notions of playfulness and entertainment. In our celebrity/scandal-obsessed culture, of course, the appeal of Caravaggio's violent and eccentric lifestyle is very strong, and so is the legacy of the Romantic myth of the link between madness and genius to which the image of the 'pittore maledetto' is strongly indebted.[20] Art historians like Stone (2002) have convincingly argued that through his self-portraits, particularly those of *David with the Head of Goliath* and *Medusa*, in which the artist presents his own severed head to the viewers, Caravaggio contributed to the development of the theory of the disturbed and gender-confused personality. Interestingly, Caravaggio occasionally features in articles on schizophrenia and other mental disorders like depression or 'black-hole' personality, and books or exhibition catalogues devoted to the Lombard painter are reviewed in scientific journals.[21] Although the idea of approaching Caravaggio from a psychological point of view is often criticized, Cropper and Dempsey argue that:

> It might gain some historical validity [...] by taking into account 17th-century attempts to characterize Caravaggio and other artists according to a theory of the humors. That theory is after all a primitive means of analyzing personality according to psychological temperament. In the case of Caravaggio, the imbalance of humors is certainly toward the choleric (not melancholic). (p. 498)

However, seventeenth-century sources are often dismissed as mere fables by art historians and this trend has contributed to perpetuation of the Caravaggio myth (Cropper and Dempsey, p. 496). According to Cropper and Dempsey, the fact that eminent Caravaggio scholars like Sir Denis Mahon, Mia Cinotti, or Giovanni Previtali, who usually represent very different critical positions, share the opinion that Caravaggio's contemporary sources (particularly Bellori and Malvasia) were inaccurate and unreliable, instead of promoting a more objective study of seventeenth-century art has encouraged the proliferation of further theories about the Lombard painter (and some of his contemporaries). Cropper and Dempsey maintain that by dismissing earlier interpretations of Caravaggio's life and works as fables, contemporary scholars feel entitled to reject what they do not agree with without 'having to refute in detail' (pp. 496–97).

Finally, we must also focus on some shifts in the art industry and in the way exhibitions are conceived as these factors have had a major impact on Caravaggio's fortune beyond the world of art history. For instance, in recent years, exhibition curators invited artists from fields other than painting to give talks or stage performances inspired by Caravaggio (Dario Fo and Franca Rame for the 2003 exhibition in Rome), or to write short stories or poems on aspects of Merisi's life and works (Camilleri for the 2006 Düsseldorf exhibition and the author of children's books Antonella Ossorio for the 2004 Naples exhibition). Film nights (London 2005) and musical evenings (Barcelona 2005) inspired by the Lombard painter have also become a common corollary of major exhibitions.[22] These are just a few examples of a significant trend in furthering the appropriation of Caravaggio by popular culture. I would argue that Ndalianis's comments on the impact of digital technologies on the film industry are also relevant to the art industry. The fact that works of art readily available on computer screens has forced the art industry to diversify and, like the film industry, to find 'new convergences between different entertainment media' ('Neo-Baroques', p. 4; *Neo-Baroque Poetics*, p. 25) in order to reduce risk and maximize profit. The various satellite events organized around exhibitions and the merchandise sold in the museum shops blur the boundaries between traditionally close spaces like those of museums and art galleries and the outside world in ways that are similar to the Baroque obsession with expanding spatial parameters, thus confirming the omnipresence of neo-Baroque poetics in our era. The huge number of viewers which all major art exhibitions seem to attract today, and which in Caravaggio's case reached 11,000 people in a single day,[23] should be seen as an example of what Perniola calls 'the expansion and complication of leisure time', a feature that began in the 1980s and 'was widely expressed in the recovery of traditional forms of painting, literature, architecture and music' (p. 3).

In terms of structure, this book consists of five main chapters and a conclusion. Except for the first and the last chapters, all the others are devoted to specific genres (fictional biographies, crime fiction and the noir, and homoerotic literature and film). Chapter 1 consists of two parts, which set Caravaggio in context. While the first part centres on biographical and historical details offering an overview of some key moments in Caravaggio's life and of the major events that shaped his era, the second part focuses on the most controversial features of his art and on Caravaggio's fortune over the centuries, with particular emphasis on the twentieth and twenty-first centuries. The debates surrounding the 1951 exhibition in Milan, where for the first time almost all the then-known works by Caravaggio were gathered together, are particularly interesting from the perspective of this study. The event generated a wealth of new critical material and an unprecedented scholarly interest in the Lombard painter. Despite its tremendous success, however, the exhibition attracted fierce criticism and Longhi (the curator) was accused of not only encouraging a 'populist' image of Caravaggio, but also of having turned the baroque painter into a kind of soap opera character. As Chapters 2 and 3 reveal, this so-called 'populist' image of Caravaggio was destined to survive and continually reappears in popular culture, particularly in fictional biographies where the dramatic and entertaining qualities of the hero are often more important than his historical credibility. We can identify another key reason for Caravaggio's current popularity by studying art-historical debates as they show that his art addresses a series of issues that are as relevant today as they were during his lifetime such as 'the preoccupation with spontaneous violence, the allure of ambivalent sexuality, the expression of doubt in matters of faith and salvation, and the immersion of the artist in his own imaginative creations' (Hunt, p. ix).

After having introduced the context and the protagonist of this book it seemed appropriate to proceed with contemporary representations of Caravaggio's life, which is why I decided to devote Chapter 2 to fictional biographies. By covering a wide range of authors, differing in age, nationality, background, and writing styles, this chapter stresses the omnipresence of the biographical genre, which, as Ossorio's text illustrates, extends to children's literature. The sample consists of Dominique Fernandez's *La course à l'abîme* (2003), Atle Næss's *Doubting Thomas* (1997), Andrea Camilleri's *Il colore del sole* (2007), Rita Guidi's *Il gigante perduto* (2004), Antonella Ossorio's *L'angelo della luce: Il giovane Caravaggio sogna il suo destino* (2004), and the 2006 docudrama *Caravaggio* produced by RAI Fiction and directed by Angelo Longoni.

The analysis of the aforementioned set of works shows how a series of factors contributed to the sudden proliferation of fictional biographies or biographical films devoted to Caravaggio. In order to understand this trend, one needs to engage with three sets of questions: (1) a general one concerning the popularity of the biographical/autobiographical genres; (2) a more specific one regarding the reasons behind the choice of Caravaggio as a subject matter for many of these works; (3) one relating to changes in the art industry. Whilst the first can be understood mainly in terms of a need to return to narrative and to reaffirm the subject in the era of 'weak thought', when such concepts are viewed with suspicion, the second set of questions demands that we look beyond the painter's biography, taking into account the rhetorical construction of his paintings and the role he himself played in the construction of one of the most popular myths about his persona, that of the 'pittore maledetto'. Finally, the boom in the production of art fiction is determined by changes in the attitude of museum and art gallery curators, who see in this genre a tool to boost revenues and to attract new visitors to their exhibitions, thus building a bridge between people and art and opening their institutions to the masses.

After fictional biographies, the most popular genre regarding responses to Caravaggio's life and works is that of crime fiction and Chapter 3 is devoted to *Caravaggio, Crime Fiction and the Noir*. As in the previous chapter, the case studies consist mainly of works published between the late 1990s and the first decade of the twenty-first century, apart from one cinematic exception, Martin Scorsese's film *Mean Streets* (1973). Such an exception seemed justified on two grounds: first, as a way of illustrating the link between the Hollywood tradition of *film noir* and hard-boiled texts, and second, as a further proof of Caravaggio's influence on cinema. The texts included are: *Murder at the National Gallery* (1996) by the American crime fiction writer and daughter of former US president Margaret Truman; *Il mistero del*

Caravaggio (2003) by Fabio Baldassarri; *The Lost Painting* (2005) by the American author Jonathan Harr; *Saving Caravaggio* (2006) by the English writer Neil Griffiths; *The Art Thief* (2007) by one of the world's leading experts on art crime and founding director of the Rome-based international Association for Research into Crimes against Art (ARCA), the young American scholar Noah Charney; and, finally, the 2008 novel by the Italo-French author Gilda Piersanti, *Jaune Caravage*. As seen in Chapter 2, what this sample reveals is how the interest in Caravaggio is a worldwide phenomenon that cannot be reduced to just a morbid fascination with the painter's violent life.

Whether we look at art-crime thrillers, noirs, or texts belonging to both genres (e.g. Baldassarri's), all the case studies endeavour to offer comments on various problems affecting our contemporary globalized world. These texts are often characterized by a shift towards the fantastic as a strategy for dealing with extreme violence and portraying evil as the non-place of our societies, thus confirming a recent trend in noir literature highlighted by La Porta.[24] As for the role of Caravaggio in the aforementioned works, apart from the obvious appeal of his dark and mysterious personality, it is the painter's ability to challenge fixed traditional boundaries (e.g. sacred/profane; life/death; inside/outside, etc.) that makes him interesting for writers and directors willing to engage with crime fiction and the noir. It is no coincidence that the most quoted of his paintings in this context is *David with the Head of Goliath*. Not only does this painting blur the boundaries between victim and victimizer but it also raises interesting questions about guilt and punishment and offers the potential for turning a noir or crime story into a philosophical or moral tale.

David with the Head of Goliath, of course, addresses also the issues of death and sexuality and is frequently quoted in homoerotic fiction and film. Caravaggio and homoeroticism is the topic of Chapter 4. One of the most controversial and most debated aspects of Caravaggio's life is the question of his sexuality. Despite the lack of concrete evidence capable of proving whether Caravaggio was heterosexual, homosexual, or bisexual, and the awareness that the phenomenon of homosexuality as we know it today is a nineteenth-century concept, there is no doubt that some of his early paintings are very sensual and could be interpreted in homoerotic terms. This chapter argues that, regardless of Caravaggio's actual sexual inclinations, what appeals to contemporary gay authors is the anti-bourgeois features of his works on the one hand and, on the other, the ability of his boy paintings to capture the liminal state between identities. Furthermore, Caravaggio's capacity to combine a depiction of the link between sexuality and death (e.g. *David with the Head of Goliath*) with a lyrical element offers gay artists an ideal platform for exploring different notions of homosexual love. The case study selected for this section consists of four fictional works: the 1982 French novel *Dans la main de l'ange* by Dominique Fernandez, the 1961 poem 'In Santa Maria del Popolo' by Tom Gunn, the 1986 film *Caravaggio* by Derek Jarman, and the 1989 novel *The Caravaggio Shawl* by the American author Samuel M. Steward. The first two texts use Caravaggio as an anti-bourgeois hero in order to stress the need to rebel against authority and those forces within society that demand a strict adhesion to pre-established norms. The last two examples use

Caravaggio and his paintings to raise questions about gender and sexuality. Of course, such features are not mutually exclusive as, by problematizing gender, one inevitably questions notions of authority and patriarchal structures, and the need to rebel against the normalizing forces of society usually leads to the questioning of gender and identity. It is just a matter of emphasis. Despite their differences, in fact, the above works share many common aspects: an interest in love, in the relationship between power and desire, sadomasochism, life and death, and the body as a sight for the production of meaning.

Many of the themes listed above (particularly those of life and death, power and desire, and the body) are also relevant to Chapter 5, which looks at Caravaggio from a postcolonial perspective. This chapter focuses on two novels by Michael Ondaatje, *In the Skin of a Lion* (1987) and *The English Patient* (1992), and the 1996 filmic adaptation of the latter by Anthony Minghella. It shows how Caravaggio has been used for reflections on the power of art in our contemporary world and to articulate some postcolonial concerns such as the tension between master narrative and alternative story, the efficiency of mimicry as a strategy of appropriation and resistance[25] when living in a dominant culture, and the need to move beyond a postcolonial literature of resistance. To date, scholars have mainly looked at Ondaatje's Caravaggism in individual works, but no real effort has been made to bring the novels and the film together and, generally, the emphasis on Caravaggio is rather limited. The analysis proceeds on two levels: on the one hand, it is a study of the personality, function, and development of the character named Caravaggio across all three works and, on the other, it contains the various intertextual references to Caravaggio's paintings, from his *David with the Head of Goliath* which, particularly as far as *The English Patient* is concerned, combines all the different intertextual levels, to *Judith Beheading Holofernes*, *St Jerome* (one of Caravaggio's favourite subjects), and *Narcissus*.

Ondaatje's novels and Minghella's film do more than simply quote Caravaggio. They actually perform his artistic lesson, as they blur various boundaries, forcing us to problematize traditional grand narratives, and in true Baroque (or neo-Baroque) style they demand the reader/viewer's active participation, which is why the Deleuzian concept of fold (as a symbol of the Baroque) has been applied as a theoretical framework to this chapter. The fold affects all materials (paper, rocks, sand, water, clouds, living tissues, and the brain) and, as a consequence, materializes form. As Bal suggests, 'the fold insists on surface and materiality [...] [and] entails the involvement of the subject within the material experience' (*Quoting Caravaggio*, p. 30). The fold also emblematizes the Baroque point of view, 'in which the subject must give up its autonomy' (p. 39). Any transformation in the object implies an equivalent transformation in the subject, as the subject is no longer something pre-given or defined but 'what comes to the point of view or rather what remains in the point of view' (ibid.). The insistence on materiality or, more specifically, in Caravaggio's case, on the materiality of paint, problematizes representation and emphasizes the idea of work as process, which is also implicit in the Deleuzian/Leibnizian fold and which, in turn, encourages self-reflection, thus showing us a link between Baroque and neo-Baroque poetics.

Finally the Conclusion offers a brief summary of the project's key findings regarding the reasons for Caravaggio's incredible popularity, reiterating the centrality of the twentieth-century rediscovery of the Baroque and the development of various forms of neo-Baroque poetics. Building on Maravall's theory of the Baroque and Angela Ndalianis's and Mario Perniola's studies on neo-Baroque aesthetics, I argue that in order to understand the legacy of the Baroque in the late twentieth and early twenty-first centuries the following features should be taken into account. First of all, we should look at Baroque culture as the product of a crisis; we should also keep in mind that the Baroque, with its interest in the audience/public, marks the birth of mass culture. The question of taste (including *cattivo gusto*) is also extremely important and so are emotions and the theory of affects as the Baroque believes in the need to move or make an impression in a direct and immediate way. We should also consider the Baroque obsession with ostentation and spectacle; its interest in realism and attention to biography; the violence of its society, the importance of movement and, last but not least, the Baroque faith in art as a tool capable of influencing public opinion. Although many of these features may seem contradictory, it is precisely in some of the paradoxical aspects of the Baroque that we find the reason for its continual appeal in our contemporary world and it is only by looking at Caravaggio's appropriation by popular culture in this context that the self-perpetuating nature of his myth can be fully appreciated.

Notes to the Introduction

1. See Laura Rorato, '"The Colour of Light": Caravaggio's *The Burial of St Lucy* Revisited by Pino Di Silvestro in *La fuga, la sosta*', Romance Studies, 23 (2005), 131–41.
2. Mieke Bal, *Quoting Caravaggio: Contemporary Art, Preposterous History* (Chicago: University of Chicago Press, 1999), p. 15.
3. David Carrier, *Principles of Art History Writing* (University Park: Penn State University Press, 1993), p. 153.
4. Giovanni Previtali reminds us that one of the earliest connections between Caravaggio and cinema was made by Longhi in 1939 in a paper that he delivered at an art history conference in London and which was later published in the volume *Ultimi studi sul Caravaggio e la sua cerchia* (1943) (in Roberto Longhi, *Caravaggio*, with an introduction by G. Previtali (Rome: Editori Riuniti, 2006), p. xxix).
5. This kind of influence can be found in the works of Zeffirelli, Greenaway, and Gibson. See Mario Dal Bello, *Caravaggio: Percorsi di arte e cinema* (Torino: Effatà Editrice, 2007), pp. 72–74.
6. Worthy of attention are also the following works and playwrights/choreographers: Frank McGuinness with his 1986 *Innocence: The Life and Death of Michelangelo Merisi, Caravaggio*; Richard Vetere, *Caravaggio* (2007); Dario Fo, *Caravaggio al tempo di Caravaggio* (2005); Dario Fo and Haim Baharier, *Caravaggio* (2011); Darshan Singh Bhuller, *Caravaggio: Exile and Death* (2003; still touring in the UK in 2011); Manfredi Gelmetti, *Caravaggio: La passione* (2010); and Massimo Pulini, *Caravaggio: Nero d'avorio* (2010). The case of Mario Bigonzetti's 2008 ballet is particularly interesting because it is clear that, for this artist, Caravaggio represents something essentially Italian. When the Staatsoper Berlin commissioned him for an Italian project with a strong cultural connotation, Bigonzetti was delighted to have the opportunity to work on something he had always wanted to do, that is to say a ballet on Caravaggio. Apart from representing a tribute to the Lombard painter, this ballet is also a homage to Bigonzetti's native city of Rome. See Mauro Bigonzetti, *Caravaggio*, Staatsballett Berlin (ArtHaus Musik, NTSC 101 463, 2009), bonus material.
7. Apart from the case studies included in this volume, the following texts are also interesting as

they show how even in the 1980s responses to Caravaggio were a worldwide phenomenon and were not confined to one genre or artistic form. See Oliver Banks, *The Caravaggio Obsession* (New York: New American Library, 1984); Christoph Geiser, *Das geheime Fieber* (Zurich und Frauenfeld: Verlag Nagel & Kinchel, 1987); Christoph Meckel, 'Wissen Sie wie Caravaggio gestorben ist?', in Christoph Meckel, *Ein roter Faden* (Munich: Hanser Verlag, 1983); Frank McGuinness, *Innocence: The Life and Death of Michelangelo Merisi, Caravaggio* (London: Faber & Faber, 1987), first performed in Dublin in 1986; Enrique Trogal, *Il Caravaggio: fábula escénica con música de Monteverdi* (Cuenca: Carboneras de Guadazaoń, 1983).
8. Angela Ndalianis, 'From Neo-Baroque to Neo-Baroques', *Revista Canadiense de Estudios Hispánicos*, 33 (2008), 265–80 (p. 268) [hereafter 'Neo Baroques']. See also Angela Ndalianis, *Neo-Baroque Aesthetics and Contemporary Entertainment* (Cambridge, MA: MIT Press, 2004), p. 17 [hereafter *Neo-Baroque Aesthetics*]. Although Ndalianis highlights different stages in the development of neo-Baroque, starting with Modernism until the present, varied manifestations of neo-Baroque (or Neo-Baroques), in this monograph the term will be used as synonymous with Postmodern (unless otherwise indicated).The importance of the Baroque in contemporary responses to Caravaggio is also highlighted by Mieke Bal and her definition of *baroque point of view* has been instrumental to the analysis of some of our case studies (see Chapter 5).
9. Fabrizio Scrivano, *Lo spazio e le forme: Basi teoriche del vedere contemporaneo* (Florence: Alinea Editrice, 1996), pp. 135–36.
10. Howard Hibbard, *Caravaggio* (Boulder, CO: Westview Press, 1985; first published 1983), p. 77.
11. See Giovanni Previtali's introduction to his edition of Roberto Longhi, *Caravaggio* (p. xxii). Marangoni's article was originally published in *Rivista d'arte*, 10 (1917–18), 1–31.
12. Elizabeth Cropper and Charles Dempsey, 'The State of Research in Italian Painting of the Seventeenth Century', *The Art Bulletin*, 69 (1987), 494–509 (p. 494).
13. John Rupert Martin, *Baroque* (New York: Harper & Row, 1977), p. 28.
14. Controversies began during his lifetime when, in 1604, whilst praising Caravaggio's achievements, claiming that following nature was 'no bad way of achieving a good end', van Mander argued that the Lombard painter was not always able 'to distinguish the most beautiful of life beauties and select it' (Carel van Mander, *Het Schilder Boek* (Haarlem, 1604, 1911), quoted in Hibbard, *Caravaggio*, pp. 344–45). In 1672, Baglione expressed very similar opinions when, in describing Caravaggio's style as 'from nature', he added that 'he did not have much judgment in selecting the good and avoiding the bad' (Giulio Mancini, Giovanni Baglione, and Giovanni Pietro Bellori, *The Lives of Caravaggio* (London: Pallas Athene, 2005), p. 54). Giovanni Previtali (p. xii) reminds us that we need to wait until the end of the eighteenth century and the beginning of the nineteenth century for Caravaggio's realism to be seen in positive terms in the works of critics like Gabriel Laviron (1806–49) or Jacob Burckhardt (1818–97).
15. Cropper and Dempsey, 'The State of Research in Italian Painting of the Seventeenth Century', p. 498.
16. John Varriano, *Caravaggio: The Art of Realism* (University Park, PA: Penn State University Press, 2006), p. 130.
17. See: Hal Foster, *The Return of the Real* (Cambridge, MA: MIT Press, 1996); Ihab Hassan, 'Beyond Postmodernism: Toward and Aesthetic of Trust', in *Beyond Postmodernism: Reassessments in Literature, Theory, and Culture*, ed. by Klaus Stierstorfer (Berlin: Walter de Gruyter, 2003), pp. 199–212; Mario Perniola, *Art and its Shadow*, trans. by Massimo Verdicchio (London: Continuum, 2004); Romano Luperini, *La fine del postmoderno* (Naples: Alfredo Guida Editore, 2005). In Italy in 2008 an entire issue of the journal *Allegoria* (no. 57) was devoted to the question of the end of Postmodernism and the return to realism. According to Perniola, this new sensibility is characterized by an interest in 'the most violent and most raw aspects of reality' and by a predilection for the themes of death and sex (Mario Perniola, *Art and its Shadow*, trans. by Massimo Verdicchio (London: Continuum, 2004), p. 4).
18. Gabriel Laviron quoted by Previtali, p. xxxi.
19. Omar Calabrese, *Neo-Baroque: A Sign of Times* (Princeton: Princeton University Press, 1992), p. 179.
20. For an interesting analysis of Caravaggio as 'pittore maledetto' see Maurizio Calvesi, *Caravaggio* (Florence: Giunti, 2009), pp. 7–16.

21. The exhibition catalogue *Saint and Sinners: Caravaggio and the Baroque Image* and Peter Robb's controversial biography of the painter *M: The Man Who Became Caravaggio* were both reviewed in the *American Journal of Psychiatry*, 157.12 (2000). In 2008, the same journal published a very short article devoted to Caravaggio by Dr Peter J. Buckley entitled 'Images in Psychiatry' (165.2, pp. 201–02). In 2001, the Italian psychiatrist Giuseppe Resca published a book entitled *La spada e la misericordia: Caravaggio e il demone della violenza*. In 2002 the Israeli criminologist Shlomo Giora Shoham published the volume *Art, Crime and Madness: Gesualdo, Caravaggio, Genet, Van Gogh, Artaud*. In 2007, the American psychologist Ronnie Mather published an article entitled 'Caravaggio and the Psychology of Schizophrenia' in the online journal *PSYART*.
22. The Spanish composer and expert in Renaissance and Baroque music Jordi Savall and the French author/art historian Dominique Fernandez collaborated on the production of a CD devoted to Caravaggio. *Lacrimae Caravaggio* (2006) consists of thirty tracks composed by Savall and inspired by the style of music which was popular during Caravaggio's life and by some of his paintings. The CD is accompanied by a booklet in which Dominique Fernandez explains the paintings with which Savall's music engages and which are often used as background projections during the live performances of *Lacrimae Caravaggio*. This work was first performed during the 2005 Caravaggio exhibition in Barcelona.
23. That was the number of visitors reported on the last day of the 2010 exhibition at the Scuderie del Quirinale in Rome, an event that lasted one 114 days and attracted a total of 582,577 people. See Goffredo Silvestri, 'Quel record sprecato alle Scuderie: Troppo breve la mostra del Caravaggio', *Repubblica*, 17 June 2010, <www.repubblica.it/speciali/arte/classifiche/2010/06/17/news> [accessed 20 October 2011].
24. La Porta, Filippo, 'Ancora sul *neonoir*', in *Roma Noir 2008: 'Hannibal the Cannibal c'est moi?' Realismo e finzione nel romanzo noir italiano*, ed. by Elisabetta Mondello (Rome: Robin Edizioni, 2008), pp. 49–58
25. Homi Bhabha, 'Of Mimicry and Man', in *The Location of Culture* (London: Routledge, 1994), pp. 85–92.

CHAPTER 1

Caravaggio in Context

> Works of art always spring from those who have faced the danger, gone to the very end of an experience, to the point beyond which no human being can go. The further one dares to go, the more decent, the more personal, the more unique a life becomes
>
> RILKE, *Letter to Clara Rilke*[1]

This chapter provides an overview of some key moments in Caravaggio's life and of the historical events that shaped his era in order to prove that his popularity is certainly related to his tormented life, while at the same time transcending it. Particular attention will be given to the issue of the painter's sexuality as this aspect features heavily in many of the fictional texts we are about to analyse. The most controversial aspects of his art will also be examined as they will help us understand some of the problems faced by art historians, which will be further developed in the next chapter. When looking at Michelangelo Merisi's life, it has often been suggested that there has never been an artist whose 'biography is more dependent on police records' (Hunt, p. ix). To do Caravaggio justice, however, we must also remember that his violent temper and behaviour must have come across as less extraordinary in his time. In brief, we must look at the context before we can judge the subject. Rome, for instance, was an extremely violent city, a place where 'stabbings and shootings were so routine as hardly to raise the eyebrow of the papal scribe'.[2] During Caravaggio's stay in the capital, from 1592 until 1606, 658 executions were carried out, most of them under the papacy of Clement VIII. Those of Beatrice Cenci (1599) and Giordano Bruno (1600) were just the most famous and controversial which attracted the largest crowds; 'public executions provided a popular form of free mass entertainment' at the time.[3] As Thomas and Elizabeth Cohen point out:

> A good public execution, with its penitential pomp, was a piece of edifying theatre. It at once execrated crime and glorified the majesty of the law and the mercy of God, who received the soul of any victim displaying the gifts of faith and contrition. Men, women and children came in throngs to see the show.[4]

In order to understand how such a climate could develop, we must step back a few decades and focus on some major historical events that affected not only Italy but also Europe.

The socio-historical context

As Helen Langdon reminds us in her seminal monograph devoted to the Lombard painter:

> The early years of the sixteenth century had been years of continual warfare. France and Spain fought for the dominance of Italy, turning northern Italy into a vast battlefield. The Medici Pope, Clement VII, attempted to maintain the balance of power, but so incompetent was his diplomacy that in 1527 an unruly army of Spaniards, German *landsknechte*, and Italians, employed by Charles V, German Emperor and King of Spain, had sacked Rome. The troops behaved with appalling brutality, the Pope was humiliated and there was outrage throughout the peninsula. Spain was left dominant in Italy, in possession of Milan, Naples and Sicily, and in 1559 this was confirmed at the Peace of Cateau Cambrésis, a settlement between France and Spain.[5]

In 1556, when Charles V died, his son, Philip II, became king of Spain and during the following decades he was often in conflict with the popes. The Vatican was hoping that the French might regain power in order to reduce the influence of Spain. When, after the assassination of the last Valois King, the Huguenot Henry IV of Navarre inherited the throne, a new problem arose. Both France and Spain were extremely hostile to the idea of a Protestant king and joined forces in the fight against Henry IV. France was devastated by a civil war. The situation changed unexpectedly in 1593 when Henry IV converted to Catholicism, thus reuniting his country. Pope Clement VIII immediately took the opportunity to recognize Henry IV as King of France and in 1598, with the Treaty of Vervins, managed to persuade Spain to do the same. This meant that the two countries were finally at peace. In the same year Clement VIII annexed Ferrara and it looked as if 'Rome was regaining her power' (Langdon, p. 2). During the sack of Rome approximately 60,000 people had died and 12 million gold ducats had been lost from various treasuries. Rebuilding the city's reputation and former glories became a priority. Between 1600 and 1640 there were probably 400–500 artists working in Rome and Caravaggio was one of them (Hunt, pp. 11–12).

The other key event that we must remember in order to fully understand Michelangelo Merisi's art is the Council of Trent, which met three times between 1545 and 1563 and condemned Lutheranism, particularly the belief that faith alone can guarantee salvation, and tried to 'revive the direct and popular appeal of medieval Christianity' (Langdon, p. 3). As a result, new religious orders and secular organizations devoted to charity and welfare, the so called confraternities (ibid.), were born. It is in such a climate that during the plague epidemic of 1576, when Caravaggio was approximately five years old, a figure like that of Carlo Borromeo could turn the city of Milan into 'a vast and highly orchestrated display of penitence and of ceaseless prayer' and become a living emblem of the sufferings of Christ, 'seeking a heroic martyrdom' in the streets of his city (Langdon, pp. 18, 19). The Council of Trent, in fact, had reasserted the status of saints as mediators between God and mankind and the importance of both good deeds and the sacraments for obtaining salvation. This rekindled enthusiasm for Christianity in general and

Catholicism in particular reached its climax on 7 October 1571 when the Holy League triumphed over the Turks at Lepanto. The true hero of this victory was Marcantonio Colonna, commander of the papal galleys and father of Costanza Colonna, known as Marchesa of Caravaggio, who was one of Merisi's lifelong patrons.

When considering the two key popes of this period, Sixtus V (1585–90) and Clement VIII (1592–1605), the former is mainly remembered for his ambitious architectural projects, which left an indelible mark on the city, and for having strengthened the papacy. The latter, instead, despite continuing the work of his illustrious predecessor with equally monumental building projects, was also interested in the fight against heresy, venality, prostitution, and moral corruption. He 'did not exactly live up to his name for clemency' (Hunt, p. 14) with his radical approach to the above-mentioned problems and his open anti-Semitism. As Puglisi reminds us, late sixteenth-century Rome was probably the 'most cosmopolitan city in Europe, boasting a unique mix of inhabitants'.[6] Whilst Rome was still relatively small in 1527, by 1600 its population had doubled to 110,000. It attracted immigrants and visitors from all over Italy, and the number of foreigners increased thanks to the capital's international affairs. Ten per cent of residents were ecclesiastics and men outnumbered women (hence the high demand for prostitutes). The city was also crowded by large groups of pilgrims, whose numbers reached half a million for the Jubilee in 1600 (Puglisi, p. 44).[7] Rome was, therefore, a place full of contrasts. What was condemned at the public level was often acceptable in the private sphere and vice versa. Clement VIII, for instance, whilst endorsing outward pomp, was actually leading a modest and pious life and was genuinely concerned about public decorum. This obsession led him to censor even religious art: 'during visits to Roman churches, he ordered images with nude or scantly clad figures to be covered or removed' (Puglisi, p. 45), something Caravaggio experienced at first hand when the first version of his *St Matthew and the Angel* for San Luigi dei Francesi was rejected.

Clement VIII, who suffered from gout, spent the last months of his life in bed; when he died, in March 1605, turmoil spread through the capital. The Conclave was divided into two factions, those who supported Spain and those who were closer to France, such as Federico Borromeo. The elderly transitional pope Leo XI was a relative of Henry IV and was strongly opposed to the Spanish faction. Unfortunately, he died in April after only three weeks in office. In May 1605 Camillo Borghese became Paul V. He was a supporter of the Spanish and Austrian ruling families (Hunt, p. 105). This was a setback for Counter-Reformation figures such as Federico Borromeo as Paul V reintroduced opulence and pompousness in the Vatican. Inevitably, for artists like Caravaggio who depended on patronage for their livelihoods, the election of a new pope could mark a drastic change of fortune. In this case, scholars are divided. According to Calvesi, with the election of Paul V the fortunes of Caravaggio, whose patrons had always been Francophiles, began to decline.[8] On the contrary, Hibbard claims:

> The papal court of Clement VIII was hostile toward Del Monte's protector, Grand Duke Ferdinand. Thus when Caravaggio obtained the Cardinal's favour he automatically lost all possibility of patronage from the Aldobrandini family.

At first the problem could hardly have occurred to him, but by 1600 he may have set his sights on other patrons in order to break out of what perhaps seemed a restrictive situation. Nevertheless he had to wait until the election of Paul V Borghese in mid 1605 in order to achieve papal favour.[9]

Regardless of whether we agree with Calvesi or Hibbard, it is clear that Caravaggio's position in Rome was rather precarious and that his talent alone was not sufficient to determine his popularity. In order to fully understand the complexity of the situation we must consider some key events in Merisi's life.

How does Caravaggio fit in this context? Key events in Merisi's early life

Thanks to archival material discovered in the 1970s, we now know that Michelangelo Merisi is likely to have been born on 29 September 1571, St Michael's day, not in 1573 as previously thought.[10] His father Fermo died in 1577, together with two other members of the Merisi family, during the plague epidemic which struck Milan in 1576. He had worked as a mason for Francesco I Sforza, Marchese of Caravaggio and was reasonably well-off. Michelangelo had two brothers and one sister and spent most of his childhood between Milan and Caravaggio. It has been suggested that the loss of male role models at a young age might have contributed to the development of Caravaggio's violent temper and eccentric personality.[11] Given the family background, Michelangelo is likely to have received a basic education and attended the grammar school. Documentary evidence suggests that he was in Milan in 1584, as he signed a four-year apprenticeship contract with the painter Simone Peterzano, who proudly signed on his frescos 'Titiani alumnus' (Hunt, p. 8). Very little is known about his apprenticeship and the following two years, until he moved to Rome in 1592. Some critics state that after leaving Peterzano's studio, Caravaggio must have painted portraits and travelled to Venice to study the works of Giorgione.[12] John Spike also reports that according to Mancini and Bellori, before the age of twenty, Caravaggio had already spent a year in jail,[13] either for having murdered a man or because of an incident 'involving a whore, a slashing, daggers and a police spy' (Prose, p. 21). His mother, Lucia Aratori Merisi, died in 1590 and Caravaggio quickly sold most of the land he had inherited, which was probably shared by his siblings. It is thanks to the money he accumulated through the sales that Caravaggio was able to travel and settle in Rome, even though, according to many early biographers, his initial stay in the capital was marked by poverty (Hunt, p. 10). However, the most significant fact of Michelangelo's youth is that he grew up during the time when Carlo Borromeo was Archbishop of Milan (1538–84). As a consequence, the particular religious and artistic atmosphere which developed in the city must have had an impact on his life. As Puglisi notes:

> When Borromeo died in November 1584, Caravaggio had been living in Milan as an apprentice for the past eight months. Since Peterzano and other Milanese workshops had fulfilled Borromeo's call for frescoes and altarpieces to decorate the city's churches, the Archbishop's death must have had some effect on Caravaggio's workplace, if only at an economic level. (p. 21)

Today, Merisi's familiarity with Borromeo's ideas and Counter-Reformation culture are considered to be of vital importance when reading his religious paintings.

Rome and other key events in Caravaggio's life

On reaching the capital in 1593, the first task for a young artist in search of success was finding suitable patrons or a position in one of the city's established studios and this is precisely what Caravaggio did. His first known patron, whom he probably got to know through his uncle, who was a priest, was Monsignor Pandolfo Pucci, quickly nicknamed Monsignor Insalata owing to his avarice. After a few months, Caravaggio left the establishment of Monsignor Pucci and his next position was with a rather obscure Sicilian painter, simply known by his first name, Lorenzo. The most significant aspect of this collaboration was the meeting with another Sicilian painter, Mario Minniti. Minniti, with whom Caravaggio lived, acted as a model for some of his paintings and later played a vital role in helping Merisi when he arrived in Sicily after fleeing Malta. For an artist with ambitions, working in Lorenzo's studio could not represent a desirable solution and Merisi left after a short period of time. He then worked in the studio of Antiveduto Grammatica, known for his portraits of Roman notables, but was not satisfied until he could join the best studio of Rome, that of Giuseppe Cesari (1568–1640) and his brother Bernardino (1571–1622). Giuseppe Cesari would soon be knighted as Cavalier D'Arpino (1600). His art represented the pinnacle of Mannerism, a style that Caravaggio, whether consciously or unconsciously, rejected (Hibbard, p. 10). Michelangelo stayed eight months in the Cesari brothers' studio (Hunt, p. 17) even though early biographers report that he was treated as a lesser artist. It is not entirely clear why the relationship between the Cesari brothers and Caravaggio came to an end, but Spike (p. 37) suggested a possible illegal activity which led the two brothers to desert a wounded Caravaggio, 'leaving him to the compassion of Lorenzo and the Ospedale for destitute persons' (Hunt, p. 24). After having been discharged from hospital, Michelangelo found himself a position with Monsignor Fantin Petrignani, but the experience was short and unproductive. Dissatisfied and unable to sell his pictures, Caravaggio's fortune seemed to decline until, thanks to his friend Prospero Orsi, he met Maestro Valentino, an art dealer who agreed to sell some his works. Orsi 'helped Caravaggio secure a venue to promote and sell paintings via Mastro Valentino' (Hunt, p. 27) and, thanks to this arrangement, Caravaggio got to know his future patron Cardinal Del Monte. The Cardinal, by taking him into his service and household in 1595, gave Merisi status and respectability, something the young painter had not experienced since leaving home three years earlier (Hunt, p. 32). Although not one of the wealthiest cardinals in Rome, Del Monte was a very knowledgeable man, passionate about art in general and music in particular, having been a guitarist in his youth (Hunt, p. 32). Thanks to Del Monte's influence, and that of his circle of friends, Caravaggio's iconography became progressively complex (Hunt, p. 34). In Del Monte's household, Caravaggio met another of his key patrons: a Genoese nobleman, the Marchese Vincenzo Giustiniani, who was to purchase many of his paintings. Another important religious patron in Caravaggio's life was the Cardinal Federico Borromeo (1564–1631), nephew of Carlo Borromeo, related to the Marchese of Caravaggio, and Protector of the Academy of St Luke, 'the painters' guild whose lectures Caravaggio might have attended as early as

1593 if he is the "Michele da Milano" recorded in the meetings' (Hunt, p. 18). Federico Borromeo was also the author of a book about painting, *De Pictura Sacra* and, according to Calvesi, Caravaggio's works are in line with the principles and ideas expressed by Borromeo in this volume (*Le realtà del Caravaggio*, pp. 51–52), thus partially deconstructing the myth of Caravaggio as the rebel artist who had no interest in his predecessors and was an isolated figure amongst his contemporaries.

If, thanks to the link with Del Monte (1594–1600), Caravaggio's prestige and popularity were rapidly growing, so did his eccentricities and violent temper: 'it is estimated that between 1598 and 1605 Caravaggio would be hauled before the police at least eleven times' (Hunt, p. 65). No document indicates why Caravaggio left the service of Del Monte in 1600. The split was probably amicable as, by then, the painter had a regular income, similar to that of a merchant. Del Monte continued to help Caravaggio for at least another year by getting him commissions through his friends. It is likely that, with his need to experience all aspects of life, Caravaggio was beginning to perceive even the cosmopolitan atmosphere of one of the most prestigious Roman households as suffocating (Hunt, p. 64). Between 1600 and 1601, however, Merisi stayed with another prelate, Cardinal Mattei. The paintings of this period seem to convey a rather paradoxical picture of Caravaggio: bellicose and abrupt, on the one hand, but humble and capable of 'a rare appreciation of humanity' (Hunt, p. 66) on the other. His style and method were soon to be identified by his contemporaries through the terms *tenebrism* (dark and shadowy effect) and *chiaroscuro* (dramatic interplay between light and darkness). Black was used to give relief to the forms and he never painted scenes in daylight (Hunt, pp. 66–67). Caravaggio's success reached its climax between 1600 and 1603, thanks to two very important public commissions, both through Del Monte's influence, those for the Contarelli Chapel in San Luigi dei Francesi (1599) and those for the Cerasi Chapel in Santa Maria del Popolo (1600). As part of his first commission, Caravaggio painted *The Calling of St Matthew* and *The Martyrdom of St Matthew* for the side walls of the chapel and, three years later, *St Mathew and the Angel* for its altar. Whilst the two lateral paintings were hugely successful, the first version of *St Matthew and the Angel* was rejected because of lack of decorum: Matthew, who comes across as being illiterate, lacked the countenance of a saint, with his dirty feet in the foreground directly facing the viewer. What is more, the old man and the angel were too close to each other, particularly since the scantly clad angel was a very sensual, almost erotic, figure. The discarded version was bought by the Marquis Vincenzo Giustiniani, but Caravaggio produced a more conventional version of the scene which is still standing in the chapel today. For the Cerasi Chapel, instead, he painted *The Crucifixion of St Peter* and *The Conversion of St Paul*. A document was attached to the contract for these two works naming Caravaggio *egregius in urbe pictor* for the first time. As Paul and Peter were the two key saints of the capital, these two paintings by Caravaggio were far more important to Rome than his St Matthew cycle for San Luigi dei Francesi. However, as Hunt points out:

> Caravaggio's innovative theological vision for both Peter and Paul does not show the Church triumphant at all. Rather it shows the defeat of Rome's patron saint, Peter, as an ageing man with a tired face being humiliated in a crucifixion

upside down by indifferent henchmen. Without a halo or any hint of martyr's crowning splendour or ministering angels waiting in heaven, darkness makes Peter's near-nakedness almost obscene. Saints are thus no more than ordinary people. [...] Paul's humiliation as the upended Saul is equally a peripety of expectation. There is no glory in either falling or being thrown by a horse and now being under its hoof. Paul, illuminated, whether the light came from heaven or not, finds his eyelids closed by blindness. In fact, the horse is far more central than the saint. (pp. 74–76)

The execution of the pictures for the Cerasi Chapel proved problematic, and the first version of both paintings was rejected. It is thought that Cerasi himself ordered the replacements, even though he did not live long enough to see the outcome of his request. The discarded works were bought by a friend of Del Monte, Giacomo Sannesio, who was also a collector of paintings and secretary of the *Consulta* (the body that administered the Papal States). What is interesting is that, at this stage, if his original conceptions failed to please, Caravaggio was given a second chance. Later, when he painted the *Death of the Virgin* (1601–03) and the *Madonna dei Palafrenieri* (1605–06), he did not meet such favours: 'his paintings were rejected outright' (Puglisi, p. 149). Although rejections were fairly common for artists in those times, 'five instances in a relatively short career suggest that Caravaggio's imagery consistently confounded the expectations of his patrons' (ibid.) and, as Hibbard (p. 147) put it, 'Caravaggio is unique in having as many Roman altarpieces refused as were accepted'. The Contarelli and Cerasi commissions reveal other key features of Caravaggio's style which are still greatly admired today. First of all we notice his ability to compose like a stage designer, to arrange his figures in a 'carefully directed light' so that the depicted scenes convey the impression of taking place in the real space of the chapel before us (Langdon, p. 188). Also, by making himself a witness in the *Martyrdom of St Matthew*, and in a way complicit in the murder of the saint, he conveys a 'personal sense of universal darkness and guilt' that recurs in his religious works and gives them extraordinary power and tension (Langdon, p. 189). Finally, we admire his gift of 'drawing the viewer in to canvas space with his controversy and unexpected presentation' (Hunt, p. 76; see also Langdon, p. 179).

The beginning of the seventeenth century constituted for Caravaggio a period of intensive work during which he produced some of his most famous masterpieces. However, two major personal events tarnished his image and damaged his popularity. The first is a lawsuit for libel which forced Caravaggio to appear in court on 11 September 1603 accused by the fellow painter and biographer Baglione of undermining his artistic merit out of jealousy. Baglione claimed that Caravaggio was the author of some vulgar satiric verses written to ridicule him. Although other defendants were included in the lawsuit (e.g. Orazio Gentileschi, Ottavio Leoni and Filippo Trisegni), Caravaggio was considered to be the main author of those verses. When Caravaggio testified on 13 September, he denied all knowledge of these poems and maintained he had nothing to do with any of the other people mentioned. This incident was to become very interesting for posterity as the painter's defence constitutes the nearest thing to a declaration of poetics he left us and the only surviving written evidence of his ideas about art and his contemporaries. He showed contempt for Baglione, claiming that he knew no painter who praised Baglione, but spared Giuseppe Cesari, Annibale Carracci, Federico Zuccaro and Pomarancio from criticism. His definition of a good painter was 'a man who can paint well and imitate natural things well' (Hunt, pp. 93–95), which was to give him his reputation as a realist. From a juridical point of view, of course, Caravaggio did not do himself any favours as, by publicly defaming Baglione, he could not avoid a jail sentence. He was imprisoned during the trial and sent to the Tor di Nona prison for approximately two weeks. As Hunt reminds us, 'Tor di Nona was a horrible place even by 17th century standards' (p. 97). Unfortunately, Caravaggio was to become all too familiar with Tor di Nona in the following years (ibid.) through a series of progressively more severe scrapes with the law. Hunt suggests that, although this escalation of incidents may not be surprising, given Caravaggio's notorious temper and pride, it may also be linked to a fairly well-known phenomenon, the 'temporary self-poisoning of artists from the grinding and mixing of painting concoctions' (p. 100). No doubt, such poisoning could affect an artist's personality, particularly if combined with frequent drinking and violent companions (ibid.).

The other fundamental episode is of a far more serious nature and ended Caravaggio's career in Rome, a city to which he would never return. It took place on 28 May 1606 in Via della Scrofa, near a tennis court close to Palazzo Firenze. Caravaggio, who had arrived in the area with some friends looking for trouble, engaged in single combat with Ranuccio Tomassoni, whose arrogant family dominated the area, and accidentally killed him. Caravaggio too was wounded but, by the following Wednesday, he had to leave Rome and seek refuge in the Alban Hills as a *banda capitale* was soon to be imposed on him (Langdon, pp. 309–14). The severity of the sentence probably reflected the elevated status of the Tomassoni family, 'who themselves got off scot-free for similar offences' (Langdon, p. 314). The Tomassoni brothers were notorious for brawling and had appeared in several local courts. Above all, however, they 'were aligned with the Farnese and Aldobrandini faction, which were Spanish-leaning' (Hunt, p. 104). With the election of Paul V in 1605, the Francophiles, including Caravaggio's patron Del Monte, ceased to be at the centre of power and 'were certainly not favourites of the Tomassoni family' (Hunt, p. 105). According to Varriano (*The Art of Realism*, p. 78), the unfortunate fight which led to the killing of Ranuccio could be seen as a product of the political tension of that period, because on the same day similar fatal incidents had taken place between the French and Spanish factions.[14] In 1990, Calvesi (*Le realtà del Caravaggio*, p. 49) had already suggested a possible political motive behind the change in Caravaggio's fortune as the decline of his popularity seemed to coincide with the ascent to power of Paul V. Regardless of the actual motives, what counts is that Caravaggio was forced to leave the capital at the height of his career and live the rest of his life as a fugitive, in permanent exile. He must have felt haunted by the fear of instantaneous execution, should he be captured. This fear was objectified in his paintings through the motif of the severed head, which became progressively more frequent after 1606 (Hunt, p. 109).

After an initial stay in the Sabine hills, north of Rome, where he received shelter from the Colonna family, Caravaggio moved to Naples in September 1606 and during 'the nine months or so that he lived in the Spanish-controlled city, [he] produced some of his most remarkable and influential altarpieces', the most famous of which, perhaps, is *The Seven Works of Mercy*, completed in January 1607 for the Pio Monte della Misericordia and still *in situ*.[15] As Hunt points out, Caravaggio probably continued to enjoy the protection of the Colonna family as

> Naples was Marzio Colonna's main residence and he was on the vice-regal advisory council there. Other Colonnas lived in Naples, including his brother Ascanio Colonna who was Cardinal Protector of the Kingdom of Naples, and Costanza Colonna, the Marchesa of Caravaggio. (p. 110)

In Naples, the papal authority was weak, which meant that Caravaggio enjoyed a certain freedom and, surprisingly for a man of his temper, managed to avoid legal problems and arrests (ibid.). The local art world welcomed him and he found himself in an environment where artists and dealers thrived thanks to the connections Naples had with other Italian cities and northern Europe (Langdon, p. 324). His fame had preceded him and 'at once he was launched into a series of increasingly lucrative commissions' (ibid.). Barely a month following his arrival in Naples, he opened a bank account and deposited a payment of 200 ducats which he had received on that very day as remuneration for one of his works (Langdon, p. 326). Despite his huge popularity and success, he left Naples sometime in the summer of 1607 and sailed to Malta, where he arrived in July 1607 (Langdon, p. 338). This must have come across as a rather puzzling decision to many of his contemporaries and, in fact, his Maltese period was neglected even by scholars until the mid-1970s, partially because of lack of access to archival material.[16] It is likely that Caravaggio travelled to Malta, hoping to be made a member of the order of St John as, in order to be knighted, he would need an official pardon for his crimes and the death sentence would have to be repealed, something he undoubtedly wanted.

The knights of Malta had arrived on the island in 1530, but, for the first thirty-five years of their stay, they could not decide whether they should settle there or move elsewhere. Things changed in 1565 when, following their victory during the Great Siege laid by the Turks, they realized that in order to survive they needed to transfer their convent to a more central location; thus plans for a new city were set into motion.[17] This city was built according to Renaissance principles and named after the hero of the siege, Grand Master Jean Parisot de la Valette (1557–68), who, however, did not survive to see his new city finished (Sciberras and Stone, p. 18). By the time Caravaggio arrived on the island, Valletta was a small but cosmopolitan place. Like Rome, it had a large male population and violence was endemic.

The Grand Master at the time was the powerful Frenchman Alof de Wignacourt, who had been elected to the Grand Magistry in 1601. As the knights were generally eager to increase their prestige by attracting famous artists, it is possible that Caravaggio's move to the island was simply the result of Wignacourt's desire to have a court painter. Whatever the reasons behind Caravaggio's decision to leave Naples for Malta, the Colonna family is again likely to have played a vital role in this scenario. Caravaggio's status was not high enough to be able to deal directly with the knights, who were members of the most prestigious aristocratic families in Europe. He would need mediators to introduce him.[18] As for the issue of knighthood, his lack of noble lineage and the fact that he had committed murder were not the only obstacles the painter had to overcome. Since becoming Grand Master in 1601, Wignacourt had been extremely reluctant to bestow the only honorific knighthood open to someone like Caravaggio, the Knighthood of Magistral Obedience, reserved for valorous men who were not members of the aristocracy (Sciberras and Stone, p. 20). However, although Caravaggio's name is never directly mentioned, scholars have found documentary evidence proving that in December 1607 Wignacourt had written to his ambassador in Rome, who would then address the papal court, requesting two dispensations, one for investing a man guilty of murder and the other for making him a Knight of Magistral Obedience. Remarkably, 'the full document of the authorization, as released by the papacy, is dated 15 February 1608', just three weeks after the receipt of the Grand Master's letter in Rome (Sciberras and Stone, p. 30). Before he could be invested, Caravaggio had to serve a twelve-month period as a novice 'in Convent'. The Grand Master must have given instructions to start counting this period from the painter's arrival on the island, as Caravaggio received the habit of the Order of St John on 14 July 1608. As Sciberras and Stone point out, Caravaggio had thus built 'a strong foundation for his eventual return to Rome' (p. 31). Unfortunately, barely four weeks after the actual investiture, on 18 August 1608, Caravaggio disgraced himself by taking part in a violent brawl during which another knight was seriously injured. As a result, he was arrested and imprisoned in Fort St Angelo, a rather imposing if somewhat derelict fortress. After a few weeks of detention, on 6 October 1608, Caravaggio managed to flee the island, thus contravening the Order's rules stating that no knight was allowed to leave the island without permission from the Grand Master. This led to his defrocking, which took place *in absentia* on 1 December 1608.[19] Although Caravaggio's escape was not an isolated incident, as other knights and slaves had succeeded before him (Farrugia Randon, p. 123), he could not have done it without help, and his accomplices were risking very serious punishments if found out.[20] The Grand Master usually ordered the immediate recapture and detention of the fugitives, so Caravaggio must have lived in fear of the knights pursuing him.

    The largest and most celebrated of his Maltese works is *The Beheading of St John the Baptist*, which he probably started painting before being invested. He donated it to the orders as his *passaggio*, instead of 'the large sum of money which was usually demanded from prospective knights' (Langdon, p. 356). *The Beheading* displays a new compositional method which Caravaggio was to develop further in his Sicilian paintings and in his last works. Sciberras and Stone effectively summarize the key features of this style by pointing out how 'a concentrated group of figures is set into a cavernous space of which the top half is left almost completely unarticulated' (p. 12). According to these two scholars, all of Caravaggio's Maltese works have a distinctive look and seem to express a new confidence in his approach to painting' (p. 69). They are 'noticeably harder, more spartan and subdued than anything that came before them' (p. 68) and 'his daring brushwork and new economy of means [...] in certain cases test the limits of what could be considered a finished work' (pp. 68–69). *The Beheading* is the first painting to display a 'mature concept of space as a positive factor [...] the overwhelmingly unpopulated area conveys a sense of vastness, a unique theatrical effect: Man is confined' (Farrugia Randon, p. 179). The moment selected is rather unusual and, when looking at the painting, we have the impression that his figures are 'posing an action' (Farrugia Randon, p. 182). In this way, Caravaggio gives 'duration to a single moment', but 'in order to arrest movement, Caravaggio had to depict volume with greater clarity' (ibid.). *The Beheading* has also been described as 'a theatre of voids, displacements and arrested actions' (Sciberras and Stone, pp. 92–94). In Farrugia Randon's view, death, in this painting, 'is not portrayed eschatologically; it is portrayed as a physical, irrational and irrevocable act. Martyrdom is simply murder' (p. 195), an idea taken up in some of the fictional works we are about to analyse (e.g. Fernandez's novels). We must also remember that this is the only painting Caravaggio ever signed. He proudly added the title Fra to his name and used the blood squirting out of the saint's head to write it. As Calvesi reminds us, the already complex symbolism conveyed by the signature is emphasized by the fact that it is written in blood. Traditionally, signing has at least three meanings: underwriting; extracting blood; crossing oneself (Calvesi, pp. 41–42). The central position of his signature is obviously an indication of his pride in receiving the Cross, whilst the blood suggests his 'penitential identification with the martyr and the order as a form of expiation for the blood of Ranuccio Tomassoni' (Hunt, p. 117; Puglisi, pp. 304–08).[21] According to Puglisi, with its unique 'amalgam of pride, piety and penance', this signature 'lends autobiographical poignancy to the Malta altarpiece, marking the moment of brightest optimism in Caravaggio's exile when social and professional rehabilitation seemed within reach' (p. 308). As previously mentioned, however, this optimistic phase was very short-lived as less than two months after his investiture Caravaggio was escaping to Sicily where, according to his early biographers, he lived in permanent fear for his physical safety, 'going to bed fully dressed and armed with a dagger' (Puglisi, p. 311).

His arrival in Sicily, in a way, bears similarities to his arrival in Naples after the killing of Ranuccio Tomassoni, for 'despite his shamed status' he was welcomed to the island and received almost immediately by the civic senate of Syracuse, who seem to have commissioned a painting depicting their patron saint Lucy and for whom Caravaggio painted *The Burial of St Lucy*, the first of four major religious works he produced in approximately twelve months (Hunt, p. 120). In Sicily, Caravaggio could also rely on the support of a friend from his youth, the fellow painter and former model Mario Minniti. Langdon suggests that it was probably Minniti who asked the Senate of his city (Syracuse) to employ Caravaggio. Caravaggio, however, was becoming increasingly more unstable and could not settle in the same place for long. After a few months, he left his friend's house and moved to Messina. Some of his paintings were now earning him more than 1,000 scudi, but, at the height of success, he got himself into trouble again. Langdon reports that, according to his Sicilian biographer, Susinno, he suddenly left for Palermo after a quarrel with a schoolteacher whose pupils Caravaggio watched playing. The teacher seems to have accused Caravaggio of homosexual inclinations, something extremely dangerous in Sicily where homosexuals were hanged (Langdon, p. 376). The painter overreacted and injured the accuser on the head, thus making himself a fugitive again. He probably sailed to Palermo, where he left some excellent works of art, but, by early autumn 1609, he was back in Naples (Langdon, p. 379). In a poignant statement about the last phases of the painter's life, Langdon points out:

> His wanderings in Sicily are full of contradiction, in part the triumphal progress of an international celebrity, admired and richly rewarded, and in part the anguished flight of a fugitive, fearing capture and possible death [...]; he was feared for his increasingly strange behaviour and was constantly described — as he was not in Rome — as mad and crazy. (p. 379)

It is likely that Caravaggio was planning to stay in Naples until he got the longed-for pardon that would enable him to return to Rome. He had been exiled for nearly three years, a customary period after which offenders could expect a pardon (Langdon, p. 379). He stayed with his old friend the Marchesa of Caravaggio in the Palazzo Cellamare at Chiaia. Unfortunately, 'his enemies were in pursuit and on 24 October 1609 he was so badly wounded in the Osteria del Cerriglio that a newspaper sent word of his death to Rome' (Langdon, p. 382). During his short stay, from October 1609 until July 1610, part of which must have been spent convalescing, he produced an impressive number of works and changed his style again (p. 383). If his Sicilian paintings seem to accentuate the style he had developed in Malta through their austerity, reduced individuality, and compactness of design (Sciberras and Stone, p. 12) but often tender mood (Langdon, p. 383), in his Neapolitan ones, the mood becomes harsher. Their theme is death and human evil: 'there is a sense of the draining of faith, of submission to the tragic faith of man' (ibid.). His figures are still and inward looking; the narrative element and colour range are both reduced to the bare minimum (ibid.). The number of self-portraits is also increasing, confirming Caravaggio's obsession with his own life and imminent death (Hunt, p. 131). Despite his success, in Naples he must have felt in danger, either from the Maltese or from the Spanish so, in the summer of 1610, he boarded a felucca at Chiaia with the intention of reaching Rome, taking with him a few paintings intended for Scipione Borghese. The felucca stopped at Palo, an isolated small port dominated by a fortress, but otherwise surrounded by malarial plains. Caravaggio disembarked but was immediately imprisoned, possibly the victim of a mistaken identity. Having bought his way out of prison with a large sum of money, he found himself in a paradoxical situation, as the felucca had set off again with his belongings (Hunt, p. 135). Almost destitute and alone, he must have decided to go to Porto Ercole in the hope of catching up with the felucca and recovering his belongings. Unfortunately, by the time he reached Porto Ercole, the felucca was no longer there and he fell horribly ill. He was probably looked after by a local confraternity, but died around 18 July 1610 of 'some lethal form of enteric fever' (Hunt, p. 136), not of malaria as previously believed. In actual fact, a halo of mystery still surrounds his death. Despite the discovery of an archival document by Maurizio Marini in 1995 which suggested that Caravaggio had been buried near the sea, in the garden of the small chapel of St Sebastian owned by the Confraternity of Santa Cruz, his actual grave was never found (Hunt, pp. 136–37). In December 2001, a new document was uncovered proving that the painter had died of illness in the hospital of Santa Maria Ausiliatrice in Porto Ercole, but it contained no further indication as to where the painter had been buried.[22] Since the list of enemies outnumbered that of his friends or supporters, Caravaggio 'was not granted the honour of a public funeral, eulogies or catafalque, as was customary for famous painters, nor was an official memorial ceremony staged in Rome' (Puglisi, p. 367). In June 2010, a group of researchers from the University of Bologna claimed to have identified Caravaggio's mortal remains among some bone fragments in the Cemetery of Porto Ercole, the town where he died.[23] The painter, however, is not destined to rest in peace. Despite the evidence provided by the research group led by Giorgio Gruppione, many Caravaggio scholars remained sceptical. Professor Vincenzo Pacelli of the University of Naples (one of the most eminent biographers of Caravaggio) was among those who dismissed the 'bone findings' and, in March 2012, proposed a new theory regarding Merisi's death: Caravaggio did not die in Porto Ercole after all, but in Palo (a town on the Roman coast now known as Ladispoli), where he was murdered by some emissaries of the Knights of Malta with the unofficial assent of the Church.[24]

As Philip Sohm points out in his seminal article 'Caravaggio's Deaths', the final demise of the Lombard painter is one of the most exploited details not only in art history, but in fiction and film alike, as 'beginnings and endings, the dual portals of narrative, are often charged with portent and revelation' (p. 2).[25] A tendency to fictionalize Caravaggio's death was already visible in the accounts of his contemporaries. For instance, although the area around Porto Ercole 'is more often rocky and swampy than sandy' (Sohm, p. 6), his seventeenth-century biographers claim that Caravaggio died on a beach in the scorching summer sun as, symbolically, the beach has often been associated with death, loss, isolation, and punishment.[26] By manipulating the story of his death, they could better characterize his life and style (Sohm, p. 2). Death became the 'explanatory mirror of artistic practice or, in Caravaggio's case malpractice'; so, according to Sohm, when Baglione wrote 'he died as miserably as he lived' he actually meant 'he died as badly as he painted' (ibid.). The image of the scorching sun was also used to create an ironic counter-element to the tenebrism of his art, which was traditionally considered dangerous and destructive (Sohm, p. 8).

After his death, the other most highly debated aspect of Caravaggio's life is his sexuality. According to Hunt, his early biographers indicate clearly that he was a homosexual, but, as we have already seen, in some cases their objectivity is debatable[27] and no surviving private or public record can help us establish his preferences. An argument could be constructed either way, depending on how we choose to read the evidence (Hunt, pp. 61–63). The case in favour of his homosexuality rests mainly on his youthful paintings of nude boys (1593–1602) and on the alleged homoerotic inclinations of his prestigious patron Cardinal Del Monte, as well as on the ambiguity of the term *bardassa* used by one of the witnesses in the 1603 libel trial. *Bardassa* could indicate either a male prostitute or a low-life companion. During the trial, however, Caravaggio denied any knowledge of such a person and the reliability of the witness was undermined by the fact that he was a personal friend of Baglione's (Hunt, p. 62). Those critics who support the homosexuality theory, such as Posner (1971) and Frommel (1971) or Bersani and Dutoit (1998), point out that, whilst Caravaggio never painted female nudes, he often stressed male nudity even in his religious paintings (Hibbard, p. 258). Sciberras and Stone suggest that his early paintings of androgynous boys, who appear to be sensuously on display, represent a subversion of the Venetian tradition of half-length, portrait-like images of sexy females posing as mythological goddesses (p. 7), thus adding an element of parody to his paintings but also the possibility for homoerotic interpretations. *Amor Vincit Omnia* (1601–02) is perhaps the painting with the highest homoerotic charge, but also his *Lute Player* (1595) and *Boy Bitten by a Lizard* (1593–94) can be easily read in such terms. The lute was an instrument traditionally associated with erotic music, and many amorous songs for lute were written in the Baroque period. In Caravaggio's *Lute Player*, the erotic message is emphasized by the fruit and vegetables, particularly by the figs and cucumber (Hibbard, p. 37). The rose behind the ear of his *Boy Bitten by a Lizard* can also be seen as an amorous invitation. What is more, both the lizard and the finger being bitten have erotic connotations; cherries too could have sexual meanings (Hibbard, p. 44). However, such pictures could equally be interpreted in very different ways. *The Lute Player*, for instance, could be seen as a symbol of harmony or as 'an illustration of the 5 senses', and *Boy Bitten by a Lizard* as a warning against the evils of life or an invitation to love with prudence (symbolized by jasmine) if we want to avoid pain and disappointment (Hibbard, pp. 37, 46). Maurizio Calvesi is among those scholars who dismiss the possibility of Caravaggio's homosexuality by claiming that even his early paintings have strong religious connotations. Such paintings, according to Calvesi, usually focus on the dichotomy between human and divine love and, to support his theory, he provides a detailed analysis of the symbolic value, in religious terms, of the fruit and vegetables which populate all of Caravaggio's early paintings (*Le realtà del Caravaggio*, pp. 6–8). *Boy Peeling Fruit*, for instance, is seen as a symbol of Christ redeeming humanity from the original sin (symbolized by the apple) through martyrdom (symbolized by the knife) (p. 9). Green and red grapes, which are extremely common in Caravaggio's early works, also have strong symbolic connotations: red grapes represent blood and death whilst white/green grapes are a metaphor for resurrection, hence the significance in those terms of the *Bacchino Malato* (1593–94) where both varieties of fruit are clearly visible (p. 14). The use of androgynous figures too is devoid of sexual meanings and has a religious overtone. The image of Christ as a child belongs to the Christian tradition; androgyny symbolizes the unity of opposites, God as unity and love as conjunction (pp. 13–14).

The main argument in favour of Caravaggio's heterosexuality is equally weak and is constructed around the fact that one of his models, Maddalena Antonietti, better known as Lena, was referred to as 'Michelangelo's girl'. Also, in July 1605, Caravaggio is said to have fought the notary Mariano Pasqualini over her. She was a street girl who used to stand near Piazza Navona, the kind of courtesan a man like Merisi could afford. Evidence suggests that Caravaggio had regular contacts with two further women, also prostitutes, Anna Bianchini and Fillide Melandroni. Of the three, Fillide was the one with the highest social status. She ran her own house and her clients included clergymen and members of the nobility. Ranuccio Tomassoni

FIG. 1.1. Caravaggio, *Amor Vincit Omnia* (*c*. 1601–02), Berlin: Gemäldegalerie.
FIG. 1.2. Caravaggio, *Lute Player* (1595), St Petersburg: Hermitage Museum.

FIG. 1.3. Caravaggio, *Boy Bitten by a Lizard* (1593–94).
Reproduced by courtesy of the National Gallery, London.

was also close to Fillide and the disagreement between him and Caravaggio might have also been tainted by jealousy. Although all three women feature in Caravaggio's paintings, they are never depicted as objects of lust or, at least, they never convey full-blown sensuality (Hunt, p. 55). Fillide is perhaps the only exception as, in the *St Catherine of Alexandria* (1597–98), she holds a sword, suggesting a sexual punning of some kind (pp. 58–59); in *Judith Beheading Holofernes* (1598) she is portrayed as a femme fatale. Hunt suggests that, like many of his contemporaries, amongst whom was Benvenuto Cellini, Caravaggio might have been bisexual, preferring men in his youth and women later on in adulthood (Hunt, p. 63).[28] Like many other aspects of his life and art, the enigma of his sexuality is likely to remain unsolved. However, it is precisely this aura of mystery that generates fertile narrative material.

Caravaggio's fortune

Although he enjoyed great attention during his lifetime, by the middle of the eighteenth century Caravaggio's art was nearly forgotten, whether because of the scandals caused by his lifestyle or the controversy provoked by his works. There were moments of interest in his style by painters such as Joseph Wright of Derby (1734–97) and Jacques Louis David (1748–1825), but, apart from isolated cases, his name was little more than an entry in art dictionaries (Sciberras and Stone, pp. 13–14). As Francine Prose points out, 'in 1789, the historian Luigi Lanzi wrote that Caravaggio's figures "are remarkable only for their vulgarity" and during the Victorian era, John Ruskin grouped him "among the worshippers of the depraved"' (p. 7). Caravaggio did not have a studio and so did not have real followers. Some artists understood his method and his passion for truthfulness and tried to follow his lesson in a very personal way. Without Caravaggio, the works of Rubens, Velázquez, and Vermeer would probably look very different, but we cannot speak of a real school.[29] In fact, the term *caravaggismo* carried negative connotations and the label was often applied to rather mediocre painters. It was mainly in the twentieth century, thanks to the writings of Roberto Longhi, that Caravaggio 're-emerged as a major personality in the history of art' (Sciberras and Stone, pp. 14–15). At the beginning of the twentieth century Caravaggio was not simply barely known, but, above all, badly known: of the six hundred or so works which were attributed to him many were not his at all, and some art historians were aware of this.[30] Until Longhi's rediscovery of his talent, Caravaggio's image was still affected by the judgement expressed by one of his first biographers, Bellori (1672), who accused him of having destroyed painting by subverting all traditions and common practices, and preventing other painters from appreciating beauty until Annibale Carracci 'venne ad illuminare le menti at a restituire la bellezza all'imitazione' [came to enlighten the minds and reintroduce beauty in imitation] (Sgarbi, p. 42). The descriptions of the early biographers fostered the idea of the *pittore maledetto*, which persisted into the twentieth century and was particularly popular during the Romantic period, especially among those scholars who wanted to stress a link between his genius and madness.[31] They also generated the myth of Caravaggio's realism, which was emphasized towards the end of the nineteenth century during the Naturalist period (*Verismo*). According to Calvesi (*Le realtà del Caravaggio*), however, the culture of Verismo led to a misinterpretation of Caravaggio's oeuvre which continued into the twentieth century and was hard to rectify. In Calvesi's view, if we cannot totally dismiss Caravaggio's realism, we must also remember that his realism had a different meaning from the one attributed to him by many nineteenth-century and contemporary scholars. Caravaggio's art can only be understood if contextualized. It must be studied in relation to the cultural climate of the Counter-Reformation and the ideas of some of his patrons, in particular those of Federico Borromeo. Caravaggio's art was aimed at the masses: it tried to appeal to ordinary people, all poor sinners, through the use of simple and realistic images, to flatter them by portraying the privileged position they occupied according to the Gospel (*Le realtà del Caravaggio*, p. 59). Behind this mass message, however, we also find an elitist discourse, a theological allegory, a learned disquisition (ibid.). Calvesi sees a similarity between Caravaggio's Baroque, symbolic imagination and Giovan Battista Marino's use of language. In both cases, the stylistic acrobatism is never purely empty, virtuous exercise but a way of emphasizing meaning (pp. 40–41). In line with the principles of the Counter-Reformation, Caravaggio stresses the 'massification' of sin, the fact that all human beings are damned and can aspire to salvation only through humility and obedience to the Church. Genius, blood nobility, and cultural superiority are of little importance as only 'the fear of God' can lead to salvation (pp. 60–61). Caravaggio's turmoil is not that of the artist as a creator but that of a poor sinner who is afraid of death and aware of his sins. According to Calvesi, in his works we see that existential consciousness of sin which Kierkegaard considered to be an essential feature of Christianity (p. 62). The sense of equilibrium between man and God typical of the Renaissance is now broken and so is the parallelism between natural truth and revealed truth. There is no longer a natural truth, that is, a logical explanation of reality. Reality is something brutal and obscure that only the light of God can shape or illuminate (pp. 62–63). Pacelli, like Calvesi, highlights the need to study Caravaggio in the context of the spirit of the Counter-Reformation, pointing out that his values and ideas appear to be close to those of the lower church but that his personality cannot easily be categorized. He also stresses the success of the 'populist' interpretation of Caravaggio's works, claiming that such an approach acquired new strength in the twentieth century, first as a result of the 1935 Paris exhibition, then during the Neorealist period and culminating with the 1951 exhibition in Milan.[32] The task of rediscovering Caravaggio after such a long period of neglect was not easy. Pacelli identifies three phases in the Caravaggio scholarship. Initially, the first phase involved putting together a catalogue of the painter's works as during the years he had been attributed works he had never painted whilst some of his originals were kept in terrible conditions in museums' or private storage rooms. The second phase involved the task of reconstructing his life by studying archival sources, establishing a correct chronology of his paintings, and studying his work in the cultural and sociological context of his time. Finally, the third stage, which began during the 1990s and is still ongoing, requires the revision of previously accepted statements as a result of new archival material becoming available (Pacelli, p. 8).

The first major attempt at revising Caravaggio dates back to 1906–07, thanks to the unfinished work of Wolfgang Kallab. Kallab was one of the first scholars to pay attention to the context and provide a detailed description of the artistic situation in Rome at the beginning of the seventeenth century (Berne-Joffroy, p. 10). Kallab is also among the first to stress the need to reassess the 'realist' label too often attached to Caravaggio (Berne-Joffroy, p. 47). However, the impact of his study was limited as, apart from a few specialists, the number of people interested in Caravaggio was small. The 1909 article by Lionello Venturi[33] marks the beginning of Italian scholarship on Caravaggio (Pacelli, p. 7). Venturi, whose father, Adolfo Venturi, in 1893 had also contributed to the re-evaluation of Caravaggio through a small book entitled *Il Museo e la Galleria Borghese*, was extremely active. He produced complex studies involving the analysis of archival material (he published Mancini and some documents found in the state archives of Modena and Mantua); a careful definition of Caravaggio's *giorgionismo*, against Kallab's theory that Caravaggio had been mainly influenced by Titian, Veronese, and Tintoretto; and a lucid analysis of the importance of the still-life genre in Caravaggio's oeuvre (previously considered to be marginal). In the 1920s, Venturi also played a vital role in the debate on seventeenth-century art initiated by De Chirico in the journal *Valori plastici* with his article 'La mania del Seicento'. According to De Chirico, far from being a landmark in the Italian tradition, the seventeenth century is responsible for the corruption/decadence of painting visible in his age. The success of seventeenth-century art is due to its easiness. In his opinion, it is a lot easier to imitate a painter like Caravaggio than Botticelli or Piero della Francesca, because Baroque painters confine themselves to a banal reproduction of reality, painting directly from models without the mediation of drawing. As a result, seventeenth-century paintings are commercially viable and modern audiences can easily identify with them.[34] Whilst major seventeenth-century scholars like Longhi and Marangoni refused to intervene in this debate and ignored the provocation, Venturi tried to deconstruct the opposition between an idealist fifteenth century and a realist seventeenth century. He pointed out that both centuries were interested in realism and had idealist moments, so much so that more traditional critics and art historians considered the fifteenth century to be realist while they labelled the seventeenth century mannerist (Storchi, p. 140). The attacks on the seventeenth century published in *Valori plastici* are perhaps more interesting than Venturi's defence, as they help us understand the importance of the Baroque in modern culture and the need to study seventeenth-century painters in the context of the Counter-Reformation culture. As Storchi points out, for instance, Suckert's article looks at the seventeenth century as a transhistorical phenomenon, marking the beginning of attitudes which survived through the centuries — such as the rejection of the equivalence between beauty, symmetry, and order, and the idea that artistic activities transcend the traditional binary oppositions of true/false and good/evil. The seventeenth century is also accused of allowing the classical Mediterranean spirit to become corrupted by northern European influences of Protestant origin, and of introducing a sense of metaphysical restlessness which was alien to the Catholic, classical spirit, features which we undoubtedly encounter in Caravaggio's paintings (Storchi, pp. 147–52). Despite the strong declarations of poetics — which in actual fact were masked political statements — by the artists collaborating with *Valori plastici*, the seventeenth century continued to be studied in the 1920s. Extremely important for the re-evaluation of Caravaggio was the *Il Seicento italiano* exhibition which took place at Palazzo Pitti in Florence in the spring 1922. According to Lionello Venturi, this exhibition represented the crowning achievement of those scholars who had been striving to place Caravaggio amongst the most important Italian artists of all times. From a practical point of view, this exhibition enabled the public for the first time to appreciate fully the Contarelli Chapel paintings — usually confined to the darkness of poor lighting of San Luigi Dei Francesi.[35] The juxtaposition of various works attributed to the Lombard painter allowed the experts to eliminate a few paintings from his corpus (Berne-Joffroy, p. 155) and to reassess the chronology of his works.

The other key scholar who is extremely active at the beginning of the twentieth century is Roberto Longhi. Although, between 1914 and 1916, he mainly wrote about followers of Caravaggio, his studies are extremely important for the appreciation of the *maestro*. His essay on Borginni (1914) sheds light on Caravaggio's middle period, the essay on Carracciolo (1915), also known as Battistello, is useful when looking at Caravaggio's last phase, and the one on Gentileschi (1916) helps us understand Caravaggio's early production (Berne-Joffroy, p. 109). The issue of the *Caravaggisti* would continue to play a prominent role in the debates of art historians until the 1970s and had a direct impact on the planning of exhibitions.[36] Scholars were divided into two factions. One faction was determined to expand the field. The other faction comprised those who, like Longhi, stressed the importance of distinguishing between a close adherence to the style of the *maestro* and the transmission of the wider, but at the same time more significant legacy with social and ethical implications. This was the case with the *Bamboccianti*, a group of Dutch painters who lived in Rome in the mid-seventeenth century famous for the lack of decorum of their subject matter and their interest in ordinary aspects of life or *bambocciate*, from which their name derives (Gregori, p. 52). Longhi wrote further important studies between 1927 and 1930, but, after two decades of enthusiasm for Caravaggio, both in Italy and abroad, scholars seemed to lose interest in the Lombard painter until the beginning of the 1940s when a new monograph by Schudt (published in Vienna in 1942)[37] was followed by an article by Giulio Carlo Argan (1943) and one by Longhi (entitled *Ultimissime sul Caravaggio*). Longhi severely criticized Schudt for having attributed some mediocre paintings to Caravaggio (whilst questioning more obviously authentic works) and Argan for his comments on Caravaggio's *Deposition* (Berne-Joffroy, pp. 314–16). The next milestone in the Caravaggio revival was the 1951 Italian translation of Bernard Berenson's *Caravaggio: Of his Incongruity and his Fame*.[38] The book was very controversial. Berenson was one of the first scholars to ignore questions of chronology or attribution in order to focus on the wider context. Berenson refused to consider Caravaggio a Baroque painter. In his opinion, Michelangelo Merisi's style was archaic (p. 69) and the only label that could describe his works is anti-Baroque (p. 81). According to Berenson, the immense popularity of Caravaggio in the twentieth century, compared to that of other great figures of his time such as Rubens, can only be explained through his eccentric and violent lifestyle: 'sono il carattere e la carriera di Caravaggio che oggi attirano tanti verso di lui e non, oso credere, le sue qualità di artista, tanto meno di pittore' [it is Caravaggio's character and career that attract so many people to him and not, I dare say, his qualities as an artist and even less as a painter] (p. 70). Berenson was also among the first to suggest that Caravaggio might have been homosexual (p. 70), something which greatly irritated Longhi, who reacted with a brief article entitled 'Novelletta del Caravaggio invertito' in which he ridiculed the idea.[39] All the post-war period scholarly efforts to promote the reappraisal of Caravaggio culminated in the 1951 Milan exhibition, which took place from 21 April until 15 July at the Palazzo Reale. The curator was Roberto Longhi, who also edited the catalogue with contributions by Baroni, Dell'Acqua, and Gregori. The event was extraordinary, because, for the first time, almost all the then-known works by Caravaggio were gathered together. This generated a wealth of new material and an unprecedented scholarly interest in the Lombard painter. The exhibition attracted a total of half a million visitors, with an average of 20,000 visitors a day, and it is estimated that 75–80per cent of the population of Milan went to see it. Suddenly, a painter who was no longer completely unknown, but not particularly popular either, was in the limelight (Berne-Joffroy, p. xii), catching the interest of ordinary people, of people who had never been to a museum before (Berne-Joffroy, p. xx). As Giorgio Galansino put it in a letter to André Berne-Joffroy, it was the kind of success normally expected only in football stadia (p. xvi); it took even the organizers by surprise, as they did not have the time to set up a statistical database (to establish the provenance of visitors and other important factors such as the relevance of the location), which would have been useful for the planning of future exhibitions (Berne-Joffroy, p. 11). Despite its tremendous success, the exhibition also attracted fierce criticism — particularly in the context of the debates on realism in art promoted by the left and the Italian Communist Party in the immediate post-war period. According to some liberal writers, such as Alfredo Mezio of *Il Mondo* or Leonardo Borghese of *Il Corriere della sera*, Longhi was encouraging a 'populist' reading of Caravaggio that could be politically manipulated by the left (Berne-Joffroy, pp. xii–xiii). Mezio was particularly critical and engaged in a personal debate with 'il Professore', as Longhi was then known, through a series of articles published in *Il Mondo* between June and September 1951. According to Mezio, the exhibition had generated 'una specie di congiura trasversale ai danni dell'arte moderna, borghese, disinteressata, non ideologica' (p. xiii), because both the left and the Catholics had used it to make Caravaggio's art match their ideologies. With time Mezio's remarks became increasingly aggressive. By the end of July, he was accusing Longhi of populism and having turned Caravaggio into a kind of soap-opera character: the title of his article, 'Anacleto il caravaggista', encourages such a connection, as Anacleto was a popular working-class character in a post-war radio programme. By August, he was blaming the left for mixing up the notions of popular and populist. He claimed that his colleagues at *L'Unità* (the Communist paper) had misunderstood Gramsci's theories and that according to Marx the proletariat should be class-conscious, something Caravaggio's characters lacked. Caravaggio's proletariat was a ' "Lumpen-proletariat", that is a proletariat of rags'

(Berne-Joffroy, pp. lxxxiv–lxxxv). Also Vittorini, who would shortly be leaving the Communist Party after a lengthy dispute, in an article in *La Stampa* dated 17 July 1951, seemed to agree with Mezio stressing, as he had done on the pages of *Il Politecnico* in 1947, that artists and intellectuals should remain independent and refrain from 'playing the fiddle of revolution' (Berne-Joffroy, p. lxxxvi). His criticism was particularly harsh as he attacked not only the exhibition but also the painter, whom he considered to be a 'fake realist' interested only in the most obvious and vulgar aspects of reality that would later inspire the worst trends of nineteenth-century painting: theatricality and expressivity (Berne-Joffroy, p. xiii). Vittorini also attacked the attitude of most viewers for their tendency to consider Caravaggio in relation to our times, rather than his time, thus inevitably gaining a very limited and misleading knowledge of the Lombard painter (p. xiv). Regardless of whether we agree or disagree with the aforementioned arguments, such remarks are extremely interesting. Not only do they represent a historical record of Caravaggio's reputation in the twentieth century, but they also capture one of the main reasons why Caravaggio's popularity could transcend the realm of art history and enter that of popular culture. To use Longhi's words, Caravaggio was 'un pittore che ha cercato di essere "naturale", comprensibile; umano più che umanistico; in una parola popolare' [a painter who tried to be 'natural', understandable; human rather than humanistic; in one word, popular] (Berne-Joffroy, p. 351). By realizing that the only way of ensuring an adequate reappraisal of Caravaggio was through a rediscovery of his 'naturalist', or better 'natural', origins, Longhi helped create a myth whose impact he could not have foreseen. As Hunt points out, nowadays 'Caravaggio is the most renowned Old Master of recent times. More articles, books, exhibitions, films and novels have been devoted to him than to all of his contemporaries combined' (Hunt, p. ix). Despite Vittorini's disapproval, one of the main reasons for Caravaggio's popularity is the fact that his art addresses 'a number of issues that are as compelling today as they were in 1600', such as 'the preoccupation with spontaneous violence, the allure of ambivalent sexuality, the expression of doubt in matters of faith and salvation, and the immersion of the artist in his own imaginative creations' (Hunt, p. ix). Caravaggio's trans-disciplinary 'potential' was already visible in 1959 when André Berne-Joffroy published his *Dossier Caravage* and in a letter to Jean Wahl, in which he discusses the reactions and comments caused by his book, says: 'mi fanno piacere gli happy few che parlano di "prima detective-story della critica dell'arte" o, come ha detto lei, di "un romanzo con flashback e flash-forward"' [I like the happy few who talk of 'the first detective story of art history' or, as you do, of 'a novel with flashbacks and flash-forward moments'] (p. lxix).

Notes to Chapter 1

1. Rainer Maria Rilke quoted in Gaston Bachelard, *The Poetics of Space* (Boston: Beacon Press, 1969), p. 220.
2. Varriano, *Caravaggio: The Art of Realism*, p. 76.
3. Francine Prose, *Caravaggio: Painter of Miracles* (New York: Harper Press, 2007; first published in 2005), p. 25. Also, according to Prose, 'the Italians' reputation for violence and banditry' was

such that 'British playwrights of sixteenth and seventeenth centuries — Caravaggio's contemporaries and near contemporaries — mined Italian street life and exaggerated the sad histories of Italy's spectacularly dysfunctional and incestuous noble families for the plots of their gory dramas' (ibid.). Our interest in the misbehaviour of the Corleone and Soprano Mafia families, Prose maintains, is the modern equivalent of the Baroque passion for revenge tragedies (ibid.).

4. Thomas V. Cohen and Elizabeth S. Cohen, *Words and Deeds in Renaissance Rome* (Toronto: University of Toronto Press, 1993; rpt. 2000), p. 16.
5. Helen Langdon, *Caravaggio: A life* (London: Pimlico, 1999; first published by Chatto & Windus 1998), pp. 1–2.
6. Catherine Puglisi, *Caravaggio* (London: Phaidon Press, 1998), p. 44.
7. According to Thomas and Elizabeth Cohen the large number of 'strangers' in Rome contributed to the widespread violence:

> Rome was a city of loose men and loose women [...]. Loosely tethered to their protectors but not much pledged down by neighbourhood, kind, group or professional association, these outsiders were often quick to fly into violence. Not all rough deeds were theirs but they did much to set the tone. (Cohen and Cohen, p. 15)

8. Maurizio Calvesi, *Le realtà del Caravaggio* (Turin: Einaudi, 1990), p. 49.
9. Howard Hibbard, *Caravaggio*, p. 31.
10. Richard Spear, *Caravaggio and his Followers* (London: Harper & Row, 1975), p. x; *L'ultimo Caravaggio e la cultura artistica a Napoli, in Sicilia e a Malta*, ed. by Maurizio Calvesi (Milan: Ediprint, 1987), p. 13. Also, in February 2007 a pensioner researching seventeenth-century painters in the Archivio Diocesano in Milan discovered a document confirming, as some scholars were suspecting, that Michelangelo Merisi was born in Milan (not in Caravaggio), in the parish of Santo Stefano in Brolo where he was christened on 30 September 1571. Pierluigi Panza, 'Caravaggio Milanese', *Il Corriere della sera*, 26 February 2007, <http://www.corriere.it> [accessed 12 October 2008].
11. Andrew Graham-Dixon, *Caravaggio: A Life Sacred and Profane* (London: Allen Lane, 2010), p. 52.
12. Giovan Pietro Bellori, *Le vite de' pittori, scultori et architetti moderni* (Rome: [n. pub.], 1872), p. 202.
13. John T. Spike, *Caravaggio* (New York: Abbeville Press, 2001), p. 22.
14. See also Hunt, p. 106.
15. Keith Sciberras and David M. Stone, *Caravaggio: Art, Knighthood and Malta* (Valletta: Midsea Books, 2006), p. 10.
16. Sciberras and Stone point out that the first seminal work on the Malta period was published by Farrugia Randon in 2004. Prior to that Caravaggio's stay on the island 'was really only accessible through a dozen or so specialized articles and essays' (p. vii). The first major Caravaggio exhibition in Malta opened in September 2007: <http://www/artinmalta.com/?p.62> [accessed 30 May 2010].
17. Philip Farrugia Randon, *Caravaggio, Knight of Malta* (Sliema: AVC, 2004), pp. 66–73.
18. Langdon points out that, according to a 1935 article by F. Ashford, the Giustiniani family had facilitated Caravaggio's move to Malta. Whilst their involvement is not to be excluded, the more widely accepted theory is that Caravaggio sailed with Fabrizio Sforza Colonna (p. 417).
19. As Sciberras and Stone point out,

> the fact that, after his expulsion from the Order, he seems to have lived with relative tranquillity at Messina, indicates that probably there was not a civil case pending against him in Malta. Thus, after the *privatio habitus*, his juridical case could have been considered concluded. The victim, Fra Giovanni Rodomonte Roero, had left the island. (p. 40)

Even though we now know that Caravaggio was not the person who inflicted the wounds, it is obvious that he had powerful friends and protectors. Farrugia Randon, however, is keen to stress that at the time of Caravaggio's arrival in Sicily the relationship between Messina and the Order was very strained and 'it was not impossible for fugitive and defrocked knights to be reaccepted with open arms within the Order' (p. 127).

20. The Grand Master himself was suggested as a possible accomplice, but he is not likely to have been involved (Farrugia Randon, p. 137). Other possible people who helped him are Fabrizio

Sforza Colonna (Hunt, p. 119) or the Procurator of Prisons who was a relative of the Carafa family in Naples who had previously protected Caravaggio (Puglisi, p. 309).
21. Catherine Puglisi points out that 'Caravaggio's macabre choice provoked various interpretations among modern viewers, foremost among the psychoanalytical' (p. 306). Despite being a stimulating exercise, applying psychoanalytical theories to someone who lived more than 400 years ago could be misleading: 'Pictorial tradition and contextual evidence offer the most persuasive interpretation of Caravaggio's unusual signature: a penitential attitude and a desire for expiating his crime' (ibid.). Puglisi suggests that Caravaggio was probably familiar with two paintings which used 'the motif of writing a message with the martyr's blood: Vincenzo Foppa's Martyrdom of St Peter Martyr and Moretto's canvas of the same subject', both illustrating the legend of the dying saint who wrote 'credo in unum deum' in his own blood. Caravaggio, however, transposed the motif and what 'in the earlier paintings had been a pious affirmation of faith can be constructed as the painter's personal statement of faith and salvation' (p. 307).
22. Giuseppe La Fauci and Gianna Anastasia, 'L'ultima verità sulla fine di Caravaggio', *Corriere della sera*, 21 December 2001, <http://archiviostorico.corriere.it/2001/dicembre/21/ultima_verita_sulla_fine_CARAVAGGIO_co_0_01122111249.shtml> [consulted 10 December 2007].
23. Antonia Bordigon, 'Caccia allo scheletro: Trovate le ossa di Caravaggio?', *Il Sole 24 Ore*, 16 June 2010, <http://www.ilsole24ore.com/art/cultura/2010–06–16/caccia-scheletro-trovate-ossa-192300.shtml?uuid=AYl5P7yB> [accessed 10 July 2010].
24. 'La morte di Caravaggio? Fu "omicidio di Stato" e avvenne a Palo nel Lazio', *Corriere del Mezzogiorno*, 31 March 2012, <http://www.corrieredelmezzogiorno.corriere.it/napoli/notizie/arte_e_cultura/2012/31-marzo-2012/morte-caravaggio-fu-omicidiodi-stato-avvenne-palo-lazio-2003902883297.shtml> [accessed 1 April 2012].
25. Philip Sohm, 'Caravaggio's Deaths', *The Art Bulletin*, 84 (2002), 449–68 (online 1–22), <http://www.collegeart.org/artbulletin> [accessed 20 January 2008]. Interesting fictional works giving Caravaggio's death a prominent role are: Dominique Fernandez, *La Course à l'abîme* (2002); Enzo Siciliano, 'Morte di Caravaggio', in *Cuore e fantasmi* (1990); Erri de Luca, 'Agguati', in *Alzaia* (1997); David Stedman, *That Terrible Shadowing* (2009); the dance theatre show *Caravaggio: Exile and Death* (2003) by Darshan Singh Bhuller.
26. Sohm points out that such associations are a constant trope in literature 'from Dante's Inferno to Thomas Mann's Death in Venice and Paul Theroux Mosquito's Coast' (p. 6).
27. Baglione, for instance, could have done with his sexuality what he did with his death and used the allegation to discredit the image of a fellow painter he hated. We must also remember that in seventeenth-century Italy homosexuality was a crime punishable by death.
28. As Prose points out,

> Sex between men in Caravaggio's time was viewed very differently than it is today [...]. It was widely understood and accepted that a man could have sex with both males and females at different stages in his life. Moreover, sex with another male was not associated with effeminacy [...] especially if one took the active role, and only with the appropriate partner, which is to say with a boy, preferably smooth-skinned and beardless and not older than eighteen. (p. 44)

During the Renaissance in Florence and the surrounding cities, homosexuality was so common that not only was a special branch of the police created to deal with sodomites, but the city fathers of Lucca legalized prostitution in the hope that the increasing numbers of available females might decrease the incidence of sodomy (ibid., p. 42).
29. Vittorio Sgarbi, *Caravaggio* (Milan: Skira, 2005), p. 43.
30. André Berne-Joffroy, *Dossier Caravaggio*, trans. by Arturo Galansino (Milan: 5 Continents Editions, 2005), p. cxix.
31. Lucia Trigilia, 'Premessa', in *L'ultimo Caravaggio e la cultura artistica Napoli, in Sicilia e a Malta*, ed. by Maurizio Calvesi, pp. 7–11 (p. 7). According to Nicola Spinosa, director of the Polo Museale Napoletano, nowadays the myth of the pittore maledetto survives out of convenience, as a marketing tool capable of attracting, with the complicity of the media, endless numbers of visitors ready to queue for hours to visit mediocre exhibitions, often 'dei veri a propri bidoni' ('real rip-offs'), to the joy of politicians, local councillors, and producers/retailers of cards,

books, and other gadgets: <http://www.caravaggioultimotempo.it/it/mostra_caravaggio.html> [accessed 10 December 2007].
32. Vincenzo Pacelli, *L'ultimo Caravaggio, dalla Maddalena a mezza figura ai due san Giovanni (1606–1610)* (Todi: Ediart, 1994), p. 201.
33. Lionello Venturi, 'Note sulla Galleria Borghese', *L'Arte*, 12 (1909), 31–50.
34. Simona Storchi, *Valori Plastici 1918–1922: Le inquietudini del nuovo classico*, supplement to *The Italianist* (2006), p. 135.
35. Lionello Venturi, *Il Caravaggio: Quaranta riproduzioni con testo e catalogo* (Rome: Società Editrice d'Arte Illustrata, 1925), p. 5.
36. Mina Gregori, 'Significato delle mostre Caravaggesche dal 1951 a oggi', in *Novità sul Caravaggio*, ed. by Mia Cinotti and Carlo Nitti (Milan: Regione Lombardia, 1975), pp. 27–60 (p. 48).
37. Ludwig Schudt, *Caravaggio* (Vienna: Anton Schroll, 1942).
38. Bernard Berenson, *Caravaggio: Delle sue incongruenze e della sua fama*, trans. by Luisa Vetrova (Florence: Electa, 1951). The original English edition was published in London in 1953. All references are from the 2006 Italian edition (Milan: Abscondita) with an afterword by Luisa Vertova, editor and translator of the 1951 edition.
39. Roberto Longhi, 'Novelletta del Caravaggio invertito', *Paragone*, 3 (1952), 62–64.

CHAPTER 2

Michelangelo Merisi's Lives: The 'Painter as Character' Genre

> Sapete invece su cosa posa tutto? Ve lo dico io. Su una presunzione [...]. La presunzione che la realtà, qual'è per voi, debba essere e sia ugualmente per tutti gli altri.
> [You know what all this relies on? I'll tell you. On an assumption [...] The assumption that reality, as you see it, must be and is the same for everyone else]
> LUIGI PIRANDELLO, *Uno nessuno, centomila*, p. 26

This chapter looks at a sample of fictional biographies or life stories and at a recent RAI docudrama devoted to Michelangelo Merisi da Caravaggio with the intention of providing a possible explanation for what could easily be described as an obsession with the painter's life and a brief overview of the interaction between the discipline of art history, the art industry and fiction, cinema or television. The examples aim to cover a wide range of authors, differing in age, nationality, background, and writing styles to stress the omnipresence of the biographical genre, which, as Ossorio's text illustrates, extends to children's literature. The sample consists of Dominique Fernandez's *La course à l'abîme* (2002), Atle Næss's *Doubting Thomas* (1997), Andrea Camilleri's *Il colore del sole* (2007), Rita Guidi's *Il gigante perduto* (2004), Antonella Ossorio's *L'angelo della luce: Il giovane Caravaggio sogna il suo destino* (2004), and the 2006 docudrama *Caravaggio* produced by RAI Fiction and directed by Angelo Longoni.[1] As suggested in the previous chapter, and as the varied nature of the aforementioned works demonstrates, this constant interest in Caravaggio's life story is such that it cannot be easily dismissed as a simple morbid fascination with a dark and mysterious individual. In order to understand the proliferation of texts engaging in one way or another with Merisi's biography, we need to address a series of questions which transcend the limited sphere of those individual works or of their authors.

First of all, it is important to look at the role played by Caravaggio himself and by his early biographers in creating the self-perpetuating myth of the *pittore maledetto*, which is still very much alive today. Second, we must consider the impact of more recent developments in art history in fashioning a 'populist' counter-image which emphasizes the painter's interest in ordinary people rather than his propensity to violence, whether in his private life or in the subject matter of many of his paintings. I will argue that both images contain a kind of autopoietic force that encourages endless variations of the same story. Significantly, many of the works engaging in one way or another with Caravaggio's life represent the first or second fictional effort of their authors. Rita Guidi's book is just one example, but we could also mention Neil Griffiths's *Saving Caravaggio*, which will be analysed in the next chapter, and which is only his second novel.[2] It is as if, in the age of 'pesniero debole' (weak thought), new authors feel the need to test their creative abilities through someone else's life story.[3]

Another vital factor that cannot be disregarded is the role played by the art industry, particularly the tendency in recent years to combine exhibitions with other cultural events such as film nights (Naples, 2004;[4] Rome, 2004; London, 2005), concerts (Rome, 2004; Barcelona, 2005); theatre performances (Naples, 2004;[5] Rome, 2004), or collections of short stories (Düsseldorf, 2006). Antonella Ossorio, for instance, was initially contacted by the Neapolitan publishing house Electa and asked to produce a children's book that could be sold together with the catalogue of the 2004 exhibition 'Caravaggio: L'ultimo tempo' hosted by the Capodimonte Museum. Camilleri, instead, originally published a short story for the 2006 Düsseldorf exhibition in the collection entitled *Maler Mörder Mythos: Geschichten zu Caravaggio*, but claims that whilst researching the topic he accumulated so much material that he decided to expand the original story into a novel. As the curators of the 2003–04 exhibition 'Caravaggio, una mostra impossibile' pointed out, in an era when art can be reproduced digitally, the museum opens to the masses and the gap between high art and popular culture becomes narrower and narrower.[6] According to Vittorio Sgarbi, the 2001–02 exhibition in Japan marked the bridging of this gap. In an interesting review of the event entitled 'In Giappone tutti pazzi per Caravaggio, da maledetto a mito Pop', Polese Ranieri pointed out how not even the terrorist attacks of 9/11 could stop the preparations for this event in Japan.[7] Despite some initial fears, the exhibition went ahead as planned, starting in Tokyo at the Teien Museum from 20 September until 16 December, and continuing in Okazaki from 22 December 2001 until 24 January 2002. Vittorio Sgarbi, who at the time was Undersecretary for Cultural Heritage, attended the opening of the exhibition, officially representing the Italian government. In his opinion, the fact that some of Caravaggio's works were shown for the first time in Japan constituted the last step towards the consecration of Caravaggio to popular culture, a process confirmed by the endless queues of visitors forming outside any Caravaggio exhibition either in Italy or abroad since the late 1990s (Ranieri, p. 31).

In 2003, Louise Govier, adult-learning manager at the National Gallery in London, stressed the importance of art fiction for museum and gallery bookshops. Using the National Gallery shop as an example, she pointed out that, in a period of eighteen months from the moment it was introduced, the fiction section had increased rapidly 'in scale and popularity' to become the part of the shop with the highest turnover.[8] According to Govier, the commercial success of this kind of fiction is determined by the fact that 'people with an amateur interest in art are hungry for a kind of writing which acknowledges the excitement and sense of wonder they feel when looking at a painting or sculpture' (p. 29). Fiction can explore aspects which are normally neglected by art historians because they are too ambiguous and elusive, such as the 'intersection between an artist's emotional experience and what they produce' (p. 29). Often these works do not promote an original interpretation of the subject matter with which they engage, but tend to reinforce by repetition or slight variation of the same theme those ideas and stereotypes already ingrained in the reader's mind, confirming Petronio's views on popular fiction.[9] However, regardless of whether we consider these books as serious literature or simply 'airport lounge fodder', they are important, Govier concludes, because they help to build bridges between people and art and allow museums and galleries to open up to the masses (p. 30).

Finally, we must look at biographies and fictional biographies in the context of postmodern literary theory and reflect on how this old and traditional genre can appeal to our contemporary world. Particular attention will be given to the 'author as character' genre, as defined by Paul Franssen and Ton Hoenselaars, of which the 'painter as character' is considered to be a variation.[10] As Franssen and Hoenselaars point out, paradoxically, this literary device 'offers a lively and economical way of not only raising but actually embodying such postmodern concerns as representation, the impossibility of historical knowledge, the share of the author in the genesis of a text, and intertextuality' (p. 11), concerns which were at least implicitly present in many of Caravaggio's works. As we shall see later, the 'author as character' is a hybrid genre that crosses various boundaries and is often difficult to define in a simple and concise way, particularly in relation to other more established genres such as biography. For the purpose of this study I selected texts whose fictional nature is unquestioned, whilst works whose status is more ambiguous, such as the controversial *M: The Man Who Became Caravaggio* by Peter Robb (2001) or *Caravaggio: Painter of Miracles* by Francine Prose (2005) will only be briefly touched upon,[11] even though they provide further evidence of the 'cult status' Caravaggio has reached in our times and of the reappropriation of his image by popular culture.

Caravaggio *pittore maledetto* versus Caravaggio the hero of the poor

In a seminal article entitled '*In Figura Diaboli: Self and Myth in Caravaggio's David and Goliath*', Stone argues that, if Caravaggio's image had already acquired dark and negative connotations during his lifetime, it is not simply due to some features of his personality.[12] His early biographers Baglione (1642) and Bellori (1672) had personal reasons for disliking Merisi, the first being 'a jealous painter who had sued the Lombard for libel', whilst the latter someone 'whose aesthetics were diametrically opposed to Merisi's' (Stone, p. 20). Both lived in an age in which to construct links between personality and art was deemed acceptable. According to a popular fifteenth-century saying, every painter paints himself, so the representation of filth, poverty, or deformity was considered to be a sign of moral depravity. As Stone demonstrates, the late seventeenth-century Florentine biographer Filippo Baldinucci also applied this theory to Caravaggio. After accusing him of filling his religious paintings with all sorts of vulgarities, which resulted in their being rejected by the original commissioners and in the vilification of art itself, he invited

Fig. 2.1. Caravaggio, *David with the Head of Goliath* (1606–07), Rome: Galleria Borghese.

FIG. 2.2. Caravaggio, *The Incredulity of St Thomas* (1601), Potsdam: Sanssouci Palace (Picture Gallery).

his readers to pardon Caravaggio because his style of painting was just a mirror image of his personality, as his manner of conversation and personal behaviour indicated (Stone, p. 22).

In Stone's view, however, Caravaggio greatly aided his biographers in constructing his dark persona, not through his outburst of temper but through his self-portraits. From his *Sick Bacchus* of 1593 to his 1609–10 *David with the Head of Goliath*,[13] it could be argued that Caravaggio himself 'made Caravaggio the explicit — and self-abasing — subject of his own paintings' (p. 23). The Caravaggio/Goliath duality is particularly interesting as 'Caravaggio seems openly to mock his detractors by this outrageous gesture of casting himself as a grimacing, screaming, bleeding and bodiless Goliath' (p. 24). According to Stone, Caravaggio created his 'witty, satirical *persona*', which his biographers, and even some modern art historians, mistook as an indication of a 'disturbed, gender-confused, violent personality' (ibid.).[14] Whilst recognizing the potential of the various psychoanalytical studies of this painting, Stone distances himself from their conclusions because according to him Caravaggio is very much in control of his discourse and, rather than self-destructive, the mode of the painting is 'provocative, witty, poetic and satirical' (p. 25). Rudolf Preimesberger, in 1998, had already pointed out the highly rhetorical construction of *David with the Head of Goliath*, stating that Caravaggio had employed a *pathos*-inducing technique which was commonly used in tribunals in order to shock but, at the same time, get the support of the public.[15] Such a technique relied on irony and Caravaggio's self-accusation can be interpreted as an example of self-irony aimed at an elite capable of recognizing this explicit ironic touch. Negative self-portraits belonged to a well-established and conventional pattern of male self-deprecation and humiliation in the presence of a pure and beautiful woman, which was particularly common in love poetry; and which was intended as a gallant and erotic homage to the lady in question. In Caravaggio, this tradition acquires a paradoxical overtone as it is applied to a relationship between two men. Even if, in order to appreciate the full significance of this gesture, we need to look at it in the context of the extremely negative and erotic connotations attached to the figure of Goliath in the Bible and in exegesis, the element of irony cannot be denied (Preimesberger, p. 66).

By ironically belittling himself, Caravaggio looked down on those who criticized him and reaffirmed his superiority (Preimesberger, p. 67). Stone also points out, through Shearman, that, from Donatello to Caravaggio, various authors had explored the homoerotic undercurrent of the David and Goliath story through the conceit of the cruel beloved, 'of the poet as victim, who suffers or even dies from the cruel indifference of his unattainable, beautiful lover' (Stone, pp. 25–26). What is more, Stone endorses the theory proposed by Posèq that 'a lost pseudo-antique statue of *Apollo with the Flayed Skin and Head of Marsyas* served as a source for Caravaggio's composition' (p. 27) and sees in the self-portrait as Goliath a possible identification with Marsyas. In this case the painting could also be seen as a comment on 'the idea of Earthly or "Low" Art (Caravaggio's naturalism) being made a martyr by Divine Art (Apollo)' (pp. 27–28). This interpretation is also made plausible by the fact that *David with the Head of Goliath* is frequently compared to the *Medusa*, another 'statement about the power of Caravaggio's naturalist art' (p. 35). Finally, Stone concludes by pointing out that 'the very choice of the *David* theme for a work of art [...] begs comparison to Buonarroti's' (p. 37), whose identification with his David statue in Florence was universally acknowledged. Throughout his career, Caravaggio adapted ideas and motifs from his namesake, sometimes in converting Michelangelo's classicism 'into a deliberately irreverent, sexually aggressive engine of disarming naturalism' (p. 37). In this light, Caravaggio's 'pictorial self-mutilation and self-abasement' become signs of 'the artist's fierce competitiveness and quest for originality' (ibid.).

As we have seen, both Preimesberger and Stone consider Caravaggio's obsession with self-portraits, but particularly his *David with the Head of Goliath*, as central to the creation of a mythical persona which inevitably influenced biographers over the centuries. The image of the tormented genius, or *pittore maledetto*, in fact, resurfaced in the Romantic period and keeps thriving in our 'celebrity-obsessed, tabloid culture', and has led to 'an international craze to hunt for documents revealing tidbits' (Stone, p. 19) of Merisi's character which culminated in the 1990s with controversial publications such as the 1994 *Caravaggio Assassino*.[16] Significantly, apart from Camilleri's book, all the fictional works we are about to analyse contain references to *David with the Head of Goliath*. It is also interesting to note that even very prestigious exhibitions, such as 'Caravaggio: The Final Years' which took place in London at the National Gallery between February and May 2005, seem to fall into this trap. As Sheila McTighe points out, 'London put on a show that dramatized the tumultuous biography of the artist' where the lighting of the exhibition space was used to create a sense of drama, even though the almost twilight darkness made some of the larger paintings difficult to see.[17] The choice to 'set off the Galleria Borghese's *David with the Head of Goliath* in a small room at the end of the exhibition' was also revealing: it presented Caravaggio's self-portrait as 'the culmination of his career, the ultimate confession, the transparent representation of his life in art', offering the masses of viewers what they wanted to see whilst avoiding the problematic question of the painting's dating, whether it was painted in Rome in 1606 or in Naples in 1610 (p. 586).

As already discussed in Chapter 1, the other more recent and, perhaps, less powerful image of Caravaggio is the 'populist' one which was promoted by Longhi in the twentieth century, particularly through his 1951 exhibition in Milan. The advocates of this image often consider Caravaggio as a product of the Counter-Reformation. They usually stress his Milanese background and the impact a figure like that of Carlo Borromeo might have had on the young Michelangelo. It generally appeals to scholars and writers who wish to highlight the political or, at least, revolutionary aspect of Caravaggio's works. Being mainly centred on his oeuvre, rather than his life, it does not feature as prominently as that of the *pittore maledetto* in the 'author as character genre'. However, since some of the texts we are about to analyse fit the definition of more than one genre, this populist image will also be present in our selected sample, particularly in Fernandez's novel. As we shall see later, in the section on *La course à l'abîme* and in the chapter on Caravaggio and homoeroticism, Fernandez is particularly interested in pointing out the multilayered nature of Caravaggio's works, which he sees as mirroring the complexities of human nature and sexuality, and which he turns into a vehicle for exploring the inner struggles of gay artists across the centuries.

The author/painter as character genre

In order to appreciate fully the significance of the proliferation of biographies, fictional biographies, and various life stories devoted to the Lombard painter, we must look at them in the context of a renewed interest in real-life, historical, and usually canonical authors in both literature and cinema. As Franssen and Hoenselaars point out, paradoxically 'the very postmodernism that proclaimed the death of the author and the demise of the character delights in resurrecting historical authors as characters' (p. 11). In her seminal contribution to Franssen and Hoenselaars's volume, Fokkema shows how in the famous 1968 essay on 'The Death of the Author' by Roland Barthes, the target was not so much the author 'but a practice of reading that construes a single or unified meaning by means of authority of the author'.[18] In other words, what we are asked to consider is a relocation and re-evaluation of the author's function, particularly 'how the discursive author can be reconciled with a personal author in clear terms that salvage, if not enrich, thinking on the subject' (Fokkema, pp. 39, 40). If we keep these facts in mind, what initially appeared to be a paradoxical situation ceases to be so and the popularity of the biographical genres acquires new connotations. It can be seen as an expression of postmodernism's major concerns such as the themes of 'writing, origin and loss, the question of representation' (p. 41), but also of issues relating to knowledge, particularly its nature and acquisition. This apparent unquenchable thirst for 'Lives' which started in the last decades of the twentieth century has brought some changes to one of the longest-standing literary genres. According to Fokkema, the postmodern fans of the biographical genre are no longer interested in new facts about their favourite authors but want 'a biographical replica of their favourite novelist's fiction, as a lost work that is recovered from a dusty attic' (p. 42). As a result, the biographer is expected to become a novelist in disguise. This explains the success of works such as Peter Robb's *M: The Man Who Became Caravaggio* or Francine Prose's *Caravaggio Painter of Miracles*. Christopher Benfey, in a review of Prose's text for *The New York Times*, for instance, says: 'a novelist's tools are as necessary here as a biographer's: an imaginative reconstruction of events, a credible portrayal of Caravaggio himself. And Prose, a superb novelist and occasional art critic, has provided both'.[19] According to the canon of scholarship, however, historical accuracy should always prevail over fiction as 'fiction in biography [...] is at best an indulgence, at worst mere aberration' (Fokkema, p. 42). And, indeed, both Rob and Prose have been criticized for their unscholarly/unauthoritative approach to biography and, particularly in the case of Robb, accused of sensationalism as the following extract from *The National Post* demonstrates:

> It wouldn't be difficult to mock Peter Robb's new biography of the great Italian painter Michelangelo Merisi of Caravaggio (1571–1610). Start with its title, which Robb never quite gets around to explaining after these opening

> sentences. For all the relevance that the letter 'M' played in Caravaggio's life — the artist certainly never used the initial — Robb might just as well have called his book 'Mike'.
>   Then there's his prose. Colloquialisms, anachronisms and profanity abound: Rome is filled with 'arselickers and time-servers,' frescoes 'took forever and were a drag,' Pope Clement VIII is a 'touchy feely pontiff,' Caravaggio's testimony before a court smacks of 'Clintonian casuistry.' This is not the usual language of biography.
>   It is, however, damn fun to read. This is biography à la Raymond Chandler, with Robb as private detective Philip Marlowe. [...] if you're looking for sober and reliable, then stick with Helen Langdon's recent critically acclaimed *Caravaggio: A Life*. Just don't forget to sneak a copy of *M* between the covers.[20]

Regarding Prose's text, instead, *The Publishers Weekly*, wrote:

> Despite her obvious love for the artist, Prose has little of substance to say about him. Once she dispatches with the basic points of the artist's life — that Caravaggio defied the fashion for mannered, pious painting with a gritty but theatrical realism that mirrored the artist's turbulent life — she resorts to the puffed-up style of a student trying to reach a term paper's required length. [...] Even those with only a casual interest in the artist would be better served by Helen Langdon's 1998 biography *Caravaggio: A Life*, which is as accessible as it is scholarly.[21]

It is interesting that both texts are compared to a canonical biography of Caravaggio by the well-established art historian, critic, and former lecturer Helen Langdon and attacked for failing to hold the comparison. According to Fokkema, postmodern biographers refuse 'to play the game': they 'question the value of factual evidence and overcome the conflict between truth and lies by treating both as versions of what can no longer be recovered' (p. 42). Endorsing Jeanette Winterson's humorous definition, Fokkema calls the postmodern biography 'a game of art and lies' (p. 44).

Having highlighted some key problems concerning biographical writings in the postmodern era, it is now important to focus more specifically on the 'author as character' genre. As Franssen and Hoenselaars point out, this genre can be 'situated at the crossroads between the historical novel, biography and the Künstelrroman' (pp. 18–19) and comprises various fictional forms including novels, short-stories, films, plays, and dramatic monologues. Usually, the main character is a writer. However, the *vie romancée*, a genre to which the 'author as character' is closely related, but which excludes all forms of writing other than the novel, extends to all sorts of historical figures. Since Caravaggio features as protagonist not just in novels, but in short stories, dramas, poems, and films, as the various works analysed throughout this volume demonstrate, I adapted Franssen and Hoenselaars's original title to coin the term 'painter as character'. The motivations which drive an author to engage with a more famous predecessor, or with another artist, range from politics to 'issues of gender, race, religion, sexual performance or aesthetic theory' (p. 24). The fact that such concerns are also a feature of Caravaggio's paintings can be seen as an extra reason for the endless series of publications devoted to Merisi's life. As we are about to see, the dialogue with other illustrious or canonical artists can take place through 'appropriation, confrontation or both' (Franssen and Hoenselaars, p. 24).

Franssen and Hoenselaars end the introduction to their volume wondering whether the same mechanisms of 'appropriation, self-projection and anxiety of influence' are at work when 'the later author and his/her subject work in different artistic fields' (p. 26). I argue that in the case of Caravaggio this is the case because, as I suggested above, there is a coincidence between the themes of many of his paintings and the motivations for engaging with the 'author as character' genre.

According to Patrice Terrone, the 'painter as character' genre seems to favour famous artists, such as Caravaggio or Vermeer,[22] whose lives are still fairly mysterious as they can be more easily turned into mythical characters or allow more easily the biographer to impose his/her image onto that of the painter whose life he/she is trying to reconstruct.[23] In many cases, fictional biographies of painters are written by art historians or scholars with a strong interest in visual arts (e.g. Fernandez and Guidi) and are often intended as a tool for correcting traditional critical discourse on the painter's works (e.g. Fernandez) (Terrone, p. 65). Alternatively, these fictional lives are used to explore the creative process, to draw a parallelism between visual arts and literature, or become a form of oblique autobiography (Franssen and Hoenselaars, p. 20). In this sense the genre is always characterized by an element of self-reflection. As Mieke Bal suggested, however, 'once self-reflection as a possibility has become a commonplace (as it has with postmodernism) reading for "narcissism" is in danger of becoming narcissistic itself'.[24] Saying that a work is about itself is no longer sufficient, and self-reference should not be a dead-end street, but an avenue leading to a 'critical perspective on the world and its changeability' (*Reading Rembrandt*, p. 256). Unfortunately, this is where some of the texts we are about to analyse fail. Our case study seems to confirm Petronio's views on 'letteratura di consumo' [popular literature] as a tool for reinforcing certain ideas and stereotypes.[25] In Terrone's view, these works contribute to the construction of a myth which every time acquires different connotations, but which has more to do with the construction of the writer's personal myth than that of Caravaggio (p. 68). Terrone concludes her article by pointing out that the most interesting aspect of the 'painter as character' genre is the use of language, how literature tries to say in words what painting says through colour, forms and symbols (p. 69). Once again, however, it is difficult to generalize and some of the examples below will reveal that the desire to reproduce Caravaggio's chiaroscuro technique through words does not always lead to meaningful outcomes.

Michelangelo Merisi and his lives: A case study

I will start this section by focusing on the earliest of the texts featuring in our sample, *Doubting Thomas: A Novel about Caravaggio* by one of Norway's foremost authors, Atle Næss.[26] The book consists of a series of witness statements gathered by a narrator/editor/writer who claims he is reproducing the translation of some archival material discovered in the Archivio Borghese in Rome, in 1996, in order to clarify what really happened on the night of 28 May 1606 when Caravaggio and Ranuccio Tomassoni fought in a duel which cost the latter his life. Like many books belonging to the 'author as character' genre, it portrays a constant tension between fiction and reality. Whilst the title of the book indicates that we are dealing with a fictional work, the way in which the documents allegedly discovered in the Secret Archive of the Vatican are referenced seems to suggest that this work should be taken seriously as it is based on authoritative sources. The book, however, ends with an 'un-scholarly comment' by the editor (*DT*, pp. 154–55). The tension between fiction and reality increases when we are told that one of the witnesses is not particularly reliable and that there is no real evidence that another one really existed (pp. 152–53). As suggested by Franssen and Hoenselaars, such claims are a common feature of the genre, and the tension is resolved by granting equal status to both factual and fictional elements. Ironically, the testimony of Innocenzo Promontorio, who is described as one of Caravaggio's intimate friends and occasional models, is rather confused. Despite being a physicist and a mathematician, and a follower of Kepler and Galileo, Promontorio has a tendency to skip vital details in his accounts of events and often reprimands himself for his lack of clarity (*DT*, p. 46). He plays a rather prominent role in the book as he is the only character who gives two statements. At the end of the novel, however, we are told that there is no evidence that this person ever existed. Such a revelation casts a doubt on the entire historical reconstruction of the Tomassoni murder: 'Innocenzo Promontorio has left no trace of himself in any contemporary source [...]. What is worse, the town he expressly names as his birthplace, Frassinocasa, does not exist. [...] Innocenzo's account may be pure fabrication' (*DT*, pp. 152–53). The editor tries to salvage Promontorio's credibility by suggesting that this name could have been used to hide the identity of someone who knew the painter but was unwilling to speak publicly about him. However, he is also forced to admit that his speculations are 'mere guesswork' (p. 153).

Further doubts are cast at the end of the chapter when the editor informs the readers that the second most authoritative witness after Promontorio, Ignazio the municipal clerk of Naples, may never have existed. The attempt to justify the lack of documental evidence by blaming the notoriously chaotic nature of the Neapolitan archives, compared to the neatness of the Vatican ones, does not come across as convincing. The editor seems aware of this as he adds that Ignazio's information on Caravaggio's stay in Naples and Malta should not be dismissed since it is in line with that 'attested to in other sources' (*DT*, p. 153). What Næss managed to do, through this series of nine imaginary statements by real and fictional characters, is to illustrate the impossibility of an objective historical reconstruction of any event, as perception varies depending on the involvement and position of the observer/viewer. He also succeeded in paying homage to Caravaggio by pointing out his revolutionary style and by inviting all viewers to shift their attention from the man to his works, as 'Caravaggio's pictures exist. [...] The pictures speak or, what is even more disquieting they are spoken through' (*DT*, p. 155). These words, which represent the novel's concluding statement, are particularly interesting as they seem to suggest a kind of autopoietic power inherent in Caravaggio's paintings. Similar remarks are to be found also in Francine Prose's text when she comments on the English tour guide in San Luigi dei Francesi who keeps speaking even when 'the most dutiful tourists have long since stopped listening' as 'the power of the paintings is drowning out her voice' (*CPM*, p. 9).

In recent years, scholars such as Elizabeth Cropper or Preimesberger have pointed out various similarities between some features of Caravaggio's works and the tradition of Petrarchan lyricism, particularly in his early paintings such as *Medusa* or *The Lute Player*. Cropper also highlights the importance of Marino, claiming that 'Marino's direct appeal to the senses, without recourse to dramatic action, [...] provides the closest parallel to the sensuality and suppression of significant action that seventeenth century Roman critics identified in Caravaggio's early work'.[27] According to Cropper, 'Caravaggio captured the irony of the new Marinesque lyricism which celebrated the simulacrum at the expense of the idea and claimed that art had the power to occupy reality' (p. 54). I would like to suggest that Caravaggio's success in literature is at least partly related to his use of literary devices and to his familiarity with literary concepts: his 'constant selection of lyric themes deriving from the Greek epigrammatic tradition suggests a more sophisticated literary consciousness than is usually attributed to him'.[28] What is more, he lived in an age which 'assumed the equivalence of painting with poetry' (Colantuono, p. 57) even when works had no specific literary content. The fact that Caravaggio's literary popularity began during his lifetime, since from Marino to Milesi and Murtola various Baroque writers wrote sonnets, epigrams, and madrigals in praise of his works, could also be seen as significant when trying to understand the constant verbal response generated by his paintings.

Interestingly, as mentioned above, many of the works falling into the category of the 'author as character' genre engage with *David with the Head of Goliath*, one of Caravaggio's most rhetorical works, and *Doubting Thomas* is no exception. Næss emphasizes David's look of reflection, the fact that 'painter and painted melt together' (*DT*, p. 148) in this picture and Caravaggio's ability to capture a moment of transition between life and death through the eyes of Goliath. The presence of a self-portrait and Næss's reference to 'reflection' make us inevitably think of Bal's analysis of self-reflexivity and of the double meaning of the term 'reflection' which indicates both the act of mirroring (inevitable in self-portraits) and that of thinking, that is, a discursive self-reflection that should lead to self-criticism (*Reading Rembrandt*, p. 258). Bal is mainly concerned with art criticism, but what she says can also be applied to any kind of writing dealing with artists and works of art: for self-reflexivity to be successful, both the self of the work and that of the critic/author should be involved in the process (ibid.). Depending on the level of entanglement of the two possible selves to be reflected, Bal identifies four potential outcomes: (a) an unconscious doubling of the work where the author/critic responds only to the self of the work, 'taking it as radically other and leaving him- or herself safely out of reach' (ibid.), and where the output is pure description; (b) a position in which the two selves are conflated, but the reflection remains non-reflective, or non-analytic and non-discursive, and the result displays signs of primary narcissism;[29] (c) a conscious position towards the work that problematizes representation, but where the reflection is limited to the self of the work, and the result is a theoretical statement as 'the text or painting becomes a theory' (p. 259); (d) a reflective position involving the self of the work, how it problematizes representation, and that of the critic/author whose position as a writer is also questioned. Although

Næss seems to be aware of Caravaggio's revolutionary style and how many of his paintings express concerns about representation, and despite his attempts, through the voice of the editor, to problematize his position as a biographer/researcher, the level of reflection/self-reflection is rather limited. His text could be summarized as a statement about the impossibility of an accurate and totally objective historical reconstruction of past events. At the end of the twentieth century, unfortunately, such an observation is almost commonplace and his invitation to the readers to engage with the paintings or let the paintings be spoken through, whilst certainly valid and interesting, seems equally dry as his text fails to provide a creative example of how this can be achieved.[30]

The second work I propose to analyse is Rita Guidi's *Il gigante perduto* (*The Lost Giant*),[31] whose title, as in Næss's case, refers to a painting by Caravaggio, in this case the *David with the Head of Goliath*. The book was published in 2004 by Bevivino, a small Milanese publishing house founded in 2002 to give a voice to young and promising authors and specializing in biographies and online publishing. Significantly Guidi's work is part of the series *I Cattivi* (*The Bad Ones*) devoted to the lives of controversial artists, musicians, directors, sportsmen, or historical figures from various ages ranging from Cleopatra, to Diego Armando Maradona, Quentin Tarantino, and Jim Morrison. For the same series, in 2005, she published the biography of Salvador Dalì. Guidi, a lecturer in Italian literature and art history, also works as a freelance journalist for various periodicals, local newspapers, and press agencies. In 2003 she came second in the selection for the 'Pietro Bianchi' journalistic prize.

In her short fictional biography/autobiography of Caravaggio, Guidi perpetuates the Romantic myth of the cursed painter whose works, like the pages of a diary, reveal his sins and the dark secrets of his tormented soul. Guidi seems to imply that the chiaroscuro typical of his style is the result of extreme contrasts in his life and she constructs Merisi's fictional biography using a language that mimics such dichotomies: 'il ricercato è ricercato' [the wanted is wanted] (*GP*, p. 55); 'Caravaggio assassino. Grandissimo artista e piccolo uomo' [Caravaggio, the assassin. Magnificent artist, mediocre man] (*GP*, p. 58) or 'la sua vita è ora su un'altalena estenuante e schizofrenica lanciata tra l'odore del sangue che ancora sente dentro e la luce di un successo che quasi lo abbaglia, fuori' [now his life is on an exhausting and schizophrenic swing, oscillating between the smell of blood he still senses inside and the light of success that almost blinds him outside] (*GP*, p. 52). Each chapter begins with either a passage taken from one of Caravaggio's early biographers or Caravaggio's imaginary reflections on some of the most crucial moments in his life, particularly just before his death, which is given a prominent role in this work. Like many other biographers before her, Guidi tells us that Caravaggio died on a beach, an image that, as Sohm explains (see Chapter 1), becomes a symbol of loss, isolation, and punishment, and is used as a mirror image of artistic practice or, rather, malpractice. The titles of the various chapters are also interesting, as they emphasize negative aspects of Caravaggio's life, works, or personality. Apart from the obvious reference in the title, 'il giante perduto', *David with the Head of Goliath* features again in the last chapter where it is interpreted as yet another sign of Caravaggio's tendency to use his paintings as an outlet for his fears, 'pronto come sempre a spalmare le ombre dei propri sinistri presagi sulla tela' [always ready to spread the phantoms of his sinister premonitions on the canvas] (GP, pp. 79–80). Unlike Næss, who at least tries to analyse his position as a biographer, Guidi does not question her role. Quite the opposite, in fact, as from the start she seems to feel entitled to focus on limited aspects of the painter's life, but at the same time expresses generalized statements from an 'authoritative' point of view:

> i nervi scossi dal timore di continue aggressioni avevano già condotto il Caravaggio oltre ogni soglia del possibile [...] È allora delle cattiverie di un valent'uomo che ci occuperemo. Tagliando senza pietà la testa al gigante (GP, pp. 7–8)
>
> [His nerves shaken by the fears of constant aggressions had already pushed Caravaggio beyond the threshold of the possible [...]. It is therefore on the wickedness of a worthy man that we are going to focus. Severing the head of the giant without mercy]

Such a deconstructive attitude is typical of the 'author as character' genre, in which 'the founding-fathers of literature must be robbed of their phallic power' (Franssen and Hoenselaars, p. 48). In the case of Guidi's book, however, it is not clear what the author wanted to achieve with her merciless beheading of the giant. Although she ended her biography with a list of respectable bibliographical references, Guidi's engagement with Caravaggio and his works is rather superficial and never goes beyond a morbid fascination with the painter's dark character. We could almost say that despite including in her bibliography texts by some of the most respected Caravaggio scholars, such as Cinotti, Calvesi, and Pacelli, her main source of inspiration was the controversial *Caravaggio Assassino* (1994) by Bassani and Bellini.[32]

Another text initially inspired by Merisi's troubles with the law and by the Marxist belief in the artistic potential of the criminal in bringing a new impulse to the creative forces is *Il colore del sole* [*The Colour of the Sun*] by the Italian crime-fiction writer Andrea Camilleri.[33] Despite actually quoting Marx's famous claim that 'the criminal produces not only crime but also [...] art, literature, novels, even tragic dramas' and, in an interview with Maddalena Bonaccorso,[34] openly declaring that Caravaggio is the kind of painter people are interested in mainly because of his dark character, Camilleri managed to create a very complex and interesting example of 'author/painter as character' fiction. First of all, like many other books of this genre, *Il colere del sole* could also be looked at from other perspectives, such as those of the detective novel or the historical novel. However, I believe that it is only when we analyse it in the context of the 'author as character' genre that we can do justice to this work.

The book begins with a declaration by the author in which he claims that in the spring of 2004 he travelled to Sicily in order to refamiliarize himself with the Catanese dialect, which he needed for one of his novels. During this visit he was approached by a strange individual who left a mysterious note in one of his pockets, inviting him to get in touch with a person who promised to reveal something interesting to him. Camilleri agreed to meet this stranger and take all the precautionary measures suggested by him. The man, who claimed to be called Carlo, told him that his late wife had come across a kind of diary written by Caravaggio which she wanted Camilleri to see in the hope that he could make some use of it since she had been a huge fan of his novels. Camilleri's books had kept her company and made her laugh, even during the final stages of her terminal illness, and she wanted to thank him. Our author is also told that Carlo's wife was related to the Minniti family, in whose household the papers were found. The mysterious Carlo said that he was forced to hide from the police as he had been implicated in some unpleasant business which did not concern him. At the end of the book, Camilleri reveals that months after his return to Rome he received a copy of a Sicilian paper in which the interview he gave during his stay in Sicily was published. Despite the intention to keep his visit as low-key as possible, the hotel concierge had informed the press of his arrival and, therefore, he had found himself in the limelight. When flicking through the Sicilian paper, Camilleri discovers a picture of the man who called himself Carlo and finds out that he had been killed by the Mafia a few months earlier. He was a well-known lawyer wanted by the police for his collusion with the Mafia. Camilleri, who had tried to get in contact with Carlo to request his permission to publish extracts from Caravaggio's papers, also discovers from the police, who were tapping his phone, that the man was suspected of having stolen the Palermo *Nativity* in 1969. Ironically, at the time of the meeting with Camilleri, Carlo was in a position very similar to that of Caravaggio just before his death, wanted by various people, in this case by the police and the Mafia. The remaining text consists of alleged extracts from Caravaggio's diary, which Camilleri had copied during his brief Sicilian stay.

By placing himself as a character in his own novel, Camilleri produces a very intricate mirroring game through which he raises issues of objectivity in the transmission of historical records and addresses themes such as realism, mortality, the Mafia in Sicilian society, and the value of literature, writing, and intertextuality. When asked by Bonaccorso, in the aforementioned interview, why he decided to feature in the first person in his book, Camilleri replied that he intended to play with the classic literary device of the found manuscript, which usually is given to the author by a friend. Usually, the author refuses to take full responsibility for the discovery. By being present in the first person, instead, he can renounce all claims to authenticity and stress the fictional nature of the text. This is why in the first part of the book, which is used to construct the fake mystery related to the finding of Caravaggio's diary, Camilleri makes no effort to create a more plausible scenario. We are dealing with 'falsi di falsi', he says, since the starting point is literature.[35] However, like Mieke Bal, Camilleri believes that such texts reveal a lot about the works and authors to which they refer.[36] Camilleri says he was interested in Caravaggio's realism, a realism that could accommodate errors of perspective caused by the use of the *camera oscura*, as what he wanted to achieve was to capture not just the outward reality but moods and feelings, impressions, the representation of death (which he felt was approaching), and to subvert stereotypes.

Fundamental to the understanding of this work are also the questions of language and authenticity. Language is seen as an essential aspect of culture and identity, which is why, for the sections in which Caravaggio is speaking, Camilleri reproduces a kind of seventeenth-century Italian capable of conveying the inner turmoil of a tormented mind.[37] At the same time, by hinting at the linguistic diversity of Sicily, when at the beginning of the novel the author declares that his main reason for returning to the island was the need to refamiliarize himself with the dialect from Catania, he educates those readers who may not be aware that the language spoken in Sicily varies considerably from area to area. He also makes sure that he gets the attention of his most faithful readers as they will be aware that 'Catanese' is not Camilleri's dialect. In the aforementioned interview with Maddalena Bonaccorso, Camilleri talked of his passion for linguistic experiments and said that his ambition would be to make a 360-degree exploration of the Italian language in order to reach a radical form of experimentation bordering on deconstruction.[38] According to Antonella Chinaglia, through language Camilleri emphasises the tension between fiction and reality by addressing also the notion of authenticity.[39] In this respect Camilleri adheres to the 'author as character' genre as he grants truth and fiction equal status. On the one hand, through his seventeenth-century Italian, he tries to give credibility to his fictional creation and, on the other, as Chinaglia points out,[40] he declares that the alleged document which he partially transcribed could contain errors and oversights and admits altering certain features of Caravaggio's uncultivated and often vulgar language (CS, p. 33).

Another interesting aspect of the 'author as character' genre is the fact that Camilleri uses Caravaggio briefly to evoke other canonical writers such as Giuseppe Tomasi di Lampedusa and Ludovico Ariosto. Caravaggio's imaginary diary, which Camilleri transcribes, in fact contains references to a meeting between the painter and Captain Mario Tomasi, the forefather of the illustrious author of *The Leopard*,[41] and to the island of Lampedusa whose literary potential had already been explored by Ludovico Ariosto (1474–1533) in his *Orlando Furioso* (1516) and which, at the time of Caravaggio, was an example of multicultural tolerance as one of its monasteries welcomed Christians and Muslims alike (CS, pp. 66–67). We must not forget that intertextual references to the works of Ariosto and Tasso (1544–95) play a key role in *The Leopard*.[42] What makes such references significant from our perspective is the fact that the two authors symbolize the tension between innovation and tradition, between two different conceptions of the world which we also find in Caravaggio. For the later author, as for Caravaggio, the world ceased to be 'a forest that he oversaw'[43] and became a theatre with many stages; life became a spectacle. If we look at the Tasso/Ariosto controversy from different approaches to the creative process we find other interesting resonances not only with Caravaggio but also with Lampedusa, Camilleri, and even the character of the Sicilian people, who are still trapped between two worlds:

> Where Ariosto invariably preserves an ironic distance from the creatures of his imagination, Tasso submits them to an emotional proximity. His is the art of the close-up and he repeatedly assumes the role of the *metteur en scène* and choric commentator. He draws his audience into the scene, openly invoking their admiration, compassion, indignation or sympathy for his actors and he evokes specific emotional effects more often than intellectual ones. (Marinelli, p. 248)

Even though, when reading the above passage, it would be tempting to replace the name of Tasso with that of Caravaggio, we must not forget that irony also played an important role in his paintings.[44] Another interesting element to keep in mind is the fact that Tasso had received patronage by many of the people who also protected Caravaggio, such as Cardinal Francesco Maria Del Monte and the Marchese Giustiniani. Although there is no evidence to suggest that Tasso and Caravaggio ever met, Tasso's poetry was certainly familiar to Caravaggio, both through his friend Giovan Battista Marino[45] and through the Flemish composer Jacques Arcadelt (1505–68). Arcadelt's music was popular in the Del Monte circle, and his madrigals feature in Caravaggio's two versions of *The Lute Player*, the one for Del Monte and the Giustiniani one. Moreover, in the introduction to his translation of Tasso's *Gerusalemme Liberata*, Anthony Esolen calls Tasso the Caravaggio of poetry.[46] Other Renaissance scholars, such as Matthew Treherne, have compared Tasso to Caravaggio for his interest in chiaroscuro techniques and the presence of strong visual elements in some of his works.[47]

As for Camilleri, both irony and empathy are essential features of crime fiction writing. Whilst as an author/investigator Camilleri has to maintain an ironic distance from the subject matter of his books/investigations, he also needs to provide close-ups and *mise en scènes*, first of all because the solution of mysteries usually lies in the uncovering of a previously neglected detail, but also in order to stimulate the interest and empathy of the readers who will determine his success as a writer. If we take such images metaphorically, similar tensions can also be seen as epitomizing Sicily, an island which, according to Camillari, took both the best and the worst aspects of the cultures of its conquerors and where in some places you can feel as if you were in Switzerland whilst just round the corner you find people killing each other.[48] Lampedusa would also agree with Camilleri: like the Principe Salina in *The Leopard*, he was a man sceptical about progress who claimed that Sicily had experienced too many foreign invasions for its inhabitants to be able to embrace the future with optimism, even though he accepted the inevitability of change. Finally, returning to *Il colore del sole*, we must point out that Mario Tomasi is also the character of another book by Camilleri, *Le pecore e il pastore*, which was published just a few months after Caravaggio's biography, and which also combines national, local, and personal history in a condensed and multilayered text.[49] In true postmodern style, Camilleri creates an inner intertextuality, inviting his readers to follow his characters in different contexts and to pursue some of the themes which are particularly dear to him from different angles.

If Camilleri has often been accused of being excessively concise, the same cannot be said of Dominique Fernandez, whose works tend to explore the full potential of the novel genre. *La course à l'abîme* (2002) [*Running to the Abyss*] is no exception: Caravaggio's life is explored in detail in nearly eight hundred pages.[50] Born in 1929, Fernandez is considered to be one of the best Italianists in France. Over the years, he won several prestigious literary awards, including the Prix Médicis (1974) and the Prix Goncourt (1982), and in March 2007 he became a member of the illustrious Académie française. Apart from novels, Fernandez also writes essays, travel memoirs, and works of criticism, and, as Tina Gianoulis points out, 'inseparable from Fernandez's identities as an academic, historian, novelist, essayist, and travel writer is his identity as a gay man who came of age during the 1950s'.[51] To date, despite his literary success, he has not received much critical attention, particularly in the English-speaking world.[52] As in the case of Camilleri's book, Fernandez's *La course à l'abîme* could be read from different perspectives, the obvious one being that of gender studies, but it is only in the context of the 'author as character genre' that the book can be fully appreciated. Also, like Camilleri's novel, his text is full of references to previous works and this inner intertextuality is used to explore various ideas in different ways. The prominent role played by Caravaggio's *David with the Head of Goliath* inevitably evokes his earlier work *Dans la main de l'ange* (1982), devoted to the life of the great homosexual writer and film director Pier Paolo Pasolini and to his obsession with some aspects of Caravaggio's work. This obsession will be analysed in Chapter 4. As we can see, Fernandez's interest in the 'author/painter as character' genre is not recent and has remained a dominant feature throughout his career.[53] Gianoulis points out that 'Fernandez pioneered the "psychobiography", a literary form that he used to imagine the lives and inner struggles of gay artists in past centuries', and to explore 'the experiential gulf between homosexuals who grew up under almost total societal disapproval and those who developed their gay identities after the gay liberation movement made public homosexuality a possibility'.[54] According to Terrone, *La course à l'abîme* gives Fernandez the opportunity to put the principles of psycho-biographical criticism into practice, showing that paintings are always autobiographical. His reading of Caravaggio's works, therefore, tries to reveal the inner mythology of the painter, his duality and the inextricable link between *eros* and *thanatos* (Terrone, pp. 64–65). As a result, however, Fernandez's novel becomes a self-justification of the author's own desires and drives, acquiring strong autobiographical connotations (p. 67).

Like Camilleri, Fernandez problematizes the tension between fiction and reality, or authenticity and lack of authenticity, but in very different ways. Unlike Camilleri, Fernandez does not include photographs of Caravaggio's paintings and, despite the wealth of details concerning the painter's life covered in this book, no attempt is made at acknowledging the sources. What is more, occasionally some vital facts are omitted. For instance, the first chapter opens with what appears to be a rather detailed description of Michelangelo's birth and death but, in both cases, although the day and the month are mentioned, the year is left out. The issue of authenticity is further explored in the chapter devoted to Fermo Merisi (Michelangelo's father) where Fernandez invents the story of his brutal murder by a gang of men who were never punished for their crime, and who had probably been sent by the Duke of Milan in order to kill the only person capable of confirming the authenticity of a certain painting. Fermo had in fact made a copy of *St John the Baptist* by Leonardo which was so convincing as to be easily mistaken for the original (*CA*, pp. 92–93). Fernandez appears to ridicule our modern obsession with authenticity, our celebrity culture, and some aspects of the art industry by pointing out that a work of art should be admired for what it is, rather than because of the man behind that piece of work (*CA*, p. 83). The dichotomy true/false is irrelevant as there is always more than one truth (ibid.). Like Camilleri, Fernandez lets Caravaggio speak in the first person. The painter tells the story of his life starting from the various hypotheses surrounding his death, exposing the absurdity of some theories with the intent of challenging and deconstructing most of the myths commonly associated with his persona. Whilst pretending to endorse the image of the violent rogue with no sense of morality (*CA*, pp. 18–19) and homosexual proclivities, he invites his audience to focus on some of the circumstances preceding Caravaggio's death, asking them to reconsider his image in view of those details. As we shall later see, in Chapter 4, Fernandez uses Caravaggio's alleged homosexuality to thematize some of his concerns about gay culture, particularly his conviction that 'permissiveness has trivialized homosexual culture' (Gianoulis), a topic he had also addressed in his 1999 novel *Le loup et le chien* [*The Wolf and the Dog*] based on the classic French tale of a wolf and a dog discussing the advantages and disadvantages of security and freedom. In *La course à l'abîme*, Caravaggio seems to epitomize this tension between the freedom of following one's instincts and the comfort of a more traditional relationship. On the one hand, he claims to be simply interested in sex, 'fucking' whoever he fancies whenever he likes, in total defiance of social and moral conventions. On the other, his long-lasting relationship with the fellow painter Mario Minniti seems to suggest the seduction of a more conventional love:

> 'Faire du sexe', car, 'faire l'amour' serait la réminiscence d'une époque dépassée [...] *Cazzo e culo*, rageusement, dangereusement. En pleine Église catholique, apostolique et romaine, braver Moïse et saint Paul, bafouer les prêtres, défier le Saint-Office, narguer le bûcher! (*CA*, p. 19)

> [*to have sex* because *to make love* would be a remnant of a past era [...] *Cazzo e culo*, furiously, dangerously. In full defiance of the Roman Catholic and Apostolic Church, challenging Moses and St Paul, scoffing priests, facing the Inquisition, laughing at the stake]

Through this passage, Fernandez seems to hint at the impossibility of being openly homosexual in Counter-Reformation Rome as homosexuality was considered a crime to be punished with a death sentence. At the same time, however, challenging conventional morality is seen as a tool for criticizing the hypocrisy of the church, to show that what was rejected in public was often enjoyed in private. Yet, according to Fernandez, this contrast between different spheres, whether public/private or legal/illegal, can have positive effects and, like crime and criminals for Camilleri, acts as a stimulus for the creative process. At the end of chapter XI, Caravaggio declares that if Protestantism had reached Italy, painting would have been doomed and in explaining his decision to move to Rome he says that:

> Les murailles du Vatican, voilà un rempart autrement solide contre l'hérésie que la barrière des Alpes. Près du trône de saint Pierre, il était sûr que la 'cogitation charnelle' de Dieu et des saints ne me serait pas imputée à crime. (*CA*, p. 151)

> [Against heresy, the walls of the Vatican were a rampart as solid as the Alpine barrier. Surely, near St Peter's throne, my 'carnal way of thinking' about God and the saints would not be held against me]

Here, as in his other 2002 book about art and homosexuality,[55] Fernandez 'advances the somewhat regressive, and certainly debatable theory, that the homophobic censorship of earlier times, which forced queer artists to conceal their true meanings, produced better art than the openly gay-themed art of the past few decades' (Gianoulis). Fernandez illustrates his notion of 'privileged pariahdom' which, as Cairns (p. 147) points out, he sees as immanent in homosexuality (and which he had already explored in previous novels including his 1987 *La gloire du paria*). All the references to the Portuguese sect, and to its symbol, the thistle flower which was usually tattooed on the shoulder of its members, or the French book the young Caravaggio received as a present from a Maltese merchant, *Le Chevalier de la charrette*, seem to indicate that shame and ignominy are virtues to be proud of, as only those who live dangerously live fully (*CA*, p. 160).

Closely related to this notion of the privileged outcast is a tendency towards the aestheticization of life, which Fernandez perceives as the other side of realism. In his view, Caravaggio teaches us that if art can imitate real life the opposite is also true. *David with the Head of Goliath* is seen as a prime example of this. According to Fernandez, the painting is about love and death, and represents Caravaggio's self-fulfilling prophecy, his desire to die in the arms of a younger lover, which eventually materialized on the beach of Porto Ercole on 18 July 1610. Despite opening with a description of all the various theories about the painter's mysterious death, *La course à l'abîme* seems to support the version that Caravaggio was killed by his younger friend and lover Mario (Minniti):

> Mario, à genoux sur le sable et toujours penché sur moi, avait commencé par pleurer. Je n'étais plus là pour lui dire qu'il rapetissait par ses larmes un geste qui avait sa source au-delà de la douleur et de la joie. Ayant compris de lui-même que ce qu'il avait fait était moins son oeuvre que le parachèvement de certains de mes tableaux, il se redressa et vit d'une autre manière ce qui n'était plus un crime. Quel éclair maintenant dans ses yeux! (*CA*, pp. 785–86)

> [Mario, kneeling on the sand and leaning over me, had started to cry. I was no longer there to tell him that his tears were diminishing a gesture which originated beyond pain and joy. Having himself worked out that what he had done was more the completion of some paintings of mine than his own work, he stood up and looked differently at what was no longer a murder. What a flash of light in his eyes now!]

According to Michelangelo, however, Mario was not alone. The scene had been observed by another of his boys, Gregorio, who, unfortunately, being more concerned about the painter's works than his safety or state of mind, had taken the liberty of ridiculing and insulting the two lovers. The book concludes by pointing out that even Gregorio's scornful attitude had been scripted, as it served to enhance the drama, and that even the Passion of Christ would not have been complete without the cruel jokes of the soldiers (*CA*, p. 786). Significantly, one of the paintings to be given greater attention is *The Martyrdom of St Matthew*. Here 'a saint seems willing to offer himself up for slaughter to a fierce but strikingly beautiful young man' (Cairns, p. 128), and the biblical scene acquires a personal significance for Fernandez's Caravaggio and his lover Mario (*CA*, pp. 461–71). As Cairns clearly illustrates, 'the association of sexual pleasure with submission and pain is [...] based on a complex psychological cluster of impulses in which enduring subjection to an inchoate Law of the Father is a not-negligible factor' (p. 127). Such a paradigm is supported by the authority of Western tradition embodied, 'in different ways and with different emphases', in figures like Oedipus, Christ, and Caravaggio (Cairns, p. 132). The image of Oedipus appears to be particularly significant as *La course à l'abîme* contains references to blindness (*CA*, pp. 137, 211), which, according to the myth, is the result of Oedipus' sense of guilt for what he has done and expresses the limit beyond which desires cannot go.[56] However, we must also remember that 'Oedipus blind, disgraced, guilty, shamed, remorseful, lonely is happier than Oedipus young, smart king and devoted family man',[57] a situation Fernandez can identify with as it was only in 1971, after divorcing his wife, that he began 'publicly to assume a gay identity' (Cairns, p. 93). Besides, Fernandez had a complex and slightly problematic relationship to his own father, Ramon, who was an extremely influential critic and biographer after the First World War. Ramon's books on Molière, Balzac, and Proust can still be purchased today, but his morality was questioned when he agreed to sit on the executive committee of the largest fascist party in France, the Partie Populaire Français. He died in disgrace in 1944.

As for the image of Caravaggio the book is trying to promote, we can say that Fernandez favours the 'populist' one. The episode in which Caravaggio confesses to Mario that the face of Christ in his *Supper at Emmaus* had been inspired by that of a prostitute he had previously used for *Mary Magdalene*, but who, since then, had been publicly disgraced, seems to prove the point. Out of fondness for the girl, the painter had decided to offer Rome a different image of his friend Anna (*CA*, p. 419), even if such boldness could lead to an accusation of heresy. Previously, Caravaggio had referred to himself as a worker, 'un auteur méticuleux, qui ne laisse pas un pouce carré de toile au hasard, et règle l'émotion qu'il veut communiquer au spectateur' [a meticulous author who does not leave a single square inch to chance and controls the emotion he wants to convey to the spectator] (*CA*, p. 196). Generally, Caravaggio is depicted as a man who spent most of his life in front of his easel (*CA*, p. 197), for whom love, work, and the simple pleasures of life are inseparable from each other (*CA*, p. 443). Fernandez particularly seems to appreciate Caravaggio's revolutionary style, his courage in representing even the cruellest aspects of reality such as the degradation of physical suffering (*CA*, p. 199). Fernandez sees in Caravaggio's interest in the poor evidence of his inclination to follow the teachings of Filippo Neri:

> Filippo Neri [...] m'a fait comprendre qu'un des moyens de renouveler la peinture serait de choisir des modèles dans une catégorie sociale où la misère fait des trous aux vêtements et laisse de la sanie dans les plaies. (*CA*, p. 199)
>
> [Filippo Neri [...] made me understand that one of the ways to renew the art of painting would be to select models belonging to a social group in which poverty left holes in clothes and pus in sores.]

Despite the fact that Fernandez manipulates aspects of Merisi's life to stress the painter's homosexuality, his detailed biography forces the reader to look at Caravaggio in his historical context and to appreciate the multilayered nature of his works. Readers are encouraged to interpret Caravaggio's works in different ways and to reflect on the birth of popular art, thanks to a new figure, the art dealer, whose importance increases during the Baroque period, and the role of genius and social ambition in the making of a successful artist.

Finally, before concluding with some thoughts on RAI's most recent production devoted to the Lombard painter, I would like to focus on a more unusual form of fictional biography, Antonella Ossorio's *L'angelo della luce: Il giovane Caravaggio sogna il suo destino* (2004) [*The Angel of Light: The Young Caravaggio Dreams of his Destiny*].[58] As mentioned in the introductory part of this chapter, this is a book for children that was published for the 2004 Naples exhibition by Electa.[59] *L'angelo della luce*'s success was also due to the beautiful illustrations by Caterina Arciprete, who incorporated actual details from Caravaggio's paintings in her colourful drawings. Arciprete's images are accessible to children but at the same time celebrate the sense of movement and swirling forms typical of Baroque art. As the title suggests, the night before leaving his mother's house to start his apprenticeship with Simone Peterzano in Milan, Caravaggio has a dream in which his destiny is revealed to him. Ossorio depicts the young Caravaggio as a bit of a rebel who doesn't easily accept hierarchical principles. Even in his dream he is rather arrogant and doubts the validity of the angel's revelations. The angel takes Caravaggio to various locations where some of the key events of his life will take place. He also shows him where he will find his artistic inspiration and teaches him that saints can be very ordinary people. After this extraordinary experience the young Caravaggio is no longer afraid of leaving the shelter of his mother's house and is ready to face his destiny. The angel expresses himself in verse and the language used by Ossorio tries to reproduce the contrasts of light and shade that characterize Caravaggio's paintings, as the following passage shows: 'Ma di andarsene, i pensieri non vogliono saperne. Stanno attaccati al suo cuore come colori alla tavolozza: pensiri bianchi, blu, rossi, ocra, però macchiati da un'ombra nera d'inquietudine' (*AL*, p. 4) [But those thoughts have no intention of leaving him. They cling to his heart like colours to the palette: white, blue, red and ochre thoughts, but stained by a dark shadow of anxiety].

Similar chiaroscuro effects can be found when the narrator tries to describe how the young Caravaggio was torn between the excitement of becoming a painter and the fear of being unable to keep the promise he made to his mother to stay out of trouble:

> È questa speranza a regalare ai suoi pensieri colori così brillanti da illuminare la notte. Come fuochi d'artificio vanno su, tra poco esploderanno in mille fiori variopinti e ... no, si sono spenti! Colpa dell'ombra nera che, accidenti a lei, stanotte ce la mette tutta a trasformare il suo entusiasmo in incertezza. (*AL*, p. 5)
>
> [It is this hope that gives his thoughts such vibrant colours that they could light the night. Like fireworks, they go up and will soon explode in a thousand multicoloured flowers and ... no, they are off! It's because of that dark shadow which, damn it, tonight is trying really hard to turn his enthusiasm into hesitation.]

Generally speaking, the images used are rather stereotypical, but in this case they work as they are the kind of images with which children can identify. Ossorio's pedagogical intent is clearly visible as the book ends with a brief biography of the painter, including a list of his major works. Considering the nature of Caravaggio's works, Ossorio's effort in making them accessible to young people is certainly praiseworthy. As she herself declared, she regularly uses this book during her school visits in order to make children interested in art as the balanced mixture between text and images seems to generate positive responses.[60]

Having studied various examples of fiction, we must now move to a different kind of 'painter as character' genre and look at RAI's most recent homage to the Lombard painter, the docudrama directed by Angelo Longoni in 2006, starring Alessio Boni in the role of Caravaggio. Before analysing this work, we should perhaps point out that the term docudrama was almost unknown until the 1970s, because until then cinematic products could easily be divided into categories of either fiction or non-fiction/documentary. The blurring of boundaries between the two spheres was a rare occurrence. However, as soon as this new genre gained in popularity during the 1980s and 1990s, so did the debate on its suitability to engage with historical figures and events. Critical responses to the genre are also interesting, because both documentary experts and film studies scholars seem to avoid engaging with docudrama as an autonomous genre.[61] The Italian term for this genre is *fiction televisiva* or, more simply, *fiction*, which inevitably seems to shift the balance between the factual and the fictional elements in favour of the latter.[62] Within this genre historical subjects are extremely popular, as RAI's various docudramas about the lives of popes or saints in recent years indicate. However, even within this subgenre, the once very important role of the historical consultant has become marginal. The historian is asked to spot mistakes and factual inaccuracies, but only the most blatant ones are removed. Unless employed as co-director, the historian has no influence on the production of the film/programme and, as a result, family tragedies, love stories, or bereavements become more important than adherence to the truth. This latest French, German, Italian, and Spanish co-production is no exception. What is interesting is the fact that, even before the programme was broadcast, RAI had sold its rights to eleven different countries: Belgium, Bulgaria, China (pending the approval of their Censorship Authorities), Croatia, Holland, Japan, Latin America (all countries), Luxembourg, Portugal, Russia, and Slovenia.[63] The actual number of viewers is also worthy of attention: 6,418,000 people, constituting the highest number of spectators per show of the entire evening (17 February 2008). The record for what Italians call 'lo share', that is to say the commercial target audience between the ages of fifteen and sixty-five, was held by the reality show *Amici* (inspired by the British programme *Pop Idol*), but *Caravaggio* 'won' for the overall viewing figures, overtaking very popular programmes such as the Italian version of *Who wants to be a millionaire?* (5,150,000). The total number of viewers remained approximately the same for the second episode, even though 'lo share' marginally declined. RAI Fiction has also envisaged a shorter version for cinema. Regardless of the quality of this docudrama, the aforementioned data offer a clear example of what I call the Caravaggio phenomenon, that is to say the appropriation of the painter's image by popular culture.

As far as content is concerned, *Caravaggio* received very mixed reviews. Toni Jop on *L'Unità* praises the docudrama for its honesty in depicting the corruption of the Vatican, its obsession with temporal power and the perpetuation of violence. At the same time, however, he also stresses the possibly excessive emphasis on the Cenci saga and on Michelangelo's affairs with women. Other episodes in the painter's life, instead, or in the lives of his patrons, were rushed through and never properly explained in either of the two episodes.[64] Similar remarks are to be found in Dal Bello's short monograph on Caravaggio and cinema.[65] Whilst praising some aspects of RAI's homage to the Lombard painter, such as Storaro's photography and the soundtrack capable of alternating between modern and old rhythms, Dal Bello points out that this work does nothing to dispel the myth of the *pittore maledetto*, which is far too popular with the general public to be discarded (pp. 64, 67). He also highlights the fact that no reference is made to the Neapolitan period, despite the fact that Caravaggio produced several masterpieces during that time, and that many episodes of the painter's life, such as his relationship to Costanza Colonna and the farewell to his mother, had been fictionalized to meet the taste of the audience (p. 62). Antonio Dipollina, on *La Repubblica*, is even less generous. Although he praises Storaro's photography for having captured the atmospheric light of Caravaggio's paintings, Dipollina questions the validity of such an expensive production. In his opinion, RAI's *Caravaggio*, apart from lingering on fights and love stories, does little to explain the painter's works and his motivations.[66] Even stronger accusations are expressed by Aldo Grasso, who claims that not even Storaro's excellent photography could save what, according to him, is a rather sloppily produced programme, with faults in the style of acting, in the direction and the script. Grasso is especially critical of certain dialogues which do not seem to match the seventeenth-century context. The term *città fantasma*, used to describe Caravaggio's impression of Rome upon his arrival in the city, is given as an example of a modern concept which could not have existed in the historical period in question. Grasso also criticizes one of the scenes involving a dispute with the Neapolitan poet Giovanbattista Marino as, in his opinion, the dialogue resembles more closely what we normally encounter in a talk show than what we could expect in the private office of an important prelate in seventeenth-century Rome.[67] Giovanni Spagnoletti talks of 'an excessively fictionalized plot which thanks to a very modern (in)sensibility becomes undistinguishable from an episode of *Orgoglio* [a very popular soap opera] or something like that'.[68] He also uses terms such as 'unbearable blindness', 'fundamental ethnocentrism', and 'extremely mediocre level'. He criticizes the producers of the programme for their lack of didactic/artistic ambitions and excessive desire to meet the taste of the public. Ultimately, however, the management of RAI Fiction has to take the blame for its inability to move beyond mainstream, bourgeois atmospheres (ibid.). According to Gianluca Nicoletti of *La Stampa*, Longoni's *fiction* was also attacked by Gay TV for having portrayed a mainly heterosexual Caravaggio, and to counterbalance this vision Gay TV showed Derek Jarman's film, which did justice to Merisi's alleged homosexuality.[69] All the aforementioned accusations are more than justified, but they become even more interesting if seen against the popularity of the programme in terms of ratings. The secret of this success lies in what Sorice calls 'emotional realism' (p. 59), a realism that is not based on the faithful or mirror-like reproduction of facts but embraces what Buonanno calls spheres of 'elaboration, identification, and fantastic projection, which are now integral aspects of our daily lives and therefore significant elements of reality and triggers of reality effects'.[70] If Buonanno's theory is correct, Caravaggio is once more an ideal subject, because his form of realism has also been described as emotional and what has just been said about docudramas can be extended to all the other fictional biographies we have analysed, which, despite their diversity, all have a strong emotional appeal.[71]

What this chapter has demonstrated is that a series of factors contributed to the sudden proliferation of fictional biographies or biographical films devoted to Caravaggio. To understand this trend we need to engage with three sets of questions: a more general one concerning the popularity of the biographical/autobiographical genres; a more specific one regarding the reasons behind the choice of Caravaggio as a subject matter for many of these works; and, last, one relating to changes in the art industry. As we have seen, the first can be mainly understood in terms of a need to return to narrative and reaffirm the subject in the era of 'weak thought' when such concepts are viewed with suspicion. This also explains why many of these works are debut pieces or are written in the early stages of an author's career. The second set of questions, instead, demands that we look beyond the painter's biography, taking into account the rhetorical construction of his paintings and the role he himself played in the construction of one of the most popular myths about his persona, that of the *pittore maledetto*. Finally, the boom in the production of art fiction is determined by changes in the attitude of museum and art gallery curators, who see in this genre a tool to boost their revenues and to attract new visitors to their exhibitions, thus building a bridge between people and art and opening their institutions to the masses.

Notes to Chapter 2

1. A two-part drama, *Caravaggio* was shot in 2006 and first broadcast by RAI Uno on 17–18 February 2008. It stars Alessio Boni and it is a French, German, Italian, and Spanish co-production. Previously, RAI had produced a six-part documentary on the life of the Baroque painter in 1967 which starred Jean Maria Volontè and was broadcast various times over the years.
2. Other examples include Noah Charney's *The Art Thief* (New York: Simon and Schuster, 2007), Roberto Fagiolo's *L'ombra del Caravaggio* (Rome: Nutrimenti, 2007), Paolo Turati's *Notturno Barocco* (Turin: Ananke, 2005), and Fabio Baldassarri's *Il Mistero del Caravaggio* (Milan: Il Ponte delle Grazie, 2003).
3. In his seminal study of biographical genres, Alessandro Iovinelli points out:

    quel che appare davvero evidente è che la tematica dell'autore non solo ha assunto un'estensione considerevole ma che ha modificato il codice retorico del genere biografico, diventando una fonte d'ispirazione costante per la narrativa contemporanea. Non vi è alcun dubbio sul fatto che mai prima di adesso la figura dell'autore abbia occupato la spazio letterario in modo tanto ossessivo quanto imprescindibile.

    [what is really obvious is that not only did the theme of the author become much more widespread, but that it also altered the rhetorical code of the biographical genre, becoming a constant source of inspiration for contemporary fiction. There is no doubt that never before has the figure of the author dominated the literary space in such an obsessive and inescapable way.] (Alessandro Iovinelli, *L'autore e il personaggio: L'opera metabiografica nella narrative italiana* (Catanzaro: Rubettino Editore, 2004), p. 20)

4. The film and theatre director Mario Martone was asked to produce a film for the occasion. His *Caravaggio: L'ultimo tempo* (41') uses texts by Anna Maria Ortese and has been

described as 'a beautiful visual poem': <http://www.filmfestivalrotterdam.com/eng/search/film.aspx?id=721dc0c0-fb25-42aa-8673-b8d5167a5b3e> [accessed 20 June 2010]. Unfortunately, it is not easily available. The Dutch director Vincent Monnikendam has also produced a documentary on Merisi's stay in Naples entitled *Souls of Naples* (2005) in which, unlike Martone, who started with the life and works of Caravaggio to end up in our times, he showed 'how much of contemporary Naples can be found in Caravaggio's work' (ibid.).

5. For the 2004 exhibition 'Caravaggio: L'ultimo tempo', the Teatro Stabile Le Nuvole in collaboration with the Museo Capodimonte put together a series of performances for children entitled *Caravaggio: La rivoluzione dell'arte*.
6. For a detailed account of this project see the following websites: <http://www.lazio.istruzione.it/offerta_formativa/allegati/caravaggio.pdf> [accessed 13 April 2008]; <http://www.caravaggio.rai.it/index_en.htm> [accessed 13 April 2008].
7. Polese Ranieri, 'In Giappone tutti pazzi per Caravaggio, da maledetto a mito pop', *Corriere della sera*, 30 September 2001, p. 31.
8. Louise Govier, 'The Fiction Phenomenon: Art in the Airport Lounge?', *The Art Book*, 10 (2003), 28–30 (p. 28).
9. Giuseppe Petronio, *Sulle trace del giallo* (Rome: Gamberetti Editore, 2000), p. 191. Petronio uses the term 'letteratura di consumo' to identify a literature written for a non-elite audience and lacking an original moral and intellectual tension (ibid.).
10. *The Author as Character: Representing Historical Writers in Western Literature*, ed. by Paul Franssen and Ton Hoenselaars (London: Associated University Presses, 1999).
11. Peter Robb, *M: The Man Who Became Caravaggio* (New York: Picador, 2001); Francine Prose, *Caravaggio: Painter of Miracles* (Hammersmith: Harper Press, 2007; first published in 2005). All references to Prose's text are from the 2007 edition; abbreviated as *CPM*.
12. David M. Stone, 'In Figura Diaboli: Self and Myth in Caravaggio's David and Goliath', in *From Rome to Eternity: Catholicism and the Arts in Italy, ca. 1550–1650*, ed. by Pamela M. Jones and Thomas Worcester (Leiden: Brill, 2002), pp. 19–42.
13. Despite appearing to support the theory that the Borghese *David with the Head of Goliath* was painted *c*. 1609–10 and was probably Caravaggio's last painting, Stone later dismisses this dating on stylistic grounds, agreeing with scholars such as Vittorio Sgarbi (2005) who date the painting to the late Roman period of *c*. 1605–06, prior to the murder of Tomassoni: 'in my view, this picture was clearly produced in a Roman context, where its allusions, conceits, homo-erotic in-jokes, and *persona*-building [...] would have been understood and appreciated by Caravaggio's close circle of friends and patrons' (Stone, p. 28).
14. Shoham, for instance, describes Caravaggio as suffering from a 'black hole' personality, a biological predisposition aggravated by the relationship to an absent mother: after the death of her husband,

    Caravaggio's mother was left with four children, the eldest barely six, for whom she had difficulty providing. She could well be described hypothetically as either a physically or mentally absent mother. Therefore, [in Caravaggio] we have a combined insatiable quest for a 'good object' to fill in the ever-augmenting 'black hole', coupled by a distrust and hatred of all the relevant others. (S. Giora Shoham, *Art, Crime and Madness: Gesualdo, Caravaggio, Genet, Van Gogh, Artaud* (Brighton: Sussex Academic Press, 2002), pp. 95–96)

15. Rudolf Preimesberger, 'Golia e Davide', in *Docere, Delectare, Movere: Affetti, devozione e retorica nel linguaggio artistico del primo barocco romano*, ed. by Anna Gramiccia and others (Rome: De Luca, 1998), pp. 63–69 (p. 67).
16. Riccardo Bassani and Fiora Bellini, *Caravaggio Assassino: La Carriera di un 'valentuomo' fazioso nella Roma della Controriforma* (Rome: Donzelli, 1994). As Stone points out, some of the so-called Caravaggio documents referenced by Bassani and Bellini were not about Caravaggio at all. However, popular writers such as Peter Robb relied on this sensationalist text (Stone, p. 19) for their work, thus adding an extra link to the endless chain of misconceptions that has characterized Caravaggio's image from the start.
17. Sheila McTighe, 'The End of Caravaggio', *The Art Bulletin*, 88 (2006), 583–89 (pp. 583, 586).
18. Aleid Fokkema, 'The Author: Postmodernism's Stock Character', in *The Author as Character*, ed. by Franssen and Hoenselaars, pp. 39–51.

19. Christopher Benfey, '"Caravaggio": The Artist as Outlaw', *The New York Times*, 2 October 2005, <http://www.nytimes.com/2005/10/02/books/review/02benfy.html> [accessed 16 April 2008].
20. Paul Mitchinson, 'Bristling with Life', *National Post*, 26 February 2000, <http://paulmitchinson.com/reviews/bristling-with-life> [accessed 16 April 2008].
21. 'Caravaggio: Painter of Miracles', <http://www.publishersweekly.com/978-0-06-057560> [accessed 16 April 2008].
22. We simply need to think of the success of Tracy Chevalier's *Girl with a Pearl Earring* (1999) and of its cinematic adaptation staring Colin Firth and Scarlett Johansson (2003).
23. Patrice Terrone, 'Portraits d'un inconnu illustre: Biographies fictives du Caravage', *Recherches et Travaux*, 68 (2006), 57–69 (p. 58).
24. Mieke Bal, *Reading Rembrandt: Beyond the Word–Image Opposition*, rev. edn (Amsterdam: Amsterdam University Press, 2006), p. 256.
25. See n. 9 in this chapter.
26. Born in 1949, Næss studied Language and Literature at the University of Oslo and worked as a teacher at various levels before devoting himself to full-time writing. His biography of Galileo won the Brage Prize for best Norwegian work of non-fiction in 2001. He also published a biography of the Norwegian painter Edward Munch. First published in 1997 (*Den tvilende Thomas: Roman* (Oslo: Gyldendal Norsk Forlag)), *Doubting Thomas* is Næss's ninth fictional work. It was a bestseller in Norway and has been translated into several languages. In-text references, referred to as *DT*, are from the following edition: Alte Næss, *Doubting Thomas: A Novel about Caravaggio*, trans. by Anne Borne (London: Peter Owen, 2000).
27. Elizabeth Cropper, 'Caravaggio and the Matter of Lyric', in *Caravaggio: Realism, Rebellion and Reception*, ed. by Genevieve Warwick (Newark: University of Delaware Press, 2006), pp. 47–56 (p. 51).
28. Anthony Colantuono, 'Caravaggio's Literary Culture', in *Caravaggio: Realism, Rebellion, Reception*, ed. by Warwick, pp. 57–68 (p. 63).
29. In psychology, primary narcissism is a defence mechanism common in the formative years (six months to six years old). It is intended to shield the infant and toddler from the inevitable hurt and fears involved in the individuation–separation phase of personal development. Online resource: <http://samvak.tripod.com/narcissismglance.html> [accessed 17 May 2008].
30. What makes Næss's final statement particularly interesting is the fact that it seems to coincide with Terrone's theory about the centrality of the paintings in the 'painter as character genre', which are seen as generating the fiction and leading to writing (Terrone, p. 60). If judged against Bal's categories of self-reflection, however, Næss's work would come closest to the position of the third group, that is a general theoretical comment.
31. Rita Guidi, *Il gigante perduto* (Milan: Bevivino, 2004); abbreviated as *GP*. All translations are mine.
32. See n. 16.
33. Andrea Camilleri, *Il colore del sole* (Milan: Mondadori, 2007); abbreviated as *CS*. Camilleri, who was born in 1925 in Porto Empedocle, in the province of Agrigento, came to writing late, publishing his first book in 1978, when he was 53. He lives in Rome where he also works as a director for the cinema and the theatre. In the 1990s his crime novels featuring Detective Montalbano and set in the imaginary city of Vigata became bestsellers. *Il colore del sole* is not his first biography. In 2000 he published with Rizzoli *Biografia del figlio cambiato*, a very personal account of Pirandello's life from the point of view of the difficult relationship Pirandello had with his father Stefano.
34. Maddalena Bonaccorso, 'Ecco la verità su Caravaggio. Ho inventato tutte le prove. "Caravaggio sono"', *Stilos*, 20 February 2007, <http://www.vigata.org/rassegna_stampa/2007/stilos_200207_1.htm> [accessed 18 May 2008].
35. Ibid.
36. See Bal, *Quoting Caravaggio*, p. 15.
37. According to Iovinelli, the use of an 'apocryphal style' is typical of 'meta-biographical' works (*L'autore e il personaggio*, p. 17). Regarding Camilleri's language, it is also worth noting that, as usual, we are dealing with an invented language comprising a mixture of seventeenth-century terms plus later ones and totally made-up words. For instance, the adjective 'acconcio' (*CS*, p. 98) is already listed in the 1623 edition of the *Vocabolario della Crusca*, but the verb 'isguardare'

(CS, p. 99) does not exist. As for 'hora' and 'istare', these forms appear respectively only twice and seven times in the *Vocabolario della crusca*, whilst the modern forms 'ora' and 'stare' are much more frequently used (677 and 299 times respectively). The verb 'isguardare', although invented, appears to have been modelled on other verbs like 'istare' or 'isaminare', 'ispignere' or 'isquartare', which were actually in use in the seventeenth century, to create an impression of authenticity.

38. See Bonaccorso, 'Ecco la verità su Caravaggio'.
39. Antonella Chinaglia, 'Camilleri A., *Il colore del sole*, 2007 — Fuga continua del Caravaggio in Sicilia?', <http://www.spigolature.org/mambo/index.php?option=com_content&task=view&id=574&Itemid=353> [accessed 27 April 2008].
40. Ibid.
41. Mario Tomasi was a man of dubious morality who hunted wanted criminals, killing them and bringing back their heads for a cash reward. Therefore, he represents an ironic counter-image to Caravaggio, whose 'passion' for severed heads is well known. The other fascinating aspect concerning Mario Tomasi is the fact that, despite being the man who brought wealth to the Lampedusa family, he fell into disgrace with his descendants, who tried to avoid commemorating him to the extent that no heir was ever named after him.
42. Two of the main characters in *The Leopard*, Angelica and Tancredi, are respectively named after characters in Ariosto's *Orlando Furioso* and Tasso's *Gerusalemme Liberata*.
43. Peter Marinelli, 'Narrative Poetry', in *The Cambridge History of Italian Literature*, ed. by Peter Brand and Lino Pertile (Cambridge: Cambridge University Press, 1996), pp. 248–49.
44. See Stone.
45. According to Maria H. Loh, Marino was an admirer of Tasso: Maria H. Loh, 'New and Improved: Repetition as Originality in Italian Baroque Practice and Theory', *The Art Bulletin*, 86 (2004), 1–41 (p. 12).
46. Anthony M. Esolen, *Jerusalem Delivered* (Baltimore: Johns Hopkins University Press, 2000), p. 1.
47. Matthew Treherne, 'Pictorial Space and Sacred Time in Tasso', *Italian Studies*, 62 (2007), 5–25. Treherne focuses particularly on 'Le lacrime della Beata Vergine' (1593), whose source of inspiration had been a painting.
48. See the section called 'Sicily' on Camilleri's official website: <http://www.andreacamilleri.net/camilleri/sicilia.html> [accessed 20 December 2009].
49. Andrea Camilleri, *Le pecore e il pastore* (Palermo: Sellerio, 2007). This book was published in March and *Il colore del sole* in January. For an interesting analysis on *Le pecore e il pastore* see the following interview: <http://www.radio.rai.it/radio1/ilbacodelmillennio/view.cfm?Q_EV_ID=209891#> [accessed 25 April 2008].
50. Dominique Fernandez, *La Course à l'abîme* (Paris: Éditions Grasset & Fasquelle, 2002); abbreviated as *CA*.
51. Tina Gianoulis, 'Fernandez, Dominique', in *glbtq: An Encyclopedia of Gay, Lesbian, Transgender, Bisexual and Queer Culture*, ed. by Claude J. Summers (2007), <http://www.glbtq.com/literature/fernandez_d.html> [accessed 28 April 2008].
52. One notable exception is Lucille Cairns's monograph *Privileged Pariahdom: Homosexuality in the Novels of Dominique Fernandez* (Oxford: Peter Lang, 1996).
53. Starting from his aforementioned *Dans la main de l'ange* (1982), with which he won the prestigious Prix Goncourt, other examples include: *L'Amour* (*Love*, 1986), about painter Friedrich Overbeck; *Le Dernier des Médicis* (*The Last of the Medicis*, 1994), about Gian Gastone; and *Tribunal d'honneur* (*Court of Honor*, 1996), about composer Pyotr Ilyich Tchaikovsky. His Franco-Mexican father, Ramon Fernandez, was also a prominent biographer and literary critic.
54. See Gianoulis, 'Fernandez, Dominique'.
55. Dominique Fernandez, *A Hidden Love: Art and Homosexuality* (London: Prestel Publishing, 2002).
56. Edith Wyschogrod, *Saints and Postmodernism: Revisioning Moral Philosophy* (Chicago: University of Chicago Press, 1990), p. 202.
57. Anna-Teresa Tymieniecka, *Phenomenology of Life and the Human Creative Condition* (New York: Springer 1998), p. 57.
58. Antonella Ossorio, *L'angelo della luce: Il giovane Caravaggio sogna il suo destino* (Naples: Electa, 2004); abbreviated as *AL*.

59. Ossorio's work is not the only children's book published by Electa that year. See also Fiorella Congedo, *Caravaggio e il segreto del Tasso Barbasso* (Naples: Electa, 2004), illustrated by Emilio Urbano. Other examples of children's books engaging with Caravaggio are: Franca Cicirelli, *Camilla e il pirata Caravaggio: una fiaba di educazione alimentare* (Molfetta: Edizioni La Meridiana, 2006); Luisa Mattia, *Caravaggio e l'incanto della strega* (Rome: Lapis, 2009). More recently, the American author and illustrator of children's books, Marissa Moss, published *Mira's Diary: Home Sweet Rome* (Brainerd, MN: Bang Printing, 2013), in which time traveller Mira is transported to Rome in 1595 where, masquerading as a boy, she mingles with Giordano Bruno, prominent cardinals, and the painter Caravaggio.
60. In February 2008 I had an informal exchange of e-mails with Ossorio, who explained her interest in Caravaggio and some aspects of her work, including the challenge of making such a complex painter suitable for young people.
61. Steven N. Lipkin, *Television Docudrama as Persuasive Practice* (Carbondale: Southern Illinois University Press, 2002), p. x. See also Derek Paget, *No Other Way to Tell It: Dramadoc/Docudrama on Television* (Manchester: Manchester University Press, 1998).
62. The term *fiction* in Italy started replacing the term *sceneggiato* during the 1980s and became commonplace in the 1990s. Unlike the *sceneggiato*, which was characterized by its strong cultural content, the *fiction* has retained a certain pedagogical ambition and an interest in cultural dissemination, but the emphasis is mainly on entertainment. The term *fiction* is also associated with the birth of private television channels. For a detailed analysis of the Italian *fiction* see Michele Sorice, 'La fiction televisiva nella prospettiva italiana', *Studies in Communication Sciences*, 4 (2004), 49–67.
63. See: 'Caravaggio nel Mondo', <http://www.film.it/news/televisione/dettaglio/art/caravaggio-nel-mondo-23953/> [accessed 12 September 2009]. Whilst this effort can be partially seen as the result of the introduction of a new law in 1998 (legge122/98) which affected the production and promotion of European products (Sorice, p. 57), the wide range of countries interested in RAI's *Caravaggio* seems to confirm the universality of the painter's myth.
64. Toni Jop, 'Caravaggio, diglielo a questi politici', *L'Unità*, 20 February 2008, p. 19.
65. Mario Dal Bello, *Caravaggio: Percorsi d'arte e cinema* (Turin: Effatà Editrice, 2007).
66. Antonio Dipollina, 'Caravaggio, un grande artista bollito dalla tv', *La Repubblica*, 20 February 2008, p. 67.
67. Aldo Grasso, '*Caravaggio*: una fiction che fa 30 ma non 31', online video: <http://mediacenter.corriere.it/MediaCenter/action/player?uuid=93dcec0c-e131-11dc-b2e4-0003ba99c667> [accessed 14 May 2008].
68. Giovanni Spagnoletti, 'Fiction Italia — Caravaggio ovvero The Dark Side of TV', online resource: <http://www.Close-Up.it> [accessed 18 May 2008].
69. Gianluca Nicoletti, 'Il Caravaggio RAI fa arrabbiare i gay: "La vera fiction? Farlo diventare etero"', *La Stampa*, 14 February 2008, p. 62.
70. Milly Buonanno, *Leggere la fiction* (Napoli: Liguori, 1996), p. 22; my translation.
71. In the last chapter of this book we will see a different response to the sensual and emotional aspect of Merisi's works in Michael Ondaatje's novels and Anthony Minghella's cinematic adaptation of Ondaatje's *The English Patient*.

CHAPTER 3

❖

Caravaggio, Crime Fiction, and the Noir

La realtà è solo il lato in luce della verità, la quale sin dai tempi dei greci ha sempre avuto un lato non rischiarabile (alétheia). È questo sottrarsi alla luce che chi scrive seriamente deve impegnarsi ad esplorare.

[Reality is only the illuminated side of truth which, since the times of the ancient Greeks, has always had a side that cannot be lit (alétheia). It is this shunning of light that (s)he who is serious about writing must endeavour to explore]

MARIO COVACHICH in *Allegoria*, 57, p. 10[1]

After fictional biographies, the most popular genre regarding responses to Caravaggio's life and works is that of crime fiction. This is hardly surprising given that, since its origin in the nineteenth century, the genre has proved suitable for 'gender, ethnic and cultural appropriation',[2] particularly in the twentieth century. Of all its subgeneric modes, that of 'hard-boiled' fiction is the most open to reformulations (Scraggs, p. 4), and the 'crime thriller', which seems to be the format favoured by most of the authors included in this chapter, is directly related to it. Before proceeding with the analysis of the individual texts and authors, this chapter will start with brief definitions of the aforementioned key terms: 'hard-boiled fiction' and 'crime thriller'. It will then address the question of the significance of Caravaggio in these contexts. Finally, by comparing and contrasting various textual examples, it will further confirm the flexibility of the crime fiction genre and offer some reflections on the reasons behind its popularity and on the notion of realism. Given the vast amount of crime thrillers engaging, in one way or another, with the Baroque painter, this work cannot offer an exhaustive picture of what is available on the market, but rather case studies based on material as varied as possible. As in the previous chapter, the sample concentrates mainly on works published during the late 1990s and the first decade of the twenty-first century, apart from one cinematic exception, Martin Scorsese's film *Mean Streets* (1973). Such an exception is justified on two grounds: first, as a way of illustrating the link between the Hollywood tradition of *film noir* and hard-boiled texts,[3] and second, as further proof of Caravaggio's influence on cinema. The texts included are: *Murder at the National Gallery* (1996) by the American crime fiction writer (and daughter of former US president) Margaret Truman; *Il mistero del Caravaggio* (2003) by Fabio

Baldassarri; *The Lost Painting* (2005) by the American author Jonathan Harr; *Saving Caravaggio* (2006) by the British writer Neil Griffiths; *The Art Thief* (2007) by the young American scholar Noah Charney, one of the world's leading experts on art-crime and founding director of the Rome-based international Association for Research into Crimes against Art (ARCA); and finally the 2008 novel by the Italo-French author Gilda Piersanti, *Jaune Caravage*. As in the previous chapter, what this sample reveals, even at a glance, is how the interest in Caravaggio is a worldwide phenomenon.

But let us begin by trying to understand the concept of hard-boiled fiction (e.g. Hammett, Chandler, Ross McDonald, etc.) and of its subgenre the crime thriller. As Scraggs explains:

> hard-boiled detective fiction developed in the early 20th century as a distinctively American sub-genre, and grew out of sources as diverse as the Western and gangster stories [...]. Such gangster stories, in which an individual from a disadvantaged background becomes rich and powerful from a life of crime, only to become a victim of the criminal world that created his success, sprang from the reality of the attraction of crime as an understandable career choice in an increasingly aggressive capitalist society. (p. 29)

Unlike the more traditional 'whodunnit' (e.g. Conan Doyle, Agatha Christie), which triumphed during the period between the two wars (commonly known as the Golden Age of Detective Fiction), the hard-boiled genre survived beyond the Second World War. By making no 'appeal to reason and logic, concentrating instead on the character of the detective in a plot normally characterized by violence and betrayal' (Scraggs, p. 28), this genre was better able to capture the anxieties and uncertainties of the post-Holocaust era. The genre's key characteristics include the use of the first-person narrative voice, a threatening and often alienating urban setting, and an interest in the language of the streets, illustrating the injustice of a world where money can buy justice (Scraggs, p. 63). As far as the private eye is concerned, despite being a professional investigator, s/he has no access to definitive solutions: 'small, local and temporary victories are all that the hard-boiled private eye can hope to achieve in a corrupt world' (ibid.). The genre offers also an interesting parallelism between detection and writing and detection and reading: the reader is like a private eye who has 'to deconstruct, decompose, deplot and defictionalize "reality" to construct or re-construct out of it a true fiction, an account of what really happened'.[4]

Thanks to its flexibility, over the years, hard-boiled fiction branched off in different directions. The one that interests us is the 'crime thriller', whose main focus is the crime and the person/s committing it (Scraggs, p. 105), because most of the texts we are about to analyse feature the theft of a work of art (usually a Caravaggio) as their focal point. In this subgenre, it is the characters with their lives and psychology that form the basis of the story (Scraggs, p. 106), but the detective no longer plays a primary role. The emphasis is on a present danger or on a situation bound to end in violence. Freeman suggested that the crime thriller is characterized by a 'highly sensational fiction' with the sole aim of making 'the reader's flesh creep'.[5] Whilst a sensationalist element is certainly present in all the novels included in our case study, I would argue with Symons that the crime thriller is often used to question some aspects of society, law, or justice.[6] As we shall later see, many of the aforementioned novels use the crime story to reflect on the ways in which organized crime operates and on the collusion between the state and organized crime. I would also argue that the art-crime novel, as a specific subgenre of the crime thriller, offers an ideal platform for combining entertainment and social criticism.[7] This mode appears to be extremely popular: even judging by our limited sample of texts, we can see that seven out eight feature the theft or loss of a painting as their central motif. It is therefore important to understand why this particular form of crime thriller is thriving. Noah Charney's studies of the history of art-crime offer some interesting explanations.[8] Since the Second World War, Charney maintains, art-crime has evolved into the third highest grossing annual criminal trade worldwide, behind only the drug and arms trade. The times of Vincenzo Peruggia's theft of the *Mona Lisa*[9] and of the possibility of art-crime being a crime of passion have long gone. Art-crime is now a cold business 'valued as high as $6 billion dollar per year'.[10] Unfortunately, most stolen works are never recovered and art criminals remain unpunished as the solution rate for art-crime is approximately 10 per cent (Mueller). There is a lack of serious statistics about art-crime and, in many cases, art-crimes are filed with other crimes, leading to a significant loss of data. Also, some museums do not report theft out of fear of damaging their reputation and of limiting their chances of receiving large donations from benefactors. In Charney's opinion, the recovery of the stolen work of art is often just an afterthought and not enough energy is invested in changing this trend. Myths originating from popular culture, such as the idea that theft is commissioned by passionate criminal collectors, are often taken for well-known facts even by the police and private investigators. Charney, however, maintains that, if used effectively by authors of fiction, this lack of information could have an impact on the real criminals, who might feel encouraged to steal art on the assumption that such a collector is easy to find. The police could pose as collectors, thus increasing their chances of recovering the stolen goods or of gaining an insight into the ways in which international organized crime syndicates operate. Whilst this theory might be perceived as rather far-fetched, it certainly contributes toward explaining the popularity of the art-crime thriller: the lack of concrete data about art-crimes, the vast numbers of unsolved cases, and the involvement of organized crime are ideal ingredients for a genre deriving from the hard-boiled mode, with an aspiration to social realism, particularly regarding issues of law and justice (Symons, p. 193). A stolen work of art also raises interesting legal questions about the ownership of art, sale, and copyright, and some psychoanalytical questions, if Charney is right in suggesting that the same technique of criminal profiling forensic psychologists use to help identify rapists and murderers should be applied to 'sketch' art thieves. Finally, since there is still a certain romance attached to art-crime, art-crime thrillers sell well and are often translated into several languages.[11]

Having highlighted some of the possible reasons behind the success of the art-crime thriller, we must now try to understand why most works belonging to this genre seem to focus on the disappearance or the recovery of a painting, rather than a sculpture or other works of art. In so doing, we must turn to psychoanalysis for help, in particular to Lacan's theory of sublimation. According to Lacan [Freud], 'we are born in a universe of signs and [...] one of its main effects is the experience of loss',[12] be it the loss of the mother through the Oedipus complex, the loss of the body's enjoyment through the constraints of education, or other forms of loss related to the acquisition of language and speech. Loss, in turn, generates desire, the longing to retrieve something we once possessed, and art 'provides a special place within civilization to symbolize and elaborate this search' (Leader, p. 75). Lacan identifies this loss in terms of a place which is always beyond what we can represent, or symbolize or give meaning to. This is something we never possessed as such, but where we project images and myths of an origin, of something that was initially there and is now inaccessible and forbidden. Lacan calls this void, or empty place, the 'Thing', and, through his theory of sublimation, he explains how the true function of a work of art is to evoke the empty place of the Thing, the gap between the artwork and the place it occupies. He actually uses the metaphor of the potter who literally manufactures an empty space (Leader, pp. 61–66). According to Freud, visual arts in general and painting in particular have a 'special relation to the dimension of loss', since a visual field is bound to be incomplete and a painting inevitably suggests that there is always something beyond its surface (Leader, p. 81). Freud also argues that 'any art form that accentuates the idea of a surface that we cannot see beyond will be ideally suited to catch our desire' (ibid.). Myths about the origin of painting seem to confirm Freud's theory, going as far as suggesting that, since the act of painting is directly linked to the outlining of a shadow and shadows cannot be grasped, painting can be defined as the 'framing of an absence' (Leader, p. 75). To reinforce this point, Leader uses the example of the Dutch expressionist painter Willelm de Koonig who:

> Borrowing from his experience as a house painter, would often lay his canvas flat and apply a thin layer of turpentine to the painted surface before sanding it down. The new surface would be smooth and polished, and the repetition of this process would reveal the images of the lost paintings that lay beneath the surface. As he continued to paint, these ghosts would propel him, showing how the creative act is not just based on an emptiness, but can systematically and actively repeat the experience of loss. (p. 91)

Also, in relation to the idea of absence generating desire, we must point out that the act of looking seems to be particularly affected by disappearances: 'vanishing objects make us look for them' (Leader, p. 90). On a more general level this means that we become interested in things when they are lost and explains why, when the Mona Lisa was stolen from the Louvre in 1911, the crowds flocked to the museum to stare at the place where Leonardo's painting used to hang. Lacan's theory of sublimation offers a more meaningful interpretation of what might otherwise come across as a simplistic perception of a rather odd phenomenon. In his view, the stealing of a famous work of art, be it Leonardo's masterpiece or a Caravaggio, draws our attention to the issue of the gap between the work of art and the place it occupies (Leader, p. 75), as we are about to see in the analysis of Charney's novel. The emptiness evoked by the work of art, or even more by its disappearance, raises also the issue of value, a feature which, as mentioned above, is important in the genre of the art-crime thriller. In Lacanian terms, such emptiness is the reason why art is extremely expensive. The exorbitant price mirrors the 'gulf that separates "natural" object and images from the symbolic universe' (Leader, p. 84); it is a reminder of the fact that to inhabit reality (or to become human, as I mentioned earlier) we need to give up something and 'let the register of signs and symbolic values mould and structure everything else' (ibid.).

Finally, before moving on to the question of Caravaggio's popularity in crime fiction, we must highlight the relationship between painting, as a form of art, and the novel. As Pedro García-Caro points out regarding the role of paintings in Peter Ackroyd's *Chatterton* and Arturo Pérez-Reverte's *The Flander's Panel*, the canvas can be seen as 'an emblem of the novel reproducing its multi-layered structure'.[13] As a result, on the one hand, the paintings introduce the element of mystery into the stories, but, on the other, they offer a 'pretext for departure from the plot of detection into a self-referential exploration of the status of the work of art' (García-Caro, p. 162) and, I would add, of the relationship between art and life or fiction and reality. As in the example of Ackroyd's *Chatterton*, most of the texts we are about to analyse (but particularly Piersanti's) show a similarity between the complex structure of the canvas and the way the novel is created: both consist of 'a series of parallel narratives and intertexts, different plots that demonstrate a parallel concern for artistic production' (García-Caro, p. 164). By raising the aforementioned issue of forgery, imitation, authorship, and originality (through the use of quotation and pastiche) and by introducing the world of art-trade, these works force the readers to reconsider their aesthetic position on different levels. Most importantly, the mysteries surrounding the paintings introduce a 'degree of uncertainty about the status of the present and its relation with history' (García-Caro, p. 165). The paintings themselves can be seen as constituting a kind of 'transhistorical palimpsest',[14] raising similar issues about identity and the relationship between past and present.

The notion of palimpsest makes us inevitably think of Caravaggio. The Lombard painter did not leave us any sketches of his paintings or preliminary drawings: he was experimenting directly on the canvas and the x-raying of his works confirmed the existence of more than one version of the same scene or of certain figures within a given scene.[15] This brings us to the final and most important aspect of the introductory part of this chapter, the question of Merisi's popularity in crime fiction. If we accept the aforementioned psychoanalytical theory of art's special affinity to the dimension of loss and of a painting as constantly suggesting the existence of something beyond its surface, it becomes clear why so many art-crime thrillers engage with Caravaggio. Over the years, several scholars, such as Posner, Hibbard, and Gash, to mention just a few, have proposed psychoanalytical interpretations of Caravaggio's paintings, often relating to Caravaggio's alleged homosexuality. Regardless of whether we agree or disagree with their views, it is clear that Caravaggio's pictures raise the issue of the gap between the work of art and the place it occupies. In his book about the theft of the *Mona Lisa*, Leader uses the example of Malevich's *Black Square* to illustrate the Lacanian notion of the gap. He argues that the Suprematist works of the Russian painter emphasize the tension between figure and background or element and place (Leader, p. 75), something that we could say of most of Caravaggio's paintings too. Whether we think of some of his earlier works such as the *Bacchino Malato* (1593/94), the Doria-Pamphilj *Penitent Magdalene* (1595/96), *Narcissus* (1597–98), or his *St Jerome Writing* (1605/06), the *Madonna of the Serpent / Madonna dei Palafrenieri* (1605/06), and the *Salome with the Head of John the Baptist* (1609), Caravaggio's paintings show a human figure, or a cluster of figures, against a plain dark background. 'Tenebrism' was the term used to describe this style of painting by critics who did not like Caravaggio's chiaroscuro technique. Such a style was also seen as a symbol of the painter's dark and violent personality.[16] Another term directly linked to the idea of tenebrism is *serrato/shuttered*, which, as Sohm reminds us, was used to refer to Caravaggio's 'cellar locations', to his artistic qualities, and to his plebeian characters and sensibility:

> The socially based 'shuttered' light of the basement also conveyed a sinister private world closed to the public forum of civilized behavior. It signaled a psychic space as much as a physical and social space, where, for example, Caravaggio could imprison Leonello to prevent his model from escaping. The word serrato recruits an interlocking set of associations including morbidity, danger, and secrecy, all connected to aspects of Caravaggio's psychobiography, so that in looking at his paintings we are reminded of the 'shadows of the shuttered tomb'. (p. 13)

Such features make Caravaggio an ideal subject for crime fiction. As we have seen, the crime thriller is considered to be a sub-mode of the hard-boiled genre that shares with its forefather an interest in realism. The French word used to describe the American hard-boiled fiction is *roman noir* and the adjective *noir* (black) 'codifies the dark, shadowy atmosphere and setting of the hard-boiled fiction' (Scraggs, p. 69). The idea of darkness is further explored in the *film noir*, both technically and thematically, through the use of lighting, by creating or emphasizing shadows on the screen, which is why Martin Scorsese's *Mean Streets* (1973) provides an ideal starting point for this study.[17]

Mean Streets: Scorsese and Caravaggio

Significantly, the title of the film derives from Chandler's famous 1944 essay 'The Simple Art of Murder', in which he discussed some of the main features of the hard-boiled genre, such as its threatening urban setting. As Arthur Wrobel points out, the term 'mean streets' was not invented by Chandler: it became popular in London at the end of the nineteenth century, where it was used to describe 'the banality, lack of purpose, and joylessness of life in the East End',[18] thanks to the successful publication of Arthur Morrison's *Tales of Mean Streets* (1894). Even though poverty, violence, and crime were present in these original stories, they did not play a prominent role as the emphasis was on the 'unproductive, unchanging banality of working-class London life' (p. 225). Something similar could be said of Scorsese's *Mean Streets* where, at first, the violence we see does not appear to be particularly destructive[19] since the film seems to be mainly interested in emphasizing the repetitive patterns of life in Little Italy. Scorsese focuses on four young men who

CARAVAGGIO, CRIME FICTION, AND THE NOIR   75

FIG. 3.1. Caravaggio, *Judith Beheading Holofernes* (1598–99),
Rome: Galleria Nazionale d'Arte Antica.

are followed in their daily routines. The characters in question are Charlie (Harvey Keitel), who is a collector for the local Mafia; the loan shark Michael (Richard Romanus); Tony (David Proval), who runs the bar where many of the film's scenes are shot; and Johnny Boy (Robert De Niro), who is presented as Charlie's crazy and irresponsible friend. Other important characters are Giovanni, Charlie's uncle and local Mafia boss, and Teresa who is Johnny's cousin and Charlie's lover. Teresa suffers from epilepsy, something that makes her doubly an outsider as in the patriarchal world of Little Italy there is very little place for women, even less for unhealthy ones. The fact that Giovanni defines her condition as 'sick in the head' is indicative of such a rejection. As for the role of Caravaggio, it is Scorsese himself who pointed out the link. In an interview with Matt Wolf for the *Royal Academy Magazine*, Scorsese said:

> If Caravaggio were alive today, he would have loved the cinema; his paintings take a cinematic approach. We film-makers became aware of his work in the late 1960s and early 1970s, and he certainly was an influence on us. [...] We felt a great influence by Edward Hopper, too, but the light and shadow there deals with buildings and rooms and objects, whereas in Caravaggio, it's the people. And though his light seems to be coming from a single source, it's not a real light, it's a dramatic light: it just lights the scene from one mysterious burst. It's like a flashbulb that just happened to pick up these extraordinary looks on the faces of the models. What hit us about his work was the extraordinary power of what seemed to be realism in that, say, you've got Judith beheading Holofernes, which is a difficult job, and you could see that in her face. The best part for us was that in many cases he painted religious subject-matter but the models were obviously people from the streets; he had prostitutes playing saints. There's something in Caravaggio that shows a real street knowledge of the sinner; his sacred paintings are profane.[20]

In the same interview, Scorsese admitted that Caravaggio was a direct source of inspiration for several of his films, including *Mean Streets* (1973), *The Age of Innocence* (1993), *The Last Temptation of Christ* (1988), *Gangs of New York* (2002), and *The Aviator* (2004). But let us return to the mixing of sacred and profane themes that features prominently in most of Scorsese's films. In *Mean Streets*, Charlie epitomizes this tension as he is constantly torn between a Christian desire to care about others, as the conversation with Teresa on the beach shows,[21] and his ambition to own a restaurant and emulate his uncle Giovanni. At the beginning of the film we see Charlie praying in a church, but thanks to the voiceover we realize that his prayers are blasphemous. He refuses to perform his penance in the traditional way. Instead of reciting his standard prayers, he prefers to make up for his sins in the street in a gesture that expresses all his arrogance and reveals this aspiring saint for what he really is, an ordinary sinner. This scene showing the respectable Charlie kneeling in front of a *pietà* in his best suit cannot but call to mind Caravaggio's *Madonna dei pellegrini*, in which two dirty beggars kneel in front of the image of the Virgin Mary holding baby Jesus. If Caravaggio elevated the status of the poor, who were traditionally considered to be unworthy sinners, Scorsese does the opposite. He shows us how problematic the morality of a respectable man is. The comparison with Caravaggio's *Madonna dei pellegrini* becomes even more poignant if we take into account Teresa, the woman Charlie loves. Like the girl who posed for Caravaggio's painting, Maddalena Antonietti (Hunt, p. 85), 'Teresa's status as a sexually active but decent young woman reconciles and transcends the madonna–whore dichotomy' (Grist, p. 86), through which all women were seen in the patriarchal and misogynistic society of Little Italy. Teresa, like many of Caravaggio's madonnas, is frequently wearing a red dress,[22] and when it comes to her name, 'parallels are often drawn between Teresa and Teresa of Ávila, a figure often discussed in relation to the confusion of religious and sexual ecstasy' (Grist, p. 225). Such blurring of religious and sexual ecstasy represents another point of contact between Scorsese and the Baroque painter, whose work weaves together two kinds of religious experience, death and sexuality.[23] Significantly, in the aforementioned interview, Scorsese mentions *Judith with the Head of Holofernes*, in which the link between death and sexual pleasure is clearly evident (Varriano, *The Art of Realism*, p. 81). Henrickson, in discussing the theme of ecstasy in Caravaggio's work, uses the example of 'St Francis in Ecstasy' (p. 4), a saint with whom Charlie identifies, even though, as Teresa points out in the previously described scene on the beach, St Francis did not 'run numbers'. I would argue with Grist that one of Scorsese's main aims in this film is to emphasize the difficulty of being moral in a morally corrupt society. The frequent references to fire are also significant. Towards the end of the film:

> The burning of a $10 bill continues the metaphoric relation of fire to Charlie's moral retribution for his secular desires. Fire here destroys the means by which Charlie had hoped to pay off Michael and hence to keep his involvement with Johnny under wraps and his hope of getting the restaurant intact. The fires of hell in turn fill the screen via the extract from *The Tomb of Ligeia*; a film Charlie and Johnny are shown watching as they lay low. (Grist, p. 90)

What is more, Charlie repeatedly places his right hand over flames in a gesture which symbolically expresses his desire for punishment and retribution, which then is actualized in the final sequence of the film when he is shot in his right hand (Grist, p. 92). As Grist points out, this scene evokes the one in the church: Charlie's wounded hand reminds us of the hand on the statue of Christ holding a red flower, which is part of the *pietà* scene in front of which Charlie is kneeling. Charlie is therefore implicitly compared to the crucified Christ and his pain suggests a kind of martyrdom (ibid.). Significantly, Grist analyses Charlie through Raymond Williams's concept of 'defensive martyrdom', a form of martyrdom which does not lead to a complete renewal of our life but to 'a positive renewal of our general guilt' (pp. 92–93).[24] Also, the insistence on fire and martyrdom in the film encourages a comparison between Charlie and St Januarius (San Gennaro), a saint who, to date, is still celebrated in New York every 19 September through a feast that lasts approximately ten days and involves a procession similar to the one we see in Scorsese's film. According to hagiographic sources, St Januarius was finally beheaded after several forms of torture, including being burnt alive and being thrown into an arena full of lions, which, however, failed to have the desired effect as the flames did not burn the body of the saint and the lions did not touch him. Just as Januarius was finally defeated by his persecutors, so was Charlie. Despite his desire to conform to Christian values, the criminal mores of Little Italy triumph over morality. As Grist suggests, the Mafia is portrayed 'not as the criminal "other" but as the dominant patriarchal norm' (p. 95), which is hard, if not impossible, to subvert.[25] The theme of decapitation, as we know, is very prominent in Caravaggio's paintings, and if we accept the association Charlie (Scorsese)/St Januarius we cannot but think of *David with the Head of Goliath*, a painting which like Scorsese's film has been interpreted through psychoanalysis and is often referred to as the best symbol of Caravaggio's desire for punishment 'in order to atone for unconscious feelings of guilt' (Hibbard, p. 262). As we shall see in greater detail in the chapter on Caravaggio and homoeroticism, and in the section of the chapter on 'Caravaggio and Postcolonial Concerns' devoted to *The English Patient*, the relationship between David and Goliath can also be read in homoerotic terms. Likewise, the relationship between Charlie and Johnny has some homoerotic overtones, as the scene following Teresa's epileptic fit shows:

> after catching up with Johnny and slapping his face and pushing him against a metal shutter, Charlie tenderly asks 'Did I hurt you?', gently rubs his tearful friend's head and puts his arm around him as they move out of shot. (Grist, p. 89)

Grist considers this scene as an example of how Scorsese explores 'tensions within masculine heterosexual identity' and as a 'representation of Little Italy's masculine subculture that clarifies both its censurableness and its ambiguous lure' (p. 90).

Figure A   Figure B

The two images in Figure A and Figure B can also be compared on a different level. In both cases, the contrast between light and shade plays a very prominent role, but, above all, it is the use of white that has striking similarities. White unites the two subjects. The white on Charlie's collar is similar to the white on David's shirt, thus stressing the ambiguity of Charlie's nature: like Caravaggio who, according to some scholars (e.g. Hibbard, Bal), identified both with the victim and with the victimizer, Charlie's interest in Johnny is unclear: on the one hand it is based on a genuine Christian compassion but, on the other it could also be seen as an expression of Charlie's desire to act out the godfather role (Grist, p. 76). What is more, if we concentrate on Johnny and follow the diagonal line of his gaze, we will notice that, despite trying to avoid Charlie, it inevitably meets the white collar of Charlie's shirt. Since white, in Leibnizian/Deleuzian terms, functions as a mirror, ironically, when Johnny's gaze meets Charlie's body it bounces back to him. Like the sword in Caravaggio's painting, which points both in the direction of David himself (his groin) and the victim,[26] Charlie and Johnny appear to be inevitably entangled

FIG. 3.2. Caravaggio, *Bacchus* (1595–96), Flornce: Uffizi Gallery.

not only at plot level but also through various visual strategies. This scene cannot but remind us of the pre-credit one in which Charlie looks uneasily at his own image in a mirror and which, according to Grist, implies 'the notion of identity as estrangement that is fundamental to Lacan's account of subject formation' (p. 74). In line with this psychoanalytical interpretation, Charlie and Johnny are also respectively described in terms of 'ego' and 'id' figures. Charlie's split subject is constantly torn between the demands of his super-ego (uncle Giovanni), his repressed self (Johnny) and external reality (Grist, p. 80). Apart from suggesting a problematization of identity and subjectivity, I would argue with Bal that Scorsese's endorsement of the kind of Baroque entanglement seen in Figure A, in which pain and suffering are bound up with sexuality (Figures A and B), hints at the possibility of scratching away 'the dust of a disembodied religiosity [...] [to] gain access again to a religious life that is much closer to bodily experience' (*Quoting Caravaggio*, p. 38).[27]

To conclude, let us return to the use of light, which is undoubtedly the most obvious point of contact between Scorsese and Caravaggio and between Caravaggio and the fictional or cinematic hard-boiled genre. Light is what allows Scorsese to combine documentary and expressionistic modes in order to convey 'a mutual sense of physical and psychic, environmental and emotional oppression', which is further emphasized through a contrasting and, at times, cacophonous soundtrack consisting of a mixture of pop, rock, Italian opera and traditional tunes (Grist, p. 73). The red light of the bar scenes, for instance, 'conveys a lurid but alluring sense of degradation and danger' (Grist, p. 70). Likewise, Caravaggio's chiaroscuro was often seen as a sign of his degenerate lifestyle and moral corruption. As we have previously seen, it has even been suggested that 'in looking at his paintings we are reminded of the shadow of the shattered tomb' (Sohm, p. 462). This reference to death makes us immediately think of *Murder at the National Gallery* by Margaret Truman, in which the unexpected recovery of a lost Caravaggio leads to four people being murdered. Deception, forgery, and corruption are the other key ingredients of Truman's text which make it a perfect example for illustrating what would become the major themes and concerns of the art-crime thriller.

Margaret Truman: *Murder at the National Gallery*[28]

Before proceeding with the analysis of the main features of *Murder at the National Gallery*, we need to have an overview of its intricate plot. The story is centred on the mysterious recovery of a lost painting by Caravaggio just before a major Caravaggio exhibition is due to open at the National Gallery in Washington. This is a tale of corruption, forgery, and greed involving a wide range of individuals including members of the Camorra, Italian officials in Washington, Italian cultural attachés and government representatives, art dealers, and members of the White House. Luther Mason, leading Caravaggio expert and Curator of the National Gallery, becomes obsessed with Caravaggio's lost painting *Grottesca* and is prepared to risk his life, reputation, and career to recover it and bring it back to the National Gallery. Through an Italian contact, he finds out that the painting is in the hands of an old Mafioso, Signor Sensi, who is prepared to sell it to Mason thanks to the mediation of their common Italian friend. Once Mason has the painting in his hands, he decides to have two copies of it made in Paris by a well-known forger as he does not intend to return the original to Italy. His plan is to give up his job at the National Gallery and retire on a Greek island with his beloved Caravaggio after giving the other copy to a corrupt art dealer (Franco Del Brasco), who is also known for his links with the local mob and who had given Mason the necessary money to bring *Grottesca* to the United States.

Unfortunately, things do not work as planned, as the panic-stricken Mason reveals all his moves to a friend, the corrupt art collector and popular television presenter Scott Pims, who betrays Luther without remorse as nothing for him is more important than the chance of making a profit. Noticing that Luther is very nervous, Scott offers to accompany him to the meeting, during which not the original but a copy of *Grottesca* was meant to be handed over to the unknowing art dealer Franco Del Brasco. Realizing that Luther was too scared to give Del Brasco the copy, Scott tries to swap the paintings behind Luther's back. At this point, however, Luther's son Julian and his girlfriend Lynn become involved. Despite owing her job at the National Gallery to Luther, Lynn had developed a grudge against the old man. Having had a brief affair with him in the hope of advancing her career, she became progressively more irritated by the delays in her promotion and blamed Luther for failing to apply his influence in her favour. As a form of revenge, she started going out with Luther's son, Julian, a greedy and angry young man who only visited his father when he wanted money. Julian is depicted as a promising artist having a Caravaggio-like personality, quarrelsome and often in trouble with the law.[29] The two lovers uncover Luther's plan and follow him to the place where the handover of the 'original' painting is meant to take place. When, having recovered the other painting from Pims's car, Luther resurfaces and walks away holding it under his arm, Lynn and Julian follow him as far as the National Gallery. When they try to snatch the painting, Luther loses his balance, falls down some wet steps, and dies of his injuries. This is only the first of a series of deaths which continue until *Grottesca* is recovered in Italy thanks to a very theatrical operation staged by Pims who, realizing that he cannot keep the painting's original, tries to transform the event into one of his live shows. The painting is indeed recovered and several people are arrested including the eccentric and dodgy Pims. However, after the initial enthusiasm nobody seems to be really interested in pursuing the case and ensuring that the right people are punished. Even Pims might escape imprisonment. All that matters is that the formerly tense Italian–American relations seem relaxed. Meanwhile, another famous Caravaggio painting (the *Madonna of Loreto*) is stolen from St Agostino's church in Rome on behalf of Sensi. As Charney maintains, not enough is done to protect our artistic patrimony and art-crime squads cannot afford to be complacent even after a major successful operation.[30]

The first thing that strikes a reader of this novel who is vaguely familiar with Caravaggio is the title of the missing painting with which Luther Mason becomes obsessed. The term *grottesca*, in fact, seems to suggest something almost completely alien to Caravaggio's style. The *Encyclopaedia Britannica* offers the following definition:

> In architecture and decorative art, fanciful mural or sculptural decoration involving mixed animal, human, and plant forms. The word is derived from

the Italian grotteschi, referring to the grottoes in which these decorations were found c. 1500 during the excavation of Roman houses such as the Golden House of Nero.[31]

Caravaggio did not paint frescoes and there are very few decorative elements in his works.[32] A closer analysis of the history of the term *grottesca*, however, will reveal the appropriateness of this title and how through one word Truman can pay homage to Caravaggio and at the same time to the forefather of detective fiction, Edgar Allan Poe, and play with irony. During the archaeological excavations which led to the discovery of Nero's palace, *Domus Aurea*, the rooms containing the aforementioned decorations were amongst the first sites to be made available. As a result, 'more because of the setting than of any qualities inherent in the designs, a consensus soon emerged according to which the designs were called *grottesche* — of or pertaining to underground caves'.[33]

Apart from the subterranean connotation, the term also acquired suggestions 'of burial and of secrecy' (Harpham, p. 32), thus providing through the idea of the tomb a first possible connection with the art of Caravaggio (Sohm, p. 6). Grotesque forms, like Caravaggio's chiaroscuro, were seen as material analogues of spiritual corruption, weakness, and sin (Harpham, p. 6). During the Renaissance this style was copied and reinterpreted by artists like Raphael and Giovanni da Udine, who collaborated on the decoration of the Vatican Loggias. Raphael, who was in charge of the overall design, had planned to depict the history of the world as told in the Bible through a series of panels on the vaults of each of the thirteen bays, with the areas surrounding the panels taken up by ornamental designs. As Harpham points out, whilst the method of depicting the narrative line of history through a series of panels was not new, the idea of combining 'a sublime Christian message and *grottesche* pagan designs — in an insubordinate position — was a bold stroke' (p. 33). Raphael assigned the decoration task to Giovanni da Udine, who produced a work that rivalled that of the panels themselves, thus challenging the centre/periphery hierarchy. Like Caravaggio's paintings, the *grottesche* required the involvement of the reader/viewer: they invited a search for meaning and at the same time drew attention to the act of artistic creation, encouraging the viewer/reader to appreciate craft and to consider alternative possibilities. Despite being often dismissed as having no point, the *grottesche* make several conflicting points and perform a number of tasks at the same time. In this respect, they are similar to the Baroque point of view, to the challenging of the subject/object dichotomy we find in Caravaggio's paintings (e.g. *David with the Head of Goliath*). Finally, the term 'grotesque', which is also related to *grottesche*, is often applied to the Gothic and the Baroque (Harpham, p. 74). Gothic, in turn, makes us think of Poe, who is considered to be the inventor of detective fiction. What is more, the adjective 'gothic' was often perceived as synonymous with confusion and disorder, something that characterizes the scenario of a detective story before the genius of the detective allows the re-establishment of order. As the summary of the novel has revealed, at plot level, Truman's text weaves together a series of stories which in their complexity resemble the intricacy of the *grottesche* or, as previously suggested, the very structure of the canvas.

Interestingly, in a play between fiction and reality, *Grottesca* (the re-discovered lost masterpiece) is described only in the vaguest of terms when Luther Mason is asked to explain how he became convinced of the painting's originality:

> 'What said to you, Luther, that this was, in fact, the lost *Grottesca*?' 'Many things. Every scrap of information I've learned about it came into play. For instance, Caravaggio's 1597 *Bacchus* has always been considered the final painting he did in his famous series using the same young boy as a model. Remember? That, too, disappeared but was found in 1917 in a back room of the Uffizi. But my research has told me — and I say this without hesitation or reservation — that *Grottesca* was, in fact, *the* final work using that same youthful model [...]. There is no question that the same model was used. Court, the painting is so alive you can feel the thorns trapping the boy and beasts, hear the anguished cries. The medium appears to be walnut oil, although that can easily be determined by Donald's lab.' (*MNG*, p. 59)

Mason starts his argument by referring to *Grottesca* as belonging to a group of early paintings featuring the same model, which includes the 1596 *Bacchus*. As Luther explains, the Uffizi *Bacchus* was indeed discovered in 1917 in one of the storerooms of the gallery. The model in question was Mario Minniti, Caravaggio's Sicilian friend/lover and fellow painter who posed more than once for Caravaggio. Significantly, the other paintings for which Mario was used as a model are all rather innovative works. They caused some controversies at the time they were produced and have been the subject of very diverse interpretations over the years. The first of the series was the 1593 *Boy with a Basket of Fruit*, which, despite being one of Caravaggio's most straightforward images,[34] attracted criticism on two levels: first of all because of the unusual amount of attention given the fruit (Hunt, p. 20) and because when we look at the boyish young man 'we cannot escape the impression, unprecedented in art, that we are seeing the boy exactly as he appeared when he was posing in the studio' (Spike, p. 34). Mario also appears in paintings produced under the influence of Cardinal Del Monte such as *The Musicians* (1595), *The Lute Player* (1595), and *St Francis in Ecstasy* (1596). All these works seem to contain references to the theme of Platonic love and, according to Spike, show how this mystical concept, which compared the union of two kindred spirits without sexual intercourse to the relationship of an individual to God, gave 'homosexual erotics a new language that was deliberately ambiguous without arousing controversy' (p. 56). The remaining works featuring Minniti are: the aforementioned 1596 *Bacchus*, the second version of *The Gypsy Fortune Teller* (1598–99), and the *The Calling of St Matthew* (1599–1600). Of these, *Bacchus* is undoubtedly the most interesting from our perspective. As we have already seen, *grottesche* have often been seen as a symbol of the artist's freedom, of his possession of space (Harpham, p. 41), and the same could be said about Caravaggio's *Bacchus*. Caravaggio seems unable to handle a conventional subject in a conventional way: despite portraying a god of the Olympus, Caravaggio cannot resist the temptation of introducing some very earthly elements such as dirty fingernails, sunburnt hands, and an old mattress camouflaged as the kind of couch used at a Roman banquet (Spike, p. 70). Like the *grottesche*, we could say that the *Bacchus* is a sight of conflicting points, as what is most noteworthy about it is the 'the juxtaposition of the ordinary with the extraordinary' (Hunt, p. 38). All these elements, of course, are partially present in the original myth, since Bacchus has traditionally been associated with the freedom and creativity of the artist and with ambiguity (human and divine; savage and civilizing; noble and corrupt). From the point of view of Caravaggio and the grotesque, if there is a grotesque element in his works it is precisely his ability to combine the ordinary with the extraordinary. It is also worth remembering that 1597 is the year when Caravaggio painted his *Medusa*, which stresses another aspect of the grotesque, that is to say, the deformation of the body, and inaugurates a long series of decapitation scenes: with her snaky hair, gaping mouth, grim brow, bulging eyes and spilling blood, she expresses shock and is 'far more frightening and emotive of horror than previous Renaissance images' (Hunt, p. 37).[35] According to Fraschini, the body epitomizes the grotesque in modern art and is the site where the grotesque constantly renews itself:

> I nostri corpi nell'arte contemporanea incarnano il principio grottesco, non finiscono alla pelle e dinvengono pura intercorporeità. Il corpo è in perenne mobilità trasgressiva, è forza metaforica che rovescia ciò che è Uno, Immutabile e Identico. È qualcosa di geneticamente dinamico: conosce la propria finitezza ma anche la propria potenza di 'seminatore di segni e simboli', per vivere si 'getta oltre', nei segni e nelle opera d'arte, perché questa è l'unica immortalità che gli è stata consentia.[36]

> [Our bodies incarnate the grotesque principle in contemporary art. The body is in a state of perpetual transgressive mobility, it is a metaphorical force that subverts what is One, Immutable and Identical. It is genetically dynamic by nature: it is aware of its finitude but also of its power as a 'spreader of signs and symbols', to live 'it flings itself beyond', into signs and works of art, because this is the only immortality it can enjoy.]

Significantly, in his only description of *Grottesca*, Mason mentions a boy and some animals trapped in thorns, suggesting that the portrayal of physical pain is so convincing that the viewer has the impression of hearing cries of anguish. Also, the kind of contamination between realism and fantasy that is typical of the grotesque points in the direction of what Mondello sees as one of the key features of contemporary noirs, that is to say the invasion of horror into reality (*Roma Noir 2008*, p. 110).

Apart from Mason's rather enigmatic description, we can argue that the real protagonist of Truman's book remains absent, particularly for the reader who is left wondering what this imaginary masterpiece might look like. Since all the murders are directly related to *Grottesca*, this absence adds an ironic and grotesque element to the plot, whilst for the reader it generates the desire to know more about it and functions as an incentive to continue reading. As we have seen, absence and value are closely related in art and the issue of value is always at the centre of this novel, whether through Mason's troubles with the National Gallery's director for his overspending on the Caravaggio exhibition (*MNG*, p. 42), or when Father Giocondi, who had been hired to act as an intermediary and make the finding of *Grottesca* seem legal, starts threatening to tell everything to the Italian authorities unless Mason gives him more money (*MNG*, p.139), or when, at the very end of the novel, the TV presenter Scott Pims turns the recovery of *Grottesca* into an episode of his art programme, ironically called *The Art Insider*. Pims, assuming now the role of the classic whodunit detective, gathers all the people involved with *Grottesca* who are still alive on a wind-swept Italian plateau in southern Italy and confronts them with all the versions of the alleged masterpiece. His 'guests' include Italian government representatives, people sent by Washington on behalf of the National Gallery and the White House's Commission of the Arts, Julian Mason, some local mobsters, and the corrupt art dealer Franco del Brasco,[37] all rather anxious and surprised at finding themselves gathered in the same location. Pims introduces all his 'guests' for the benefit of the audience and, in so doing, reveals their 'relationship' to what they thought was the original *Grottesca*. By focusing on issues of forgery and authenticity, Pims also reveals various dealings amongst his players, all involving extraordinary amounts of money, such as the two million dollars Luther Mason is demanding from the White House representative in exchange for 'his' *Grottesca* (MNG, p. 350). The tension reaches its climax when one of the copies is hit by a bullet. In a farcical scene worthy of *Mean Streets*, Del Brasco, believing he is in possession of a copy, throws the original to the ground and orders his men to recover what he believes is the authentic version of the painting. His partners in crime take out their guns and point them at the White House's representatives Mac and Annabel Smith, but, thanks to Julian's intervention, end up shooting Mason's son and the *Grottesca* he was still cradling in his arms (MNG, p. 351):

> The bullet passed through the chest of the sensuous young model in *Grottesca* and entered Julian's chest to the left of centre. He slumped silently to the ground, first on his knees, then toppling forward on top of the Jacques Saison's forgery. The uniformed police from Aquila opened fire. The blond thug was hit in the shoulder and thigh, his revolver sent spinning into the air. His companion, who'd fallen to the ground unhurt, pushed his weapon away from him, covered his head with his hands and pleaded not to be hurt. (MNG, p. 351)

In true postmodern style the book is full of irony, self-irony, and intertextual references. The image of Julian being shot through one of Caravaggio's models in a painting which does not exist seems a grotesque reiteration of the aforementioned similarities between Mason's son and the Baroque painter. What is more, if Julian is often in trouble with the law, his father Luther Mason is also not beyond reproach since, for the sake of *Grottesca*, he was ready to risk his career and reputation, and get involved with organized crime. His name seems a parodic take on Perry Mason, the well-known fictional lawyer, crime solver, and main character in several novels by Erle Stanley Gardner, a radio crime serial, various films, and a television series. If Perry Mason was a specialist in getting people out of trouble, Luther dug himself deeper and deeper into trouble until his untimely death towards the end of the book. Also, like Gardner's Perry Mason novels which, apart from featuring the same protagonist, have very similar titles beginning with 'The case of . . .', all Truman's books belonging to the 'Capital Crime Series' have titles starting with 'Murder. . .'. Like Truman, Gardner was often dismissed by critics as a bad novelist. His readers, however, were of a different opinion: in the mid-1950s, his novels were selling at the rate of 20,000 copies a day. At the time of his death in 1970, Gardner was the most widely read of American authors and the most widely translated writer in the world.[38] Even though the figures are much more modest, the same can be said for Truman: whilst critics are sceptical about her works, readers' ratings are usually very high (ranging between four and five stars).[39]

What makes *Murder at the National Gallery* particularly interesting in the context of this study is that it seems to illustrate all the main features of the art-crime novel even before Charney wrote about them. Despite all its stereotypes and implausibility, the book contains a core of truth: too little is done to recover lost masterpieces; the world of art dealing is extremely corrupt and often this corruption extends to high government officials. Particularly in the south of Italy the mafia is often behind the stealing of art. The recent case concerning bribes and payoffs for the advertising of exhibitions in New York and Italy reported by *Il Corriere della sera* in March 2008 could be taken from one of Margaret Truman's books.[40]

The involvement of the mafia in art-crime is also at the core of the next book we are about to analyse, which in terms of structure, themes, and, at least as far as Italy is concerned, setting is very similar to *Murder at the National Gallery*. It was written in 2006 by the British author Neil Griffiths. As in Truman's novel, the main protagonist of the story, a painting by Caravaggio, remains absent. In this case, however, it is hardly surprising, since the work in question is Caravaggio's stolen *Nativity with the Saints Francis and Lawrence*.

Neil Griffiths: *Saving Caravaggio*[41]

Like Truman's novel, *Saving Caravaggio* has a very intricate and complex plot which we need to understand before focusing on some of its key features. In this case, all the works of art mentioned exist and the main character is a detective investigating various crimes against art. The story begins with art policeman Daniel Wright travelling to Calabria to recover from the Ndrnagheta a stolen painting by Turner. Whilst negotiating an agreement with a local boss, Daniel is shown Caravaggio's *Nativity*, 'the world's most famous stolen painting. Cut out of its frame from above an altar in a chapel in Palermo in 1969' (*SC*, p. 6). From this moment onward Daniel becomes totally obsessed with the idea of recovering the lost Caravaggio and is prepared to ruin his marriage, career, and even his life for the sake of it. Daniel's ambition was to become an art historian. He had always been a passionate art lover and, as a student, had written a dissertation on Caravaggio. Having failed to find a job in the art world in London, he decided to join the police and devote his life to the recovery of lost masterpieces. He partially blames his working-class background for his failure as, in his opinion, the art world is very class-conscious. The difference in social background is also one of the causes of tension between Daniel and his upper-middle-class wife, Sarah, who works for Langdon's,[42] a prestigious auction house in London. Against the advice of his superior (Jim), Daniel returns to Italy, officially to investigate a possible corruption case at the Uffizi in Florence but, in actual fact, because he is hoping to make the right contacts that will enable him to save Caravaggio. In Florence, Daniel meets Francesca Natali, the senior curator of the Uffizi who, being single and dissatisfied with her life, takes a personal interest in Daniel. Despite finding Francesca attractive, Daniel does not want to yield to her charm as he is still hoping to save his marriage.

Daniel's obsession with Caravaggio leads him away from his official assignment. He travels to Naples where he meets an old informant, Italo Nenni, who is a lesser member of a Mafia clan and whose marginality is aggravated by the contrasts with the leader of his clan. Italo Nenni agrees to provide Daniel with the name of the person who has Caravaggio's painting, following the death of the man who had previously shown Daniel the *Nativity*. This operation takes longer than expected and eventually Daniel returns to Florence. One night, however, whilst dining with Francesca, Daniel sights Nenni, who had travelled to Florence to give him the promised name. In exchange for this favour, Daniel has to sell some Greek vases — illegally recovered from southern Italy — on the black market. Daniel agrees and disappears without saying anything to Francesca, his wife, or his boss. Having succeeded in this part of the operation, Daniel asks Sarah for money (€50,000) as his plan is to find the *Nativity*. Sarah, whose financial situation is comfortable enough to take risks, gives him the requested money but becomes very suspicious of Daniel's odd behaviour and speaks to his boss, who tries to dissuade him. Daniel, however, is not prepared to listen and decides to go ahead with his plans against all advice. Meanwhile Francesca, who had seen Daniel with Nenni, informs him that she had recognized that man on the news when the umpteenth Mafia settling of scores had been reported. Both Nenni and his wife Maria had been brutally murdered. Consequently, Francesca is weary of Daniel, who had previously claimed to be a writer researching some paintings exhibited in the Uffizi. Despite finding out that Daniel is a police officer obsessed with Caravaggio, Francesca decides to help Daniel in order to escape the boredom of her life. In the meantime, Daniel strikes a deal with a man called Storaro, a dodgy art collector and Caravaggio fanatic he had met through Francesca. Storaro agrees to supply the necessary money to recover the *Nativity* provided he gets to keep the painting as a reward.

Daniel and Francesca travel together to Calabria where, unfortunately, things get nasty. Daniel is badly beaten and ends up ruining his chances of getting closer to Caravaggio. Having put Francesca's life at risk too, he is forced to realize that the painting would never be offered to an outsider:

> I will never be offered the Caravaggio. It is there to read in Lomazzo's reflection. For him the deal has been done and the Caravaggio has not been offered. [...] And I know why. I am an outsider. And no matter what I offer [...] the painting is on the inside. (*SC*, p. 314)

Griffiths illustrates some of the issues discussed by Charney, such as the concrete obstacles police officers encounter when investigating art-crimes, particularly when organized crime is involved. Organized crime syndicates prefer to barter stolen works of art for other illegal goods, such as drugs or weapons, or to keep them as a sign of power and prestige. As Daniel points out, members of the Mafia or other criminal organizations are not interested in works of art for their aesthetic qualities but only for their monetary value:

> My guess is that whatever the symbolic value of the Caravaggio they still don't care. [...] I have seen the way these people treat works of art. They are just interested in the money [...] As a piece of art — they really don't care. Don't care at all. (*SC*, p. 246)

The reference to the mishandling of works of art raises another important question, the fact that the men paid to carry out the actual thefts do not understand the nature of what they are stealing and therefore often end up damaging the goods in question. If we are to believe Francesco Maria Mannoia, the former Mafia heroin refiner and witness in the Andreotti trial in 1996,[43] this is precisely what happened to Caravaggio's *Nativity*. Mannoia confessed that:

> As a young man he had been one of those who stole the Caravaggio *Nativity*. It was, he said, a theft on commission, carried out so clumsily that the painting on the huge and crudely folded canvas — more than five square metres — was irreparably damaged. The person it was stolen for had burst into tears when he saw the ruined work and refused to take it.[44]

Even though Mannoia's version of events was met with much scepticism, particularly amongst art historians, including the leading Caravaggio scholar Maurizio Marini,[45] it remains a possibility.

Another obstacle in the fight against art-crime, Griffiths seems keen to point out through his art policeman Daniel Wright, is the lack of recognition for the work done by police officers: 'even now as a policeman and central to the recovery of many great paintings I am regarded as little more than a bit of muscle needed to make the exchange' (*SC*, p. 21). Griffiths appears to blame the traditionally snobbish and elitist art world for this lack of appreciation. Unfortunately, as Charney suggests, the cooperation between law enforcement officers and art experts is essential if the fight against art-crime is to succeed. Chances of success are particularly low in a country like Italy due to the ubiquitous presence of the mafia[46] in certain parts of the country: 'the one thing you learn about Calabria, the *Ndrangheta* is built into the fabric of the community — there is no "them and us"' (*SC*, p. 245). This idea is further emphasized through the name of one of the characters, Italo Nenni. The surname of Daniel's informant in Naples inevitably evokes the figure of Pietro Nenni (1891–1980), the Italian socialist politician and former leader of the PSI (Socialist Party) in the post-war period. Nenni was in politics at a time when there were strong tensions between the PSI and the PCI (Communist Party), and even within the PSI itself, which eventually led to the creation of a new political party, the PSD (Socialist Democratic Party). This is obviously an ironic comment on Italian politics: it seems to suggest that the tensions within political parties resemble those within Mafia clans, or even a possible collusion between the Mafia and the world of politics. However, the surname Nenni applied to a member of the Mafia whose first name (Italo) is symbolic of the entire nation seems also to stress the omnipresence of organized crime in Italian society.

Significantly, the book concludes with Daniel travelling to Naples alone with the intention of killing the mafia boss Savarese[47] in order to be accepted by the Ndrangheta as an insider. Even though Daniel tries to justify this crazy enterprise by seeing it as a way to 'make right the deaths of Nenni and his wife, deaths that could have been avoided if only I hadn't been thinking about myself, the grand plan — the Caravaggio' (*SC*, p. 337), deep down he knows that killing a man will not yield the desired outcome (*SC*, p. 338). The story has an open ending as we do not know whether Daniel carries out his murderous plan. What is clear, however, is that he seems to be driven by a self-destructive impulse (*SC*, pp. 145–46). The last few weeks of his Italian adventure seem to mirror the last phases of Merisi's life, always on the run, always fearing for his own safety (*SC*, pp. 286–88). The language and images used also seem to mirror the contrasts of the chiaroscuro technique. Daniel imagines confronting Savarese with a gun, forcing him on the ground and delaying the final moment when the trigger will be released to let him know why he has to die. However, Daniel, in a scene which seems to stress his identification with the man he wants to kill, also envisages a sudden outburst of energy in Savarese. In a gesture of self-defence, the Mafia boss extracts a blade and penetrates Daniel's lower abdomen just as Daniel is ready to shoot his victim:

> But then I am neither pulled down nor pushed back, only entered into. A blade — making space inside of me, a place of division, desperation, sadness. The two sides of dying. I see this happen in the heavy shadows of the black walls in the brown light of a long, long dawn, in an old Naples. (*SC*, p. 336)

The reference to the blade and the ambiguous role of executioner and victim evoke what is perhaps the most quoted of Caravaggio's paintings, that is to say *David with the Head of Goliath*. Ironically, in trying to save Caravaggio, Daniel seems to be led to his own damnation. As in Truman's book, there are frequent references to the fact that anybody becoming involved with Caravaggio appears to be cursed (*SC*, p. 178), thus perpetuating the image of the *pittore maledetto* whose spell extends beyond his person and persecutes all those concerned with his works over centuries. Apart from this classic stereotype, which for obvious reasons is extremely popular in crime fiction, what makes *Saving Caravaggio* interesting is the fact that it is written in the first person and in places it comes across as Daniel's confession or imaginary dialogue with the painter (*SC*, pp. 280, 339). In this sense the book can also be seen as a quest for identity and a great homage to the power of Caravaggio's art, which, even after centuries, is still capable of speaking to modern viewers, challenging their role of passive spectators and forcing them to take responsibility for their own actions. Griffiths stresses Caravaggio's ability to capture human nature. When Daniel looks at Caravaggio's paintings he is struck by the fact that:

> It is the human condition — that old-fashioned term — that is disclosed by every one of them. Each face displays a set, a range of feelings which I think help us understand what it is to be human — the varieties of pain, conflict, joy, bravery, submission, responsibility. Caravaggio paints the recognitions — ours in others and therefore ourselves. Caravaggio is us. (*SC*, p. 145)

This aspect of Caravaggio's realism encourages Daniel to embark on the quest for his own identity, a process that forces him to realize that what matters in life is the constant self-questioning which results in risk-taking and sacrifice: 'only through work, risk, sacrifice will I be able to redeem myself. It is only through these things that I will restore the earlier passions to the heart of myself. And become something Caravaggio might want to paint' (*SC*, p. 201). From this perspective Daniel's lack of success in saving the *Nativity* is less of a failure. What counts is the motive behind one's actions and the ability to deal with the consequences of one's deeds. The book's concluding remarks are therefore particularly significant: 'Believe me when

I tell you, maestro, please believe me. It was never for the glory. It was always for love' (*SC*, p. 339).

Forgery and revenge: Baldassarri's *Il mistero del Caravaggio* and Noah Charney's *The Art Thief*[48]

This section is devoted to two debut works which in many ways are rather similar, since both of them feature forgery, justice, and revenge as key themes. Also, both novels are rather ambitious and seem to confirm La Porta's theory that many contemporary detective novels or noirs, despite containing several stereotypes and limitations related to the nature of the genre (e.g. overly melodramatic plots), engage with high moral questions.[49] Charney's novel represents a further exposition of his theories about art-crime and an attempt at implementing his idea of fiction as valuable aid in preventing and, in some cases, even solving art-crimes. As a result, it is possibly the weaker of the two texts. In places, the didactic intent is too obvious (e.g. when the author explains the relationship between art theft and organized crime or raises the issue of security in art galleries and museums: *AT*, pp. 45–46 and p. 133 respectively), whilst in others, despite the author's realist intent, the plot is far too implausible.[50] The book was inspired by the figure of Rodolfo Siverio, one of the greatest art detectives of the 1950s who was also a member of parliament. In the 1980s Siverio collaborated with the English writer Peter Watson who, pretending to be an art collector, tried to persuade the Mafia to sell him Caravaggio's stolen *Nativity*. His plan failed, but he managed to recover a Bronzino which is now exhibited at the Academy of Fine Arts in Florence. Art-crime police are often ridiculed in Charney's book: his investigators seem uninterested in the cases assigned to them and often display amateurish behaviour.[51] *The Art Thief* focuses on three separate investigations which at first seem unrelated. Caravaggio's *Annunciation* is stolen from the church of Santa Giuliana in Rome,[52] the first of Malevich's series *White on White* goes missing from the basement vault of the Malevich Society in Paris, and in London the National Gallery's most recent acquisition, which, significantly, is also a Malevich, disappears just a few hours after it was purchased at a Christie's auction. Eventually, what seems to be the genuine Caravaggio, but turns out to be a fake, reappears underneath a forged Malevich (*AT*, p. 227), whilst a real Malevich is found underneath a copy of Caravaggio's *Annunciation*. The real Caravaggio, instead, ironically, had been hidden under a layer of white chalk (*AT*, p. 289).

The three investigations reveal that not only is a leading expert on the Baroque (Professor Barrow) corrupt, but also the curator of the National Gallery in London (Elizabeth Van Der Mier) and the director of the Malevich Society in Paris (Geneviève Delacloche). Regarding the curator of the National Gallery, her lover, Lord Malcolm Harkness, was in serious financial trouble. To enable him to save his family home and pay off his debts, but also out of greed (*AT*, p. 272), Ms Van Der Mier accepted Lord Malcolm's criminal plan. This involved putting a real Malevich, legally owned by Lord Harkness, for sale at Christie's and getting Elizabeth to buy it at the auction on behalf of the National Gallery for £6.3 million and stealing it back from the museum shortly after the purchase. Not happy with all this, Malcolm had also commissioned an expert forger and art thief to steal Caravaggio's *Annunciation* on his behalf. However, this part of the plan did not develop according to his desires: not only did he not get his Caravaggio but he had no idea where it was (*AT*, p. 273). After volunteering to pay the ransom for the fake Caravaggio hidden underneath the forged Malevich and having blackmailed the already corrupt Professor Barrow to identify the painting as the original *Annunciation*, Harkness lost track both of his 'art thief' and of the real Caravaggio. It transpired that Dr Gabriel Coffin, the art thief and forger in question who is a former member of the Carabinieri and of Scotland Yard (*AT*, p. 41), had decided to keep the real Caravaggio. What is more, out of revenge, he made Malcolm retrieve a copy of the Malevich, not his own original. Malcolm had apparently been responsible for the arrest of Coffin's girlfriend and partner in crime, Daniela Vallombroso, during her last job, and this was the couple's retribution. As Daniela points out:

> The man who framed me for arrest during my last job, and got me sent to prison, has been deprived of the painting he loves and which he hired you to steal for him, the Caravaggio. We've also deprived him of his family's greatest treasure, his original Malevich *White on White*. And he has been tricked. The justice may not be biblical, but it is poetic. (*AT*, p. 289)

As if all this was not enough, the reader finds out that the director of the Malevich Society in Paris, Geneviève Delacloche, also is corrupt. She took advantage of all the mayhem surrounding the disappearance of *White on White* and allowed her American boyfriend to keep the original Malevich which, thanks to Dr Coffin's intervention, was hidden under the fake Caravaggio, and made sure that a copy of *White on White* was returned to the society. To avoid further investigations, she verified its authenticity (*AT*, p. 277).

Before analysing some of the most interesting features of Charney's novel, let us briefly look at Baldassarri's text. As the book cover explains, sixteen masterpieces of Western painting represent the initial inspiration for this intricate novel in which a missing-person investigation turns into a major international operation involving the secret services and revealing links between some local criminals, the art trade, and Islamic terrorism. The first two chapters of the book are set respectively in Italy in 1969 and in Algeria in 1996 during periods of violence and unrest for both countries. As far as Italy is concerned, Baldassarri is particularly critical of the period of Italian history known as *anni di piombo* (years of the bullets) marked by outburst of violence initiated both by left- and right-wing extremist movements. Significantly, Baldassarri refers both to the killing of the Milanese police officer Antonio Annarumma on 19 November 1969, who was the first public official to die in a riot organized by left-wing demonstrators, and to the murder of Aldo Moro, who was first kidnapped (on 16 March 1978) and then killed on 9 May 1978 by the Red Brigades. The assassination of the leader of the Christian Democrats and former Prime Minister Aldo Moro did not mark the end of political violence, but at least indicated the beginning of a clampdown on terrorism which led to a loss of popular support for the Red Brigades. Interestingly, one of the novel's main characters, Maggiore Fabbri, had been inspired to join the police force as a fifteen-year-old boy, after witnessing a students' assembly during which the participants officially condemned the killing of Moro. Through the character of Bruno Barent, who in the novel is the person who killed Annarumma, Baldassarri instead seems to condemn the superficiality and mediocrity of many individuals who joined the various terrorist groups, pushed more by the conflict culture of that period than by genuine ideological convictions. As a result, many demonstrators/terrorists, like Barent, were surprised at the consequences of their own actions:

> Bruno Barent rimase senza conoscenza per quasi un giorno. [...] Aveva ucciso un uomo? Se lo domandava nella confusione e nel torpore che lo assaliva, nel dolore fisico che adesso provava. Aveva ucciso qualcuno. Oppure no. Gli era sembrato di averlo fatto, ma poi era scappato e non aveva potuto accertarsene [...] Non aveva fatto niente di male, si disse, prima di perdere nuovamente i sensi.[53] (*MC*, pp. 18–19)

> [Bruno Barent remained unconscious for nearly a day. [...] Had he killed a man? He kept asking himself this question in the confusion and slumber that was coming over him, in the physical pain he felt. He had killed someone. Maybe not. He thought he had, but then he'd run away and could not check [...] He had done nothing wrong, he told himself, before losing consciousness once again.]

The most shocking aspect in Barent's case is his moral shallowness.

Apart from the prologue and the aforementioned two initial chapters, the rest of the novel is set in an unspecified present ('oggi'/today) in the provincial seaside resort of Viareggio.[54] As in Charney's case, Baldassarri explores several themes ranging from the common fear of terrorist threats to issues of value and the relationship between narrative and images, greed in human nature, but also concepts of justice. Most importantly, Baldassarri reflects on the thin line dividing the executioner from the criminal, a theme clearly illustrated by Caravaggio in his *David with the Head of Goliath*. As the anonymous professor of art history[55] delivering a lecture on the Baroque painter in Oriveto in 1959 points out, if an inexperienced viewer came across Caravaggio's *David with the Head of Goliath*, s/he might overlook the clear signs pointing at David as the hero and at Goliath as the monster:

> Se non aveste mai letto un rigo della Bibbia e vi capitasse per caso di vedere quest'opera, potreste tranquillamente dedurne che Davide sia un semplice assassino e Golia una vittima. Tutto sarebbe in mano alla vostra immaginazione, alla capacità evocative dell'opera; e guardate che questo accade per qualsiasi opera, di ogni tempo e ogni luogo, purché sia un capolavoro. (*MC*, pp. 10–11)

> [If you had never read a single line of the Bible and you happened to see this work by chance, you might easily conclude that David is an ordinary assassin and Goliath his victim. Everything would depend on your imagination, on the evocative power of the painting; and please remember that this happens with any work of any time and place, provided it is a masterpiece.]

Apart from providing the philosophical framework for the novel, *David with the Head of Goliath* is also at the centre of the mystery mentioned in the title. Major Franco Fabbri of the Secret Services is forced to investigate what turns out to be the brutal murder of his ex-wife Francesca, who had been missing for a month and had last been seen boarding her old but beloved sailing boat, enigmatically named 'Caravaggio'. Like Caravaggio's Goliath, Francesca had been beheaded (*MC*, p. 52). Her remains had been put inside a bin liner and dumped in the sea and the killer had disappeared with her boat. Initially, nothing makes sense in this horrific crime as the victim was an ordinary woman leading an ordinary life and an unlikely victim of any crime. Francesca was far from wealthy. Occasionally she struggled to make ends meet and during the summer she often worked for a sailing school in order to get an extra income. She had never expressed an interest in art and nobody could understand why, shortly before going missing, she had renamed her boat Caravaggio. Maggiore Fabbri is at a loss, but it soon becomes clear that Francesca had accidentally fallen into a net of art criminals and international terrorists. Her only faults were her naivety and her greed, which made her pursue the dream of an easy fortune. As a result, when Paolo Rossi, one of her clients, becomes infatuated with her and offers her a precious painting in exchange for one night of passion, the usually reluctant Francesca becomes interested in the proposition. The painting in question is *David with the Head of Goliath*: after studying a few catalogues Francesca becomes convinced she is being offered the second version of that painting, the one that can be admired at the Galleria Borghese in Rome (*MC*, pp. 210–11). Unfortunately for Francesca, her suitor's gesture infuriates his superiors, who take their revenge on Francesca by torturing and murdering her.

Ironically, Paolo Rossi had made his 'generous' offer to Francesca because he believed that the Caravaggio in his hands was a copy of the original, thus revealing, as Noah Charney would put it, the incompetence of many art criminals (*AT*, p. 240), who usually can be divided into two categories: extremely stupid, like Nenni in Griffiths's novel, or extremely clever like Dr Coffin in Charney's book and Kateb El Djebar in Baldassarri's work. As Maggiore Fabbri is about to discover, in fact, stealing and forging all the greatest masterpieces of Western art was part of the plan of a notorious Algerian terrorist, Kateb El Djebar, who, despite being wanted by various police forces throughout the world, had turned a desert island off the coast of Turkey into an impregnable fortress, which he would use as a base while planning his revenge against the West. Dreaming of becoming a hero of the Islamic world and, possibly, the new president of Algeria, Kateb El Djebar's planned to replace the greatest masterpieces of Western art with perfect copies, and destroy all the originals, during a televised event that would make him famous:

> Il mio porgetto prevedeva una certa spettacolarizzazione dell'evento. [...] Ero in contatto con la CNN per l'esclusiva. [...] Se lo immagini: il mio esercito che tiene sotto tiro i cameramen, il regista, i giornalisti e i tecnici della troupe, mentre io prendo dalla rastrelliera del forziere *Il ritratto del dottor Gachet* e lo faccio a pezzi, poi *La dama dell'ermellino* di Leonardo da Vinci e la brucio, e su quel falò continuo a buttare opere di Raffaello, di Velázquez, di Michelangelo e Giotto, di Picasso, di Monet, di Bosch, di Dürer, di Rubens e Modigliani, di Vermeer e di El Greco, di Goya, di Mantegna. (*MC*, pp. 259–60)

> [My project envisaged a kind of spectacularization of the event. [...] I was in touch with CNN for the scoop. [...] Just imagine: my army holding the cameramen, the director, the journalists and the technician of the troupe at gunpoint whilst I take from the rack inside the safe the *Portrait of Dr Gachet* and

I destroy it, then *Lady with Ermine* by Da Vinci and burn it, and on that bonfire I keep throwing works by Raffaello, Velázquez, Michelangelo and Giotto, Picasso, Monet, Bosch, Dürer, Rubens and Modigliani, Vermeer and El Greco, Goya, Mantegna.]

Such a gesture would inevitably cause a major political crisis as all Western governments would look foolish and incompetent. However, it would also have a much deeper and universal effect as it would destroy the conditions that allow the transformation of a simple artefact into a work of art in the eye of the beholder. As Kateb El Djebar admits:

> È lì, negli occhi di chi la guarda che l'arte diventa tale. [...] Così ho immaginato di colpire, nel vostro mondo, proprio quell'attimo, distruggendo le fonti dell' esperienza [...] perché avrei potuto colpirvi tutti insieme, nei sentimenti comuni a tutti i vostri popoli. (*MC*, pp. 260–61)
>
> [It is in the eyes of the beholder that art becomes such. [...] So, I imagined to hit, in your world, precisely that moment, destroying the sources of the aesthetic experience [...] because I could have hit you all, in the feelings common to all your peoples.]

As we have seen, the issue of forgery is central also to Charney's book, not only in the sudden proliferation of the missing masterpieces but also in Lord Harkness's admiration of Coffin's skills. Whilst Harkness is simply surprised at the number of Coffin's paintings hanging in various museums throughout the world 'in place of the stolen originals' (*AT*, p. 273), Elizabeth Van Der Mier acknowledges the subversive power of forgery when she expresses her fear that a right-wing group might be responsible for the recent outburst of crimes involving the stealing of famous works of art and the production of perfect copies (*AT*, p. 198). What is particularly shocking about forgery and plagiarism is that they interfere 'with the language of those who exert aesthetic and representational power, ranging from previous canon to the art market' and show the unreliability/artificiality of bourgeois values and reality.[56] The traditional concepts of author, authority, and authenticity are challenged and so is the notion of value which depends on hierarchies created by the interplay of those three parameters (Allmer, p. 11). In particular, 'the forgery, like the trompe l'oeil, radically undermines notions of the sublime, of the aesthetic aura, since it asserts that the specific aesthetic ability to evoke the sublime can be imitated and reproduced' (Allmer, p. 7).[57] Significantly, Allmer illustrates her point through Lacan's example of the ancient Greek tale of Parrhasius who entered in competition with his rival painter Zeuxis by painting a drape which was so convincing that even Zeuxis was fooled by it. Zeuxis asked Parrhasius to remove the fabric from the canvas and show what he had selected as a subject for his painting. When he realized that the drape was the subject of the painting, Zeuxis acknowledged the superiority of his rival by saying that whilst his realistic portrayal of grapes had only deceived some birds, Parrhasius had deceived an artist. Lacan used this tale to stress man's attraction to 'something that incites him to ask what is behind it'[58] or, as Magritte put it, the very nature of our human condition, as our gaze is 'always trying to go further, to see the object, the reason for our existence'.[59] These statements, apart from confirming the shrewdness of Kateb el Djebar's plan, make us inevitably think of the Malevich series *White on White* in Charney's novel. Like Parrhasius' drape, the white on white reveals the impossibility of going further; it denies any interpretation beyond what it represents. In other words, it allows the 'viewer to risk the gaze into nothingness' and in so doing 'it subverts the Western privileged position of the gaze' (Allmer, pp. 7, 8). As Jagodzinski points out, this kind of art is 'depleted and stripped of all desire'; it is pure 'artifice' and 'more visible than visible such objects have nothing to see "in" them'.[60] If, on the one hand, such works undermine the very notion of the aesthetic experience and seem to suggest the end of art (*AT*, p. 288), the constant game of juxtaposition of Malevich's *White on White* and Caravaggio's *Annunciation* seems to suggest a possible similarity between the two. I would argue with Jagodzinski that the kind of hyperrealism to be found in many of Caravaggio's paintings produces an effect that is equivalent to that of Parrhasius's veil in the sense that his paintings make us want to look behind what we actually see (Jagodzinski, p. 237).[61] However, the fact that the real Caravaggio is kept hidden under a 'veil' of white chalk seems to suggest that iconographic art is much more dangerous than the negation of iconography represented by the white surface. Daniela Vallombroso explains to Gabriel Coffin in *The Art Thief*: 'the point, Gabriel, is that you and your iconographic paintings, and your logical observation-based deductions are prone to manipulation' (*AT*, p. 288). This statement appears to be in line with Kateb El Djebar's motivations (in Baldassarri's text) for wanting to destroy all the greatest masterpieces of Western art in his possession. He is particularly hostile towards religious art, that is to say towards all those paintings that capture the essence of Christianity — particularly its consolatory power — and all those works, like Caravaggio's, capable of speaking the language of the heart, of appealing to the poor and giving hope to people (*MC*, p. 263).

The events leading to the final showdown between Maggiore Fabbri and Kateb El Djebar are as extraordinary and implausible as those of a James Bond movie. More specifically, we could argue that the story of Fabbri and Kateb El Djebar are reminiscent of the 1962 cinematic adaptation of Ian Fleming's novel *Dr No*, in which an investigation concerning a missing colleague leads James Bond to the fortress island of the mysterious Dr No, who is planning to take his revenge against the West by ending the US space programme. Like Kateb El Djebar, Dr No represents 'the idea gone wrong; the site of disavowal'[62] and, like Baldassarri's book, the film raises the issue of justice and revenge. According to Christian Lindner, although James Bond seems to kill villains on behalf of society, its 'fantastic fictional expression takes the form of a right to punish that is more closely related to the vengeance of the sovereign' and as such, like a public execution, does not re-establish justice but merely reactivates power (Lindner, p. 145). Initially, in Baldassarri's book, justice seems to acquire a biblical proportion as the Algerian terrorist is beheaded with an ancient sword that in the ninth century had been used by the governor of Toledo against the Muslims. However, we soon realize that, unlike the Bible, Baldassarri does not present us with a clear distinction between good and evil. Provoked by Kateb El Djebar's direct reference to the *David with the Head of Goliath* stored underneath a seat on board the *Caravaggio*, Maggiore Fabbri grasps the precious weapon and turns into a modern David, thus avenging the death of his ex-wife and that of some of his colleagues who had been brutally murdered by the Algerian's acolytes. For Maggiore Fabbri, however, revenge brings no relief, just the acute awareness of being a faithful servant of an imperfect justice (*MC*, p. 269).

As in a James Bond movie, the elimination of a villain can only reactivate power (in this case the authority of Maggiore Fabbri), but even this knowledge brings no sense of triumph. Significantly, the chapter concludes with an image of Maggiore Fabbri throwing up, shocked by his own action and unable to find any comfort since not even the sea can eliminate the nauseating smell of blood:

> Il Maggiore Fabbri restò immobile un tempo che non avrebbe saputo precisare. Poi uscì all'aperto [...] saziando la sua fame d'aria con la brezza salmastra, riempendosi le narici per cancellare l'odore dolciastro del sangue appena versato. Il mare era lì, e come sempre seguiva il proprio ritmo musicale o chissà che altro: una logica matematica o il caos, o qualche dio beffardo. Il caso, magari. Il Maggiore Fabbri restò un attimo a guardarlo. Poi vomitò: aveva uno strano sapore, in bocca. (*MC*, p. 269)

> [Maggiore Fabbri remained still for a time he could not quantify. Then he went out in the open [...] satisfying his hunger for air with the salty breeze, filling his nostrils to eliminate the queasy smell of the just-spilled blood. The sea was there and, as always, it followed its own musical rhythm or goodness knows what else: a mathematical logic, chaos or a capricious god. Chance, perhaps. Maggiore Fabbri stopped and looked at it for a moment. Then he threw up: he had a strange taste in his mouth.]

The reference to chance is particularly interesting as it undermines the significance of Fabbri's success. It is also in line with Turnaturi's idea of the noir as a genre that narrates the present, rather than the future, and chaos, rather than a re-established order. If, as we have just seen, the ending of the last chapter is significant, so is the opening of the penultimate chapter in which the final confrontation between Fabbri and Kateb El Djebar begins. Baldassarri devotes the introductory paragraph of this chapter to a brief description of *Takka Takka* by Roy Lichtenstein. In this 1962 work, the artist depicts military aggressiveness in an absurd light: 'A Guadalcanal, per l'oro e l'onore di una patacca, dal folto delle felci un tracciante si stacca. Ogni bossolo un botto, ogni morto una tacca. E un cielo blu allegro fa da sfondo alla mitraglia che attacca' (*MC*, p. 230) [In Guadalcanal, the gold and honour of a tacky medal, from the thick of ferns a tracer is shot. Each cartridge case a bang. A firing machine gun and in the background a cheerful blue sky]. Baldassarri seems to suggest that if the splatter surrounding the fight between Maggiore Fabbri and Kateb El Djebar is absurd and implausible so is the very thought that violent conflicts can be solved through military aggression or further violence. The reference to the Guadalcanal campaign, one of the most violent military operations of the Second World War, involving the army, the navy and the air force, which marked the first significant success of the Allied Forces against Japan, makes the reader reflect on the striking similarity between fiction and reality. As in the case of *David with the Head of Goliath*, if the reader is unfamiliar with the history of the Second World War, s/he will miss the connection to a real historical situation. Furthermore, in our media-dominated society, even the most educated reader/spectator has become immune to violence. The contrast between the firing machine gun and 'the cheerful blue sky' seems to act as a warning against our indifference. Recent historical events (particularly the events of 9/11) have demonstrated that reality can be stranger than fiction and there is no place for complacency when violence is involved.

Apart from the aforementioned reflections on the notion of work of art and the nature of human justice, Baldassarri addresses the question of the relationship between word and image. As we have seen, each chapter opens with a brief and often impressionistic description of a famous painting which represents a commentary on what happens in the rest of the chapter and expresses the point of view of the author. The inclusion of *Takka Takka* by Roy Lichtenstein is interesting also in this context since, as Wendy Steiner notes, 'by constantly evoking narratives and undercutting their narrativity, Lichtenstein reveals another important function of narrative in regard to images. As in commercials where the product is embedded in a story, image products require narratives in order to have value'.[63] Art-crime fiction, therefore, contributes not only to educating the general public about the problems faced by those investigating crimes against art or, in many cases, their inadequacy, as suggested by Charney, but helps preserve the status of a work of art. By focusing on missing masterpieces, art-crime fiction, in fact, emphasizes the gap between the artefact and the place it occupies and ensures that even lost works of art do not lose their status and value.

The next section is devoted to a rather anomalous art-crime thriller which is entirely based on true events, that is to say the research surrounding Caravaggio's *The Taking of Christ* (1602), which was accidentally found in a Jesuit convent in Ireland in 1990 by Sergio Benedetti, senior conservator of the National Gallery of Ireland.

When truth is stranger than fiction: Jonathan Harr's *The Lost Painting*[64]

The painting in question represents Jesus Christ being captured in the Garden of Gethsemane by soldiers who were led to him by Judas. Caravaggio focuses on the moment of betrayal and on Christ's humble acceptance of his fate, an attitude that would encourage the viewer to place forgiveness before revenge. As the entry for the 1999 Boston exhibition *Saints and Sinners in Baroque Painting Explains*:

> Caravaggio presents the scene as if it were a frozen moment, to which the over-crowded composition and violent gestures contribute dramatic impact. This is further intensified by the strong lighting, which focuses attention on the expressions of the foreground figures. The contrasting faces of Jesus and Judas, both placed against the blood-red drapery in the background, imbue the painting with great psychological depth. Likewise, the terrorized expression and gesture of the fleeing man, perhaps another of Christ's disciples, convey the emotional intensity of the moment. The man carrying the lantern at the extreme right, who looks inquisitively over the soldiers' heads, has been interpreted as a self-portrait.[65]

The painting, originally owned by Ciriaco Mattei, had been erroneously attributed to Gerard van Honthorst (also known as Gerardo delle Notti), a Dutch painter

Fig. 3.3. Caravaggio, *The Taking of Christ* (c. 1602), Dublin: National Gallery of Ireland.

and follower of Caravaggio, in 1793. By that time the Mattei family was already in serious financial difficulties and the inventorist they hired was either extremely incompetent or lazy and, regarding the attribution of works of art to be found in the Mattei's household, relied on a popular guidebook of Rome written by Giuseppe Vasi which, unfortunately, was full of mistakes and inaccuracies (*LP*, p. 95). A copy of the painting (by some considered to be an original) was to be found in Odessa until 1 August 2008 when it was stolen from the Museum of Western Art in the Ukrainian city. The Odessa version of *The Taking of Christ* had been found in Paris in 1870. After a thorough but not uneventful restoration the Dublin version was officially recognized as the original, which had been purchased in 1802 by the Scotsman Hamilton Nisbet from Ciriaco Mattei (*LP*, p. 128).

The book is based on the story of Francesca Cappelletti, whose work, together with that of her colleague Laura Testa, was very important in tracing the ownership of the painting after it left the Mattei family. Thanks to her determination, she was able to demonstrate that Longhi's intuition about Hamilton Nisbet was correct: in 1802 the Scotsman had bought a Caravaggio believing it was a Honthorst. Cappelletti willingly spoke of her Caravaggio adventure to Jonathan Harr, who fully acknowledges the importance of her contribution in his book. Another unusual aspect of *The Lost Painting* is that it features all major Caravaggio scholars, from Maurizio Calvesi to Mina Gregori, including Sir Denis Mahon. The book reads like a thriller. As Bruce Handy put it in his 2005 review for *The New York Times*, it 'even kicks off with the ritual opening: a brief prologue suggesting the high stakes of the game afoot followed by the introduction of an unlikely and unprepossessing but, in the end, surprisingly resourceful heroine'.[66] Handy speaks of 'an art historian's version of C.S.I.' (ibid.). The book is divided into four parts. The first presents the main characters, in particular the 91-year-old Sir Denis Mahon. The reader is introduced to the antagonism between Longhi and Sir Denis Mahon, whose first major disagreement dated back to 1951 when Sir Denis disputed the authenticity of another painting by Caravaggio, *St John the Baptist* from the Doria Pamphilj collection in Rome (*LP*, p. 6). The second part is devoted to Francesca and Laura's work in the archive of the Mattei family in Recanati, where the two young scholars managed to befriend an old marchioness usually reluctant to let visitors into her palazzo. This part covers also Francesca's trips to the Warburg Institute in London and pays tribute to her ability to work on different projects at once, 'fulfilling her obligations for the Warburg grant [...], pursuing the fate of the Mattei paintings' and, between projects, looking for 'information on William Hamilton Nisbet and his art collection' (*LP*, p. 106). The third section introduces Sergio Benedetti, his discovery of the painting, the events concerning the restoration process, and the various steps leading to the authentication. Finally, the last section is devoted to the 1993 celebrations in Dublin when the painting was unveiled and put on display at the National Gallery of Ireland after the Jesuits had agreed to grant the gallery an indefinite loan.

Although, technically, Harr's book is a non-fiction narrative, it has many features in common with the previously analysed art-crime thrillers. As the reviewer for *The Economist* pointed out shortly after its publication, 'Jonathan Harr has taken the story of the lost painting, and woven from it a deeply moving narrative about history, art and taste — and about the greed, envy, covetousness and professional jealousy of people who fall prey to obsession'.[67] *The Taking of Christ* is one of Caravaggio's most frequently copied works so, like the previously analysed novels, Harr's book engages with issues of originality and authenticity. Harr seems to believe that if Mahon's theory that a painting is the expression of the mind of the artist is correct, when we are looking at the works of a genius 'no copy, however good, could reveal those depths' (*LP*, p. 10). *The Lost Painting* is successful because Harr is capable of making the reader follow Francesca's and Laura's work with the same suspense and anticipation the two scholars must have felt whilst carrying out their research. What is more, a certain element of mystery is present until the very end of the book, since Harr included the 1997 incident involving an infestation of biscuit beetles which, had they not been spotted in time, could have damaged the painting only four years after its restoration:

> *The Taking of Christ* became the Gallery's biggest draw, attracting thousands of visitors a year. One of those visitors, gazing at the painting on a warm day in April 1997, happened to notice a tiny dark brown speck on the inner edge of the gilt frame. It would not have caught the visitor's attention had the speck not started to move in erratic circles, and then suddenly take wing. [...] As senior restorer, O'Connor assumed the task of tackling the problem. He had all the paintings in the Italian room of the gallery taken down. He inspected each in turn for signs of infestation, but found none. *The Taking of Christ* was the sole painting afflicted by the biscuit beetle. (*LP*, pp. 260–62)

This curious case was the source of amusement amongst ordinary people and journalists as the following headline demonstrates: 'Beetles show excellent taste by selecting £30m painting for snack'.[68] The beetle had been attracted by a kind of organic glue, rich in starch, used to reline the painting. Despite the apparent triviality of the case, the biscuit beetle is a well-known hazard for museums and libraries. Significantly, the director of the National Gallery of Ireland, Mr Keaveney, said: 'We spend all our time worrying about men in balaclavas coming in to steal our paintings and then you find this tiny thing wreaking havoc. In many ways they are a lot more destructive' (ibid.). Harr adds extra spice to his narrative by including another story related to the biscuit beetle incident, that is to say the rumours of how Benedetti nearly ruined the Caravaggio and of the National Gallery's lack of modern equipment for relining paintings.

Harr reports that, according to some National Gallery sources, Benedetti had taken the unusual decision of using Irish linen to reline the painting instead of ordering some from Italy which would have been much closer to the original canvas. Also, given that the Gallery did not own heat tables and low-pressure tables capable of sealing one canvas to another through partial vacuums, Benedetti had decided to use a very traditional and old-fashioned technique for relining the painting. He made his own glue, 'he thickened it with quantities of flour, adding water until it had a gruel-like consistency. He added more molasses for greater elasticity. When the glue had cooked, he brought the pot to the table and spread it on the back of *The Taking of Christ*, using a wooden spatula with shallow notches in it' (*LP*, p. 186).

Unfortunately, during the ironing, which was the last but also most difficult phase of the lining, things went wrong and the surface of the painting began to crack (*LP*, p. 188). In the end, Benedetti had no choice and was forced to subject the painting to another relining. This time he ordered some Italian canvas and the operation was successful. The cracks did not vanish completely, but even an experienced observer would have mistaken those marks as a sign of the painting's age (*LP*, p. 195). Naturally, Benedetti never admitted he experienced problems in relining the painting and 'the few people at the Gallery who knew what had happened did not discuss it in Benedetti's presence and he never brought up the issue himself' (*LP*, p. 189).

To conclude, I would argue that Harr's book — by raising the issue of some aspects of security usually ignored by people outside the art trade — performs one of the key functions of the art-crime thriller (as identified by Charney), which is the ability to educate the reader whilst entertaining him/her. Furthermore, Harr seems to confirm what in the introduction to this study we called the Caravaggio phenomenon — that is to say: on the one hand, the ability of a name like Caravaggio to attract even people who would not normally visit art exhibitions; and, on the other, a need for museums to capitalize on the popularity of certain artists, which led to the birth and expansion of a satellite industry of books and artefacts related to certain event. As we have seen in the previous chapters, whereas, in the past, the curators of an exhibition or a museum were only concerned with producing an attractive and informative critical catalogue, today this is no longer enough: in order to provide variety in what they offer, they started to commission fictional works capable of appealing to a wider audience, particularly an audience of non-specialists. To explain this phenomenon, Harr borrows an expression from Francesca Cappelletti and calls it 'the Caravaggio disease' (*LP*, p. 31). The expression is rather powerful as it captures how, in the second half of the twentieth century or, more precisely, since the 1951 exhibition in Milan, Caravaggio's 'rebirth into the world of art was swift, the mirror image of his disappearance three centuries earlier' (ibid.). Harr rightly points out that this phenomenon initially started amongst art historians when 'Caravaggio scholarship suddenly, miraculously, blossomed into an industry' (ibid.). Francesca and Laura are prime examples of the contagious nature of this 'disease'. Probably, if scholars had not taken an interest, the current reappropriation of Caravaggio by popular culture would have never taken place.

Finally, as we started the chapter by pointing out the connection between the hard-boiled genre and the film/'roman' noir through the analysis of Scorsese's *Mean Streets* we will conclude it with a section devoted to a recent noir that, in many ways, resembles Scorsese's work, particularly in the way it quotes Caravaggio.

Gilda Piersanti's *Jaune Caravage*[69]

From the point of view of the plot and of intertextual references, this is by far the most complex of the previously studied works, but also the one for which the idea of the canvas as a metaphor for the way in which a novel is structured is best suited.[70] The novel spans one week, from Saturday 9 September to Saturday 16 September

2006. The book is divided into thirty-eight chapters and one epilogue, each devoted to just a few hours or a very specific moment of a given day (e.g. 'Midi'/Midday; 'Peu Avant Midi'/Shortly before Midday). One week is the time it takes inspectors Mariella Deluca and Silvia Di Santo to solve the case of the mutilated body of a young woman which was accidentally discovered on the banks of the river Tiber by the dog of an elderly gentleman (Eugenio Proietti) during one of their early morning walks. The murder was shocking and puzzling at the same time. Although the young woman had not been sexually assaulted, the assassin, after strangling her, had carefully removed her eyes and must have mysteriously disposed of them as they could not be found anywhere near the body, not even in the murky waters of the river. The victim was Eva, the daughter of a Russian immigrant, Katja Ismaïlova, who had moved to Rome with her husband Serguei̇̈, a drug dealer who eventually left her for a much younger woman and returned to Russia. In order to raise her child, Katja had been forced to accept all kinds of jobs but was always struggling to make ends meet. She had a difficult relationship with her beautiful daughter who, like many seventeen-year-old girls, was desperate for some independence and was aspiring to a lifestyle beyond their means. Katja's relationship with men was also problematic. After Serguei̇̈ had left, she started seeing Boris, another unscrupulous character of Russian origins who was a lot younger than Katja and who, behind her back, started sleeping with Eva.

During the investigation, apart from Katja, the main source of information about Eva is Leonora Rapisardi, Eva's schoolmate and best friend. Like Eva, Leonora lived with her mother: her father, an established architect, had left the marital home to start a relationship with a younger woman. Unfortunately, after the separation, Leonora's mother developed a form of severe depression and lived the life of a recluse. Unlike Eva, Leonora was a very diligent student and an excellent musician, but she was shy and lacked confidence about her looks. Eva, on the other hand, had the opposite problem. As a result, the two girls had started to influence each other and seemed to complement each other. Things went well until Eva had the crazy idea of persuading Boris to take care of Leonora's sexual education and the two began to exchange jokes via e-mail about Leonora's shyness and naivety, about the fact that she seemed to be falling in love with Boris instead of simply enjoying sex. Unfortunately, Leonora accidentally discovered Eva's password and saw how the two people she loved the most ridiculed her. This experience was extremely traumatic for Leonora, who became obsessed with the idea of revenge. Gradually, she was transformed from model student and ideal daughter into murderer. Not only did she kill both the people who had betrayed her (Eva and Boris), but she was also planning to kill her mother and, if Silvia had not arrived in time, Mariella would have been her next victim.

Apart from the main story relating to Eva's death, the novel follows further stories, including that of Mariella's problematic relationship to Paolo, an art lover who introduced her to Caravaggio, and that of Fausto, the intruder Mariella discovered in her house, who turned out to be a friend of Giuliano's, the superintendent's missing son. Fausto and Giuliano had been childhood friends, since Fausto was the son of Superintendent D'Innocenzo's housekeeper, and they had grown up together. Both young men were homosexual and both had families who could not accept their sexuality. Despite their close friendship, Fausto and Giuliano had never been lovers. According to Fausto, who was the last person to have heard from the superintendent's son, Giuliano had probably died of AIDS in India. Fausto, who after Giuliano's death started to suffer from depression, began to occupy Mariella's flat when she was away because that was Giuliano's last address before he disappeared.

In order to understand Piersanti's novel, it is important to focus on her introduction to the series 'Les Quatre Saisons Meurtrières'/'The Four Deadly Seasons' of which *Jaune Caravage* is part:

> Quatre histoires, quatre enquêtes policières qui débutent sur des lieux communs du noir pour les déjouer grâce à un dénouement surprenant [...].Rome plane sur les histoires et sur les personnages: Rome, ville déroutante de splendeur qui pendant quatre saisons se plaira à brouiller les pistes du climat familier [...].Composée de quatre épisodes, la série vise à explorer les possibilités littéraires du polar au-delà des codes du genre: respectés, mais déplacés.[71]

> [Four stories, four police investigations that start with the clichés of the noir only to elude them thanks to a surprising ending [...] Rome glides over the stories and the characters: Rome, a city puzzling in its splendour which throughout four seasons enjoys blurring the trails of its familiar atmosphere. [...] Consisting of four episodes, the series intends to explore the literary possibilities of the detective novel beyond the codes of the genre: respected, but altered.]

As we can see form this brief description of her series, Piersanti is attracted by contrasts, by the dark side of reality, the relationship between past and present, the idea of tradition and the need to innovate it, features which are also typical of Caravaggio. Although references to Caravaggio are present in some of the other books belonging to 'Les Quatre Saisons Meurtrières'/'The Four Deadly Seasons', particularly in *Bleu Catacombes* (2007), *Jaune Caravage* is particularly interesting because it is the one that engages more deeply with the Baroque painter. The fact that 'Caravage' appears already in the title is significant. The colour yellow, of course, is an obvious reference to the warm light we find in Caravaggio's paintings[72] and, inevitably, when we mention light we also think of shade. Piersanti's book is entirely built on the opposition between contrasting elements, such as private/public, good/evil, fair/dark, and even the characters seem to be grouped in pairs according to contrasting qualities similar to those of a chiaroscuro technique. Eva and Leonora, Mariella and Paolo, Katja and Eva, or Giuliano and Fausto, to mention just a few, all seem to be the opposite of one another and therefore to complement each other. However, the same dichotomies that characterize each character pair are to be found within each single individual and the chiaroscuro seems to become a metaphor for life.

As the author herself pointed out in the passage quoted above, another important aspect of the novel is the setting (Rome). Like Scorsese, Piersanti tries to reproduce the kind of realism we find in many of Caravaggio's paintings. Piersanti focuses on a contemporary version of the Roman underworld Caravaggio would have been familiar with in his time, and depicts the life of ordinary people who live at the margin of legality in a world where violence is all too familiar. Significantly, the story takes place in the district of Testaccio and in its neighbouring area, Ostiense, a working-class area of Rome associated with trade and commerce, thanks to its ancient port on the Tiber which connected the city to the sea (Ostia). The area was frequently flooded and infested with malaria. It has traditionally been inhabited by poor people, particularly peasants and artisans. In line with the parameters of the noir genre, Piersanti gives a very detailed and accurate description of this area of Rome as it is today (the novel is set in 2006):

> À partir de la deuxième moitié du XIXe siècle, avaient surgi sur la Via Ostiense les industries et les dépôts: charbon, coke, gaz, halles, chemins de fer, abattoirs. Puis, peu à peu, Testaccio était devenu le quartier dortoir des ouvriers travaillant à Ostiense. À l'est s'ouvrait le no man's land des anciens Mercati Generali: les travaux de démolition en vue du chantier pharaonique de la Cité des jeunes, don't l'ouverture était prévue pour 2010, venaient de commencer. (*JC*, pp. 223–24)

> [Industries and warehouses started to develop along the Via Ostiense as of the second half of the nineteenth century: coal, coke, gas, food markets, railways and slaughterhouses. Little by little, Testaccio had turned into a dormitory town for the labourers who worked in Ostiense. To the east, the no-man's land of the old Mercati Generali began: the demolition work for the pharaonic building site of *Città dei Giovani*, the opening of which was planned for 2010, had just started.]

From this point of view, Piersanti's text seems to confirm Turnaturi's thesis of the importance of space in contemporary noirs (see Turnaturi, p. 48) and also the idea of the noir as a social novel. Through the aforementioned reference to the 'Città dei Giovani' [City of Youth] project, and through the voice of Eugenio Proietti, a man who was born and lived all his life in Ostiense, Piersanti raises the issue of the contrast between the problem ordinary young people are facing and what public authorities think should be done to solve them. No matter how skilled and qualified the people behind projects such as those of the Città dei Giovani are, they seem to have lost touch with reality and with the needs of people. As a result, through their work, planners and developers perpetuate the already existing gap between the public and the private sphere (*JC*, p. 209). Eugenio is particularly critical of the architects who are in charge of the restoration of degraded areas of the city and calls the man who won the contract for the 'Città dei giovani' 'l'architecte du chaos' [the architect of chaos] (*JC*, p. 13). Like Baldassarri, Piersanti seems to blame greed and the dream of an easy fortune for many of our current social problems (*JC*, p. 210). Eva's story is emblematic in this respect. Like Francesca in Baldassarri's novel, Eva and, even more so, her mother, Katja, are ready to accept any compromise for the sake of money. When the sixteen-year-old Eva decides to pose as a model for a controversial fashion designer producing wrought-iron underwear, her mother signs the necessary documents without even trying to stop her underage daughter from pursuing her dream of fame. Through her characters, Piersanti addresses another major source of social problems, which is the myth of happiness. Once again, young people seem to be more vulnerable: instead of reflecting (or, perhaps, unable to reflect) on the causes of their discontent, they seek refuge in drugs, particularly those which, like the notorious 'angel's powder', are capable of producing a feeling of lightness and of heightened emotions similar to those experienced by Step and Babi in the 1992 novel *Tre metri sopra il cielo* by Federico Moccia (*JC*, p. 145).[73] Through Eva's blog, Piersanti offers the reader a rather bleak picture of the world of young people:

> À un moment donné, elle a même créé un blog qui s'appelait: 'L'Ange aux ailes brisées'. C'était son sanctuaire gothique à elle: le temple de ses fascinations macabres et de ses sombres délires [...]. Un mode où l'on mélange l'horreur et la beauté, où l'on exalte la solitude, le désespoir et la souffrance. Romantisme noir, fantastique et magie ... Bref, un tas de clichés. (*JC*, pp. 232–33)

> [At a certain point, she created her own blog which was called: 'The Angel with broken wings'. It was her personal gothic sanctuary: the temple of her morbid fascinations and bleak fury. [...] A fashion that mixed horror and beauty, which exalted loneliness, despair and suffering. A black, magical and grotesque Romanticism ... In short, a load of clichés.]

Apart from helping the reader to better understand Eva and young people of her age, this passage offers an example of two aspects of the noir genre identified by scholars who participated in the symposia organized by the University of La Sapienza in Rome in 2007 and 2008. First of all, the reference to the fantastic seems to confirm the idea of the noir as a genre that represents realistically the dissolution of the traditional image of reality, a reality that is governed by new laws and has established a new relationship with the fantastic. Whereas in the past the image of reality was dominated by positive models, nowadays we see a contamination between reality, horror, and the grotesque. According to Cristina Storini, this move towards the fantastic was necessary to escape from apocalyptic visions which would be too depressing to encourage a reflection on our contemporary world. The critic uses the example of *Un giorno perfetto* (*A Perfect Day*) by Melania Mazzucco[74] and argues that if the reader were to perceive Mazzucco's characters in realistic terms, s/he would be forced to recognize himself/herself in them. Such a process of identification would generate at the most an emotional but not a critical response. In this case, despite its realistic intent, the novel would run the risk of reinforcing existing fears and prejudices instead of challenging them.[75] Paradoxically, a grotesque text can be more subversive in terms of promoting a critical appraisal of society than a realistic one. As we have already seen through the analysis of the various stories that form *Jaune Caravage*, grotesque is a term that can be applied easily to Piersanti's work, not only regarding the plot but also the sphere of intertextuality. The tattoo of a crow on Eva's lower abdomen, the expression 'nevermore' used by Boris to encourage Eva to give up drugs, and the name Leonora, are all direct references to a poem by Edgar Allan Poe, 'The Raven', written in 1845. Significantly, the expression 'nevermore' and the image of a crow appear on Poe's original tombstone in Baltimore. Like many of the characters in Piersanti's novel, Poe became severely depressed during his wife's illness, which led to her death of tuberculosis in 1847. Instead of looking for the strength to get on with his life, he drowned his sorrows in alcohol and seemed unable to overcome the trauma. He never fully recovered his mental stability and spent the rest of his life courting two women at the same time. He was found badly wounded and in a state of confusion along a road on 3 October 1849 and died in hospital four days later. Unfortunately, he never recovered consciousness so he was unable to explain what had happened to him and the exact cause of death is still a mystery.[76]

The similarity between the way Poe and Caravaggio died is also significant and is used by Piersanti to underpin two of her key themes: that of the effect of a trauma on the human mind (including the mind of a genius) and that of the notion of tragedy. According to Piersanti a tragedy is always the result of the contrast between passion and reason, but tragic also is the way in which guilt is transmitted from one generation to the next. Apart from functioning as an intertextual reference to Poe, the image of the crow/raven is important as, traditionally, the crow is an ambiguous symbol. Within the Bible itself the crow has contrasting connotations. In the episode of Noah and the flood, the crow was sent to earth to inspect the situation but failed to inform Noah that the flood was over: as a result, the crow is seen as selfish. The crow can also be seen as symbolizing original sin as, according to the legend, crows became black and started eating carrion after Adam and Eve were driven from the Garden of Eden. However, the crow can also represent divine providence and both St Benedict and St Oswald have the crow as their symbol. What is more, in China and Japan crows bring light to the world and symbolize the creative principle, a theme which is also at the core of Piersanti's book.[77]

In what is perhaps the least convincing aspect of the novel, Piersanti explores the question of creativity through fashion and religion and seems to suggest that fashion has become both a new religion (*JC*, p. 233) and a new form of art, in actual fact the only art capable of producing the kind of shock effect many of Caravaggio's contemporaries experienced when looking at his paintings for the first time (*JC*, pp. 82–83).[78] In Piersanti's view, the most striking similarity between art and fashion is the amount of money associated with both activities and the consequent corruption that frequently characterizes both worlds: 'dans la mode, c'est comme dans l'art: c'est un domaine où l'argent circule à flots, et à force de circuler, il perd sa mauvaise odeur' [Fashion is like art: it is a sphere where money flows and, by flowing, loses its bad smell] (*JC*, p. 82). The fashion designer is the twenty-first-century artist par excellence, as the example of J. A. Diamant, alias Santino Coddanzinu, demonstrates. J. A. Diamant, whose fashion house is called J(esus) & J(udas), is a Caravaggio-like character who epitomizes all the contradictions and chiaroscuros which are typical of his profession. Starting from the clash between his very ordinary, and even slightly ridiculous, name and his glamorous professional name (meaning diamond) we see the industry's aforementioned obsession with value and money:

> — 'Jesus & Judas'. Ce que je voulais t'expliquer, c'est qui il s'agit d'une mode transgressive, qui mise sur le choc visuel et jouit d'ailleurs des faveurs de certains milieux aux marges de la légalité. [...] — J. A. Diamant est par example le styliste préféré de la mafia russe. (*JC*, p. 82)
>
> [— 'Jesus & Judas'. What I wanted to explain is that it is a transgressive kind of fashion that relies on the visual shock and, besides, enjoys the favours of

certain groups at the margin of legality. [...] — J. A. Diamant, for instance, is the Russian Mafia's favourite designer.]

Despite the image of brilliance, purity, and preciousness projected by his name, Coddanzinu is a rather dark and unscrupulous character. He is ready to exploit underage girls like Eva but, once a particular project is finished, he does not care about the future career or welfare of his models and in many cases he does not even remember their names. His latest line of wrought-iron underwear, for which Eva posed, shows that he identifies with Vulcan, the Roman god of fire and craftsmanship. The myth of Vulcan is closely modelled on that of the Greek god Hephaestus. According to some legends, Hephaestus was the creator of Pandora, a woman who, like Eve in the Christian tradition, brought evil to the world and caused mankind's downfall.[79] Within the novel, of course, Eva is responsible for Leonora's downfall, but Piersanti's message is that it is impossible to distinguish clearly between good and evil or light and darkness. Despite the difference in social background, looks, and personality, Leonora and Eva are fundamentally very similar: both suffered from the lack of positive male role models in their childhood, both lived with hyper-protective mothers and were extremely insecure. As a result, they resorted to violence. Ironically, the extroverted, outgoing Eva, who liked excesses, was fascinated with morbid thoughts and was driven by self-destructive impulses, whilst the introverted Leonora directed her violence towards those who betrayed her. Piersanti seems to have a very bleak view of human relationships, and the schizophrenia with which Leonora is diagnosed at the end of the book becomes a symbol of our human condition. Human beings are fundamentally alone, and growing up implies coming to terms with betrayal.[80] Only art can bring some solace and help people accept the harsh reality of human life. Once Leonora is deprived of her musical instruments she loses touch with the outside world, 'son cerveau se réfugia en lui-même, en deçà de toute relation avec le monde extérieur' [her brain found refuge within itself, cutting all ties with the outside world] (JC, p. 278).

Significantly, Leonora is not the only character for whom art is important. Mariella, for instance, has a passion for drawing and painting and when her boyfriend Paolo takes her to Villa Borghese and introduces her to Caravaggio, she is so struck by Caravaggio's *Basket of Fruit* that the following day, without telling Paolo, she returns to the museum to copy the painting (JC, p. 153). As a detective, Mariella is fascinated by a painting which had been praised and criticized for its excessive realism and attention to the least attractive aspects of reality. Painting or drawing has a therapeutic function for Mariella. It enables her to deal with emotional difficulties or a personal crisis like the loss of her assistant Lucio (JC, p. 203), who had been stabbed in the stomach and bled to death during an investigation. Finally, for Paolo, Mariella's lover, art is also something extremely personal. The secret chamber in his house, which had triggered Mariella's worst fears,[81] turns out to be a small studio full of paintings and a few books. Amongst the books Mariella discovers a study of still lives and a volume entitled *La pittura in cucina* in which an art historian, a chef, and a food journalist reproduced thirty-seven seventeenth- and eighteenth-century still lives, mainly by Italian and Flemish painters, providing a detailed commentary on each one of them, and a recipe inspired by the ingredients depicted in the painting in order to add an extra aesthetic dimension to the experience of a work of art. In line with the original concept of still life, the aim of the book was to provide the reader/viewer/eater with a complete sensorial experience.[82] To Mariella's surprise, Paolo had obviously relied on that book in order to impress her and a few friends with his culinary skills, as she discovers the recipe for their anniversary cake, which he had always refused to disclose to his guests. Even though it is not entirely clear why Paolo is so secretive about his collection of Baroque paintings, what matters is that for Piersanti's characters art plays an important part in their daily lives.

Interestingly, apart from *Basket of Fruit* and *Boy with a Basket of Fruit*, the other Caravaggio evoked in the novel is *The Calling of St Matthew* (*JC*, p. 129). With an ironic twist, Piersanti subverts the theme of election: instead of the light of salvation touching and rescuing a sinner, we have Eva, who epitomizes the world of experience, selecting and thus corrupting the world of innocence represented by Leonora. The theme of light, both in the metaphorical sense and as a reference to the warm light that through a window illuminates the table around which Matthew and the other publicans are sitting in the painting, brings us back to the title of the novel, *Jaune Caravage*, and to Eva's eyes whose yellow/green colour made them seem as bright as stars (*JC*, p. 183). The importance of Eva's eyes and of the theme of sight/blindness is obvious from the very beginning of the novel as the reader is immediately informed that the assassin had performed a perfect enucleation of the victim's eyes. It could be argued that this gesture represents Leonora's ultimate revenge: not satisfied with simply taking Eva's life, she had deprived her former friend not only of the most attractive part of her body but also, more significantly, of the tool that had enabled her to play the role of the artist/creator. Blindness, however, is also a key theme in Piersanti's most important intertextual reference, 'The Waste Land' by T. S. Eliot. Significantly, the novel opens with a quote from the second part of the 'The Waste Land' ('A Game of Chess'), which in turn is a quote from William Shakespeare's *The Tempest* (1. 2. 400–06): 'I remember | Those are pearls that were his eyes'.[83] Whilst in Shakespeare, those verses signify hope and the possibility of redemption, for Piersanti, as for Eliot, there is no such hope. Piersanti's characters are 'postmodern' wastelanders who live in extreme decadence. They are affected by a spiritual and moral blindness which prevents them from recognizing the Absolute and leads them to believe in superficial and ephemeral things such as fashion. For Eva in particular, 'life is like a game [...] meant for sexual and physical pleasures in which [she] finds no spiritual consolation'.[84] If, on the surface, Leonora's gesture of killing Eva and burying her eyes in a pot of basil could be interpreted as the wish to be freed from hedonism and worldly desires, the novel's ending seems to deny any kind of spiritual regeneration. Leonora is locked away in a mental institution and, like the corpse buried in the Waste Land's garden, the basil flourishing in the soil where Eva's eyes have been buried does not symbolize spiritual rebirth but simply the spreading of death. As we have already seen, in the space of a week the once innocent Leonora turns into a multiple murderer.

Inevitably, the image of basil cannot but make us think of Boccaccio's story in which Lisabetta da Messina, having discovered where her brothers had buried the corpse of her lover Lorenzo after killing him, detaches his head from the rest of the body, buries it in a pot of basil, and spends most of her time weeping over the plant and looking after it. Once her brothers find out the reason for her attachment to that plant, they take it away from her and Lisabetta dies of a broken heart (*Decameron*, IV. 5). If, as argued by Terzoli, Boccaccio's story contains a reference to the origin of the cult of relics as everything about Lorenzo in the text bears strong similarities with the image of a martyr,[85] there is nothing holy about Eva and the 'cult' of relics from her body can only make the similarity between Piersanti's characters and the inhabitants of Eliot's wasteland more obvious. What is more, Lisabetta was not responsible for the death of her lover and, as a result, her gesture was not perceived as shocking by Boccaccio's narrator/audience/reader. Leonora's fetishistic attachment to Eva's eyes, instead, comes across as sick, as further evidence of the decadence of the society to which she belongs. Also, from the point of view of interpretation, this is one of Boccaccio's most open novellas: like many of Caravaggio's paintings, 'il testo non ci appare mai bloccato su una verità ultima e definitiva [...], resiste ad una decifrazione del tutto appagante' [The text never appears to be stuck on an ultimate and definitive truth [...], it resists a fully satisfying interpretation] (Terzoli, p. 194). The same could be said of Piersanti's book and of Mariella and Silvia's investigations as reality is too complex to fit into a single story. Finally, this novella of Lisabetta da Messina is a rewriting of the Sicilian popular ballad 'Qualesso fu lo malo cristiano' composed in Messina in response to the story of a rather gruesome local crime.[86] Apart from illustrating the power of cross-fertilization between popular culture and high art,[87] the act of rewriting folklore recreates in the macrotext that very process that within the story turns corpses into plants, 'teste into testi, Sicilian ballads into Latinate prose masterworks', thus stressing the consolatory power of art,[88] a theme which, as we have seen, is extremely important in Piersanti's work. What is more, Piersanti, like the Boccaccio of the fifth novella, seems to identify in the 'dismemberment' of the traditional family one of the main causes for the social evils and moral decline she portrays in her books.[89] It is also worth mentioning that, as Filippo La Porta points out (p. 58), the best noirs in recent years are those which address philosophical or moral questions, and this is precisely what Piersanti's novel does.

To conclude, we can argue that whether we look at art-crime thrillers, noirs, or texts belonging to both genres (e.g. Baldassarri's), all the works included in our case study endeavour to offer comments on various problems affecting our contemporary globalized world. As a result, there are no major national differences and all attempts at classifying these texts from a national/geographical perspective (like the concept of Mediterranean noir that could be applied to Baldassarri's text) remain unconvincing as too vague. This, of course, does not mean to say that the location has no role to play. Quite the opposite: the location (or setting) is extremely important as it represents the 'realist' element that ties these works to a specific society and functions as a comment on that particular world. The term 'glocal' could be applied to many of the noirs or art-crime thrillers we have analysed as they mix realist elements with extremely complex and highly implausible plots. These texts are often characterized by a shift towards the fantastic as a strategy for dealing with extreme violence and portraying evil as the non-place of our societies.[90]

Fig. 3.4. Caravaggio, *Basket of Fruit* (1596),
Milan: Pinacoteca Ambrosiana.

Fig. 3.5. Caravaggio, *The Calling of St Matthew* (1599–1600), Rome: Contarelli Chapel in San Luigi dei Francesi.

Regarding the presence of Caravaggio, apart from the obvious appeal of his dark and mysterious personality, it is his ability to challenge fixed traditional boundaries (e.g. sacred/profane; life/death; inside/outside, etc.) that makes him so interesting for writers and directors willing to engage with crime fiction and the noir. It is no coincidence that the most quoted of his paintings in this context is *David with the Head of Goliath*, which, apart from blurring the boundaries between victim and victimizer, raises interesting questions about guilt and punishment and offers the potential for turning a noir or crime story into a philosophical or moral tale (*Roma Noir 2008*, p. 58).

Notes to Chapter 3

1. All translations from sources written in languages other than English are mine.
2. John Scraggs, *Crime Fiction* (London: Routledge, 2005), p. 30. Further references will be given in the text.
3. According to Scraggs, the relationship between hard-boiled fiction and cinema brought a new vitality to the genre and helped its survival (p. 69).
4. Steven Marcus, 'Dashiell Hammett', in *The Poetics of Murder: Detective Fiction and Literary Theory*, ed. by Glenn W. Most and William W. Stowe (New York: Harcourt Brace, 1983), pp. 197–209 (p. 202).
5. Austin R. Freeman, 'The Art of the Detective Story', in *The Art of the Mystery Story: A Collection of Critical Essays*, ed. by Howard Haycraft (New York: Carroll & Graf, 1992), pp. 7–17 (p. 9).
6. Julian Symons, *Bloody Murder: From the Detective Story to the Crime Novel*, 3rd rev. edn (New York: The Mysterious Press, 1993), p. 193.
7. According to Elisabetta Mondello, the readers of detective fiction (and particularly of historical detective novels) are looking both for entertainment and for tools to interpret reality. See Elisabetta Mondello, 'Finzione narrativa ed "effetto realtà" ' in *Roma Noir 2008: 'Hannibal the Cannibal c'est moi?' Realismo e finzione nel romanzo noir italiano*, ed. by Elisabetta Mondello (Rome: Robin Edizioni, 2008), pp. 13–48 (p. 44).
8. Noah Charney's articles and non-fictional writings are available on his personal website or on the ARCA website: <http://www.noahcharney.com/> [accessed 1 February 2009]; <http://www.artcrime.info/> [accessed 1 February 2009].
9. Vincenzo Peruggia is the man who stole the *Mona Lisa* on 21 August 1911 and hid it in his apartment, first in Paris and then in Italy, for two years. When finally questioned by the police he claimed that he had stolen the painting for patriotic reasons; the reduced sentence he received seems to confirm the authorities believed him. For further details see: <http://damforstmuseum.org/stolen.html#monalisa> [accessed 1 February 2009].
10. Tom Mueller, 'To Sketch a Thief', *The New York Times Magazine*, 17 December 2006, <http://www.nytimes.com/2006/12/17/magazine/17art.t.html?fta=y> [accessed 6 February 2009].
11. Jonathan Harr's *The Lost Painting*, for instance, has been translated into Chinese, German, Italian, Japanese, Korean, Polish, Serbian, and Spanish.
12. Darian Leader, *What Art Stops Us from Seeing* (Washington, DC: Shoemaker & Hoard, 2004), p. 75. Further references will be given in the text.
13. Pedro García-Caro, 'Behind the Canvas: The Role of Paintings in Peter Ackroyd's *Chatterton* and Arturo Pérez-Reverte's *The Flanders Panel*', in *Crime Scenes: Detective Narratives in European Culture since 1945*, ed. by Anne Mullen and Emer O'Beirne (Amsterdam: Rodopi, 2000), pp. 160–70 (p. 164).
14. The term was first used by Susana Onega in her book *Myth in Peter Ackroyd's Novels* (New York: Camden House, 1999), pp. 71–72.
15. The most famous case is perhaps that of *The Martyrdom of St Matthew*, which was X-rayed in Milan in 1951 when the art historian Lionello Venturi persuaded the governmental authorities to allow such an examination after he became convinced that he could identify an overlapping of paint surfaces around the fallen figure of St Matthew. The X-rays revealed

what looked at first glance like a chaotic triple exposure. Studied closely, the pictures showed that Caravaggio had unmistakably started two earlier versions of his famous painting on the same canvas, and covered them over. The experts isolated parts of ten figures, deduced which of them belonged to each version, and filled them out in painstaking sketches. (<http://www.time.com/time/magazine/article/0,9171,889574,00.html> [accessed 28 February 2009])

Another interesting aspect of this study is the fact that the three versions of the painting differed significantly in both style and composition.

16. Philip Sohm (p. 462) reminds us of how some of Caravaggio's contemporaries, or near contemporaries, used psychologically charged terms to attack the painter's tenebrism on the basis of his biography. Francesco Algarotti (1756), for instance, described Caravaggio's style as 'cutting' (*tagliente*) and 'gloomy', 'savage', and 'dirty' (in its many senses of turbid, troublesome, or obscene).
17. Mary Wood, for instance, claims that the chiaroscuro technique of Baroque painting, which was eventually rediscovered by artists of the twentieth century as a way of expressing the tensions of the modern world, particularly 'feelings of solitude and alienation', has always had an influence on the Italian *film noir* (p. 242). Wood does not offer specific examples, as the topic is beyond the scope of her study, but points out that even in the *giallo politico* (the political thriller) of the 1970s the tensions between power/order and revolt/disorder are expressed through 'a baroque visual excess' (p. 255). (Mary P. Wood, 'Italian Film Noir', in *European Film Noir*, ed. by Andrew Spicer (Manchester: Manchester University Press, 2007), pp. 236–72.)
18. Arthur Wrobel, 'The Origin of Chandler's "Mean Streets"', *American Notes and Queries*, 7 (1994), 225–30 (p. 225).
19. Leighton Grist, *The Films of Martin Scorsese, 1963–77: Authorship and Context* (London: Macmillan Press, 2000), p. 82. Further references will be given in the text.
20. Extracts from the Matt Wolf interview were reprinted in 2005 in an article in *The Times*: <http://entertainment.timesonline.co.uk/tol/arts_and_entertainment/article517517.ece> [accessed 20 September 2008].
21. <http://www.imdb.com/video/screenplay/vi429261081/> [accessed 12 August 2008].
22. Apart from the already mentioned *Madonna dei pellegrini*, other paintings featuring a Madonna in red are *La Madonna dei palafrenieri* (for which Maddalena was also used as a model) and the controversial *Death of the Virgin*, whose model had been a poor woman who had drowned in the Tiber.
23. Paul Henrickson, 'Caravaggio and Sexual Adjustment' (1961, repr. 2005), <http://www.glbtq.com/arts/caravaggio.html> [accessed 28 February 2009], p. 6. As Henrickson explains, 'these responses are often related, especially in a Judaic-Christian context, insofar as sensuality encourages feelings of guilt and these, in turn, suggest punishment and death' (ibid.). On Caravaggio's erotic depiction of ecstasy see also John Gash, *Caravaggio* (London: Chaucer, 2003), p. 15.
24. Henricksen identifies the weaving together of sensuality and death as one of the key themes running through most of Caravaggio's works. As a result his paintings encourage a sense of guilt in the viewer, who is likely to be conditioned by the Judaic-Christian tradition according to which sensuality inevitably evokes feelings of guilt 'and these, in turn suggest punishment and death' (p. 6).
25. As we are about to see, this is also a main feature in Neil Griffiths's novel.
26. Bal, *Quoting Caravaggio*, p. 47.
27. Interestingly, this kind of religious experience is explored in greater detail in *The Last Temptation of Christ* (1988), a film in which references to Caravaggio are also prominent.
28. Margaret Truman, *Murder at the National Gallery* (New York: Random House, 1996); hereafter referred to as *MNG*. Margaret Truman was the only child of former American president Harry Truman. Her career as a published author began in 1956 with her autobiography *Souvenir*. She commented at the time that writing was 'hard work', but she stayed with it. She was a college junior when her father became president in 1945. She also took singing lessons and made her professional debut with the Detroit Symphony Orchestra in 1947. Two years later, she performed at Carnegie Hall. She was never particularly successful as a singer so, after a few years, she abandoned the musical career. In 1956, she married the journalist/reporter Clifton Daniel, who later became managing editor of the *New York Times*. The couple lived in New York and had

four sons. One of their children died in an accident involving a taxi in 2000, shortly after the death of his father (who was 87 and died of a stroke). Margaret Truman wrote twenty-three Washington-based mysteries, beginning with *Murder in the White House* in 1980. Follow-up books took place in other famous D.C. sites, such as the Smithsonian and Supreme Court. In addition to the novels, she published nine works of non-fiction, including a book on White House pets in 1969.

29. The following passage offers a clear example of the similarity between Julian and Caravaggio:

> 'What is it, Julian?' He [Luther] asked.
> 'I'm in jail.'
> 'Did you hear me?' Julian asked, his voice surly. 'I'm in goddamn jail.'
> 'Why?'
> 'Because I was arrested. I got into a fight at a bar.'
> 'Good Lord,' Luther muttered.
> 'I need bail money' (*MNG*, p. 123)

30. Noah Charney, 'Chasing Dr No: Art-crime Fact and Fiction-1', <http://www.noahcharney.com/pdf/ArtCrime-Fact&Fiction-1.pdf> [accessed 1 February 2009].
31. <http://www.britannica.com/EBchecked/topic/246790/grotesque#ref=ref197320> [accessed 28 February 2009].
32. According to John Varriano, the two versions of the *Supper at Emmaus* (1600 and 1606) are the only two works by Caravaggio with prominent decorative elements. However, in line with his style, Caravaggio deviated from the conventional treatment of some details using an abstract ivy-like motive for the central medallion of a specific type of pitcher called *boccaletto*, which traditionally should have contained a more figurative element (e.g. a fish). (John Varriano, 'Caravaggio and the Decorative Arts in the Two Suppers at Emmaus', *The Art Bulletin*, 68 (1986), 218–24 (p. 222).) For an interesting study of decorative elements in Caravaggio's works see also Clovis Whitfield, *Caravaggio's Eye* (Washington: University of Washington Press, 2011).
33. Geoffrey Galt Harpham, *On the Grotesque Strategies of Contradiction in Art and Literature* (Princeton: Princeton University Press, 1982), p. 31. Further references will be given in the text.
34. John T. Spike, *Caravaggio* (New York: Abbeville Press, 2001), p. 33. Further references will be given in the text.
35. It is interesting to point out that the image of Caravaggio's *Medusa* was selected for the hardcover of the first edition of Truman's novel (*Murder at the National Gallery* (New York, Random House, 1996)).
36. Paola Cristina Fraschini, *La metamorfosi del corpo: Il grottesco nell'arte e nella vita* (Milan: Mimesis, 2002), pp. 12–13; my translation.
37. The name Franco Del Brasco cannot but make us think of Donnie Brasco, the undercover name of Joseph Pistone, an FBI agent who in the 1970s infiltrated two of the leading five New York Mafia families by presenting himself as a jewel thief.
38. William Marling, 'Erle Stanley Gardner', <http://www.detnovel.com/Gardner.html> [accessed 10 January 2008].
39. Ellen Ryan's comments on another book in the Capital Crime Series are particularly interesting: Truman is compared to Pelecanos (the much younger and more famous author of several detective novels set in Washington) and dismissed as inferior. According to Ryan, Truman's books are of interest only to residents of Washington looking for a hometown holiday easy-reader:

> Margaret Truman is no George Pelecanos. But if your taste in Washington mysteries runs more to mind candy and name dropping than to guts and grit, Truman's books may be for you [...]. There are amusements [...] and subplots [...]. Most wrap up too quickly at the end. But if you are looking for a hometown beach reading, what the heck? (Ellen Ryan, '*Murder at the Opera* by Margaret Truman', *The Washingtonian.com*, <http://www.washingtonian.com/bookreviews/187.html> [accessed 12 January 2008]

40. <http://corrieredelmezzogiorno.corriere.it/campania/cronache/articoli/2008/03_Marzo/17/sede_regione_news.htm> [accessed 15 March 2008]).
41. Neil Griffiths, *Saving Caravaggio*, 2nd edn (London: Penguin Books 2007). All quotations are from this edition, later abbreviated as *SC*. Neil Griffiths was born in 1965. He lived for extended

periods in New York and Paris. His first novel, *Betrayal in Naples*, was published in 2004. It won the Authors' Club Best First Novel Award and was short-listed for the Pendleton May Award and the Waverton Good Read. *Saving Caravaggio* was short-listed for the 2006 Costa Novel of the Year Award. Neil Griffiths also writes for radio and film. He lives in London. According to the author, his first book was very well received, but sales were not that good. *Saving Caravaggio*, instead, sold out and had to be reprinted.

42. This is an obvious homage to Helen Langdon, the author of one of the most acclaimed biographies of Caravaggio, but also to Dan Brown, whose novels *Angels and Demons* (2000) and *The Da Vinci Code* (2003) feature a fictional professor of religious iconology and symbology called Robert Langdon who works at Harvard University.
43. Giulio Andreotti, several times Prime Minister of Italy, was accused of collusion with the Mafia but was eventually acquitted.
44. Peter Robb, 'Will We Ever See It Again?', *The Daily Telegraph*, 4 February 2005, <http://www.telegraph.co.uk/culture/art/3636386/Will-we-ever-see-it-again.html> [accessed 12 January 2008].
45. See Celestine Bohlen, 'Mafia and a Lost Caravaggio Stun Andreotti Trial', *The New York Times*, 8 November 1996, <http://www.nytimes.com/1996/11/08/world/mafia-and-a-lost-caravaggio-stun-andreotti-trial.html?n=Top/Reference/Times%20Topics/People/A/Andreotti,%20Giulio> [accessed 12 January 2008].
46. Here by 'mafia' we understand any organized crime syndicate similar to the Sicilian 'Mafia', the Ndrangheta, the Camorra or the Sacra Corona Unita. Whenever used in this generic term the word will not be capitalized.
47. In this case the name Savarese adds a touch of irony as the reader is reminded of Lou Savarese, the American heavyweight boxing champion who is also an actor and appeared in series such as *The Sopranos*. Interestingly, *The Sopranos* revolves around mobster Tony Soprano and the difficulties he faces as he tries to balance the often conflicting requirements of his home life and the criminal organization he heads. The mobsters in the series are depicted as tough, savvy, and street-smart, but lacking heavily in formal education and a deeper understanding of themselves and their world. Italo Nenni is described as stupid (*SC*, p. 62).

Savarese is also a popular comic hero created by Robin Wood in 1978 and modelled on Joe Petrosino, the Italo-American police officer who in January 1909 went to Sicily in order to investigate the relationship between the Mafia and organized crime ('la mano nera' or black hand), but was killed by two hitmen on 12 March 1909. For further details on Petrosino, see John Dickie, *Cosa Nostra* (London: Hodder & Stoughton, 2004), pp. 195–212. This additional intertextual layer reinforces the idea of the omnipresence of the mafia and highlights the dangers of underestimating the brutality of such criminal organizations.

It is also worth remembering that almost all the characters' names in Griffiths's book have interesting intertextual resonances. Apart from those already mentioned, we could add that the name of Storaro inevitably evokes one of the cinematographers more frequently associated with Caravaggio (see Chapter 2 of this book for further details on Storaro and Caravaggio). The more sophisticated reader will also remember that Lomazzo was the painter/art historian who probably influenced Caravaggio's use of darkness. See Claudio Strinati, *La [vera] vita di Caravaggio secondo Claudio Strinati* (Naples: Arte'm, 2009).
48. Fabio Baldassarri, *Il Mistero del Caravaggio* (Milan: Il Ponte delle Grazie, 2003); later referred to as *MC* (all translations are mine). Fabio Baldassarri was born in Orvieto in 1963 and works as a pharmacist in Pistoia where he lives with his wife, who is an art historian. He claims to have been inspired to write a novel by three passions: literature; painting, and adventure. Noah Charney, *The Art Thief* (London: Simon & Schuster 2007), later referred to as *AT*.
49. Filippo La Porta, 'Ancora sul *neonoir*', in *Roma Noir 2008*, ed. by Mondello, pp. 49–58 (p. 50).
50. According to the *Australian Book Review*, the greatest strength of Charney's book is in the discussion of the paintings themselves whilst the plot is too convoluted, revealing Charney's inexperience. This review is available on Charney's website: <http://www.noahcharney.com/pdf/AussieReview-art_thief.jpg> [accessed 27 February 2008].
51. True to national stereotypes, the Italian inspector Claudio Ariosto wears designer suits and a gold chain in Poirot style (*AT*, p. 24), whilst the French inspector Jean-Jacques Bizot does not

like to have his meal consisting of three portions of oysters interrupted by the buzzing of his mobile phone which reminds him of the need to resume his duties (*AT*, pp. 17–19).
52. This is one of Caravaggio's last works, painted possibly in Sicily and rejected by the Messina senate. There is a lack of documentation surrounding this painting, which is now in the Museé des Beaux-Arts in Nancy (France). According to Patrick Hunt, this is a very solitary work which reflects the painter's state of mind before his last attempt to reach Rome in 1610 (p. 129). The iconography is only partially traditional: 'although Caravaggio follows convention in having the Madonna *lilium album* in the angel's left hand, there is no dove of the Holy Spirit to represent conception, a startling omission' (Hunt, p. 130). Furthermore, Mary's flat profile seems to suggest a Byzantine aspect of Marian tradition and, if Hunt is right in suggesting that the cloud on which Archangel Gabriel hovers represents the face of God, we are looking at an example of 'Caravaggian genius' (ibid.).
53. Although this chapter focuses mainly on left-wing violence, Baldassarri is critical of all kinds of violence, as demonstrated by the fact that he opened the chapter with a description of *Guernica*, a painting depicting the atrocities of right-wing movements.
54. The important role played by the sea and, as we are about to discover, the gruesome nature of some of the murders seem to suggest that Baldassarri's novel could be studied not only in the context of the art-crime thriller but also as an example of Mediterranean noir according to the definition of the genre given by Gabriella Turnaturi. See Gabriella Turnaturi, 'Mediterraneo: Rappresentazioni in nero', in *Roma Noir 2007: Luoghi e nonluoghi nel romanzo nero contemporaneo*, ed. by Elisabetta Mondello (Rome: Robin Edizioni, 2007), pp. 47–68.
55. When interviewed by Laura Rorato on 25 August 2009, Baldassarri declared that he wanted to use this character to pay homage to Roberto Longhi, the scholar responsible for the rediscovery of Caravaggio in the twentieth century.
56. Patricia Allmer, 'La Reproduction Interdite: René Magritte and Forgery', *Papers of Surrealism*, 5 (2007), 1–19 (pp. 7, 9).
57. Here the term 'sublime' is to be understood as 'that which is behind and beyond representation' (Allmer, p. 8).
58. Jacques Lacan, *The Four Fundamental Concepts of Psycho-Analysis*, ed. by Jacques Alain Miller and trans. by Alan Sheridan (Harmondsworth: Penguin, [1977] 1987), p. 112.
59. René Magritte in Sarah Whitfield, *René Magritte* (London: South Bank Centre, 1992), p. 139.
60. Jan Jagodzinski, *Postmodern Dilemmas: Outrageous Essays in Art and Education* (Mahwah: Lawrence Erlbaum Associates, 1997), p. 237.
61. Although Jagodzinski applies this argument to the sculptures of Daune Hansons, I would argue that the same can be said about many of Caravaggio's paintings. As in Hansons's works, in many of Caravaggio's paintings 'the detail has been promoted to a radical centrality' (Jagodzinski, p. 237): e.g. the dirty fingernails in the *Bacchus* or the pilgrims' soiled feet in the *Madonna dei Pellegrini*.
62. Christian Lindner, *The James Bond Phenomenon: A Critical Reader* (Manchester: Manchester University Press, 2005), p. 142. Further references will be given in the text. Lindner's remarks are interesting as they seem to confirm La Porta's theory about evil as the true 'non-place' of our age and of noir fiction. According to La Porta, evil represents the imploded self, left alone with its spectres; it is the outcome of extreme loneliness and of a poor imagination that generates unreality and turns the world into a desolate place. Filippo La Porta, 'Ancora sul *neonoir*', in *Roma Noir 2008*, ed. by Mondello, pp. 49–58 (p. 58).
63. Wendy Steiner, *Pictures of Romance Form against Context in Painting and Literature* (Chicago: University of Chicago Press, 1998), p. 6.
64. Jonathan Harr, *The Lost Painting* (New York: Random House, 2005); later referred to as *LP*. Writer and journalist, Harr taught non-fiction writing at Smith College Massachusetts. His *A Civil Action* (1996) became a national bestseller in the States and was turned into a film (1998) starring John Travolta.
65. < http://www.nga.gov/exhibitions/caravbr-2.shtm> [accessed 20 September 2008].
66. Bruce Handy, '*The Lost Painting*: The Caravaggio Trail', *The New York Times*, 13 November 2005, <http://www.nytimes.com/2005/11/13/books/review/13handy.html> [accessed on 5 August 2007].

67. 'Caravaggio: The Discovery of Temptation', *The Economist*, 24 November 2005, <http://www.economist.com/books/displaystory.cfm?story_id=E1_VNTPQQT#subscribe> [accessed on 5 August 2007].
68. Audrey Magee, 'Beetles show Excellent Taste by selecting £30m Painting for Snack', <http://www.museum-security.org/97/artcrime7.html> [accessed on 6 August 2007].
69. Gilda Piersanti, *Jaune Caravage* (Paris and New York: Le Passage, 2008); later referred to as *JC* (all translations are mine). Gilda Piersanti was born in Italy but has been living in Paris for more than twenty years. After a PhD in philosophy, she worked as translator of French literary works, literary critic, and exhibition curator. Since 1995 she has been devoting herself exclusively to creative writing. To date, she has published five novels, all in the noir genre. Piersanti writes exclusively in French, even though she has retained a strong attachment to Rome and claims to enjoy her condition of being 'entre-deux'. *Jaune Caravage* is the last in the series entitled 'Les Quatre Saisons Meurtrières' [The Four Deadly Seasons]. More information on the author and her works can be found on her website: <http://gildapiersanti.free.fr/index.php?id=1> [accessed on 12 September 2008].
70. In *Jaune Caravage*, intertextuality is extremely complex and varied, but the author, in places, guides the reader through a series of footnotes. Piersanti establishes a dialogue not only with her other three novels belonging to the series of 'the four deadly seasons', but also with works by Boccaccio, Poe, T. S Eliot, the Russian symbolist poet Alexander Blok, Caravaggio, and various texts and films belonging to popular culture, plus pieces of classical, pop, and rock music. Apart from the intertexts, the paratext is also extremely important. Except for the first page of each chapter, all other pages of the novel have a header containing a single word. If read in isolation or as a series these words may seem odd or insignificant. In actual fact, each one is a repetition of one of the words used within that particular page of the novel and acts as a refrain, helping the reader to focus on a key detail of the plot, an important feature of one of the characters, or a particularly relevant place.
71. <http://gildapiersanti.free.fr/index.php?id=1> [accessed on 10 September 2008].
72. Perhaps it is also a pun on the Italian *giallo* (yellow), which since 1929 has become synonymous with the detective novel.
73. Federico Moccia, *Tre metri sopra il cielo* (Rome: Il Ventaglio, 1992). This novel became such a cult among young people that a shorter version of it was later republished by Feltrinelli in 2004. In 2004, the novel was also turned into a film by Lucini.
74. Monica Cristina Storini, '"Antonio c'est moi?" Sul realismo di *Un giorno perfetto* di Melania Mazzucco', in *Roma Noir 2008*, ed. by Mondello pp. 89–112 (p. 108). Mazzucco's *Un giorno perfetto* (Milan: Rizzoli, 2005), like Piersanti's book, is set in present-day Rome and tells the story two families who meet through work and whose lives are about to disintegrate. The characters in question are a woman who tries to regain control of her life, a police officer who cannot accept the end of his marriage and becomes totally obsessed with the memories of his family, and their children who are confused and feel torn between the two parents. There are also a twenty-year-old boy who dreams of a better world and a politician whose power is in decline and who is too busy to realize that also his family is falling apart. Naturally, this is also a world dominated by violence.
75. Elisabetta Mondello, 'Introduzione', in *Roma Noir 2008*, pp. 23–24. Interestingly, Mondello maintains that the noir, compared to its origins, is losing its subversive power (p. 23). Concerning the question of realism and the moral responsibility of the writer see also Antonio Pascale, 'Il responsabile dello stile', in *Il corpo e il snague d'Italia*, ed. by Christian Raimo (Rome: Minimum Fax, 2008), pp. 52–95.
76. For a full account of Poe's life see: Peter Ackroyd, *Poe: A Life Cut Short* (London: Chatto & Windus, 2008), pp. 139–60; Hope B. Werness, *The Continuum Encyclopaedia of Animal Symbolism in Art* (New York: Continuum, 2003), p. 106.
77. On the various symbolic meanings of the raven see F. R. Webber and Ralph Adams Cram, Church Symbolism, 2nd edn (Cleveland: The Central Lithograph, 2003), p. 376.
78. Piersanti uses as an example the fashion house Dolce & Gabbana, whose advertising campaigns have been banned in several countries in recent years. More information on Dolce & Gabbana's banned advertisements can be found at: <http://www.fashionunited.co.uk/Content_by_Mail/

Received_content/New_D&G_ads_banned_in_UK_20070110747/> [accessed on 12 September 2008].
79. See 'Vulcan' and 'Hephaestus', Encyclopedia Mythica Online, <http://www.pantheon.org/articles/v/vulcan.html>; <http://www.pantheon.org/articles/h/hephaestus.html> [accessed 20 September 2009].
80. No matter how close people are, betrayal is inevitable. Leonora and Eva had promised each other never to separate (JC, p. 130) and Fausto and Giuliano had seen themselves as brothers, yet, in both cases, the relationships ended with a betrayal. By preferring to go and die in India, Giuliano had denied Fabio the possibility to look after him and be part of his life, thus betraying him (JC, p. 201). As for Eva, she started drifting apart from Leonora the moment Eva decided that Boris should also be part of Leonora's life.
81. Mariella is inevitably reminded of the French tale of Bluebeard, the wealthy aristocrat who was married several times; he killed all his wives, hiding their remains in a secret chamber which nobody was allowed to enter except himself. One of his wives decided to ignore the prohibition and entered the room, where she discovered parts of the bodies of Bluebeard's previous wives. Horrified by her discovery, she rushed out of the room, not noticing that she had stepped into blood and was leaving a trail of footprints behind her. Bluebeard threatened to behead her, but she locked herself in the highest tower and, just as Bluebeard was about to kill her, she was saved by her two brothers and inherited Bluebeard's immense fortune.
82. Luca Mariani, Agata Parisella, and Giovanna Trapani, *La pittura in cucina* (Palermo: Sellerio, 2003).
83. T. S. Eliot, 'The Waste Land', ll. 125, in *The Waste Land and Other Poems* (London: Faber and Faber, 1972), p. 27.
84. Nazia Iftikhar, 'A Journey through "The Wasteland": A Masterpiece of T. S. Eliot', *Journal of Research (Faculty of Languages and Islamic Studies)*, 3 (2003), 57–65 (p. 60).
85. Antonietta Terzoli, 'La testa di Lorenzo: Lettura di *Decameron* IV, 5', *Cuadernos de filología italiana*, special issue (2001), 193–211 (p. 201). As in the case of Poe's 'The Raven', Piersanti condenses in a single intertextual reference all her major themes and concerns. Significantly, Lisabetta is the name of a saint whose son, John the Baptist, was beheaded and whose execution was famously depicted by Caravaggio. Terzoli also sees a similarity between Lisabetta and Mary Magdalene (another personality beautifully interpreted by Caravaggio), particularly in the way she looks after Lorenzo's head by bathing it in her tears and scented water. In Leonora's case, however, there is no remorse, just a strong need for revenge.
86. Michelangelo Picone, 'La "ballata" di Lisabetta' (*Decameron*, IV. 5), *Cuadernos de filología italiana*, special issue (2001), 177–91 (p. 180).
87. According to Marcus, 'folklore, Boccaccio is telling us, enriches the imaginative soil of literary creation, stimulating the growth of new forms which may be inestimably nourished "from below"' (Millicent Marcus, 'Cross-Fertilization: Folklore and Literature in *Decameron* 4,5', *Italica*, 66 (1989), 383–98 (p. 388)).
88. Marcus, p. 393. Marcus argues that 'what Lisabetta achieves at such human cost becomes the stuff of supreme artistic consolation' (ibid.).
89. According to Marcus, in the story of Lisabetta da Messina, 'the family as a corporate unity is "decapitated" by the pre-narrative death of the father. [...] Boccaccio attributes the family's woes to its headlessness and rootlessness to its absence of father and fatherland' (Marcus, p. 389) as Lisabetta's family had moved from San Giminiano to Sicily.
90. La Porta, 'Ancora sul *neonoir*'.

CHAPTER 4

Caravaggio and Homoerotic Concerns

Voi sapete ch'io v'amo, anzi v'adoro,
Ma non sapete già che per voi moro,
Che', se certo il sapeste,
Forse di me qualche pietate avreste
Ma se per mia ventura
Talhor ponete cura
Qual stratio di me fa l'ardente foco,
Consumar me vedrete a poco a poco

JACOB ARCADELT, *Four Madrigals*

★ ★ ★

Il mio fanciullo ha le piume leggere.
Ha la voce sì viva e gentile.
Ha negli occhi le mie primavere
Perdute. In lui ricerco amor non vile.

Così ritorna il cuore alle sue piene.
Così l'amore insegna cose vere.
Perdonino gli dèi se non convine
Il sentenziare sul piume leggere

SANDRO PENNA, *Poesie inedite*, 1927–55

As we have already mentioned in the first chapter, one of the most controversial and most debated aspects of Caravaggio's life is the question of his sexuality. Despite the lack of material evidence capable of proving whether Caravaggio was heterosexual, homosexual, or bisexual, and the awareness that the phenomenon of homosexuality as we know it today is a nineteenth-century concept,[1] there is no doubt that some of his early paintings are very sensual and could be interpreted in homoerotic terms. The works at the core of such a debate are five paintings that Caravaggio made in Rome during the initial stages of his career: *Boy Bitten by a Lizard*, 1593–94 (London: National Gallery); *Bacchus*, c. 1595–96 (Florence: The Uffizzi); *The Lute Player*, c. 1595 (St Petersburg: The Hermitage); *St John the Baptist*, also known as *Youth with Ram*, c. 1602 (Rome: Galleria Doria Pamphilj); and *Victorious Love*, c. 1601–02 (Berlin: Gemäldegalerie). The first critic to suggest that Caravaggio might have been homosexual was Bernard Berenson (1951), whose tentative remarks offended Roberto Longhi, who dismissed them in an article significantly entitled 'La novelletta del Caravaggio invertito' ['The Little Tale of the

Gay Caravaggio'].[2] Whilst in Italy the question of Caravaggio's sexuality remains a sensitive issue, outside Italy, scholars have regularly proposed homoerotic readings of Caravaggio's paintings since the 1960s. Particularly interesting are the studies of Christopher Frommel (1971), on the relationship between Merisi and Cardinal Del Monte, and that of the same year by Donald Posner who argued that 'Caravaggio's youths do not merely address themselves to the spectator — they solicit him'.[3] Like Frommel, he also saw a connection between our painter's early Roman works and the alleged homosexual inclinations of his patron Francesco Maria Del Monte (Posner, p. 306). According to Andrea McTigue, these studies, which are the product of the success of the Gay Liberation movement in the 1970s, led to 'a rather more dramatic reception' of Caravaggio's works' by fictional writers in 1980s who started 'to dwell on the feature of light and dark' in Caravaggio's pictures, often to stress the 'overwhelming sexuality' of those works, but above all their anti-bourgeois nature.[4] This chapter will argue that, regardless of Caravaggio's actual sexual inclinations, what appeals to contemporary gay authors is, on the one hand, such anti-bourgeois features and, on the other, what Warwick calls the 'open-ended address' of Caravaggio's boy paintings, that is to say their ability to capture the 'liminal state between identities'.[5] The case study selected for this section consists of four fictional works: the 1982 French novel *Dans la main de l'ange* by Dominique Fernandez, the 1961 poem 'In Santa Maria del Popolo' by Tom Gunn, the 1986 film *Caravaggio* by Derek Jarman, and the 1989 novel *The Caravaggio Shawl* by the American author Samuel M. Steward. As we are about to see, the first two texts use Caravaggio as an anti-bourgeois hero in order to stress the need to rebel against authority and those forces within society that demand a strict adhesion to pre-established norms. The last two examples instead use Caravaggio and his paintings to raise questions about gender and sexuality. Such features, of course, are not mutually exclusive as, by problematizing gender, one inevitably questions notions of authority and patriarchal structures, and the need to rebel against the normalizing forces of society usually leads to the questioning of gender and identity. It is just a matter of emphasis. Despite their differences, in fact, the above works share many common aspects: an interest in love, in the relationship between power and desire, sadomasochism, life and death, and the body as a site for the production of meaning. Since *Dans la main de l'ange* is the longest and the most complex text in our case study, it represents an excellent starting point for a reflection on why gay artists are interested in Caravaggio.

Dominique Fernandez's *Dans la main de l'ange*[6]

Fernandez's passion for Caravaggio, which eventually led him to devote an entire novel to our painter in 2003 (see the section on Fernandez in Chapter 2 of this book), had manifested itself already in the early 1980s through a fictional biography of one of the most important figures of twentieth-century Italian culture, the gay writer, director, and left-wing intellectual Pier Paolo Pasolini, who was murdered in the outskirts of Rome by a young male prostitute on 2 November 1975. The connection between Pasolini and Caravaggio is a well-known one: not only did Pasolini study with Longhi, the scholar who rediscovered Caravaggio in the twentieth century, but it has also been suggested that he modelled his rebellious image on the Roman phase of Caravaggio's life. Other points of contact between the two artists are their physical and violent connection to Naples; allegedly, the manner in which they died[7] and a sense of persecution which increased towards the end of their lives.[8] Finally, I would add that the works of both artists are characterized by the juxtaposition of sacred and profane elements and by an interest in the 'voluptuousness of the human body', in its fleshiness in order to convey a sense of 'raw physicality'.[9]

More importantly, however, we may want to ask why an author like Fernandez should select Pasolini and Caravaggio as alter egos for one of his psychobiographies (a genre for which, as we have seen in the second chapter of this book, he became famous in the 1970s). In order to answer this question, we need to situate Fernandez in the context of homosexual discourses in France. Fernandez's attitude to his own sexuality was not always easy. In 1961, he married Diane Jacquin de Margerie. They had two children, but the marriage did not last and the couple divorced in 1971. Fernandez finally came out in 1974. He claims he felt liberated as he could finally live an authentic life and it was for him 'a way of being politically engaged'.[10] From the mid 1970s onwards, not only did he write openly homosexual works, but he also collaborated with gay journals like *Gai Pied* and wrote one of the first novels about AIDS in France (*La gloire du paria*, 1987). It could be argued that the development of his career coincided with the key steps in the history of the gay liberation movements in France, the importance of which increased in the aftermath of 1968. After 1978, Fernandez became interested in the 'cultural and psychological dimensions of homosexual desire at those times in the past when boundaries had to be crossed and transgressions to be committed'.[11]

Fernandez's notion of liberation seems to be similar to that of another important French gay writer, Guy Hocquenghem, who was writing in the 1970s and 1980s, despite being much younger than Fernandez. Both authors seem to believe in the paradoxical nature of liberation, which, like most revolutionary movements, ends up creating new orthodoxies and, we could add, new forms of repression. Fernandez, like Hocquenghem, seems to favour the condition of marginality or alienation, which can acquire a subversive value since 'the best tools of the revolution are those that the dominant structure provides'.[12] It is precisely such convictions that must have drawn Fernandez to Pasolini and to Caravaggio in the first instance. Apart from obvious thematic affinities, Pasolini's and Fernandez's lives were also similar in some respects. Both men, for instance, disliked their fathers' involvement with fascism, both loved India, and many of Fernandez's works, like those of Pasolini, were misunderstood by critics. Despite what is now a very successful academic and writing career (in 2007 he became a member of the prestigious Académie Française), in 1958 Fernandez was forced to resign from his teaching post at the French Institute in Naples due to a scandal caused by his lecture entitled 'Eroticism and communism in the work of Vailland'.[13] As we all know, Pasolini's career as a secondary-school teacher was often disrupted by scandals relating to his sexuality or inappropriate behaviour. For all these reasons, it is no surprise that Fernandez should select Pasolini as the protagonist for one of his novels.

Dans la maine de l'ange is written in the first person: PP[14] tells his own story as if it were a sort of testament or confession to his young Neapolitan friend Gennariello (the one the real Pasolini addresses in his pedagogical treaty of 1975, now published in *Lettere Luterane*).[15] However, as the opening quote by Chateaubriand suggests, 'on ne peint bien que son propre coeur, en l'attribuant à un autre' [one can only depict one's feelings well by attributing them to someone else], the book is also about Fernandez and in fact, in an interview for *The Nouvel Observateur*, the author of *Dans la maine de l'ange* said that writing that novel had been a form of exorcism, a way of keeping at bay masochistic and suicidal temptations.[16] In Lacanian terms, this remark seems to suggest that Fernandez is trying to defer the 'lethal encounter with *jouissance*' through fantasy and the imaginary construction of his book.[17] As we are about to see, Fernandez's statement provides one of the key elements for reading *DMA* as it explains the origin of the fascination with death that dominates the novel. However, before moving further into the analysis of the book's complex themes, a brief reflection on some of its stylistic features will enhance our understanding of Fernandez's work and of the interaction between Fernandez, Pasolini, and Caravaggio. Significantly, the style of *DMA* is evocative of the *chiaroscuro* technique of Caravaggio's paintings, a technique that can be described as the visual expression of Pasolini's poetics based on 'analogy and opposition' but also as 'the quintessential trait of the Italian Baroque'.[18] This movement, as we have seen in the introduction to this volume, appeals to authors willing to challenge traditional binary oppositions and embrace pluralities whilst retaining a critical perspective. In this way they avoid the pitfalls of some postmodern theories whose openness can be seen as complaisant with 'the given fluidities of consumer capitalism' which they originally intended to criticize.[19] As suggested above, another important aspect connecting Pasolini, Caravaggio, and Fernandez is the correspondence between words and facts, that is to say, between art and life.[20] However, it is through a series of reflections on the protagonist's name that some of Fernandez's main concerns are being explored. His notion of homosexuality, the need to rebel against conformism and the tension between life and death appear to be already present in the name Pier Paolo, which inevitably evokes the two fathers of the Church, St Peter and St Paul. According to PP, the aura of these two very different saints, also depicted by Caravaggio, seems destined to generate a kind of schizophrenic split in the mind of a person named after them:

> Pierre et Paul! Comme si on pouvait vivre uniment sous deux patronages aussi opposés! Pierre: qui fit de Rome la ville du pontificat et transforma l'évangile de Jésus en religion de l'autorité. [...] Et Paul, tout le contraire: inquiet, mystique, excessif [...]. (*DMA*, p. 18)

> [Peter and Paul! As if one could live in harmony under two such opposite patronages! Peter: Who made Rome the city of the pontificate and transformed the gospel of Jesus into a religion of authority. [...] And Paul, completely the opposite: troubled, mystical, and excessive [...].]

Such a split could be interpreted as a manifestation of a notion of the subject as division which, according to the French philosopher Alain Badiou, is what characterizes the Christian discourse as synthesized by Paul.[21] The narrator seems to be tormented by the weight imposed on him by his name and later in the opening chapter he claims that after a certain moment in his life he became obsessed with St Paul, particularly with the saint's decapitation which, unlike that of other saints, had attracted no attention: 'il resta à peu près ignoré [...] Presque personne avant le xvie siècle ne s'appela de son nom' [he was almost forgotten [...] Hardly anybody before the sixteenth century had heard of him] (*DMA*, p. 18). His troubles with the law, PP explains, were connected to his obsession with Paul, with his desire to seek a violent death in order to do Paul justice.

St Paul, of course, was very important for the real Pasolini who saw in him the creator of a new and oppressive law and 'a closeted homosexual who becomes sick with a devastating and mysterious disease when he first senses his homoerotic desire'.[22] This 'sickness', as Resca would put it, is similar to the horror Caravaggio must have felt when he discovered his lethal sadomasochistic drive which constantly surfaces in his paintings depicting violent scenes. According to Resca, Caravaggio perceived violence as ubiquitous in his world and the Church as an embodiment of power was far from innocent. Even the act of conversion, Resca argues, can be seen as a form of violence as it forces the individual to give up his freedom (which in extreme cases is also the freedom to kill) (p. 52). Resca identifies Caravaggio's works devoted to St Paul and his *David with the Head of Goliath* as the two poles marking the beginning and the end of Caravaggio's own attempts at deferring 'the lethal encounter with *jouissance*', that is to say, his death drive. Resca relates Caravaggio's obsession with decapitation to his fascination with Paul's destiny. He compares the two versions of *The Conversion of St Paul* (1600–1601) noting how, whilst in the Odaleschi one (the first version) the conversion manifests itself as 'violenza imperiosa' [majestic violence], in the one which is now in San Luigi dei Francesi, it is depicted as a kind of seduction or 'prepotenza suasiva' [persuasive forcefulness]. He finds the second version of the painting particularly interesting as there Caravaggio seems to identify with his subject, telling us that he is awaiting the revelation, something capable of making him convert and, as a result, obey the Church. This moment, however, is not coming as something in him makes him resist the calling (the idea of having to conform).[23] In Pasolini's script *St Paul* the apostle is presented as a sodomite whose role in society is to spread an apocalyptic message which clashes with his efforts to impose a new religious repression. According to Maggi, another interesting feature of Pasolini's Paul is that he perceives his homosexuality as the apprehension of new language capable of challenging that of the law and of power, a language, however, that translates itself into a physical illness that finally 'undoes its speaker' (Maggi, p. 11) as its utmost form of expression is death (Maggi, p. 12). Pasolini's Paul symbolizes 'the flesh that needs to die and resurrect' (ibid.) and as such it is a highly subversive figure because the body constitutes what cannot be codified (Maggi, p. 23).

As suggested above, in order to comprehend fully the significance of St Paul in Pasolini, Fernandez, and Caravaggio, Alan Badiou's understanding of the saint will prove very useful. The French philosopher argues that Paul's conversion represents the subjective sign of the 'truth event', that is the resurrection of Christ (Badiou, p. 17). The resurrection is not a fact (as it cannot be demonstrated) (Badiou, p. 49);

it is a pure event, marking a complete break with tradition and the start of a new epoch.[24] The most important feature of this event is that it transforms the relation between possible and impossible by stressing the possibility of overcoming death. When talking of life and death, however, we must remember that Paul is not interested in their biological equivalents. For Paul, life and death are thoughts or ways of being (Badiou, pp. 68–69); the *real* is 'that which is thought in a subjectivating thought' (Badiou, p. 55) and can be 'grasped by the two paths that constitute the subject', that is to say 'flesh' (death) and 'spirit' (life) (ibid.). In this sense, Christianity is to be understood as a *new* discourse based on a notion of the subject as division (Badiou, p. 57),[25] on the overcoming of the law (as an expression of particularity, of conformity) and, as a result, on the decline of the figure of the master (whether the prophet of the Jewish discourse or the wise man of the Greek discourse). The key figure of the Christian discourse is the apostle who is neither a witness nor a memory but simply he who names the possibility of defeating death, someone 'who claims his legitimacy only from himself' (Badiou, p. 44).

From the point of view of trying to understand Pasolini and Fernandez, the most interesting aspect of Badiou's theory is his definition of Christ as ' "a coming," [...] what interrupts the previous regime of discourses' or, in other words, 'what happens to us' and relieves us of the law (p. 48). In this way, Badiou argues, the event (that is the resurrection) is what gives rise to a universal 'becoming son' (p. 49). As a result, the son can be defined as 'he whom an event relieves of the law and everything related to it for the benefit of a shared egalitarian endeavour' (p. 60). In brief, Paul's message could be summarized as an invitation to 'depose the master and found the equality of sons' (p. 59). Interestingly, in order to stress the relevance of St Paul for our contemporary world, Badiou uses the example of Pasolini's identification with the apostle, arguing that, for Pasolini, homosexual desire has as its aspiration the advent of an egalitarian humanity in which the equal (non-hierarchical) position of the sons challenges the authoritarian symbolism of the fathers (embodied in institutions like the Church or political parties) and favours the love of the mother (p. 43). Significantly, the title of Fernandez's novel seems to suggest precisely this submission to the law of the mother. As we are about to see, the term 'ange' has various meanings, but it is used above all to refer to many of the young boys the protagonist is falling in love with, or has sex with, starting with the young Sven (the love of his life whom he met in his native Friuli), to Agnolo or Danilo, the boy PP had nicknamed 'Angelo' [angel], prior to discovering his true identity, because of the angelic quality of his voice (*DMA*, p. 294).[26] And, it is precisely through Danilo/Angelo that we realize, as Maggi explains, that for Pasolini (whether the real man or Fernandez's fictional double) sex with young men represents a way of evoking the absent mother: 'the encounter with the mother can only take place in the "shadows" of the world (an open field at night) and through the bodies of men who are sons, that is, men whose presence recalls the absent mother (they carry the smell of the mother' (Maggi, p. 210). When PP takes Danilo home his mother immediately realizes that the boy was not one of her son's usual guests (students, aspiring actors or writers, employees of Cinecittà) and, as a result, welcomes him as a son by offering him some nourishing food:

Elle avait disposé sur le plateau non seulement deux tasses de café mais deux parts de tarte, faveur insigne dont je n'avais vu bénéficier avant Danilo aucun de mes hôtes, familiers ou inconnus.
— Mangez, mes enfants, dit-elle en poussant la plus petite des tables gigognes devant le fauteuil où il n'osait se caler. (*DMA*, p. 333)

[She had put on the tray not only two cups of coffee, but also two pieces of cake, a remarkable gesture which had never been bestowed upon any of my guests, whether familiar or little known, before Danilo.
— Eat, my children, she said pushing the smallest of the nest tables in front of the armchair on which he didn't dare sit back.]

The attachment to the mother is also visible in PP's attitude towards women in general. What he usually values in his female friends is their motherly feelings, as the case of Wilma demonstrates: PP likes watching her play the cello as she touches her instrument with a 'douceur maternelle' [a motherly tenderness] (*DMA*, p. 101). Apart from the personal sphere, PP's devotion to his mother manifests itself also in his attitude to space and language. Despite the physical distance, his native Friuli retains a prominent (almost mythical) place in his mind. Significantly he writes his first collections of poems in Friulian:

Vers écrits en frioulan, circonstance qui ajouta quelque éclat à ma chétive couronne de poète, bien que la volonté politique de m'opposer à la langue officielle comptât beaucoup moins dans ma vocation dialectale, comme tu sais, que mes démêlés avec mon père et le désir de lier ma destinée d'artiste à l'idiome maternel. (*DMA*, p. 86)

[Lines written in Friulian, fact that adds some sparkle to my meagre poet's crown, even though, as you know, the political will to oppose the official language influenced my decision to use the dialect far less than the disputes with my father and the wish to tie my artistic destiny to the language of my mother.]

As the above quote demonstrates, adhering to the law of the mother means rejecting the establishment and patriarchy. Such a rejection is already implicit in the word 'ange' of the title because, as PP explains, angel means he who announces or he who brings the good news (*DMA*, p. 283) and therefore is very similar to Paul's definition of the apostle (Badiou, p. 44). As Badiou would put it, through the title of his novel Fernandez declares his 'fidelity to the possibility opened by the event' (p. 45) and, in so doing, identifies with the apostle and with the protagonist of his book who carries (at least in part) the apostle's name. This process of identification is confirmed by the frequent references to Christ and to martyrdom. Significantly, in trying to explain the importance of accepting one's destiny, PP declares:

Homme, accepte ton destin! Le mien est d'être diffamé, vilipendé, crucifié. J'ai eu tort de frapper ce fasciste. Christ s'est-il révolté contre aucun de ses bourreaux? Il a dit à Pierre: Rentre au fourreau ton glaive. (*DMA*, p. 265)

[Man, accept your destiny! Mine is to be slandered, vilified, and crucified. I made the mistake of beating that fascist. Did Christ rebel against any of his attackers? He said to Peter: Put your sword back into its case.]

Since, as previously mentioned, the advent of Christ can be seen as a universal 'becoming son' (Badiou, pp. 48–49), which inevitably implies the demise of the 'master discourse', we could argue that Fernandez, like the real Pasolini, is stressing the importance of creating a more egalitarian society. His novel, however, like his protagonist's name, represents the tension between the need to transcend authority and the seduction of patriarchal structures like those of the Church or of political parties. The Communist Party, for instance, becomes for PP a surrogate father (*DMA*, p. 157). In order to understand fully the split between the need for subversion and conformity, we must focus on PP's relationship to his biological father, a violent, abusive man, and (like Fernandez's father) a supporter of the Fascist regime, who epitomized power and the law. PP keeps stressing his aversion for this man and often expresses it in spatial terms, as a conflict between centre and periphery. PP's desperate need for alternative lifestyles represents his dissatisfaction with the world of order, norms, and customs and his desire to embrace a more ex-centric position (symbolized by the mother). The shadow of the father, however, keeps haunting PP throughout his life. The very fact that he decided to settle in Rome, the symbol of patriarchal authority par excellence, can be read as an indication of PP's inability fully to reject patriarchal structures. PP is fully conscious of the contradictory nature of his choice and becomes more and more obsessed with the need to show his opposition to the normative forces of society by looking for male prostitutes outside Rome central station, and by favouring sordid and abject places (*DMA*, p. 59). PP's dilemmas and behaviour become more understandable if we consider Maggi's comments on the significance of the mother in Pasolini's opus. In defining the mother as 'the cornerstone of Pasolini's poetics' (p. 282), Maggi points out how, for Pasolini, the mother represents an order that changes depending on whether she is alive or dead (Maggi, pp. 282–83). Since in Pasolini the mother is 'the locus of prohibition' and (similar to the Lacanian symbolic) lacks expression, whilst alive her 'order' is to turn the son into a kind of apostle announcing her 'request for (love) expression' and demanding his complete submission to her (Maggi, p. 282). Her death, however, changes the nature of this order, which becomes a command to mourn her absence. Although the son is aware that the mother and the mythical 'place of an original fusion between mother and son' no longer exist, she survives as an imposition, as 'a perverse request' that turns her also, Maggi argues, into 'a synonym for the father' (pp. 282–83). The ambivalent position of the mother in Pasolini's poetics helps us understand PP's ambiguous attitude towards his father, which crystallizes in his obsession with the image of the postcard his father sent from Africa during the war depicting a young explorer being devoured by a tiger (an animal with a very complex and ambivalent symbolism).

This image represents one of the novel's key motifs and can be interpreted in different ways.[27] First of all, since the figure of the explorer is inevitably linked to the colonial experience, it could be seen as representing the demise of master discourses. However, since the tiger symbolizes maternal love in medieval bestiaries, the picture can also be read in psychoanalytical terms, as a reference to Kristeva's notion of the abject. As Keltner explains, for Kristeva, abjection represents 'the *infans*'s initial confrontation with an ambiguous maternal place that is both the condition and a threat to the infant's own being'.[28] The abject can therefore be defined as that through which 'a rudimentary position is demarcated which establishes the possibility of not being [...] swallowed by the Other' (Keltner, p. 46). This interpretation seems to be confirmed by the fact that PP identifies this image as the source of his death drive, as death and the abject are strongly connected. For Kristeva, in fact, the corpse symbolizes 'the utmost of abjection'.[29] In the case of PP, the Other he wants to exorcise is his father (the man responsible for introducing him to the picture of the tiger and the explorer). This becomes particularly obvious when as an adult, several years after receiving the African postcard, PP travels to Africa in order to present one of his films and is introduced to the Italian consul in Kenya, a former friend of PP's father Carlo Alberto. In his official welcoming speech, the consul stresses how, had he been alive, Carlo Alberto would have been proud of his son's success. Forced to acknowledge the truth of such a remark and realize that, despite all his efforts in convincing himself of the opposite, his father had retained a prominent role in his life, PP becomes extremely unsettled and develops an obsession with the abject. He starts to go out at night, returning to his four-star hotel room at dawn, badly bruised and covered in blood (*DMA*, pp. 320–21). However, as Keltner explains, there are two sides to the abject — on the one hand, it is that which challenges laws and, on the other, it is that which, through an act of rejection, re-establishes boundaries and norms: 'it is also the permanent "outside" that preserves personal and social boundaries' (Keltner, p. 45). It could therefore be argued that the abject, here, sheds light on the schizophrenic tension present in PP's name, in Pasolini's poetics and in Caravaggio's chiaroscuro, that is to say the impossibility of overcoming certain paradoxical situations that characterize life and the dichotomy between good and evil. In terms of space this tension is mirrored in the contrast between Africa and Rome (or Rome and Friuli). Africa represents abjection as the possibility of turning 'the death drive into a start of life, of new significance' (Kristeva, p. 15) or, to use PP's words, into a new dawn of the world (*DMA*, p. 404). Rome, instead, reveals how abjection, by creating permanent outsiders like the boys of the 'borgate' (the city slums) or those male prostitutes PP meets around Stazione Termini, can be used to reinforce the status quo. This is why, according to PP, abjection is taken to the extreme only in Rome: 'ici, c'en était le déclin, le pourrissement, la décomposition ultime' [here there was decline, rotting and the ultimate decomposition] (*DMA*, p. 404).

Finally, particularly if we consider the aforementioned significance of such an image for the real Pasolini, the postcard with the tiger and the explorer can be read in masochistic terms. Despite the fact that almost the entire body of the explorer has been swallowed by the tiger and only his head and upper torso protrude out of the beast's mouth, the victim seems somehow to enjoy his torture. This explains why, on a different level, the impact of this unusual image translated itself into PP's pathological interest in Caravaggio, to the point that every night he actually embarked on a Caravaggio trail (*DMA*, p. 410) in the hope of reliving Caravaggio experiences. Regarding Caravaggio's paintings, PP favours all scenes of martyrdom, particularly his *David with the Head of Goliath*.[30] Like Caravaggio himself, PP identifies with Goliath, whom he describes as a pariah with bleeding eye sockets (*DMA*, p. 335), thus reinforcing his obsession with the abject. He regularly inspects his eyes in the mirror in order to detect any resemblance to those of Goliath, because he is convinced that he will die in circumstances similar to those of the biblical warrior (*DMA*, pp. 288–89). When, one day, his mother tells him that one of his eyelids is drooping he becomes convinced that his days are numbered (*DMA*, p. 436). In the aforementioned psychoanalytical study of Caravaggio's works, Resca endorses the theory that both David and Goliath are portraits of the artist and therefore reads this work as a proof of the painter's drive to kill and be killed (p. 54) or, in other words, of his sadomasochistic tendencies.[31] Significantly, towards the end of the novel, PP's desire to engage in sadomasochistic practices seems insatiable: he takes his young friend Danilo to the Idroscalo (a rather abject area of Rome) and forces the boy to hit him and to make love to him in humiliating positions, something the boy cannot understand and only reluctantly agrees to, often begging PP to stop and come back to his senses (*DMA*, p. 430). As Richardson explains, in patriarchal societies male masochism is seen as dangerous to the social order as it collapses the gender divide between male and female. What is perceived as particularly problematic is the fact that the masochist constantly puts his body on display (whether beaten physically or morally) as he needs a witness and an external agency to inflict pain upon him. This undermines the myth of the autotelic masculine subject revealing that his subjectivity is determined by the Other. As a result, he needs to be controlled and 'safely re-inscribed back into acceptability'.[32] Religion, particularly Christianity, represents the perfect tool to control masochism: the idea that Christians should endure pain on earth in order to be rewarded in another life can be seen as a tamed version of the masochistic principle of 'pleasure in pain' (Richardson, pp. 102–03). By turning suffering or sacrifice into a sign of compliance to the will of God, Christianity eliminates the subversive element of sadomasochism: the façade of the church is used to mask 'a rejection of phallic autonomy' (ibid.), which would otherwise be 'a dangerously emasculating activity' (ibid.). For PP, masochism represents his final act of rebellion, the only gesture capable of showing his dissatisfaction with the hypocrisy of Italian society, his refusal to become part of the establishment. This is why he considers the staging of his own death as his final masterpiece, one which, unlike his other works, will escape oblivion:

> Mon voeu le plus secret venait d'être accompli. J'avais remis ma vie entre les mains les plus indignes de la recevoir, rétabli entre Pierre et Paul l'équilibre d'une fin ignominieuse, servi de jouet sanglant à l'ardeur homicide d'un imberbe, expié autant mes fautes que celles de l'humanité. L'artiste aussi pouvait se dire sauvé. Dans aucun de mes livres, dans aucun de mes films je ne m'étais montré à la hauteur de mes ambitions. Mais maintenant je m'en allais tranquille, ayant organisé dans chaque détail ma cérémonie funèbre et signé ma seule oeuvre assurée de survivre à l'oubli. (*DMA*, p. 455)

> [My most secret desire had just been fulfilled. I had placed my life in the least worthy hands that could have received it; I had re-established the balance between Peter and Paul through an ignominious death, turned into a bleeding toy for the homicidal fury of a kid, and had atoned both my sins and those of humanity. The artist too could consider himself saved. I had never managed to accomplish my ambitions in any of my books or films. But now, I was going in

peace, having organized my funeral down to the very last detail and signed my only work guaranteed to survive oblivion.]

Once again we are reminded of Kristeva's statements on the abject. On the one hand, we are presented with the revolutionary power of the abject, with its ability to corrupt and take advantage of rules and laws 'to deny them' (Kristeva, p. 15). On the other, PP's gesture seems a confirmation of Kristeva's idea that only death can save the writer of the abject from his condition of waste and reject (Kristeva, p. 16). This is why death is for PP the only way of being coherent, of remaining faithful to his life mission, which had consisted in going against the grain of society, in saying no when everyone else was saying yes, in seeking darkness when everyone else was seeking light (*DMA*, p. 429), in order to reveal the hypocrisy of Italian society. Through PP's reflections, Fernandez offers his readers a very critical analysis of the key events that characterized Italian politics and society since the end of the Second World War. All the major political parties which dominated the political scene during the 1950s and 1960s, be it the Christian Democratic Party, the Socialist Party, or the Communist Party, are depicted in negative terms, and so are key figures like Luigi Longo, Aldo Moro, or Giuseppe Saragat (*DMA*, p. 291).[33] Like Pasolini, Fernandez seems to blame the economic boom of the 1960s and the ever-increasing power of consumerism for the loss of sound moral values, so much so that even the 1968 movement is seen as a failed revolution (*DMA*, pp. 355–74).[34] PP, like the Pasolini of 'Gennariello' (*Lettere Luterane*, pp. 20–21), comes to the conclusion that all the battles he had fought throughout his life had led to a worse rather than a better society (*DMA*, p. 429). Fernandez's protagonist is particularly disappointed with the so-called sexual liberation, which instead of generating a real tolerance for alternative forms of sexuality led to the ghettoization of gays, as the proliferation of gay bars and discotheques, like the Blue Angel (*DMA*, p. 421), demonstrates. Interestingly, the Pasolini of 'Gennariello' had expressed similar ideas: in describing himself as different from his young pupil, he attacked the ghetto mentality resulting from a society that allegedly tolerated ethnic or sexual minorities but which, in actual fact, blamed them for their difference as much as those who openly rejected outsiders (*Lettere Luterane*, pp. 23–24). As a result, PP/ Fernandez develops a sense of nostalgia for a time when homosexuality was publicly condemned but, paradoxically, individuals had more freedom and could enjoy their condition as privileged pariahs. The pariah (or the abject) is privileged because, as Kristeva explains in one of her later works, difference becomes a form of resistance that manifests itself in a tension, a dynamism that challenges hierarchy, order, and identity by refusing to be codified into a meaning.[35]

Through his engagement in progressively more extreme sadomasochistic practices, it is as if PP were trying to prove on his own skin the negative effects of a permissive society by revealing the illusory nature of tolerance and the ubiquitous presence of violence:

> — Si tu crois que tout est permis aujourd'hui, tu dois aller jusqu'au bout de ce qui est possible!
> Je mis la ceinture dans sa main et lui présentai ma poitrine nue.
> — Frappe! ordonnai-je à haute voix. (*DMA*, p. 405)

[— If you believe that everything is allowed today, you must go up to the limit of what is possible!
I put the belt in his hand and offered him my naked chest.
— Hit! I commanded in a loud voice.]

In Deleuzian terms, what PP is doing is to endorse the instruments of the law in order to challenge its validity:

> A close examination of masochist fantasies or rites reveals that while they bring into play the very strictest application of the law, the result in every case is the opposite of what we expect (thus whipping, far from punishing or preventing an erection, provokes and ensures it). It is a demonstration of the law's absurdity.[36]

As a result, what on the surface appears to be positive and liberating often turns out to be part of a very conservative political project as the Baroque movement teaches us. According to PP, Caravaggio's era and the modern age are very similar. For instance, what seemed to be bizarre and to go against the norms in Baroque ornamentation was actually a device to protect orthodoxy against the possible seduction of the Lutheran doctrine. As PP explains, 'fools' were dazzled with wealth and power so that the austerity of Lutheranism would look unappealing (*DMA*, p. 179). Similar devices to retain power and influence were used by the church in the 1960s, thus showing continuity between Caravaggio's age and the modern one (*DMA*, p. 272). Throughout history, whether in real life or in fiction, an unwillingness to conform has always led to social exclusion as figures like those of Giordano Bruno, Tommaso Campanella, Mario Cavaradossi (the protagonist of Puccini's *Tosca*), Antonio Gramsci, or Caravaggio have shown us (*DMA*, p. 182). One of the key lessons we can learn from Caravaggio's life and works, PP/Fernandez seems to point out, is that history is always a history of violence and a distortion of the truth (*DMA*, p. 113). According to Resca, Caravaggio, in fact, was the first to understand that the constant presence of violence is the only truth in history, thus going against centuries of religious propaganda devoted to the glorification of good and the criminalization of evil (p. 24).

But let us return to the above-quoted passage in which PP begs Danilo to slash him on his chest. This could also be read as a declaration of guilt and a request to be punished. Significantly, Caravaggio's *David with the Head of Goliath* was for many years seen as a kind of public confession in which the painter presents his own severed head to his audience as a sign of penance in the hope that influential people like Scipione Borghese might plead his case for pardon with the pope.[37] Guilt, as Richardson explains, is a product of Christianity: it represents the attempt at turning shame (the shame at being flawed individuals) into something transitory that can be atoned for through confession and various forms of penance or, in other words, through masochism (Richardson, p. 112). PP/Fernandez seems to suggest that the metamorphosing of shame into guilt pertains to all master discourses as it can be found even in secular societies, like our contemporary Western ones, where Jesus has been replaced by Freud and atonement by treatment (*DMA*, pp. 42, 273). Scientific language is particularly revealing in this respect: 'Je sors en jean? "Aggresivité". Je me chausse avec de baskets? "Fétichisme". Je joue au foot?

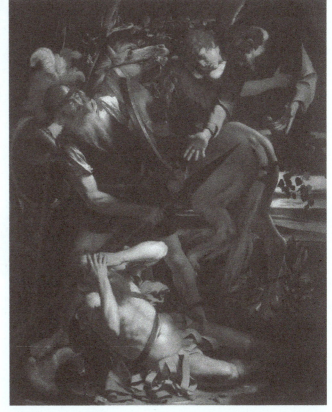

FIG. 4.1 (above). Caravaggio, *The Beheading of St John the Baptist* (1608), Malta: Valletta, St John's Cathedral.
FIG. 4.2 (right). Caravaggio, *The Conversion of St Paul* (c. 1600–01), Rome: Odaleschi Collection.

Fig. 4.3. Caravaggio, *The Conversion of St Paul* (c. 1600–01), Rome: Cerasi Chapel in Santa Maria del Popolo.

"Hypersthénie". Je préfère les légumes cuits à l'eau? "Autopunition"' [I go out in jeans? 'Aggressiveness'. I put on trainers? 'Fetishism'. I play football? 'Hypersthenia'. I prefer steamed vegetables? 'Self-punishment'] (*DMA* p. 276). Such a language turns every little idiosyncratic feature of the individual into something pathological. Masochism is the only possible answer to all this because, as Deleuze has taught us, it is more successful as a subversive than a restraining tool and power can only be antagonized by showing its 'own unacknowledged *jouissance*' (Vighi, p. 78). This is why PP has to stage his own death in the end.

Significantly, the reference to the act of 'signing' in the novel's concluding paragraph,[38] in which PP anticipates that he will be killed by a much younger man, seems to suggest the conflation of two paintings: *David with the Head of Goliath* and *The Beheading of St John*, the only painting Caravaggio ever signed. By using the blood gushing out of the saint's head to sign his work, Caravaggio presents us with a double identification. On the one hand, his 'bloody' signature tells us that he is the author of a criminal act (the beheading); on the other, his signature suggests that he was identifying with the victim, a process that acquires even more significance if we consider that St John the Baptist is seen as the precursor of Christ. This double identification can be interpreted as a reference to the necessity of death in order to resurrect and start a new life. As argued by Iovinelli, metabiographical texts grant their authors a new life as the truth of the novel is more important than the biographical one (*L'autore e il personaggio*, pp. 270–71).

To conclude, if we were to summarize Fernandez's novel in one sentence, it could be argued that it represents a homage to Paul's theory of the resurrection and, as we are about to see, Paul is also the protagonist of the next text in our case study, Thom Gunn's 'In Santa Maria del Popolo'.

Thom Gunn[39]

Although the poem 'In Santa Maria del Popolo' was published before most of the other case studies (since it was first published in 1958, subsequently reprinted in 1961 as part of the collection *My Sad Captains*, and then again in the late 1980s in the volume *Collected Poems*), it is significant for an understanding of the impact of Caravaggio on the poetry of Thom Gunn, which is much wider and deeper than this individual work. 'In Santa Maria del Popolo' is the only poem in which our painter is explicitly mentioned. However, Caravaggio was undoubtedly an important influence during the early stages of Gunn's career and echoes of Caravaggio can be found in other poems such as 'Lazarus not Raised' (1952) and a lesser-known poem entitled 'Apocryphal' (1954), which was published only once in *Botteghe Oscure*.[40] Despite the fact that these poems seem to be confined to the 1950s, I would argue that many aspects of Caravaggio's poetics (such as the tension between life and death and between sacred and profane, the representation of violence and a preoccupation with mortality) are to be found also in Gunn's later productions, including his last collection, *Boss Cupid* (2000), which contains even 'acts of cannibalism and libidinous homicide'.[41] Like Caravaggio, Gunn had an interest in 'street people', including prostitutes and drug dealers. Finally, as we are about to see, 'In Santa

Maria del Popolo' and the aforementioned poems are extremely interesting from the point of view of the relationship between Caravaggio and homoeroticism.

As Jeffrey Meyers points out, after completing his degree in Cambridge in 1953, Gunn won a small travel grant which allowed him to spend some time in Rome, where he actually saw *The Conversion of St Paul* and was so struck by it that he decided to write a poem about the painting.[42] Gunn's interest in Caravaggio and the Baroque is hardly surprising if we keep in mind that he aspired to become 'the John Donne of the 20th century'[43] and that the often sharp contrast between his strict and formal use of metre and the non-idealized, prosaic subject matter could be seen as the poetic equivalent of Caravaggio's chiaroscuro technique.[44] Like Caravaggio, who was able to make use of tradition in a creative and innovative manner, 'in Gunn's hands the inherited forms and conventions seem utterly natural and breathe with his own modernity'.[45] What is more, Caravaggio would appeal to Gunn as our poet was often interested in the contrast between artistic geniality and formal control on the one hand and, on the other, a tendency towards anarchy in the personal sphere.[46]

As we can see from the title and from the first stanza, 'In Santa Maria del Popolo' is not just about Caravaggio's *Conversion of St Paul* but also about the location where the painting is displayed and, therefore, about the experience of the viewer.

In Santa Maria del Popolo

Waiting for when the sun an hour or less
Conveniently oblique makes visible
The painting on one wall of this recess
By Caravaggio, of the Roman School,
I see how shadow in the painting brims
With a real shadow, drowning all shapes out
But a dim horse's haunch and various limbs,
Until the very subject is in doubt.

But evening gives the act, beneath the horse
And one indifferent groom, I see him sprawl,
Foreshortened from the head, with hidden face,
Where he has fallen, Saul becoming Paul.
O wily painter, limiting the scene
From a cacophony of dusty forms
To the one convulsion, what is it you mean
In that wide gesture of the lifting arms?

No Ananias croons a mystery yet,
Casting the pain out under name of sin.
The painter saw what was, an alternate
Candour and secrecy inside the skin.
He painted, elsewhere, that firm insolent
Young whore in Venus' clothes, those pudgy cheats,
Those sharpers; and was strangled, as things went,
For money, by one such picked off the streets.
I turn, hardly enlightened, from the chapel
To the dim interior of the church instead,

> In which there kneel already several people,
> Mostly old women: each head closeted
> In tiny fists holds comfort as it can.
> Their poor arms are too tired for more than this
> — For the large gesture of solitary man,
> Resisting, by embracing, nothingness. (*CP*, pp. 93–94)

When dealing with 'In Santa Maria del Popolo', most critics focus on how Gunn, a self-professed agnostic, interpreted Caravaggio's religious painting in secular terms. Michelucci argues that 'even though the poem is set in a church, the religious feeling is utterly lacking' as the poet 'offers [...] a problematic interpretation of the painting by means of an oxymoronic and ambiguous rendering of Saul's theophany', which turns Saul into one of his 'sad captains' doomed to failure (p. 83). Meyers also interprets the 'nothingness' of the last stanza in Sartrean terms, stressing the influence of the French philosopher on Gunn's poetry (p. 589).[47]

However, whilst these readings are certainly interesting and justified, I would argue that, if we look at 'In Santa Maria del Popolo' through the perspective of some recent interpretations of Caravaggio's painting, we will gain a better understanding of Gunn's relationship to Caravaggio and of the significance of the poem within the collection *My Sad Captains*. Gregg Lambert, for instance, in his seminal work on the Baroque in the modern era, uses *The Conversion of St Paul* to illustrate the concept of Baroque sublime and the role of the spectator in Baroque culture. Lambert emphasizes the concept of conversion by pointing out how 'the very "emotion" that is constructed as the linchpin of the "High Baroque" aesthetic is constantly described by critics in terms of the drama of "conversion."'[48] This concept, Lambert maintains, is to be understood beyond its religious significance, 'in a more contemporary psychoanalytic sense in which the body's agitated convulsion represents the perception of the unconscious in the discourse of the hysteric' (p. 22). According to Lambert, we should reflect on the way affection operates as this will enable us to understand the psychological characteristics of the spectator and 'the rhetoric of power which belong to the new determination of the art-work from the early modern period onward' (ibid.). Taking the position of the Spanish historian José Antonio Maravall as his starting point, Lambert elaborates on the idea that the concept of sublime (derived from the older notion of *furor*) is central to Baroque aesthetics and that the mechanisms of this new form of the sublime reveal the ideological slant of Baroque culture, but also 'the way in which culture as a whole becomes instrumental and directive within the spectator's own life-history' (p. 28). In line with Maravall, Lambert presents the Baroque sublime as referring to 'both the inner mechanisms of the cultural work (in the sense of its creative technique), as well as physical and psychological descriptions of the "movement" which takes place in the consciousness of the spectator' (ibid.). Such remarks make us easily understand why Caravaggio's *Conversion of St Paul* has been used to illustrate the 'baroque mechanism'. However, if Caravaggio's painting can be read as a statement on the nature of spectatorship and of the aesthetic experience, the same could be said for Gunn's poem. This explains the emphasis on the location in the title and in the first stanza where the dark 'recess' in which *The Conversion* is positioned prevents the spectator from responding to (and being converted by) the work of art. This also explains the interest in the ordinary people praying in the church in the last stanza, who are also potential spectators and likely to be affected by the painting (even though not in the same way as the poetic I). Interestingly, in the second stanza, Gunn stresses how Caravaggio captures the very process of the conversion, 'Saul becoming Paul' (*CP*, p. 93), which is stressed by the use of the gerund 'becoming'. This idea is emphasized by the reference to the Odaleschi version of the painting where the moment of transition was expressed through 'a cacophony of dusty forms' which becomes a single 'convulsion' in the Cerasi one Gunn admired in Santa Maria del Popolo.[49]

These two powerful images of chaotic movement seem also to evoke the notion of a 'limit-experience' and a blurring of boundaries that closely resembles Lambert's definition of the Baroque sublime as something that 'gathers together the boundaries that belong to the limit-experience of human consciousness: the sensible and affective limits of visibility and perception, the stark limitations of individual will, self-feeling, movement and repose' (Lambert, p. 31).[50] The reference to the limits of human will seems to be particularly important as it is one of the key features combining Caravaggio's *Conversion of St Paul* and Gunn's poem. What is more, the epigraph to *My Sad Captains*, the collection in which 'In Santa Maria del Popolo' was originally published, is a quote from Shakespeare's *Troilus and Cressida*, engaging precisely with the theme of will: 'The will is infinite and the execution confined | the desire is boundless and the act a slave to limit' (*CP*, p. 91). As Michelucci points out, Gunn's interest in *Troilus and Cressida* dates back to his first collection *Fighting Terms*, where the poem 'The Wound' represents the poet's response to reading the Shakespearean play (p. 56). However, whilst dealing with the Trojan War, 'The Wound' can also be read as an exploration of 'the psychological condition of anxiety' (ibid.), a condition which in Caravaggio's *The Conversion of St Paul* is expressed through the 'dark and mysterious force of night, with its swirling shadows' (Lambert, p. 22). It is also worth remembering that *Troilus and Cressida* (which is believed to have been first published in 1603 and, therefore, is contemporaneous with Caravaggio's two versions of the 'Conversion' which are dated 1600/1601), apart from belonging to Shakespeare's so-called 'problem plays', is also considered by critics and readers to be one of the playwright's most modern works. Like many of Caravaggio's paintings, *Troilus and Cressida* problematizes notions of hierarchy and love. Critics also stress the demanding nature of the play in terms of reception as 'Shakespeare invites tragic, comic, satiric, intellectual and compassionate responses all at the same time'.[51]

Like the spectator of *Troilus and Cressida*, the poetic I of 'In Santa Maria del Popolo' is puzzled and cannot understand the meaning of Paul's 'wide gesture of the lifting arms' (*CP*, p. 93). According to Lambert this kind of *aporia* is an essential feature of the sublime as 'it is precisely this state of incomprehension that causes the subjective responses of wonder, marvel and astonishment; and these affects must be understood in all their force as what the sublime itself produces [...] as a distinct form of experience' (p. 31). Another aspect of *The Conversion of St Paul* that makes it a prime example of Baroque aesthetics is the use of anamorphosis (in this case characterized by the absence of God and by the general darkness that dominates the picture). This technique demands the active participation of the viewer to complete the 'picture-event'.[52] Although in Gunn's poem the poetic I seems to be unable to engage with the painting at this level as in the first line of the last stanza he claims to feel 'hardly enlightened', Lambert would argue that 'the more the spectator resists, the more powerful the affective determination of the experience becomes' (p. 29). And, in fact, in the final couplet of the last stanza not only does the poet return to Paul's gesture, providing an interpretation of it, but uses it as a symbol of the key message of his poem: the need to keep fighting even when confronted with the meaninglessness of life or in the face of adversity, like a phoenix that rises from its ashes.[53] Significantly, if we read the last line of the poem, 'resisting by embracing nothingness' (*CP*, p. 94), through Badiou's idea of Paul's conversion as a founding event and a total break with tradition (p. 27), we see how Gunn's secular interpretation of the painting does not differ much from the religious one.[54] What happens within Paul, Badiou argues, 'is the (re)surgence [(re)surrection] of the subject' (p. 17). The word 'resisting', in Badiou's terms, means not succumbing to death (or overcoming death) by dismissing the discourse of the father (associated with the Law and the subjective path of death) to embrace what Gunn calls 'nothingness', that is a 'new beginning' (and total break with tradition), symbolized by the process of 'becoming son' (p. 59). The idea of resistance as a way of opposing the discourse of the father is in line with most critics' interpretation of the ending of 'In Santa Maria del Popolo' and seems to confirm that with *My Sad Captains* begins 'some kind of critique of the heroic' (Michelucci, p. 85). Of course, the need to embrace 'nothingness' could also be seen as an affirmation of risk as that which gives life a meaning and a legacy of Existentialism in Gunn's poetry (Michelucci, p. 84).

But let us go back to the last stanza of 'In Santa Maria del Popolo'. If we keep Badiou in mind, it could be argued that Gunn is also offering a reflection on the arbitrariness of grace and of faith, and that through the contrast between the 'hardly enlightened' (*CP*, p. 94) poetic I and the old women praying in the church, he is illustrating the tension between scepticism and faith (as faith is an essential feature of the process of conversion).[55] This tension, as Klawitter points out, is at the centre of another of Gunn's biblical poems, 'Lazarus not raised' (p. 210), which, although not always associated with Caravaggio, I would argue, has much in common with his *Raising of Lazarus* (1608–09).[56]

> *Lazarus Not Raised*
>
> He was not changed. His friends around the grave
> Stared down upon his greasy placid face
> Bobbing on shadows; nothing it seemed could save
> His body now from the sand below their wave,
> The scheduled miracle not taking place.
>
> He lay inert beneath those outstretched hands
> Which beckoned him to life. Though coffin case
> Was ready to hold life and winding bands

Fig. 4.4. Caravaggio, *The Raising of Lazarus* (c. 1608–09), Messina: Museo Nazionale.

At his first stir would loose the frozen glands,
The scheduled miracle did not take place.

O Lazarus, distended body laid
Glittering without weight on death's surface.
Rise now before you sink, we dare not wade
Into that sad marsh where (the mourners cried)
The scheduled miracle cannot take place.

When first aroused and given thoughts and breath
He chose to amble at an easy pace
In childhood fields imaginary and safe —
Much like the trivial territory of death
(The miracle had not yet taken place).

He chose to spend his thoughts like this at first
And disregard the nag of offered grace,
Then chose to spend the rest of them in rest.
The final effort came, forward we pressed
To see the scheduled miracle take place:

Abruptly the corpse blinked and shook his head
Then sank again, sliding without a trace
From sight, to take slime on the deepest bed
Of vacancy. He had chosen to stay dead,
The scheduled miracle did not take place.

Nothing else changed. I saw somebody peer,
Stooping, into the oblong box of space.
His friends had done their best: without such fear,
Without that terrified awakening glare,
The scheduled miracle would have taken place. (*CP*, pp. 7–8)

The most interesting feature of the poem is Lazarus's gesture of rebellion, the fact that he chooses death over life. Since Lazarus is a precursor of Christ, it could be argued that Gunn is presenting a rather bleak image of Christianity according to which the miracle of the resurrection is just a planned show. Such a vision would particularly appeal to an agnostic like himself because, as Žižek explains, one of the fundamental questions that arises when we reflect on the meaning of Christ's death on the cross is 'the subjective status of Christ: when he was dying on the cross, did he know about his Resurrection-to-come' (p. 101)? If that was the case, Žižek concludes, 'then it was all a game, the supreme divine comedy, since Christ knew that his suffering was just a spectacle with a guaranteed good outcome' (ibid.). This, however, seems too simplistic an interpretation, which is why it is important to look at Gunn's poem in connection with Caravaggio's *Raising of Lazarus*.

Caravaggio's Lazarus, like Gunn's, seems to be 'glittering without weight on death's surface' (*CP*, p. 7). Although his open left hand has just dropped the skull (symbolizing death) that lies beneath it, thus suggesting that he is ready to return to life, the gesture of his right hand is more problematic. If, on the one hand, it could be seen as a salute,[57] and therefore as a sign of acceptance of Jesus' exhortation to rise, on the other, it could be seen as a gesture of resistance, a request for time. His body is still affected by the *rigor mortis* and his stretched arms cannot but make us think of the cross, an image that creates a further connection between this late

Sicilian painting and the early Roman *Conversion of St Paul*. Significantly, Hammill reads both paintings in the context of biblical stories (see also *The Calling of St Matthew*) that present the voice of Jesus as irresistible (p. 76). Caravaggio's paintings, instead, he argues,

> show posed bodies that tend *not* to follow the voice that impels group formation, and in the process they reconfigure that impelling voice into something potentially disruptive of group formation, something materialized as eccentric to the diegetic space afforded by the canvas. (ibid.)[58]

According to Hammill, by making the voice opaque and eccentric, Caravaggio's works also present the 'voice as something that produces longing for an illicit unarticulated enjoyment, a longing embodied in the pose of the one who is called' (ibid.). This is particularly visible in *The Conversion of St Paul* where, as Gunn put it, 'the painter saw what was, an alternate candour and secrecy inside the skin' (*CP*, p. 93), thus turning Paul's gesture into a kind of 'erotic convulsion or perhaps an experience that belongs to that realm [...] where the ecstasy of the soul becomes one with that of the body'.[59] Hammill too focuses mainly on Paul's erotic pose in *The Conversion*, suggesting that his open-legged and open-armed body encourages us to imagine a lover whose spatial outline is blocked out by the large body of the horse and by the servant (p. 76). Klawitter, however, convincingly argues that the figure of Lazarus in the Bible is sufficiently ambiguous to be interpreted in homoerotic terms: he is not married and lives with two maiden sisters (p. 212). Klawitter also points out that an early apocryphal gospel, known as 'the Secret Gospel of Mark', and predating the official Gospel of Mark, contained a story 'rich in homoeroticism that can help us understand Gunn's affinity for Lazarus' (p. 213). The story in question, according to Father Clement (c. 300 CE), was about a young man who, having been resurrected by Jesus, as soon as he saw his saviour 'loved him and began to beseech him that he might be with him' (ibid.). Although Gunn's poem was written in 1952 and therefore predates the poet's coming out, 'the chronology of his sexual awakening [...] does not preclude the Lazarus poem form being gay-themed' (Klawitter, p. 212). Starting with the title, which can be interpreted as an erotic pun on 'raised', the poem can be seen as the story of a man 'who is afraid to make a commitment to sexual maturation' (p. 212) and therefore as a statement on sexual initiation.[60]

This view of sexuality is particularly relevant to 'In Santa Maria del Popolo', particularly if we keep in mind that the term 'will', which features so prominently in *My Sad Captains*, in Shakespearean times, was synonymous with 'penis'.[61] Another feature common to the aforementioned poems and Caravaggio's paintings is a focus on male bodies which, as Hammill puts it, 'demand a certain vocalization that is eccentric to the call of the historical [...] a vocalization that has no content' (p. 80) or, in Lacanian terms, 'a demand for voice as *object a*' (ibid.). As Hammill explains, the *object a* is the object of the drive and the cause of desire. Unlike desire, which seeks satisfaction through the constant search for an impossible object that, if it were to materialize, would put an end to desire, 'the drive achieves satisfaction through the repetition of its own aim' (p. 80). This definition of *object a* is remarkably similar to Badiou's notion of *sin*. In his book on St Paul, Badiou defines sin as 'the life of desire as autonomy, as automatism' (p. 79), emphasizing also that 'the Law fixes the subject of desire, binding desire to it regardless of the subject's "will"' (ibid.) and that it is 'this objectal automatism of desire [...] that assigns the subject to the carnal path of death' (ibid.). Significantly, when Hammill analyses Caravaggio's depiction of Saul/Paul's supine body, he argues: 'this pose resurrects the flesh that Paul relinquishes (Gal. I: 16)' (p. 79). Gunn's reference to sin in the third stanza of 'In Santa Maria del Popolo', therefore, can also be read from a psychoanalytical perspective, a reading that is in line with other explorations of the theme of desire to be found throughout his oeuvre,[62] including his last collection *Boss Cupid*, but above all in another of his early poems, 'The Allegory of the Wolf Boy', which was included in his second collection, *The Sense of Movement* (1957). This is a very personal poem in which the poet reflects on his own youth, on how he used to lead a double life, playing tennis and drinking tea during the day, whilst during the night becoming prey to 'shameful, uncontrollable impulses written on a body that is, on its surface, "open and blond," but inside its clothes, the victim of a tormenting itchiness (". . . the familiar itch of close dark hair" *CP*, p. 61)'.[63] The similarity between these images of the wolf boy and 'the candour and secrecy inside the skin' (*CP*, p. 93) of 'In Santa Maria del Popolo' is rather striking and helps us understand Gunn's fascination with St Paul. The connection between the two poems acquires an extra significance when we consider the last two lines of 'The Allegory of the Wolf Boy': 'Only to instinct and the moon being bound, | Drops on four feet. Yet he has bleeding paws' (*CP*, p. 61). As suggested by Michelucci, despite the fact that the metamorphosis from boy to wolf is complete, the poem's concluding images indicate that the boy has not been transformed into 'a strong animal to hunt his prey, able to reject and overturn the social and cultural codes that are so alien to his nature' (p. 134) but a victim whose bleeding paws 'become [...] stigmata that crucify him' (ibid.). Like Fernandez and Pasolini, Gunn in his youth must have perceived homosexuality as 'a mark of sickness and division'.[64]

As we are about to see, the contrast between desire and the need to repress it is also the subject of one of Gunn's lesser known poems, 'Apocryphal', which is usually excluded from the 'canon' as it was only published once in 1954 in the magazine *Botteghe Oscure* edited by Marguerite Caetani and reprinted in 1974 in the volume *Botteghe Oscure Reader*.[65] A discussion of 'Apocryphal' will add both to our understanding of Gunn's poetry (e.g. the early presence of gay themes) and Caravaggio's modernity and homoerotic appeal.

Apocryphal

Now Abraham lifted the blade and as he lifted
He saw in his shining a shining stranger walk.
Isaac lay motionless, counting already as object.
So Abraham turned, and watched the stranger climb
Up the hill, an angel, not God's but Abraham's angel
(He could not know this): the angel frowned, saying 'Hold!
Man of no faith.' And his frowning shadowed the world.

> Now Abraham answered, his voice an indignant prophet's,
> 'My faith is so great that I kill my only son — '
> And he pointed to Isaac swooning upon the hilltop,
> Isaac, his neck self-offered to the sun,
> Isaac, his eyes closed ignorant of fearing.
> 'So what is this mockery levelled against my faith
> More strong than thought, more solid than life itself?'
>
> The stranger pointed, his hand lay upon the valleys:
> 'Observe', he said, 'the wild unquestioning course
> Of that river, which knows in its rushing not men nor angels;
> My frown, your wonder, as light as bouncing stones.
> What is your greatest faith concerning that river?'
> On its surface were tossed huge branches, a dead goat,
> Which Abraham saw with his old clear eyes, but said:
>
> 'Imagine that river a mighty circling whirlpool,
> So faith may turn its waters upon itself:
> Imagine its level lowering until only,
> Hard earth and cracks its solitary bequest,
> A cloud of vapour floats to the straight horizon.
> My faith is greater than matter, above the world,
> My faith is essence which meets God outside space.'
>
> Isaac had opened his eyes and gazed bewildered
> Upon the stranger, his father, the dropped knife.
> 'Come', said the angel, 'you too look on this river.
> Do you believe it can dry at the fire of faith?'
> 'Why', said the boy, 'it will flow, I suppose, for ever.
> For it is in the nature of rivers to flow.
> It is strong as itself. What force could be more strong?'
>
> Now the angel turned to Abraham, and turning
> Softened his voice a little and said:
> Do not be angry, as he is of your begetting
> So I am too, and a creation of your will.
> His answer is mine and, the strength of our two answers
> Is yours against your own.' He strode away,
> While Abraham walked with Isaac down the hill.[66]

This is another of Gunn's biblical poems in which the poet engages with the story of the sacrifice of Isaac; according to Klawitter, Gunn was directly inspired by Caravaggio's rendering of the same story in his 1603 eponymous painting (p. 216). As suggested by the poem's title, Gunn deviates from the official version of the story of Abraham and Isaac by turning the angel into a figment of Abraham's imagination, who instead of calling him from heaven follows him up the hill to confront him with a mystical riddle about a local river. The angel addresses both father and son, inviting them to express their views on the river by asking each of them in turn the same question: 'What is your greatest faith concerning that river?' (*BOR*, p. 179). As Klawitter points out, Abraham's answer is dogmatic and suggests a belief in 'power as the vehicle for living life righteously' (p. 214). Isaac's reply, instead, seems to indicate the need to accept the nature of the river and respect it for what it is without trying to subject it to someone else's will. The angel seems to agree with Isaac but, seeing Abraham's disappointment, he tells him that he should not feel disheartened as the riddle was internal to him; it was the manifestation of the struggle going on in his mind 'over freedom of the will' (p. 215). The angel's reassuring words in the poem's last stanza are even more interesting because they show us how, by turning the angel into Abraham's alter ego, Gunn is able to stress the topos of the challenging of mastery already present in Caravaggio's painting and in many of the works hitherto explored. The decision not to follow God's request to sacrifice Isaac becomes entirely Abraham's, with no mediation from a supernatural being that might justify his rebellious gesture. The image of the angel as Abraham's angel (rather than God's angel) is further reinforced through the fact that Gunn chooses to make the angel first appear to Abraham as a reflection on the blade of his knife (Klawitter, p. 215). Klawitter sees strong similarities between Gunn's 'Apocryphal' and Caravaggio's *The Sacrifice of Isaac*, including the position of the shining knife which, half way between the angel and the boy, 'could very well have just reflected the approach of the angel, just as Gunn describes the reflection in his poem' (p. 216). More similarities between the two works emerge when we consider a possible 'gay sub-current' (ibid.). In both cases, we are dealing with 'a totally male milieu' and a scene of 'bondage and sacrifice' (p. 215). Similarly, when commenting on Caravaggio's *Sacrifice of Isaac*, Hibbard emphasizes the contrast 'between a naked angel and a rather impressive, bald old man' (p. 166), suggesting that, as in many others of Caravaggio's Roman paintings, 'the combination of youth and age [...] seems sexually suggestive, sometimes is tinged with sadomasochism, and often implies ridicule toward the older men' (pp. 158–59).[67]

The erotic nature of the painting is picked up by Hammill, who argues that 'the cloaked and voided engagement between Abraham's lower front and Isaac's lower rear suggests anal sex' (p. 88) with the knife being 'a substitute for the penis' (p. 89) and that the painting should be read as an illustration of the tension between the bright, 'constructed and aestheticized space of civilization' (p. 88) and the dark primordial nature of desire, here embodied in 'the fantasmic scene of pederastic anal sex' (ibid.). Significantly, Hammill reads *The Sacrifice of Isaac* as the counterpart of *Amor Vincit Omnia* (also known as *Victorious Cupid*) (1601–02), contending that both works 'introduce a conceptual difference into the carnality that is for post-Pauline Christianity the fleshy embodiment of the Jew [...] and encode it through the fantasy of anal sex' (p. 88). Both paintings confront us with gaps and discontinuities. These are particularly visible in *The Sacrifice of Isaac* where, for instance, the darkness of Isaac's open mouth, Hammill contends, functions as a syncope, that is 'an obfuscation in an aesthetic and sexual field of desire that, in introducing an ego-annihilating *jouissance*, has the potential to change that ego's relation both to itself and to group formation' (p. 90). If in music a syncope can be described as 'a note that lags behind and anticipates the rest of the movement',[68] in psychoanalysis the syncope is related to primary narcissism, the mirror phase and dynamic of the imago. Catherine Clément describes the syncope as 'that mysterious place "between expectation and relaxation": a place in which fusion and separation, animal and human, individual and collectivity, are indefinitely reversible' (p. 121). Also, if in music the conclusion of the syncope leads to harmony, at the conclusion of initiation we have 'a brand new outfit for the new man' (Clément, p. 121). These words seem to capture the essence of St Paul (at least as seen by Badiou), of Gunn's poetry and of many of Caravaggio's paintings. Both Gunn's poetry and Caravaggio's paintings, however, seem to resist any attempt at closure, preferring to stress the gap or the liminal state. Another fundamental feature common to both Gunn and Caravaggio (particularly his early 'boy' paintings) is an emphasis on poses, poses that appeal to us because, as Hammill claims regarding Caravaggio (but could extend to Gunn's poetry), they 'resist easy recognition and conscription by a group who wants to read them as transmitting its sense of identity and value' (p. 69). Hammill defines such openness as 'queer' and this notion of queerness (based on Eve Sedgwick's theory) is central also to our next case study, the 1986 film *Caravaggio* by the British director Derek Jarman.

Caravaggio and Derek Jarman

As in the case of Fernandez and Gunn, the relationship between Jarman and Caravaggio is a complex one which extends beyond his 1986 film devoted to the Lombard painter and is part of Jarman's wider interest in the Renaissance. As Ellis reminds us in his seminal work on the cinematography of the British director, Jarman started to work on the script for *Caravaggio* as early as 1978 and 'there would be about sixteen subsequent drafts of the screenplay with at least three substantially different approaches to the story'.[69] What is common to all of them is Jarman's strong sense of identification with Caravaggio from both the biographical and artistic point of view. Apart from Caravaggio's presumed homosexuality, as noted by Ellis, there are many parallels between Jarman's and Caravaggio's lives (p. 117). Caravaggio's status as a 'scandalous outsider' and his troubles with the law must have reminded Jarman of his own reputation in the 1980s when his name was 'being used in the House of Commons to put forward new obscenity legislation' (ibid.). Also, Caravaggio's difficult relationship with the art establishment of his time could be compared to Jarman's uneasy relationship with the British film industry and, finally, both Caravaggio's relationship to Cardinal Del Monte and his way of quoting Michelangelo bear similarities to Jarman's way of engaging with his early patrons (e.g. Ashton and Gielgud) and other directors who had an impact on his artistic development. According to Ellis, if Hibbard is right in saying that Caravaggio's way of acknowledging his admiration for Michelangelo was to ' "tear away Michelangelo's idealizing mask and to expose the true source of his devotion to male nudes," Jarman's more explicit representations of homosexual desire might be seen as doing the same thing to Cocteau and Pasolini' (p. 118).[70] As for the artistic legacy of Caravaggio on Jarman's works, the most obvious feature is the use of light: like Scorsese, Jarman saw in Caravaggio the inventor of cinematic light and during the production of *Caravaggio* worked very closely with his lighting designer in order to reproduce as faithfully as possible the lighting of the original paintings (p. 118). Other prominent similarities between the two artists are the tendency to focus on single objects and the 'relative lack of interest in settings' (ibid.). The limited use of props, Ellis maintains, ensures that the objects used acquire a stronger

Fig. 4.5 (above). Caravaggio, *The Sacrifice of Isaac* (c. 1603), Florence: Uffizi Gallery.
Fig. 4.6 (below). Caravaggio, *Medusa* (1597), Florence: Uffizi Gallery.

significance, which in Jarman's works becomes almost fetishistic: the use of the knife in *Caravaggio*, for instance, is a prime example of this phenomenon (p. 119).[71] The treatment of space is also a point of contact between Jarman and Caravaggio. As noted by many art critics,[72] Caravaggio was not interested in (or, according to some, incapable of) applying the rules of Albertian perspective to his paintings, preferring instead to work on the front plane of the canvas even though, when combined with his use of dark backgrounds, this eliminated the sense of a believable receding space that one would expect in a realist painting. Ellis identifies Jarman's '*tableau vivant*-style compositions' (p. 120) and lack of long shots as part of the Caravaggio legacy which enabled him to move away from 'the period's film dominant style of realism [...] in favour of a more self-consciously stylized approach to the past. Finally, the most important feature Jarman admired in Caravaggio, and which impacted heavily on his cinematography, is the relation between painting and viewer' (p. 120).

Quoting Friedlaender and Hibbard, Ellis stresses how Caravaggio forces the viewer to engage with what s/he observes by turning the spectator into a witness and making him take part in the painted drama (pp. 120–21). According to Ellis, many of Caravaggio's works produce an almost paradoxical situation where 'the world of the painting pushes outward the viewer, at the same time that it makes the spectatorial relation (and hence the spectator) one of the subjects of the paintings themselves' (p. 121). Jarman seems to have internalized this lesson and often uses devices (like Michele's finger pointing at the camera/viewer during the scene of Lena's death in *Caravaggio*) to make the audience the subject of his films. The main outcome of these techniques is the prevention of the passive 'consumption' of a work of art. In both artists this is achieved also through the insertion of anachronistic details and, particularly in Caravaggio's case, through a gap between signifier and signified visible in the dirty finger/toe nails, deformed fingers or bored look of some of his models posing as mythological figures or saints (e.g. *Bacchus*; *Victorious Love*; the 1602 *St John the Baptist*) which constantly remind us that we are dealing with real people (young boys and women, even prostitutes) 'pretending' to be someone else. In Jarman's films in general, but particularly in *Caravaggio*, the insertion of anachronistic props, such as the golden calculator held by Giustiniani or the typewriter Caravaggio's contemporary art critic and arch-enemy Baglione uses to write about his rival, have a similar effect and create an interesting dialogue between past and present.

Before focusing on the film, a quick overview of the vicissitudes of the screenplay will enhance our understanding of Jarman's relation to our painter and of the major themes eventually addressed in *Caravaggio*. The following accounts are taken from Ellis's in-depth study of Jarman's scripts. The first version of the *Caravaggio* script is a more or less straightforward depiction of the painter's life from the moment he moved to Rome and started working as a copyist, attracting the attention of prominent patrons like Cardinal Del Monte. The first crisis occurs when Michele obtains his first important public commission to paint *The Martyrdom of St Matthew*, but is unable to finish the painting until he falls in love with Ranuccio, who is a thief and a hustler. Michele makes him pose as the executioner for the painting. Ranuccio, however, is attached to Lena, who betrays him with Scipione Borghese, a very jealous lover who murders her when he discovers that she is pregnant. However, it is Ranuccio who gets the blame; he is arrested and convicted of Lena's murder, so Michele, in order to save the man he loves, agrees to paint a portrait of the pope, provided Ranuccio is released. To Michele's surprise, instead of being pleased, Ranuccio is furious with him for having compromised with Lena's murderer. The two men end up fighting and Michele accidentally kills Ranuccio. This version of the film was supposed to end with an account of the last years of Caravaggio's life by Cardinal Del Monte during a dinner party. As Ellis reminds us:

> This early script picks up on some of the elements of Jarman's first three feature films. It claims Caravaggio for a gay historical tradition, putting his sexuality at the centre of his artistic genius, and putting that at the centre of an aesthetic revolution that is opposed by the critic Baglione [...] It connects this story of an alternative aesthetics with a fairly romantic gay love narrative [...] (p. 111)

Interestingly, the theme of romantic gay love was also meant to be explored through a reference to Caravaggio's *David with the Head of Goliath* in a 'dream sequence in super 8' (p. 112) where, as in the painting, Goliath was Caravaggio but (unlike the painting) David was a young shepherd called Jerusaleme with whom the protagonist had previously had sexual intercourse. As we are about to see, the character of Jerusaleme will also feature in the actual film but in a more ambiguous and, at the same time, more prominent role.

The 1981 version of the script is very different from the original as it juxtaposes past and present in interesting and complex ways. The opening scene features Jarman talking to an American producer who is trying to persuade him to make a pornographic film about Caravaggio, something that would appeal to both gay and heterosexual audiences and would suit the video market. The producer invites Jarman to think of Joe Orton[73] as a model as he sees various similarities between the two artists. The script also introduces a photographer who makes images of male nudes in the style of Caravaggio; Jarman travels with him to Italy to research the life and works of our painter. Like the initial version, this script insists on Caravaggio's homosexuality, highlighting that all great artists of the past (Plato, Leonardo, Michelangelo, Shakespeare, etc.) were gay, and the same is true of many great film-makers of our times (Ellis, p. 112). Interestingly, Baglione's criticism of Caravaggio's works is juxtaposed with negative reviews of Jarman's films, thus stressing Jarman's identification with the painter — which is confirmed by the ending of the film featuring 'Derek holding the hand of the young Caravaggio' (p. 113). As noted by Ellis,

> the final image of Jarman and Caravaggio holding hands imagines artistic influence within a gay tradition not as an antagonistic relation, as it is often figured in mainstream tradition, but as a kind of cruising which insists on the centrality of sexuality in the artistic process. (p. 114)

In this version of the script, Jarman seems determined to draw a comparison between the pressures faced by gay artists in the 1980s and those of 'the homosexual artist of the Renaissance' (p. 113), pointing out that in both cases one of the key dangers was 'the compromising complicity that comes with the funding agencies, whether these happen to be the Catholic Church or Channel 4' (p. 113).

In 1983, Jarman began yet another major rewriting of the script which after several revisions would become the final one, even though the actual film differs slightly from the script. He abandoned the present-day narrative and focused exclusively on Caravaggio's life and works. As we know, Jarman is not always accurate in his reconstruction of the painter's life. He is mainly interested in the Roman period, whilst other phases of Caravaggio's existence are briefly evoked through flashbacks during the scenes devoted to Michele's death. These scenes are very important as they feature regularly throughout the film, including the beginning and the end, thus giving it a circular structure which, as we shall later see, is used to reiterate the key images associated with death throughout the film, like the vortex. The most obvious 'biographical liberty' Jarman takes is the introduction of a mute boy (initially named Gianni and then Jerusaleme) who prepares the painter's colours and becomes his life companion (and perhaps lover). In this version of the script it is Ranuccio (and not Scipione) who kills Lena and, according to the text, the film should have ended with a *tableau vivant* of *The Raising of Lazarus* featuring Caravaggio himself as the digger and Ranuccio as Lazarus (pp. 114–15). This scene was removed from the actual film and replaced with the one in which the young Caravaggio and the older boy with whom he had fallen in love (named Pasqualone[74]) see a tableau vivant of *The Entombment of Christ* where the face of Christ is that of the older Caravaggio. Another significant change from earlier versions of the script is the fact that the killing of Ranuccio is no longer accidental but intentional. The evolution of the relationship between the protagonist and his model/lover/rival Ranuccio through the various scripts seems to indicate an interest in the Freudian concept of masochistic narcissism as that which allows the ego to cope with its mistrust of the world through identification with the hated object.[75] According to Ellis, we see also an emphasis on masochism as an essential aspect of the creative process (p. 115), a feature which is explored on different levels throughout the film through references to various paintings by Caravaggio, but, particularly, in the sections engaging with *The Martyrdom of St Matthew* and *The Entombment of Christ*. For all their differences, if taken together, the scripts for *Caravaggio* reveal that the painter acted as a trigger for Jarman to reflect 'on his own artistic practice and in particular the ways in which politics, sexuality, and economics were intertwined with it' (Ellis, p. 116). But let us now focus on the actual film.

The film is divided into ten sections and each one of them is devoted to a particular work by Caravaggio as 'the narrative of the film is constructed from the paintings'.[76] Of all the literary and cinematic works devoted to the Lombard painter, Jarman's *Caravaggio* is the one that has been studied most in depth by various eminent critics. Building on existing scholarship, for the purpose of this book, I would like to focus on the film's opening section, 'Medusa', as I believe it is much more significant than hitherto acknowledged. Not only does 'Medusa' condense most of the key themes present in the film (ranging from questions of power structures to the relationship between art and life, to death, mourning, love, desire, and identity formation), but it also offers an ideal tool to understand Jarman's fascination with Caravaggio as the painting itself contains many of the features Jarman admired in Caravaggio, such as the treatment of space, the relationship between beholder and object observed, the nature of the aesthetic experience, and the life–death dichotomy.

Before proceeding any further, it is important to summarize briefly this section, which lasts eight and a half minutes including the credits. Interestingly, the first image the viewer sees is that of a dark surface being painted with vertical and horizontal brush strokes, which have the effect of either reflecting the light or making the surface evenly black, an obvious reference to Caravaggio's chiaroscuro technique, but also an invitation to see an analogy between the canvas and the screen. This initial shot, focusing on the necessary treatment of the canvas before it can be used by the artist for his work, alerts the viewer to the importance of surfaces and to the materiality of paint. It also seems to encourage a form of haptic visuality, that is, 'a visuality that functions like the sense of touch' and blurs intersubjective boundaries.[77] As the credits come to an end, we hear a voiceover mentioning all the locations associated with the last four years of Caravaggio's life (Malta, Syracuse, Messina, Naples, Porto Ercole) and the date of his death (18 July 1610). Significantly, the next image is that of a close-up of Michele's scarred and bruised face on his deathbed. Before we realize what is happening, Michele's eyes reveal to us that he is fighting between life and death: his right eye is closed as the whole area surrounding it is red and swollen; the left one is open but its look is glazed. If we linger on this image, we notice that Michele's nose seems to protrude into the space of the viewer, forcing him/her to concentrate on the black holes of his nostrils which, owing to the camera's angle, appear to be exceptionally large (as we are about to see, all these details represent direct quotations from Caravaggio's 'Medusa', even though the spectator has not yet been introduced to the painting which gives its name to the section). The next shot is also a close-up, this time of a hand holding a blade of dry grass flat on a rough wooden surface (a table) and a knife cutting it into small pieces. As we have already mentioned, the knife is one of the film's leitmotifs and the index finger with a rim of dirt around the nail makes us immediately think of the hands of many of Caravaggio's models. Once again, the viewer is confronted with various structures and textures which invite a form of haptic visuality. Immediately afterwards the camera recedes and we realize that the hand belongs to Jerusaleme, Michele's life companion, who is keeping a vigil on his dying master in a large, barren, dirty, and harshly lit hospital room. There is no dialogue, but the voiceover conveys Michele's last thoughts as he is rescued from the sea by a fisherman on the beach at Porto Ercole: 'salt water drips from my fingers leaving a trail of tiny tears on the burning sand [...] I can hear you sobbing Jerusaleme. Rough hands warm my dying body snatched from cold blue sea'.[78] Like the images, these words invite the spectator to engage with more surfaces and textures, a process which is interrupted only by Jerusaleme's sobbing.

In order to understand fully the significance of these initial scenes, we must consider the Medusa myth and Caravaggio's rendering of this story in his 1597 painting which was commissioned by Cardinal Del Monte as a present for his friend Cosimo De Medici, and which is now exhibited in the Uffizi in Florence. Three features of this painting appear to be particularly relevant to our discussion: first, its three-dimensionality, which derives from the fact that it was painted on canvas, but mounted on a convex round wooden frame or 'rotella'; second, the fact that this is a self-portrait of the artist; finally the paradoxical fact that it represents both the moment of terror prior to the act of decapitation and its aftermath. As noted by Mieke Bal, the convex nature of this object turns it into a 'meeting place of representational space and representation of space' (*Quoting Caravaggio*, p. 135) because like Michele's nose (and the snakes on the Gorgon's head), it protrudes into the viewer's space. This feature creates problems for museums and art galleries who want to exhibit it as it cannot simply be hung on a wall. Interestingly, the curators of the Uffizi solved this problem by displaying it on an easel, a device which reminds the viewer of the common tradition of easel painting and its tendency to 'flatten representation into two-dimensionality' (*Quoting Caravaggio*, p. 136).[79] As a result, it can be argued that Caravaggio's painting challenges the distinction between two- and three-dimensional forms of representations. The fact that we are dealing with a self-portrait raises even more interesting questions regarding subjectivity and the distinction between subject and object: the subject painter (male) and the object monster (female) are conflated and so are gender positions. The viewer, who is addressed in more than one way through various indexical signs, 'is also the object of representation, since this myth is about looking' (*Quoting Caravaggio*, p. 138). As we are about to see, Jarman quotes this aspect of 'Medusa' literally through the character of Jerusaleme. Another vital feature of the painting as a portrait is the trope of 'facing'. As Bal explains, 'facing is a crucial, perhaps primary index pointing at the viewer in a relation to space that is not incorporative but dialogic' (p. 138). However, if Medusa's head is supposed to embody this indexicality, it 'is without power because it is without look' (p. 140). Medusa does not look at the viewer; she looks away and because we are dealing with a convex object it is hard to tell whether she is 'staring inward or looking over your shoulder at something terrifying behind you' (p. 140). In Bal's view this generates a kind of spatial ambiguity very similar to the temporal one caused by the paradoxical act of representing both the moment preceding the decapitation and its outcome. This spatial ambiguity suggests a third possible relationship to space (neither incorporative not dialogic) which Bal calls 'recoiling' (p. 140). As we have already mentioned, when looking at the painting we notice that the snakes on Medusa's head project forward and represent what the monster sees when she catches a glimpse of herself and becomes so frightened that she is turned into stone. Since Medusa appears to be petrified by the same thing that frightens the viewer, the viewer's immediate reaction is to recoil and recoiling, Bal maintains, is the result of heteropathic identification that is a form of identification with the other that puts the self at risk.[80] Kaja Silverman, in her work on male subjectivity, pointed out a strong link between heteropathic identification and masochism.[81]

Another important consequence of the gender confusion caused by a male painter posing as a female figure is that it 'allows a sensitization to the fright, not provoked but undergone by Medusa'.[82] Also, by looking away, it is as if Medusa is enticing the viewer 'to look with her for the true source of the fright located in the ideology that turns women [and in the case of Jarman, homosexuals] into monsters' (p. 60). Since in psychology Medusa is often confused with Judith (another figure associated with beheading as a symbol of castration), Bal argues that the power of Caravaggio's *Medusa* to challenge mastery becomes more obvious if we consider it in connection with his *Judith Beheading Holofernes* (1598). What both paintings have in common is a very unrealistic portrayal of the blood spurting out of the victims' heads, which acquires the status of index as in both cases it looks more solid than liquid and resembles a bundle of arrows. The blood in these paintings has the function of making us question the relationship between violence and suffering. What is more, since in *Judith* the blood 'arrows' run parallel to the blade that severed Holoferne's head, one would expect the blood to follow the sword

> as its consequence [...] Visually, however, according to the eye's itinerary into the representation, being closer to the picture's plane, the blood precedes the sword as its visual 'cause': because we see blood, we subsequently see the sword. (*Double Exposure*, p. 293)

According to Bal, not only does Judith force us to question causality but she also challenges 'our certainties about what it is and how it is that we can know' (ibid.). In *Medusa*, this is achieved through the recoiling relation to space which 'undermines the humanist individual who ruled over objective knowledge, the knowledge that effectively had an object' (*Quoting Caravaggio*, p. 164). Through the snakes protruding into the viewer's space, the painting is performing a negative address: it produces a 'shock that enforces awareness of the address in our bodies at the threshold of vision and touch' (*Quoting Caravaggio*, p. 157).

In Jarman's film, the audience is introduced to the painting of Medusa when Michele takes home the young Jerusaleme for the first time, having just bought him from a family of shepherds who had no use for a mute boy. As Michele and the boy enter the studio, Jerusaleme is immediately attracted to the *Medusa* resting on an easel; he starts mocking (or we should say mirroring) her expression and then picks up the shield running around Michele's studio in order to scare him. Michele plays the game of pretending to be shocked but then pulls the shield off Jerusaleme's hands, imitating Medusa's expression as if he wanted to frighten the boy. Sitting on a windowsill, next to the basket Jerusaleme's grandmother had given him when he picked up the boy, Michele places the painting beside it, resting it partly against the wall and partly against the window. If at first this scene suggests that Jarman is mocking the myth's central theme of the dangers of looking and being looked at by turning it into a childish game, the following images produce in the viewer the recoiling effect Bal was describing in connection with Caravaggio's painting; thus the issue of the look and the gaze is reinscribed into the film. Jerusaleme falls asleep in Michele's arms and, a few seconds later, Michele dozes off too, placing his hand on the boy's head in a gesture of affection and peacefulness (have they both been petrified by the Gorgon?). The next shot focuses again on the painting resting against the wall and on the wicker basket next to it. This time, however, we see a snake coiled around the basket's handle. The animal slowly turns its head towards Medusa, thus suggesting that she died as a result of having seen the reflection of her own head. Immediately afterwards, Michele seems to wake up, but the scene is interrupted by an image of a much older Jerusaleme lying on a bed of straw next to a goat. A voiceover (representing Michele's voice) compares the boy to a true

St John brought from the wilderness. As the voice keeps describing how Michele taught Jerusaleme how to grind and mix colours, the camera returns to the scene of Michele asleep on the windowsill, holding the younger Jerusaleme in his arms: this time, however, the snake is crawling under the blanket covering Jerusaleme, dangerously close to his neck. The following shot is of the same scene, but this time the snake has disappeared. These apparently insignificant images (lasting only a few seconds) are in actual fact extremely important as they reveal to us how Jarman engages with the key features of Caravaggio's *Medusa* in order to introduce the major themes he wants to address in his film. At this particular moment of the first section of his film, by making Michele compare Jerusaleme to St John, Jarman is conflating the identities of John the Apostle and St John the Baptist. The images of Jerusaleme resting his head on Michele's shoulder seem to allude to the description of the last supper in the Gospel of St John, according to which John sat next to Jesus and leaned his head on Jesus' chest (John 13:23–25, ESV). As argued by Wymer, John, 'the disciple whom Jesus loved', represented 'a Biblically sanctioned example of male love which Jarman liked to use to challenge the modern Church's hostility to homosexual relationships'.[83] However, Jerusaleme is also explicitly compared to St John the Baptist and, later in the film, so is Ranuccio (the man Michele murders when he discovers he was responsible for Lena's death, and with whom he had a violent homoerotic relationship). It could also be argued that the conflation of the two St Johns allows Jarman to explore two kinds of homosexual love: one based on sadomasochistic practices and one based on tenderness. I agree with Bersani and Dutoit that 'however undeveloped, these scenes interestingly suggest that through painting (or more specifically through "Medusa", we could add), Michele — and Jarman — discover a connectedness independent of desire' (*Caravaggio*, p. 66). Interestingly, Bersani and Dutoit describe tenderness as:

> one version of a 'reaching toward the other in space'. Tenderness *is* that movement; it escapes the violence of human desire by enacting its independence from either the demands or the presumed secrets of subjectivity. Because of subjectivity, however, tenderness is a difficult form of contact for human subjects. It may, Jarman also suggests, depend on a certain degree of self-recognition in the object we reach toward. [...] what might have been seen as a specular narcissism should rather be read as the subject's recognition that in approaching otherness, he is also moving toward himself. (pp. 71–72)

This brings us back to the concept of haptic visuality. The reference to narcissism is particularly important from our perspective because Medusa is a self-portrait of the artist which involved both a literal and a metaphorical engagement with the mirror. By multiplying this mirroring game,[84] the film blurs the boundaries between self and other, between subject and object of the gaze. Through the element of game it also encourages the bonding between Michele and the young Jerusaleme, a bonding which is based on friendship and loyalty, rather than desire and sexual intercourse.[85] If there is an element of eroticism in these images, it is the kind of eroticism described by Noelle Oxenhandler in her work on the eroticism of parenthood in which she argues that eroticism comprises a whole range of relationships (only one of which is sexual) and that the intensity of emotion experienced in a parent–child relationship rivals that of adult lovers.[86] These relationships are based on touch and, as Barker reminds us, haptic touches, whether in the form of a caress, a scrape, or a smear, imply 'the opening of one body onto another that is erotic, but they may express a panoply of possible attitudes' (p. 39). What is more, the haptic style of touch is not necessarily always positive: 'the pleasures and horrors evoked by haptic tactility are anything but mutually exclusive' (p. 39). In *Caravaggio*, Jarman seems to explore all the ranges of haptic tactility through Michele's relationship to Jerusaleme and to Ranuccio. Just think of the violent fight that breaks between the Michele and Ranuccio after Ranuccio has finished posing for one of Michele's paintings: the brawl ends with Ranuccio stabbing Michele and Michele smearing his blood on Ranuccio's face and declaring that they are now 'blood brothers'. At the end of the film when Michele kills Ranuccio after he confesses to having murdered Lena, the dying Ranuccio smears his own blood on Michele's face as he falls lifeless in his arms.[87] Through Michele and Jerusaleme, instead, the film promotes that particular kind of haptic visuality that Marks calls 'the caressing gaze' and which, in Barker's view, is used by Marks to counterbalance the excessive emphasis on masochism and abjection in most theories about cinematic tactility (particularly in Steven Shaviro's one) (p. 169).

As mentioned earlier, haptic visuality implies a reciprocity between film and viewer, as the viewer must be receptive to the haptic images offered by the film (or any other art form). Jarman's *Caravaggio* encourages this kind of reciprocity by addressing the viewer in various ways, through various indexical signs such as Michele's finger pointed at the camera during one of the scenes devoted to Lena's death, the silver panel (the Medusa shield?) Jerusaleme uses to reflect the light and dazzle the audience, Michele's knife or Jerusaleme's whistle. Above all, however, it is through the character of Jerusaleme that the viewer is implicated. By encouraging the identification of Jerusaleme with John the Apostle, who according to 'the letters of John' in the New Testament and the book of Revelation was one of the witnesses to the life and work of Jesus (1 John 1:1–5, Bible NIV), the role of Jerusaleme as spectator is officially sanctioned. Jerusaleme becomes the spectator par excellence of the deeds of the Christ/artist. In depriving Jerusaleme of a voice, however, Jarman seems to be quoting again from Caravaggio's *Medusa* in order to comment on the nature of the aesthetic experience, stressing how this should transcend narrativity.

In an interesting book entitled *Medusa's Ear*, Dawne McCance proposes an alternative reading of the Medusa myth based on the account given by Ovid in his *Metamorphoses*. According to this interpretation of the story, Medusa is 'an icon of speechlessness'.[88] She is not 'a woman temporarily dumbfounded but incapable of speech, altogether mute' (p. 4). McCance reminds us that the term *gorgon* (commonly used to identify any of three sisters of which Medusa was the only one without the gift of immortality) means 'fearful shriek, roar or shout' (p. 4).[89] Quoting Enterline, McCance argues that 'in Ovid's texts it is not Medusa's "head", or even her gaze that petrifies. Rather, it is primarily her silenced "face" or "mouth" (*os, oris*)' (p. 4); since in Western culture the voice represents the very essence of identity, 'modernity's subject remains haunted by the fear of an *os mutum*, the fantasy of a mouth that cannot speak and of a voice that has been lost' (p. 5). Similarly, in an article comparing Caravaggio, Bacon, and the 2002 American psychological horror film *The Ring*, Davide Panagia focuses on Medusa's open mouth, claiming that like all other open mouths in Caravaggio's paintings, the Gorgon's mouth suggests an oscillation between life and death (and we have already seen how Caravaggio depicts both the moment prior to Medusa's decapitation and the one after). Panagia is also keen to define the scream not only in terms of sound but also bodily. From this perspective, the scream is an open mouth, a spasm, a movement or, in other words, a deformation of the body. Deformed bodies show us the effect of forces upon them and in so doing they collapse 'the correspondences between organs of perception and modes of apprehension'.[90] As a result, they deny the comfort of either narration or figuration: the horror of the scream is the horror of not having a story to tell (par. 26). According to Panagia, this is the kind of horror Poussin saw in Caravaggio's works when he accused him of having destroyed the art of painting: Caravaggio 'painted the effects of seeing without telling stories' (par. 26) and made 'narrativity insufficient to aesthetic experience' (par. 28). Caravaggio's works, instead, promote haptic visuality: 'his paintings ultimately insist on the force of the surface, on the invisible sensation emanating from a thinly textured patina that impresses itself upon the senses; they insist, in the end, on rendering force by confounding the distinction between the act of representation and the subject of representation' (par. 21), which is why Jarman was fascinated with them. Jarman saw in Caravaggio's style the equivalent of what he wanted to achieve through the medium of film. We have already suggested that the initial images of the opening section entitled 'Medusa' represent a quotation of Caravaggio's painting; now we see even more clearly why. The close-up of Michele's swollen and bruised face, or that of Michele's nose protruding into the viewer's space, with gigantic nostrils suggesting a doubling of Medusa's mouth,[91] exemplify Panagia's concept of 'deformed body', as they draw attention to the forces that impacted upon that body, a body that has been reduced to a single function: sensation. This impression is confirmed by the voiceover expressing Michele's thoughts just before he dies. As we have already seen, it evokes haptic images: water dripping on the sand, rough hands rubbing Michele's skin, etc.

But let us return to Jerusaleme and to Jarman's conflation of various identities. As we have seen, Jerusaleme's dumbness makes him similar to Medusa. Since in the original painting Medusa is a portrait of the artist, this (con)fusion adds an extra dimension to the blurring of the distinction between the subject and the object of representation. It seems to suggest that Jarman, like Caravaggio, was aware that the first viewer to experience the effect of a work of art is always the artist. As illustrated by Fried, regarding the significance of Caravaggio's decapitation scenes, a direct consequence of the artist-viewer topos is that the life of an artist is always conditioned by his works (to the point that, as we have seen in Pasolini, Fernandez, and Gunn, it anticipates life) as he/she can never be fully severed from them.[92] For Jarman, as for the other authors we have analysed in this chapter, it is not art that imitates life but the opposite. Particularly significant in this respect is the last section of the film, entitled 'The Entombment', in which a young Michele dressed as an angel for the Easter procession invites his older friend Pasqualone to follow him into a dark room where a tableau vivant of *The Entombment of Christ* is being staged. The most striking detail of this tableau vivant is the fact that the face of Christ is that of the older Michele. Jarman is pushing the theme of the relationship between art and life a step further by introducing the idea of the artist murdered by his own art. This notion, of course, was already present in the Medusa painting if we look at it as a self-portrait of the artist. As noted by Bersani and Dutoit, although Christ was not martyred by art, his identity has been 'at once exalted and martyred by centuries of representation' (p. 48). The same can be said of Medusa as 'she lives after death through literary and artistic representations' (Murray, p. 141). The idea of the artist murdered by art would particularly appeal to Jarman as, like Caravaggio, he was often in trouble as a result of his works: Caravaggio's paintings were often rejected by the original commissioners and Jarman's films were frequently highly controversial. In an interview with Derek Malcolm on the night of the premiere at the British Film Institute, Jarman complained that film critics often used his films as a platform for launching personal attacks against him as an individual,[93] a declaration that immediately reminds us of the section of *Caravaggio* in which Baglione uses the excuse of writing about Michele's works to slander his personality and accuse him of corruption. According to Baglione the 'second Michelangelo' had stolen the commission for the first St Matthew painting in a 'conspiracy between church and gutter' (58:08–58:15).

The last section of the film is also interesting in terms of its allusions to the opening one. The image of Michele holding the young Jerusaleme in his arms returns at the very end of the film as one of Jerusaleme's flashbacks whilst he is trying to tell the story of Michele's life through sign language. The circular structure is important as it represents a reiteration of the theme of death (or the oscillation between life and death), which plays a prominent role throughout the entire film and is explored through circular movements recalling either those of the vortex or of the 'danse macabre'. In section 3, for instance, we see Michele dressed as the personification of death surrounded by Jerusaleme and another young man on a horse who frantically dances around the painter's studio. Jerusaleme, who wears a death mask on the back of his head, laughs and blows his whistle. At the same time, he waves a big red flag with big circular movements, which remind us of Michele's gesture in the previous scene when, having difficulties with one of his paintings, he takes out his knife and draws huge circular lines that join two characters, one of which (the one on the right) looks more like a skull than a person. The sense of oscillation between life and death is emphasized by Michele's use of the knife, which, as we have already seen, is a highly symbolic object expressing precisely both life and death.[94] Significantly, in section 3 ('Stillness'), a black screen twice marks the transition from one image to the next and darkness is synonymous with both death and desire. Jarman seems to use Caravaggio in order to stress the connection between art, death, and sexuality/desire.[95] As Michele shows us, there is no art without passion: he is finally able to complete the *Martyrdom of St Matthew* only after having met Ranuccio, to whom he is physically attracted. Art, however, is similar to death, not just because of its affinity to the concept of *jouissance* as an identity-shattering experience, but, because it reveals to us the limits of representation, the limits of mimesis. As Michele keeps reminding us, there is more to flesh and blood than a clever combination of pigments skilfully applied on canvas can express. In section 5 ('He loves me, loves me not'), after the fight with Ranuccio, which leaves him with a stab wound on his side, Michele says to Davide who is drying him and cleaning him: 'in the wound the question is answered; all art is against lived experience. How can you compare flesh and blood with oil around pigment?' (38:43–38:57). The comparison of art with death returns in section 7 ('Unveiling'), where the unveiling of *Profane Love* takes place in a basement, or better catacomb-like environment, dominated by dust and images of death (skulls, bones, cobwebs, mummified saints, circular dances, etc.). This can also be seen as an allusion to the section of the 'Medusa' chapter when Michele buys Jerusaleme and the boy's grandmother, whilst counting Michele's money, says rather enigmatically: 'the stars are the diamonds of the poor; rich men hide their diamonds in vaults, embarrassed to compare them to the riches of the Lord that sparkle in the sky' (04:02–04:18). Taken in conjunction with Caravaggio's *Profane Love*, a painting that shows culture, the arts and military glory defeated by 'a love that has nothing spiritual about it',[96] the old woman's words become a comment on the impossibility for art to imitate life. However, they also seem to suggest that despite the futility and transience of all material wealth, no human being is free from lust for money and other symbols of power. For all her wisdom, she is carefully counting the 'thirty pieces of silver' Michele gave her which, as noted by Pencak, was 'the price Judas received for betraying Christ'.[97]

The other image of death that recurs throughout the film, the vortex, is particularly prominent in the scenes involving Lena's death and, significantly, when her body floats in the river, the voiceover compares her to Medusa: 'your hair streams out, dark as the Medusa weed' (1:05:27). A few minutes later, when Lena's body has been taken out of the water and cleaned so that Michele can use her as a model for 'Death of the Virgin',[98] the voiceover reporting Michele's thoughts as he is embracing Lena for the last time says:

> I float on the glassy surface of the still dark lake, lamp-back in the night, silent as an echo; a mote in your eyes. You blink and send me spinning. Swallowed in the vortex, I shoot through the violent depths. The unutterable silence of these waters. A tear forms and drops; a ripple spreads out beyond the farthest horizon, beyond matter, scintilla, star. I love you more than my eyes. (1:11:10–1:11:44)

Building on Murray's notion of 'wounded rotation', Bersani and Dutoit suggest that circular movements represent 'a "return" in death to the intrauterine immersion in a liquid which originally nourished us into life and which has now become a death shared with the mother in a devouring vortex' (*Caravaggio*, p. 77). Since, as we have already seen, Michele identifies with Christ and Lena is used as a model for the Virgin Mary, the scenes devoted to Lena's death represent Michele's (Jarman's) homage to the (his) mother; or better, they represent a longing for the mother that 'proposes a modification of the classic view of homosexual desire as deriving from an Oedipal configuration in which the boy's primary love is for the father and the mother is in the position of the rival' (*Caravaggio*, p. 78). This homage acquires an extra significance if we consider, as noted by Wymer, that Tilda Swinton (who plays Lena) 'had a definite physical resemblance to Jarman's own mother' (p. 105).

Like Bersani and Dutoit, Wymer concludes that Jarman uses *Caravaggio* to depict homosexuality as 'an inconsolable heterosexuality' (Wymer, p. 105; Bersani and Dutoit, p. 78). I would also argue that through the identification of Lena with both the Virgin Mary and Medusa, Jarman subverts the myth of Medusa as 'the Terrible Mother archetype, like Kali, Hecate or Circe, from whom the (male) hero must free himself or risk being devoured and rendered powerless' (Wymer, p. 100). Jerusaleme's mother is another female figure who could be perceived as potentially evil, as she is prepared to sell her own son. However, like McCance's Medusa, she is portrayed as powerless. At the beginning of the first section, when Michele purchases Jerusaleme, she stands silently to one side. Towards the end of that scene, the camera focuses on the movement of her head as she watches her son leave, tears streaming from her eyes. This is an image that encourages the viewer to sympathize with her, rather than look at her with hostility. Neuroscientific research on mirror neurons, in fact, has demonstrated that movement in imagery enables empathetic responses. 'The mirror neurons provide a basic link between the viewer and the seen'; since they are situated in the area of the brain responsible for emotion and emotional expression, 'seeing and making a particular facial expression of an emotion and experiencing that emotion involves the same area of the brain'.[99] Tears, as we know, are very important in the whole film; they represent one of the elements that connect its various sections, promoting haptic visuality.

The aforementioned sequence devoted to Michele's erotic embrace of Lena's dead body is seen by Murray as a direct quotation of Pasolini's *Oedipus Rex*, 'in which shattered heroes embrace lifeless female doubles' (Murray, p. 151). This reference to Pasolini is important not just as evidence of Jarman's fascination with the Italian director, but because, as suggested by Torlasco, Pasolini turns Oedipus into a kind of detective who does not want to see, 'repeatedly covering his eyes with his left hand to shield himself against the blinding light, desperately trying not to know'.[100] References to blindness and to a reluctance to look abound throughout Jarman's film. We only need to think of the scene when Jerusaleme turns towards the camera holding a reflective panel to blind the viewer and protect himself and the spectator (of which he is the embodiment) from something he does not want to see/acknowledge, that is, Michele's homoerotic attraction to Ranuccio. Similarly, when, during the section devoted to *Profane Love*, Michele and Lena passionately kiss each other in front of Pippo (the girl who posed as Cupid) and a jealous Ranuccio, Jerusaleme, unlike Ranuccio, averts his eyes; when Lena dies and Cardinal Del Monte closes her eyes, Jerusaleme does not want to look at her and holds a white lantern towards the camera which shelters the viewer from the sight of Lena's lifeless face. Jarman, like Lacan, seems to suggest that 'Oedipus reminds us that we cannot understand ourselves except through words, metaphors, which are deceptive and ambiguous signs'.[101] Like Caravaggio's paintings, they invite interpretation, but will always leave a gap between signifier and signified for alternative readings. Also, if, as Kenneth MacKinnon suggests, it is possible to interpret the dread underlying Sophocles' *Oedipus Rex* (on which Pasolini's film is based) 'as anxiety at watching the ideas of democracy being betrayed by Athens', we could argue that the references to Oedipus in *Caravaggio* are the expression of

Jarman's anxiety concerning the loss of traditional values in British society during the Thatcher era (1979–90). This kind of reading seems justified if we consider one of the most powerful references to blindness and Oedipus in the film, namely the image of Michele's corpse whose closed eyes are covered by coins. As we know, money, in the form of savings, cuts, and deregulation, was always an essential and controversial factor of many government policies during the Thatcher era, which led to a less fair society with an increased gap between the rich and the poor (a society which, in a certain way, could be said to resemble that of Baroque Italy). References to money, as we have already seen, are omnipresent in *Caravaggio* and represent one of the elements connecting all the sections of the film. Money is presented as the darker side of desire, a form of desire even more powerful and destructive than its sexual counterpart. All human relationships in the film are conditioned by money, even the most unselfish one between Michele and Jerusaleme, as Michele initially bought his assistant/companion. If we take Michele, Ranuccio, and Lena we see how money is what determines changes in the dynamics of their relationships: when Michele first meets Ranuccio he buys his (and to a certain extent Lena's) attention by offering him a gold coin. Coins again play a prominent role when Ranuccio is posing for Michele's *Martyrdom of St Matthew*. Coins function as erotic toys between Ranuccio and Lena; later in the film, Ranuccio tells a jealous Lena that he 'fucks' Michele for money. Lena passionately kisses Michele only after he gives her a pair of pearl earrings. Another interesting example of the pervasiveness of lust for wealth is Lena's attitude towards Scipione Borghese. She becomes interested in him only when she finds out that he is the nephew of the pope and when she discovers she is pregnant by him she triumphantly informs Michele and a dismayed Ranuccio that her child 'will be rich beyond avarice' (1:05:06). Finally, Davide accuses Michele of wanting the impossible and Lena tells Ranuccio that she wants much more than he could possibly imagine.

References to money are also used to illustrate another important theme: the relationship between art and power. In the section of the film entitled 'Bacchus', the young Michele tries to arouse sexually one of his clients by telling him that he (that is, his body) is an art object and a very expensive one, whilst putting the blade of his knife in his mouth in a gesture that cannot but make us think of Foucault's remarks on sadomasochism and the Greek male at the end of *The Use of Pleasure* (the second volume of the *History of Sexuality*).[102] When Michele agrees to paint the portrait of Paul V, the pope tells him that art is always connected to power and that there is no such thing as a revolutionary art: 'revolutionary gestures in art can be a great help to us. Bet you hadn't thought about that, you little bugger. Keeps the quo in the status. Never heard of a revolution made with paint brushes' (1:19:30–1:19:44). When Cardinal Del Monte has dinner with Marquis Giustiniani and complains that the Vatican is concerned about the expensive loan rates he is proposing, Giustiniani replies that Caravaggio's fees are also expensive and reminds Del Monte that he purchased the rejected *St Matthew* and he is commissioning *Profane Love*. Ellis, commenting on the golden calculator Giustiniani holds in his hands, points out that this anachronistic detail functions as a reminder of how 'commerce was just as much a factor in the production of art then as it is now' (p. 122). Murray proposes

CARAVAGGIO AND HOMOEROTIC CONCERNS 159

FIG. 4.7. Caravaggio, *The Martyrdom of St Matthew* (c. 1599–1600), Rome: San Luigi dei Francesi.

a very interesting interpretation of 'Michele's shining eyes of death', suggesting that they 'can be understood not only to allude to the sublime supplement of economic rationality but also to signify their affinity to the specifically *ocular* economy of sexual difference imprinted in Western letters since Oedipus' (p. 128), which the film tried to demystify. Similarly, Richardson highlights the contrasting functions the gold coins have in the film. The fact that they are used both as 'toys of heterosexual foreplay between Lena and Ranuccio', and as Michele's 'means of seducing Ranuccio' (p. 98), makes them similar to 'the blinding light shone directly into the camera', which prevents the spectator from making reductive readings, particularly in questions of sexuality and identity. Focusing on Michele, Ranuccio, and Lena, Richardson argues that 'the narrative offers neither a "gay romance" nor a "homosocial triangle". It deliberately confuses issues of love, sexuality and sexual identification' (p. 96) and concludes by saying that: '*Caravaggio* attests to the power (and danger) of desire to dissolve sexual identities and, ultimately, render its subjects unclassifiable'.[103]

As noted by Cropper, the group of Caravaggio's paintings most frequently associated with homoeroticism (his early 'boy'/musical paintings) are interesting also for their literary associations, particularly those to Petrarchan lyricism.[104] By the mid-1590s (Caravaggio completed his 'Lute Player' in 1596), however, the overused voice of Petrarchism had been changed and revitalized in a virtuoso and highly self-conscious way by the poet Giambattista Marino (a friend of Caravaggio's), who had provided a model for a new kind of *poesie per musica*. Marino's madrigals, instead of addressing the absent beloved, were full of references to Amphion and Orpheus or Pygmalion and Medusa; they problematized the power of music and art (Cropper, p. 51). Cropper interprets Caravaggio's musical paintings, through references to Marino, as comments about the value of beauty without piety or love. Unlike Petrarch's, Caravaggio's and Marino's images are too vividly real to be able to alleviate loss (pp. 52–53). According to Cropper, Marino and Caravaggio tend to include lyrical moments in historical or religious themes. Interestingly, our final case study for this chapter, the 1989 novel *The Caravaggio Shawl* by the American writer Samuel M. Steward, features an imaginary Caravaggio painting that addresses the issue of desire but, through the inclusion of a lyrical moment, provides also a model of interaction that 'escapes the violence of human desire by enacting its independence from either the demands or presumed secrets of subjectivity'.[105] The subject of the painting is Orpheus leading Eurydice out of Hades, another myth about the gaze, the voice, and the power of art.

Samuel M. Steward's *The Caravaggio Shawl*

Despite having being described by David Bergman as 'a remarkable figure in gay literary history',[106] Samuel M. Steward (1909–93) is almost unknown outside American Gay and Lesbian Studies and his life story is one of 'obsession, isolation and failure'.[107] From the moment Steward obtained his PhD in 1934, he taught for several years at various colleges and American universities including Washington State University, Loyola University of Chicago, and De Paul University. However, he found that creative writing and teaching were becoming progressively more incompatible. As early as 1936, the depiction of prostitution in his novel *Angels on the Bough* (1936) cost him his job at the State College of Washington, so, in the 1950s, he decided to quit academia to start a new career as a skid-row tattoo artist, setting up a parlour in a seedy district of Chicago. As a writer, he is best remembered as Phil Andros (an obvious pun on the Greek terms for 'love' and 'man'), the pseudonym 'under which he wrote, starting with *$tud* in 1966, a celebrated series of pornographic novels in the voice of a well-read indefatigable hustler' (Bergman, p. 151). Steward was obsessed with sex and, from a very early age, documented every single sexual encounter (including Rudolph Valentino) and experience, particularly after meeting Alfred Kinsey (the founder of the Sex Research Institute at Indiana University) in 1949. When he died of a pulmonary disease in 1993, he left behind a wealth of material in terms of diaries, photographs, drawings, and various sexual paraphernalia. If considered as 'a single lifelong body of work', as Justin Spring stated in his biography of Steward, these documents represent an attempt 'to demystify homosexuality for generations to come' (p. 14) and are an important resource for anybody interested in researching homosexual lives in the first half of the twentieth century. In fact, according to Spring, Steward 'evoked the world in which he moved more vividly than any anthropologist or social historian' (p. 13). Spring considers Steward's preoccupation with the nature of his homosexuality to be directly linked to the austere Puritanism of two maiden aunts who brought him up after the sudden death of his mother when he was only six years of age and his father (an alcoholic and drug user) was unable to care for his children (p. 17).

Apart from writing erotica, Steward was also the author of two murder mysteries (inspired by the whodunit genre) featuring Gertrude Stein and Alice Toklas as detectives. *The Caravaggio Shawl*[108] is the second volume of what was meant to be a series of four books, only two of which were completed. The first volume, entitled *Murder is Murder is Murder*, was published in 1985. Steward started corresponding with Stein and Toklas in 1932 when he was still a student and he met them in Paris in 1937. From a literary perspective, these are highly disappointing works of fiction 'of little value even to those interested in the lives of Stein and Toklas' (Spring, p. 396), but *The Caravaggio Shawl* deserves to be mentioned in this book as evidence of how Caravaggio has been appropriated by popular culture, and also because it sheds light on the features in Caravaggio's works which appeal to homoerotic authors. As in the case of the other artists we analysed in this chapter, Steward's interest in Caravaggio is multifaceted. Given Steward's background, it is obvious that he must have seen in the Lombard painter a kindred spirit who, through the creative process, was trying to tie up 'his disrupted personality components into a meaningful coherence'.[109] As for Caravaggio's works, the death drive and sadomasochistic traces visible in many of his works such as *David with the Head of Goliath*, *The Sacrifice of Isaac*, or *The Flagellation of Christ* must have appealed to Steward. Most of his fictional writing, in fact, focuses on sadomasochism as the only possible way for men to deal with the weakening of masculinity caused by the disappearance of the 'Hero' from 'a "modern world" that has been despoiled by "automation"'.[110] However, Steward must have also been aware of the lyrical element present in most of Caravaggio's paintings, and particularly in those early works with mythological or musical subjects, which, as mentioned above, are full of allusions to Petrarch. Interestingly, apart from writing novels and short stories, Steward was also a poet and, in 1933, he had published an essay on Petrarch in the *Sewanee Review*.

In terms of plot, the novel begins with Gertrude (Stein) and Alice (Toklas) visiting the Louvre to see a newly discovered Caravaggio painting which Italy had donated to the French government in exchange for a lucrative trade agreement on the export of perfumes and fragrances that would make Italy the leading perfumer in Europe. The work in question, which is entitled *Orpheus leading Eurydice out of Hades*, dates approximately to 1590 and represents an example of Caravaggio's early style of painting. Unfortunately, shortly after its unveiling in the Louvre, the *Orpheus* is stolen and replaced with a copy without anyone from the famous art gallery noticing the substitution. The crime is accidentally discovered by Alice when she returns to the museum with the mundane intention of comparing the colour of a few woollen yarns to the shade of pink on Orpheus's heel, which Gertrude had admired the previous day, as she wants to knit a scarf for her beloved friend. Naturally, the area around the painting is cordoned off, and there are signs forbidding viewers to get too close to the work of art. However, Alice, who is used to dusting and cleaning masterpieces of all kinds in her own house, ignores the prohibition in order to get a colour match as accurate as possible for her scarf. In doing so she realizes that the painting is still wet as 'the snippet of yarn clung like a small pink caterpillar to the left foot of Orpheus' (*TCS*, p. 34). Alice alerts the public and one of the guards that what they are admiring is not the same painting she had seen the previous day, but a forgery. While waiting to be seen by the museum's curator, she also discovers the dead body of a man which turns out to be that of Claude Duval, the husband of Alice's and Gertrude's housemaid Madeleine: 'it lay on its side, the face turned partly away [...] The skull was broken — a horrid grey mass showed through' (*TCS*, p. 39). The rest of the novel consists of Gertrude's and Alice's attempt at solving both the theft and the murder as they promised Madeleine they would 'find the beast that killed Claude' (*TCS*, p. 73). Thanks to Alice and Gertrude, in the end, the reader discovers that both crimes were connected and that Claude had been killed by the thief for having turned up in the wrong place at the wrong time (*TCS*, p. 202). The painting had been stolen by a greedy and violent police officer who was acting on behalf of a corrupt collector named François Rideau. Rideau, also a film-maker, had commissioned a mediocre painter to copy the original Caravaggio, persuading him to accept the task by promising him an exhibition in a major gallery and some buyers for his works. Significantly, his name is Vain Bénitier, which means empty holy-water font (*TCS*, p. 48), as if to stress that his desire for fame is inversely proportional to his artistic mediocrity. Like Jarman, Steward seems keen to suggest that greed is one of the prime motors for all human activities, but particularly in the art world. Bénitier, who is also a lover of the corrupt police officer, is the one who, in the end, reveals enough details to Alice and Gertrude to enable them to solve both crimes. Once the police officer realizes that he is about to be found out, he tries to set a trap for Alice and Gertrude and is planning to kill them in a room above the Arc de Triomphe. The two old ladies, however, go to the appointment well prepared and have him arrested. Unable to deal with the shame, he hangs himself in his prison cell.

All the characters have same-sex relationships and, with the exception of Alice and Gertrude, all are obsessed with sex or, more precisely, with sadomasochistic sex. Even the names of several male protagonists have sexual connotations: the corrupt police officer is called Renculé, an obvious allusion to the French slang term 'enculé', which means 'bugger', 'cocksucker', 'prick'; one of the police officer's several lovers is called Jaquot, a colloquial term for dildo; the traffic warden who works opposite the Church of St Germaine des Près is called Quisse, meaning 'thighs'; and Bénitier, apart from meaning 'holy-water font', is also 'a horrid argot name for an unmentionable part of a woman's anatomy' (*TCS*, p. 48). No reader could ignore the sexual meanings of these names as the author provides the English translation. The sexual acts these characters perform are rather brutal: Renculé, for instance, has the habit of piercing the buttocks of his lovers with a corkscrew twice during intercourse and invites them to 'wear their wounds' with pride. Similarly, the language they use to address each other is often vulgar and aggressive; derogatory terms relating to their sexuality such as 'enculé' or 'pédé' feature prominently whenever they speak.

As already mentioned, the first thing of interest to us is the title of the imaginary Caravaggio, *Orpheus Leading Eurydice out of Hades*, and the alleged dating (1590), which would make it belong to Caravaggio's early Roman works. Orpheus, as a mythological figure, is commonly associated both with music and writing. Also, according to the legend, having failed to rescue his wife Eurydice out of Hades, Orpheus forswore the love of women and took only youths as his lovers. As Alice suggests, Orpheus 'introduced homosexual love into Greece', but in her reading of the ancient myth, 'he deliberately freed himself of Eurydice so that he might return to his copins' (*TCS*, p. 18). Alice's remarks seem to endorse Bernstock's views that with the death of Eurydice Orpheus 'appears to have withdrawn the narcissistic libido he had invested in her back into his own ego, which identified with the lost object — Eurydice — and begun to form homosexual relationships'.[111] Orpheus, of course, was also the subject of a poem by Marino (belonging to the 1620 collection of idylls, *La zampogna*) and the title of one of Monteverdi's operas (first performed in 1607). Finally, *Orphée* is also a film by Jean Cocteau (1949) starring Jean Marais (who was also his lover). Interestingly, both Cocteau and Marais feature in *The Caravaggio Shawl* as friends of the art collector Rideau and the police officer/thief/murderer Renculé. As noted by Bernstock, Cocteau 'was most interested in the death and rebirth of Orpheus which he expressed in the phoenix, his favourite symbol for his own life and art', particularly 'his post-opium returns to life and creativity' (p. 165). It could be argued that, like Cocteau, Steward, who was also a drug user, identified with Orpheus to reflect on the nature of the creative process. In the novel, however, no reference is made to Orpheus' death. If there is an Orpheus-like character, this is Alice, who challenges the law (the signs and the cordon around the painting) to pursue knowledge. However, like Orpheus, who did not 'succeed to see Eurydice "in the flesh"' but only 'Eurydice receding into her own image',[112]

Alice is confronted with a copy of the original painting. Like Orpheus, who transgresses the law 'in order to fulfil his undying passion for Eurydice',[113] Alice's motivation in ignoring the museum's regulations is her love for Gertrude: she wants to knit her a scarf or better a shawl, as the title of the novel suggests, using the exact shade of pink Caravaggio had used for Orpheus' heel. Unlike Orpheus, though, Alice is not an artist. Nevertheless, it could be argued that, as Gertrude's alter ego, in a way she is, and that through these two characters Steward is trying to tell his readers that, if desire is central to artistic inspiration in everyday life, only a love that goes beyond desire can allow the individual to transcend the limits of subjectivity. As the following quote seems to suggest, without Alice's devotion and self-effacing nature, the success of Gertrude's 'autobiography' of her lover and companion would not have been as great:

> And Alice — who before her 'autobiography' appeared had confined herself to the shadows of love, always caring for Gertrude, typing, running errands, cooking — Alice of the shadows was dragged into daylight to share modestly in the new wave of recognition and fame. (*TCS*, p. 12)

Here, of course, it is Gertrude who, like Orpheus, betrays Alice, when at the end of the 'autobiography' she confesses that she is its author. She thus consigns Alice, if not entirely to the shadows, at least to the semi-shadows.

But let us return to this allegedly newly discovered painting of Orpheus leading Eurydice out of Hades. Although the only description of the work should convey Alice's and Gertrude's impressions as they attend its official unveiling in the Louvre amongst a 'crowd of notables' (*TCS*, p. 16) including De Gaulle, the perspective is clearly that of a gay male whose gaze enjoys lingering on the well-built and totally naked figure of Orpheus.[114] The reference to Orpheus' genitals, fully visible despite a 'filmy gauze' trying to conceal them, and the detail of his penis with the foreskin 'retracted over the glans' (*TCS*, p. 19), are meant to arouse the male viewer/reader. This kind of gaze is encouraged by the work itself as Eurydice features only as 'a shadowy and vaguely feminine form standing nearly waist deep in a horrid pool of decay' (*TCS*, p. 18). As far as Orpheus is concerned, we are told that apart from his nudity the most striking aspect was the expression on his face: 'an expression almost as enigmatic as that of the Mona Lisa, a kind of cruelly sexual half-smile suggesting that he was pleased to be rid of the woman who had taken him to the underworld in his love for her' (*TCS*, p. 18). On the one hand, this passage reminds us of Blanchot's interpretation of Orpheus' task of rescuing Eurydice as an impossible one[115] and, on the other, it make us think of Foucault's remarks on the nature of homosexual love in a 1983 interview. As Heather Love points out regarding the 1983 interview:

> Foucault speculated that the 'best moment' in the life of a homosexual is 'likely to be when the lover leaves in the taxi'. Foucault links this feeling to the availability of homosexual contacts [...] But at the moment he invokes this explanation, Foucault also gestures toward a history of queer feeling grounded in the social impossibility of homosexual love. Foucault's desire for the boy has a queer specificity [...] He wants the love of *that* boy, already receding into the distance — not the daytime love, the easy intimacies of a domestic partner. He wants him in the taxi, just as Orpheus wants Eurydice in the night, in the underworld.[116]

As we have already mentioned, all the male characters in the novel are obsessed with sex and have no difficulty in finding partners, sometimes even more than one in the same day, but the 'social impossibility of homosexual love' was certainly a reality Steward experienced. As Spring notes in the afterward to Steward's biography, Steward grew up in world in which sexuality was not discussed and his determination to be true to himself came at a price; the files documenting his sexual activities over the years demonstrate 'just how difficult a set of circumstances and prejudices surrounded and shaped his everyday existence' (Spring, p. 409). Having lost his mother when he was very young and having had an extremely problematic relationship with his father, Steward had been deprived of close emotional relationship during his childhood and adolescence and struggled to develop intimate bonds with people for the rest of his life. It could be argued, though, that in *The Caravaggio Shawl*, which was published only five years before he died, Steward was expressing a longing for a form of love based on tenderness. The last five chapters of the book seem to suggest the need to transcend the sadomasochistic model of interaction between two adults. The character through which such desire is voiced is Johnny, one of Alice's and Gertrude's American friends. Like all male characters in the novel, Johnny is a homosexual who enjoys both inflicting and having pain inflicted during intercourse. However, Johnny's personality reveals also a romantic touch. Whenever he wants to meet a man in the hope of finding a new sexual partner, he sends him a love poem (usually a sonnet[117]) with his telephone number written on it. Also, when Johnny and the traffic warden Quisse finally meet, Johnny's fantasies involve 'the mysterious magic of high romance' (*TCS*, p. 184) and he wishes that 'one could live entirely by remembering the best quotations for every event that transpired in one's life' (*TCS*, p. 184). A few lines further down, reflecting on his relationship with Quisse, Johnny says: 'this very encounter could be covered perhaps by a mélange of Shakespeare, Whitman, Gide, Mann and a few others, perhaps some songs from the *Arabian Nights* ... even lines from the Bible, the *Song of Solomon*' (*TCS*, p. 184). Such remarks, of course, come across as ironic and could be interpreted as a need to aestheticize his normally brutal sexual practices or, as Varriano said about Caravaggio, 'to justify his most shocking imagery through imitation' (Varriano, p. 63). However, they also seem to suggest something else. The fact that the novel begins and ends with a reference to the Caravaggio shawl forces the reader to focus on a different form of love, that between Alice and Gertrude, which is not based on eroticism but affection and tenderness. The shawl of the title is precisely the symbol of such tenderness, as the passage in which Alice finally gives her knitted garment to Gertrude reveals:

> 'For you, Lovey,' said Alice. She draped it gently around Gertrude's neck. 'Don't you remember? You admired the colour on the Caravaggio painting, and I made it for you. Every stitch put in with love, all my love.' [...] 'We shall call it the Caravaggio Shawl' said Gertrude. 'Or perhaps it is a sharf or a scawl — since it is wider and yet narrower than either' (*TCS*, p. 209)

To conclude, what the analysis of these very diverse authors and film-makers has shown is that the homoerotic reappropriation of Caravaggio transcends the debates on the painter's sexuality. It is the open-ended nature of many of his paintings that makes Caravaggio particularly attractive to queer discourses. Whether we think of his early Roman paintings or some of his later religious works, they all resist restrictive, universalizing readings and force the viewer to question any preconceived ideas. Also, Caravaggio's chiaroscuro technique can easily be turned into a metaphor for the tension between life and death, or civilization and desire, as all the fictional works we have analysed in this chapter have shown. Finally, Caravaggio's ability to add a lyrical moment to the depiction of the links between sexuality and death (e.g. *David with the Head of Goliath*) offers gay artists an ideal platform for exploring different forms of gay love. What emerges in these contemporary reinterpretations of our Baroque painter is the subversive power of his works, which is why his influence extends also to postcolonial discourses, as the case of Ondaatje and Minghella reveals.

Notes to Chapter 4

1. Michel Foucault, *The History of Sexuality*, 3 vols, trans. by Robert Hurley (London: Penguin Books, 1998), I, 101.
2. Berenson, *Caravaggio: Delle sue incongruenze e della sua fama*, p. 70. For full bibliographical references see chapter 1, note 38. What is interesting about the word 'novelletta', a diminutive form of 'novella', is that it carries the connotation of 'gossip' or 'slander', whilst the use of the diminutive suggests something unimportant, of little value.
3. Donald Posner, 'Caravaggio's Homo-erotic Early Works', *The Art Quarterly*, 34 (1971), 301–24 (p. 302). For further homoerotic readings of Caravaggio's paintings, see also Howard Hibbard, *Caravaggio* (Boulder, CO and Oxford: Westview Press, 1985); Leo Bersani and Ulysse Dutoit, *Caravaggio's Secrets* (Cambridge, MA and London: MIT Press, 1998).
4. Andrea McTigue, '"Resisting, by embracing, nothingness": Reflections of Caravaggio (1573–1610) and his Art in Contemporary Literature', in *Text into Image: Image into Text*, ed. by Jeff Morrison and Florian Krobb (Amsterdam: Rodopi, 1997), pp. 95–104 (pp. 96, 97).
5. Genevieve Warwick, 'Allegories of Eros: Caravaggio's Masque', in *Caravaggio: Realism, Rebellion, Reception*, ed. by Genevieve Warwick (Newark: University of Delaware Press, 2006), pp. 82–90 (p. 88). In her seminal article, Warwick suggests that Caravaggio's early paintings should be analysed in terms not only of their historical context but also of the tension between ordinary and often easily recognizable models used and the role they played, which prevented the viewer from totally identifying them with their mythological personas, thus exposing 'an uncomfortable gap between the cultural aspiration of his patrons projected onto singers, actors, and models, and the social world of the street from which many of these performers came' (p. 83). In this way, Warwick concludes, these paintings 'both evoke the literary anesthetisation of courtly Socratic love by a courtly, poetic culture and unveil it as constructed around a social order of patronage relations and power' (p. 88).
6. Dominique Fernandez, *Dans la main de l'ange* (Paris: Bernard Grasset, 1982); abbreviated as *DMA*. All translations into English are mine.
7. Despite the popular myth about his death, Caravaggio was not killed by an attacker. He died of a viral infection in a hospital in Porto Ercole, and not on the beach as previously believed.
8. Cesare Garboli, 'Ricordo di Longhi', *Nuovi Argomenti*, 1 (1970), p. 39.
9. Significantly, these remarks were used by Chris Stephens to characterize Bacon and Caravaggio for the catalogue of the 'Caravaggio Bacon' exhibition which was held at the Galleria Borghese in Rome in 2009–10: *Caravaggio Bacon*, ed. by Anna Coliva and Michael Peppiatt (Milan: Federico Motta, 2009), p. 67. The works of Bacon are one of the many meta-narrative allusions in Pasolini's film *Teorema* (1967).
10. Frédéric Martel, *The Pink and the Black: Homosexuals in France since 1968* (Palo Alto: Stanford University Press, 2000), p. 147.
11. Robert Aldrich, *The Seduction of the Mediterranean* (London: Routledge, 1993), p. 197.

12. Lawrence R. Schehr, *Parts of an Andrology: On Representations of Men's Bodies* (Palo Alto: Stanford University Press, 1997), p. 159.
13. Robert Aldrich and Garry Wotherspoon, *Who's Who in Contemporary Gay and Lesbian History*, II: *From World War II to the Present Day* (London: Routledge, 2001), p. 131.
14. From now on the name Pasolini will refer to the historical figure whilst the abbreviation PP will be used to refer to the protagonist of Fernandez's novel. It is also worth remembering that despite the similarity between Pasolini and Fernandez's character, *DMA* is a fictional work. On the relationship between Pasolini and Fernandez's character see Iovinelli, p. 268.
15. Pier Paolo Pasolini, 'Gennariello', in *Lettere Luterane: Il progresso come falso progresso* (Turin: Einaudi, 1976 and 2003), pp. 15–67. Interestingly, the pedagogical treaty entitled 'Gennariello' could be summarized as an invective against conformism, which, as we are about to see, is also a main feature of *DMA*.
16. Frédéric Vitoux, 'Dominique Fernandez parle de l'homosexualité, du sida et du roman', *Nouvel Observateur*, no. 1165 (6 March 1987), p. 55.
17. Fabio Vighi, *Traumatic Encounters in Italian Film: Locating the Cinematic Unconscious* (Bristol: Intellect, 2006), p. 86. As Vighi explains, it is through this fantasy or imaginary construction that 'the subject regulates its relationship with the non-discursive kernel of the Real' (ibid.).
18. Armando Maggi, *The Resurrection of the Body* (Chicago: University of Chicago Press, 2009), p. 28. As we shall later see, the Baroque is very important for Fernandez's PP as he draws an interesting comparison between his contemporary world and Caravaggio's era.
19. Owen Heathcote, Alex Hughes, and James S. Williams, *Gay Signatures: Gay and Lesbian Theory, Fiction and Film in France, 1945–1995* (Oxford: Berg, 1998), p. 54.
20. 'tu veux que les mots correspondent à des faits' [you want words to correspond to facts] (*DMA*, p. 13). In an interesting study of the relationship between art and life in Caravaggio, Giuseppe Resca argues that the work of art (that is the mental process) anticipates life (the moment of action) and that for Caravaggio life must coincide with what he believes since life is truth. Giuseppe Resca, *Caravaggio e il demone della violenza* (Rome: Armando Editore, 2001), p. 18. Regarding the relationship between literature and biography in Pasolini see Maggi, p. 343.
21. Alain Badiou, *St Paul: The Founder of Universalism*, trans. by Ray Brassier (Palo Alto: Stanford University Press, 2003), pp. 55–64.
22. Maggi, *The Resurrection of the Body*, p. 11. Also, Lucille Cairns suggests that for centuries the Pauline texts were considered to be responsible for the introduction of 'the language of sodomy as abomination': Lucille Cairns, *Changing Conceptions of Male and Female Homosexuality: A (French Oriented) Theoretical Perspective*, <http://www.well.ac.uk/cfol/homosexuality.asp> [accessed 12 March 2011].
23. Resca, *Caravaggio e il demone della violenza*, p. 54. Resca also points out that the second version of the *Conversion of St Paul* lacks the element of the sacred; the conversion has become a private affair, something happening in the mind of the saint rather than in public (ibid.). For the significance of this remark, see this chapter's section on Badiou's idea of the conversion as a subjective manifestation of the resurrection of Christ.
24. According to Badiou, Paul's main message is that Jesus (the son of God) died on the cross and was resurrected. Jesus' life, miracles, and teachings are of no interest to Paul as 'the paradox of faith must be brought out as it is, borne by prose into the light of its radical novelty' (p. 33).
25. For Paul, the Christ event is heterogeneous to the law, pure excess over every prescription, grace without concept or appropriate rite. [...] For him who considers that the real is pure event, Jewish and Greek discourses no longer present [...] the paradigm of a major difference for thought. [...] To declare the non-difference between Jew and Greek establishes Christianity's potential universality; to found the subject as division, rather than as perpetuation of a tradition, renders the subjective element adequate to this universality by terminating the predicative particularity of cultural subjects. (Badiou, p. 57)
26. Interestingly, Garboli once described Pasolini as 'un angelo provocatore dalla voce di flauto e miele' [a provocative angel with a flute-and-honey-like voice]: <http://www.pierpaolopasolini.org/prefa.htm> [accessed 13 March 2010]. The word 'angelo' of course is also part of Caravaggio's first name (Michelangelo) and angels featured prominently in his pictures. Angels in fact were often at the centre of controversies such as the one in the first version of the *St Matthew and the*

Angel, where the proximity of the angel to the saint was one of the reasons why the painting was rejected and Caravaggio was accused of 'being disrespectful of the conventions of decorum' (Maurizio Calvesi, 'L'arte eccelsa di un pittore calunniato', in *Caravaggio Bacon*, p. 61).

27. It is worth pointing out that the main intertextual references for this image are Pasolini's *Appunti per un film sull'India* (1968) and his collection of essays *Empirismo eretico* (1972). In his documentary on India, Pasolini engages with the mythical story of an Indian maharajah who let himself be devoured by the cubs of a starving tiger during a harsh winter. In *Empirismo eretico*, as Sam Rohdie reports, Pasolini recalls an episode in his childhood involving an image of a tiger, very similar to that of *DMA*, which Pasolini identifies as one of his early experiences of homosexuality:

    I was five years old and my family was living in Conegliano... One Sunday evening, mum, dad and I had just come back from the cinema. I was waiting for dinner to be ready and I leafed through some advertising handouts that had been given to us at the cinema. I recall only one illustration but I remember it with an exactness that still disturbs me today. How I was riveted by it! ... The illustration represented a man upside-down in the paws of a tiger. Only his head and his back could be seen; the rest of him had disappeared (as I imagined it) in the jaws of the beast. (Sam Rohdie, *The Passion of Pier Paolo Pasolini* (Bloomington: Indiana University Press, 1995), p. 67)

28. S. K. Keltner, *Kristeva* (Cambridge: Polity Press, 2011), p. 46.
29. Julia Kristeva, *Powers of Horror: An Essay on Abjection*, trans. by Leon S. Rudiez (New York: Columbia University Press, 1982), p. 4.
30. The other painting PP is very interested in is the *Martyrdom of St Matthew*, in which he admires the saint's passivity, the absolute lack of any expression of terror for what is about to happen: 'Cette stupeur médusée de l'apôtre devant la jeunesse et la splendeur de son bourreau me laissait tout rêveur' [the apostle's paralysed stupor when confronted with his young and magnificent executioner left me in a state of wonder] (*DMA*, p. 186). Resca has argued that the presence of Caravaggio's self-portrait in this painting shows that Caravaggio had already discovered in himself the drive to kill and be killed and was universalizing in a historical scene his own inner conflict (p. 13).
31. According to Resca, the drive to kill and be killed symbolizes the impossibility of overcoming the dichotomy between good and evil (p. 111), which can be seen as another facet of PP's life paradox: the fact that the more shocking and critical of bourgeois values his works were, the more he seemed to become part of the establishment (*DMA*, p. 59). The term paradox has also been used to describe the life and career of Dominique Fernandez. Aldrich and Wotherspoon, for instance, sketch the following portrait:

    Fernandez is [...] something of a paradox: a gay, formerly married man who had the courage to divorce and come out, who did his bit for the early activist cause, who strongly supported the campaign in France for the variously named *contrat d'union civile* [...]; and yet also a distinguished writer who, in the artistic sphere, laments the passing of age of gay marginality as the loss of the pariah's glory. (*Who's Who in Contemporary Gay and Lesbian History*, p. 132)

32. Niall Richardson, *The Queer Cinema of Derek Jarman* (London and New York: Tauris, 2009), pp. 102–03.
33. Luigi Longo (1900–80) was a prominent Communist politician and leader of the Italian Communist party from 1964 until 1972. Aldo Moro (1916–78) was twice prime minister of Italy, first from 1963 to 1968 and then from 1974 to 1976. He was the leader of the Christian Democratic Party. In 1978 he was kidnapped and after fifty-five days of captivity killed by the Red Brigades (see also Chapter 3 in this book, section on Baldassarri). Giuseppe Saragat (1898–1988) was president of the Italian Republic from 1964 to 1971. He was also the founder and leader of the Italian Democratic Socialist Party.
34. It is worth remembering that Fernandez expressed his disappointment with the 1968 movement in his novel *L'Etoile rose* (1978): this is the story of David, a writer and a teacher, and of his twenty-year younger lover, Alain, a militant Communist who devotes himself passionately to the revolutionary cause only to encounter prejudice and hostility on grounds of his sexual

orientation. Like the Hocquenghem of *L'Après-Mai des faunes*, Fernandez seems to come to the conclusion that 'after May fags are still fags' (Schehr, *Parts of an Andrology*, p. 159); for a perceptive analysis of *L'Etoile rose*, see Marie Thérèse Noiset, 'Dominique Fernandez', in *The Contemporary Novel in France*, ed. by William Thompson (Gainesville: University Press of Florida, 1995), pp. 313–30 (p. 323).Other aspects of the Italian socio-political life attacked in *DMA* are: the involvement of politicians and of members of the Roman high society in sex and drug scandals, as the case of Wilma Montesi demonstrated as early as the 1950s (*DMA*, pp. 318–23); the power of the Church in the 1960s (*DMA*, p. 272); the role of intellectuals (*DMA*, p. 226); the events of Piazza Fontana (DMA, pp. 387–97).

35. Catherine Clément and Julia Kristeva, *The Feminine and the Sacred* (New York: Columbia University Press, 2001), p. 37. On Kristeva's concepts of the abject and of the sacred see also Todd Kesselman, 'The Abject, the Object and the Thing', *Styles of Communication*, 1 (2009), 1–5.
36. Gilles Deleuze, *Masochism* (New York: Zone Books, 1991), p. 88.
37. Calvesi, 'Caravaggio: The Excellent Art of a Slandered Painter', in *Caravaggio Bacon*, ed. by Anna Colivaand Michael Peppiatt, p. 65.
38. 'Mais maintenant je m'en allais tranquille, ayant organisé dans chaque détail ma cérémonie funèbre et signé ma seule oeuvre assurée de survivre à l'oubli' [But now I go in peace, having organized my funeral down to the very last detail and signed my only work guaranteed to survive oblivion] (*DMA*, p. 455).
39. Thom Gunn (1929–2004) was born in Kent (England), the eldest son of two journalists. His parents divorced when he was ten and his mother committed suicide in 1943 whilst Thom was still in his teens. After spending two years in national service and six months in Paris, he registered for a degree in English at Cambridge in 1950. His first collection of poetry (*Fighting Terms*) was published in 1954; in the same year he moved to the United States where he spent the rest of his life. Apart from writing, Gunn held teaching positions at various American universities. Like Dominique Fernandez, Gunn came out only in the 1970s; from that moment onward he wrote openly not only about his sexuality but also about his drug use (mainly his experience with LSD). In the 1980s and 1990s he wrote also about AIDS; one of his most acclaimed collections is *The Man with Night Sweats* (1992), in which he tried to preserve the memory of many of his friends who had fallen victim to the disease. During his career, Gunn was awarded several prizes and awards, both in America and in the UK, including the Levinson Prize, an Arts Council of Great Britain Award, a Rockefeller Award, the W. H. Smith Award, the PEN (Los Angeles) Prize for Poetry, the Sara Teasdale Prize, a Lila Wallace-Reader's Digest Award, the Forward Prize, and fellowships from the Guggenheim and MacArthur foundations. He died in his sleep on 25 April 2004 in his home in San Francisco. Unless otherwise indicated, all references to Gunn's poems are from Thom Gunn, *Collected Poems* (London: Faber and Faber, 1994); abbreviated as *CP*.
40. George Klawitter, 'Piety and the Agnostic Gay Poet: Thom Gunn's Biblical Homoerotics', *Journal of Homosexuality*, 33 (1997), 207–32 (p. 214).
41. Stefania Michelucci, *The Poetry of Thom Gunn*, trans. by Jill Franks (Jefferson, NC: McFarland, 2009), p. 133. The series of poems 'Troubadour: Songs for Jeffrey Dahmer' was initially published privately and only in a second stage included in *Boss Cupid*. The poems are written from the perspective of Dahmer, the American serial killer and sex offender who was beaten to death by an inmate in 1994 and whose abominable crimes included rape, necrophilia, dismemberment, and cannibalism.
42. Jeffrey Meyers, 'Thom Gunn and Caravaggio's *Conversion of St Paul*', *Style*, 44 (2010), 586–90 (p. 586).
43. 'Thom Gunn 1929–2004', *Poetry Foundation*, <http://www.poetryfoundation.org/bio/thom-gunn> [accessed 10 May 2010].
44. Interestingly, Neil Powell begins his section on the poetry of Thom Gunn with the analysis of a poem by Fulke Greville (a contemporary of Caravaggio) in which the author 'defines clarity by describing the workings of confusion', a chiaroscuro style that could 'illuminate Gunn's interest in Greville and at the same time indicate possible approaches to Gunn's own poetry' (Neil Powell, *Carpenters of Light: Some Contemporary English Poets* (Lanham: Rowman & Littlefield Publishers, 1980), p. 19). Michelucci instead argues that in Gunn's early collections his

'existential vision manifests itself in the polarity between inertia and action, between closure and openness, between submission and challenge, generating a deep ambivalence which is partially overcome in the later collections' (p. 54).
45. Clive Wilmer, 'Gunn, Shakespeare, and the Elizabethans', in *At the Barriers*, ed. by Joshua Weiner (Chicago and London: University of Chicago Press, 2009), pp. 45–67 (p. 47).
46. Colin Gills, 'Rethinking Sexuality in Thom Gunn's *The Man with Night Sweats*', *Contemporary Literature*, 50 (2009), 156–82 (p. 168).
47. Alfred Corn links Gunn's interest in existentialism to his homosexuality; existentialism provided 'a philosophical justification to for a sexual propensity already active in his psyche' (Alfred Corn, 'Existentialism and Homosexuality in Gunn's Early Poetry', in *At the Barriers*, pp. 35–44 (p. 38)).
48. Gregg Lambert, *The Return of the Baroque in Modern Culture* (London and New York: Continuum, 2004), p. 22.
49. Interestingly, in describing the two versions of *The Conversion* for his monograph on Caravaggio, which was published more than twenty years after 'In Santa Maria del Popolo', Hibbard uses images that are remarkably similar to those used by Gunn, particularly when presenting the Odaleschi version: 'everything is caught at a split second of crisis that we actually seem to hear. The details are overpowering: gestures ribbons, leaves, plumes' (p. 121). Later, when presenting the Cerasi version he says: 'But when comparing the Odaleschi Paul with the painting in the Cerasi Chapel, which is powerfully simplified, chary of detail, and without divine personification, there seems to be no point of contact' (p. 122).
50. Interestingly, in her analysis of the Cerasi *Conversion*, Jane Taylor argues: 'the painting is all about the loss of boundaries, of mystery, and of rupture'. Jane Taylor, ' "Why do you tear me from myself?": Torture, Truth and the Arts of Counter-Reformation', in *The Rhetoric of Sincerity*, ed. by Ernst Van Alphen, Mieke Bal, and Carel E. Smith (Stanford: Stanford University Press, 2009), pp. 19–43 (p. 42).
51. Roger Warren, '*Troilus and Cressida* (1976)', in *Aspects of Shakespeare's 'Problem Plays'*, ed. by Kenneth Muir and Stanley W. Wells (New York: Cambridge University Press, 1982), pp. 152–53 (p. 152).
52. Lambert, p. 73. Hammill also stresses how Caravaggio's early paintings 'structure their reception through a sense of unknowingness sustained through the viewer's inability to say what it is the painting seems to want its viewer to say' (Graham L. Hammill, *Sexuality and Form: Caravaggio, Marlowe, and Bacon* (Chicago and London: University of Chicago Press, 2000) p. 73).
53. Michelucci, p. 86. On the idea of risk as 'the very excess of life' see also Slavoj Žižek, *The Puppet and the Dwarf: The Perverse Core of Christianity* (Cambridge, MA: MIT Press, 2003), p. 95.
54. On the lack of transcendental meaning in Caravaggio's *Conversion* see Jonathan Goldberg, *The Seeds of Things: Theorizing Sexuality and Materiality in Renaissance* (New York: Fordham University Press, 2009), p. 11.
55. Interestingly, in commenting on Caravaggio's *Conversion* for the Cerasi chapel in Santa Maria del Popolo, Hibbard notes:

> The light that blinds Paul in the painting is joined in the afternoon by real sunlight from the transparent window. When we visit the chapel at that time and look up at the source of light, we see first the vault of the entrance vestibule, where the dove of the Holy Spirit is painted in the centre of a burst of heavenly light. The Holy Spirit was the particular repository of Love. The evil Saul was blinded and converted by the light of God to become the Paul who later defined Love as the chief Virtue, greater even than Faith of Hope (I Corinthians 13:13). With hindsight, we may imagine that Caravaggio skewed the sense of the painting in his own psychological direction; some of his pictures seem to show a longing for an overwhelming, undeserved Grace. (pp. 128–29)

56. Michelucci, for instance, is one of the critics who make no mention of Caravaggio in connection with this poem.
57. Hibbard, p. 243. Hunt sees in this gesture a 'quotation of Michelangelo's Sistine Chapel God and Adam motif' and stresses that, despite its morbidity, this is a painting about faith (Hunt, p. 125).
58. In other words, Caravaggio's paintings challenge fixed identity politics thus creating that liminal

space between identities that Warwick sees as essential in generating 'the suspension of gender' typical of many of Caravaggio's early works (Warwick, p. 88).

59. Michelucci, p. 84. Goldberg in commenting on Bersani and Dutoit's take on Caravaggio's *The Conversion of St Paul* points out how, according to the two theorists, Paul seems to represent something that escapes formulation. What cannot be named, however, is 'called up' in various ways, but the insistence on this 'condition of unnamability' recalls 'the well-known formulation about Sodomy as the crime not to be named among Christians' (*The Seeds of Things*, p. 11).
60. In Gunn, however, sexuality is also used as a metaphor for the isolation and alienation of the individual and his inability to communicate with others (Michelucci, p. 45).
61. Wilmer also points out that the collusion between the philosophical and 'bluntly sexual' meanings of terms like 'will' and 'desire' is prominent in *Troilus and Cressida* (p. 57).
62. See Wilmer, p. 52. Also, in her comments on the second and third stanzas of 'In Santa Maria del Popolo', Michelucci argues that Gunn turns a religious experience into 'the expression of a supreme, perhaps sinful desire, that cannot be ritually exorcised by the redemptive effect brought by Ananias, who in the Bible restores Saul's sight' (p. 84).
63. Michelucci, p. 133. Michelucci identifies similarities also between this poem and 'Iron Man', one of the poems of *Boss Cupid* devoted to the adolescent Dahmer (p. 149).
64. Maggi, p. 83. As we know, for St Paul, homosexuality was perceived as a sign of excessive lust connected to impurity and uncleanliness: Dan O. Via and Robert A. J. Gagnon, *Homosexuality and the Bible: Two Views* (Minneapolis: Fortress Press, 2003), pp. 14 and 55.
65. The multilingual literary magazine *Botteghe Oscure* was published biannually in Rome between 1948 and 1960. As the front cover of issue 18 (Autumn 1956) says, it was 'an international review of new literature' collecting 'unpublished works by the most important writers in prose and poetry of our time'. It was edited by Princess Marguerite Caetani (1880–1963), an American woman who lived in France. In 1911, she married the composer Roffredo Caetani, a member of an ancient aristocratic family from Rome. Marguerite and her husband moved to Rome in 1932. Botteghe Oscure is the name of the street where the Caetanis lived after the Second World War. In a 1990 interview with Michelucci, Thom Gunn claimed that when he first went to Rome for six months in 1954 the only person he knew was Princess Caetani (Michelucci, p. 162), so it is no surprise that Caetani included two of his poems ('Apocryphal' and 'Excursion') in issue 14 in autumn 1954 (pp. 173–75). Significantly, 'Apocryphal' and 'Excursion' were also included in the volume *Botteghe Oscure Reader* (Middletown: Wesleyan University Press, 1974), edited by George Garrett in honour of Caetani's work. For further details on Marguerite Caetani and her husband see Helen Barolini, *The Other Side: Six American Women and the Lure of Italy* (New York: Fordham University Press, 2006), pp. 177–232.
66. Thom Gunn, 'Apocryphal', in *Botteghe Oscure Reader*, edited by George Garrett (Middletown: Wesleyan University Press, 1974), pp. 179–80. All references are from this volume, abbreviated as *BOR*.
67. Through this reference to the weaker position of the older men, Hibbard highlights the previously discussed topos of the challenging of mastery, a feature that, according to Mieke Bal, represents one of the main reasons for the appeal of Caravaggio's *The Sacrifice of Isaac* to contemporary artists: Bal, *Quoting Caravaggio*, p. 147.
68. Catherine Clément, *Syncope: The Philosophy of Rupture* (Minneapolis: University of Minnesota Press, 1994), p. 119. It is also worth remembering that this notion can also be extended to aesthetic practices. It seems to match Gunn's idea of writing as 'a reach into the unknown, an adventuring into places you cannot have predicted, where you find yourself using limbs and organs you didn't know you possessed' (Thom Gunn, *The Occasions of Poetry: Essays in Criticism and Autobiography* (Ann Arbor: University of Michigan Press, 1982), p. 183).
69. Jim Ellis, *Derek Jarman's Angelic Conversations* (Minneapolis: University of Minnesota Press, 2009), p. 89.
70. As noted by Bersani and Dutoit,

> Pasolini is at least in part a stand-in for Jarman himself. Since Pasolini's 'emotional force' is something that Jarman clearly sought to achieve in his own films, we might say that a reincarnated Caravaggio could just as well be Derek Jarman as Pier Paolo Pasolini. (Leo Bersani and Ulysse Dutoit, *Caravaggio* (London: BFI Publishing, 1999), p. 7).

71. According to Richardson, the knife symbolizes 'the tension between art (which, especially in the case of Christian art, is supposed to evoke a sense of transcendence beyond the physical) and the rough, earthly body' (p. 93).
72. Spear; Hibbard; Varriano; Warwick (2006).
73. Joe Orton (1933–67) was a controversial English playwright who became famous for his shocking dark comedies. He was killed at the age of 34 by his lover Kenneth Halliwell. After the murder, Halliwell committed suicide, indicating in his suicide note that Orton's unfaithfulness had driven him to destruction: <http://www.joeorton.org/Pages/Joe_Orton_Intro.html> [accessed 9 September 2011].
74. Bersani and Dutoit remind us that the character Pasqualone has nothing to do with the real Pasqualone (the notary Caravaggio attacked in 1605), but was inspired by Davide, the Italian boy with whom Jarman had become infatuated when, as a child, he briefly lived near Lake Maggiore (p. 33).
75. Leo Bersani and Ulysse Dutoit, *Caravaggio's Secrets* (Cambridge, MA and London: MIT Press, 1998), p. 41.
76. Timothy Murray, *Like a Film* (London: Routledge, 1993), p. 123.
77. The concept of haptic visuality was developed by Laura U. Marks in her seminal work, *The Skin of the Film: Intercultural Cinema, Embodiment and the Senses* (Durham, NC: Duke University Press, 2000), pp. 22 and 188.
78. The rest of the voiceover represents Michele's recollections of his childhood, his mother, and the love of his life, Pasqualone.
79. Significantly, in Jarman's film the painting is also resting on an easel.
80. According to Max Scheler, in heteropathic identification, a form of identification akin to ecstasy and opposed to the Freudian incorporative model, the following happens:

> 'I' (the formal subject) am so overwhelmed and hypnotically bound and fettered by the other 'I' (the concrete individual), that my formal status as a subject is usurped by the other's personality, with all *its* characteristic aspects; in such a case, I live, not in 'myself', but entirely in 'him', the other person — (in and through him, as it were). (Max Scheler, *The Nature of Sympathy* (Piscataway: Transaction Publishers, 2010), p. 19)

81. Kaja Silverman, *Male Subjectivity at the Margins* (London: Routledge, 1992), p. 264. It is worth noting that masochism is one of Jarman's main themes throughout the film and becomes particularly visible in the relationship between Ranuccio and Michele.
82. Mieke Bal, *Double Exposure: The Subject of Cultural Analysis* (London: Routledge, 1996), p. 60.
83. Rowland Wymer, *Derek Jarman* (Manchester: Manchester University Press, 2005), p. 103.
84. Jerusaleme mocking Medusa; Michele mocking Medusa and Jerusaleme; and, later in the film, Jerusaleme blinding the audience with a reflective shield.
85. Significantly, the word 'loyal' is used by Jerusaleme's grandmother when bidding goodbye to him: 'the gentleman is conferring a great honour to our family. Be faithful and loyal, like the men of our country'. 'Friendship' is the term that in Michele's mind captures his relationship to Jerusaleme. The voiceover conveying to the viewer Michele's thoughts just before he dies says: 'to think Jerusaleme that our friendship should end in this room, this cold white room so far from home'. The only time we see Michele kissing Jerusaleme in the film (section 3) it is a tender, non-erotic kiss. Michele kisses Jerusaleme on his forehead and Jerusaleme (who is lying on the floor) in return embraces Michele's legs.
86. Jennifer M. Barker, *The Tactile Eye: Touch and the Cinematic Experience* (Berkeley and Los Angeles: University of California Press, 2009), p. 38.
87. As Richardson reminds us, although at the time of *Caravaggio* Jarman was not yet aware of being HIV positive, the scenes involving Michele and Ranuccio smearing blood on each other's bodies can be seen as a reference to 'the threat of death in the midst of a contagion transferred through fluids' (pp. 190–91).
88. Dawne McCance, *Medusa's Ear: University Foundings from Kant to Chora L* (Albany: State University of New York Press, 2004), p. 4.
89. In this context, Jerusaleme's whistle acquires a new connotation.
90. Davide Panagia, 'The Effects of Viewing: Caravaggio, Bacon and *The Ring*', *Theory & Event*

(Baltimore), 10 (2007), 1, par. 25: <http://proquest.umi.com/pqdweb?did=0000001561933718&Fml=3&clientId=43168&RQT=309&VName=PQD> [accessed 16 October 2011]. Interestingly, apart from *Medusa*, amongst the pictorial examples Panagia uses to illustrate Caravaggio's interest in the liminal space between life and death we find also *St Jerome* (par. 17). Moreover, the penultimate section of Jarman's film is entitled 'St Jerome' and features Michele's last battle between life and death.

91. Interestingly, an almost identical shot of Michele's nose and eyes reappears later in the film in section 5 ('He loves me, loves me not': 36:04–36:13). Here, we have a contrast between the stillness of Michele's head and the movement of his eyes, which rotate and wander from the right to the left and back to the right in quick succession as if in search of something. As Marks would put it, the horizontal movement of Michele's eyes encourages a caressing gaze as it forces the viewer to linger on the eyes and follow their movement.

92. In his analysis of Caravaggio's *David with the Head of Goliath*, Fried reads the painting as an 'allegory of the "failure" of the project of severing, the proffered head — a figure for the finished painting — bearing for all time the tormented features of its maker' (Michael Fried, *The Moment of Caravaggio* (Princeton: Princeton University Press, 2010), p. 209).

93. This interview is part of the extras included in the DVD edition of the film.

94. The knife represents death as it is the tool Michele uses to kill Ranuccio, but also life, as it is equally a symbol of creativity and Michele uses it as a painting tool (Richardson, pp. 92–93).

95. The words 'sexuality' and 'desire' are used deliberately here because, as we are about to see, the film explores also other forms of desire such as that for wealth and power. It is also worth pointing out that the connection between darkness and desire is emphasized in section 7 ('Unveiling') when Michele, on his deathbed, reminisces about his 'true love' Pasqualone and remembers the first time he masturbated him:

> Pasqualone yawns into a blue sky. Time stops for no man, he says, caressing himself. I watch the ripples in his trousers. Then I put my hand in: the words fall over themselves with embarrassment. Pasqualone sighs and removes his hand without looking at me. I kneel beside him and reach timidly into the dark. There are holes in his pocket. My hand slides in; his cock grows warm in my hand; Pasqualone says his girl, Cecilia, holds it harder. 'Harder, Michele!' The air hisses through the gap in his golden teeth. 'Touch mine! Touch mine!' My mouth is dry and the words refuse to come; an ice-cold bead of sweat forms and trickles down my back. The seed spurts. His body tightens. He swallows. Harder Michele, harder. The violent words fly around me like the marble splinters in my father's workshop, stinging my cheek. Do it! Do it now!' (59:30–1:00:53)

96. Jean-Louis Chrétien, *Hand to Hand: Listening to the Work of Art* (New York: Fordham University Press, 2003), p. 32.

97. William Pencak, *The Films of Derek Jarman*, trans. by Stephen E. Lewis (Jefferson: McFarland, 2002), p. 83. As we are about to see, lust for wealth and material artefacts is one of the key features of most characters in the film.

98. In his comment on Caravaggio's *Death of the Virgin*, Jover points out that 'the message emanating from this woman's corpse laid out amid the silence of tears is that of a new dignity, the dignity of the human in its flesh and in its dying' (Manuel Jover, *Caravaggio* (Paris: Terrail, 2007), p. 146).

99. Kajsa Berg, 'Empathy and Movement in Caravaggio's Paintings', *Communicare*, 1 (2009), 17–29 (pp. 18–21).

100. Domietta Torlasco, *The Time of Crime: Phenomenology, Psychoanalysis, Italian Film* (Stanford: Stanford University Press, 2008), p. 75.

101. Bradley W. Buchanan, *Oedipus against Freud: Myth and the End(s) of Humanism in Twentieth-Century British Literature* (Toronto: University of Toronto Press, 2010), p. 152.

102. Michel Foucault, *The Use of Pleasure* (London: Penguin, 1992), pp. 252–53: 'for [the Greeks], reflection on sexual behaviour as a moral domain was [...] a means of developing [...] an aesthetics of existence, the purposeful art of a freedom perceived as a power game'. As noted by Suzanne Gearheart, according to Foucault, 'through his sado-masochistic mastery of his own sexuality, the Greek becomes the ultimate expression of his will to power and his own self-

created work of art' (Suzanne Gearheart, 'Foucault's Response to Freud: Sado-masochism and the Aestheticization of Power', *Style*, (Fall 1995), <http://findarticles.com/p/articles/mi_m2342/is_n3_v29/ai_18096757/> [accessed 6 December 2011].

103. Richardson, p. 96. Richardson is also keen to point out that 'although *Caravaggio* questions the cliché of the rough trade figure as being simply his body, the film also challenges the idea of this body as straight identified' (p. 93).
104. Elizabeth Cropper, 'Caravaggio and the Matter of Lyric', in *Caravaggio*, ed. by Warwick, pp. 47–56 (p. 49).
105. Bersani and Dutoit, *Caravaggio*, p. 71.
106. *Gay American Autobiography: Writings from Whitman to Sedaris*, ed. by David Bergman (Madison: University of Wisconsin Press, 2009), p. 151.
107. Justin Spring, *Secret Historian: The Life and Times of Samuel Steward, Professor, Tattoo Artist and Sexual Renegade* (New York: Farrar, Straus and Giroux, 2010), preface.
108. Samuel M. Steward, *The Caravaggio Shawl* (Boston: Alyson Publications, 1989); abbreviated as TCS.
109. S. Giora Shoham, *Art, Crime and Madness: Gesualdo, Caravaggio, Genet, Van Gogh, Artaud* (Brighton: Sussex Academic Press, 2002), p. 98.
110. David Savran, *Take it like a Man: White Masculinity, Masochism, and Contemporary American Culture* (Princeton: Princeton University Press, 1998), p. 234.
111. Judith E. Bernstock, *Under the Spell of Orpheus: The Persistence of a Myth in Twentieth-Century Art* (Carbondale, IL: SIU Press, 1991), p. 164.
112. John Gregg, *Maurice Blanchot and the Literature of Transgression* (Princeton: Princeton University Press, 1994), p. 50.
113. Leslie Hill, Brian Nelson, and Dimitris Vardoulakis, *After Blanchot: Literature, Criticism, Philosophy* (Newark: University of Delaware Press, 2005), p. 65.
114. Markowitz rightly argues that, despite the gender of the main protagonists, the narrator's perspective in Steward's murder mysteries is always that of a gay male. Judith A. Markowitz, *The Gay Detective Novel: Lesbian and Gay Main Characters in Mystery Fiction* (Jefferson: McFarland, 2004), pp. 227–28.
115. Maurice Blanchot, 'Orpheus's Gaze', in Maurice Blanchot, *The Space of Literature*, trans. by Ann Smock (Lincoln, NB: University of Nebraska Press, 1982), pp. 170–76 (p. 171).
116. Heather K. Love, 'Emotional Rescue', in *Gay Shame*, ed. by David M. Halperin and Valerie Traub (Chicago: University of Chicago Press, 2009), pp. 256–76 (p. 273).
117. It is worth noting, for instance, that Shakespeare's sonnets are often cited as examples of queerness as 'they take the reader to "a point at which one is not quite sure who is male and who is female, who is addressed and why"' (*Queer Renaissance Historiography*, ed. by Vincent Joseph Nardizzi, Stephen Guy-Bray, and Will Stockton (Farnham: Ashgate, 2009), p. 56). Shakespeare's sonnets are important also in Jarman's cinematography: in his 1985 *The Angelic Conversation*, fourteen of Shakespeare's sonnets are juxtaposed, and used as a voiceover, to a series of slow-moving images portraying love between two men, against the backdrop of harsh rocky landscapes and cityscapes. As noted by Fuller, the film can be described in intention as a queer homage to the Sonnets: David Fuller, *The Life in the Sonnets: Shakespeare Now* (London: Continuum, 2011), p. 59.

CHAPTER 5

Deleuzian Folds: Michael Ondaatje's and Anthony Minghella's Caravaggio

> Artists are presenters of affects, inventors and creators of affects. They not only create them in their work, they give them to us and make us become with them [...] whether through words, colours, sounds, stone, art is the language of sensations.
> DELEUZE AND GUATTARI, *What is Philosophy?*, p. 175

This chapter focuses on two novels by Michael Ondaatje, *In the Skin of a Lion* (1987) and *The English Patient* (1992), and the 1996 filmic adaptation of the latter by Anthony Minghella. My aim is to show how Caravaggio has been used for reflections on the power of art in our contemporary world and to articulate some postcolonial concerns such as the tension between master narrative and alternative story, the efficiency of mimicry as a strategy of appropriation and resistance[1] when living in a dominant culture, and the need to move beyond a postcolonial literature of resistance which, by insisting on the centre/periphery dichotomy, is seen by some postcolonial critics as too implicated in the dominant narratives to function successfully as a counter-discourse.[2] To date, scholars have mainly looked at Ondaatje's Caravaggism in individual works, but no real effort has been made to bring the novels and the film together and, generally, the emphasis on Caravaggio is rather limited.

My analysis will proceed on two levels. On the one hand, it is a study of the personality, function, and development of the character named Caravaggio across all three works. On the other, it looks at the various intertextual references to Caravaggio's paintings, starting from his *David with the Head of Goliath*, which, particularly as far as *The English Patient* is concerned, 'serves to bring all the centrifugal intertextuality of the narrative into alignment'.[3] It also considers *Judith Beheading Holophernes*, *St Jerome* (one of Caravaggio's favourite subjects),[4] and *Narcissus*.

I maintain that both Ondaatje and Minghella do more than simply quote Caravaggio. They actually perform his artistic lesson and, in doing so, they engage with some key aspects of the Baroque. In order to appreciate fully Caravaggio's appeal in a postcolonial context, the Deleuzian concept of fold will provide a useful theoretical framework to my argument. As we have already seen, Caravaggio's paintings transgress the limits between 'aesthetic, illusionistic and erotic pleasures', but also the 'boundary between pleasure and non-pleasure'.[5] According to Deleuze, this constant breaking of boundaries constitutes the operative concept of the Baroque, which can best be summarized through the image of the fold. The fold affects all materials (paper, rocks, sand, water, clouds, living tissues, and the brain) and, as a consequence, 'becomes expressive matter, with different scales, speeds, and different vectors [...]. It determines and materialises form'.[6] As Bal suggests, 'the fold insists on surface and materiality [...] (and) entails the involvement of the subject within the material experience' (*Quoting Caravaggio*, p. 30). The fold also emblematizes the Baroque point of view 'in which the subject must give up its autonomy' (*Quoting Caravaggio*, p. 39). This is because 'the transformation in the object refers to a correlative transformation in the subject' (*The Fold*, p. 21), as the subject is no longer something pre-given or defined but 'what comes to the point of view or rather what remains in the point of view' (ibid.). The insistence on materiality or, more specifically, in Caravaggio's case, on 'the materiality of paint' (*Quoting Caravaggio*, p. 42), problematizes representation and stresses the idea of work as process, which is also implicit in the Deleuzian/Leibnizian fold (*The Fold*, p. 39) and which, in turn, encourages self-reflection. The notion of process is, of course, also important in postcolonial studies. According to Helen Tiffin, for instance, 'decolonisation is process, not arrival' as it implies an ongoing dialectic between hegemonic discourses and their 'postcolonial dis/mantling'.[7]

As we shall see later, all the aforementioned concepts are explored through various medium-specific tools by Ondaatje and Minghella in an effort to move beyond subjectivity and embrace what Barbara Kennedy calls 'an experimental *pragmatics of becoming*'.[8] In the two novels, for instance, but above all in *The English Patient*, Ondaatje uses ekphrasis in order to 'collapse [the] distance between subject and object' and to encourage self-reflexivity, as 'in the verbal regime of the visual (that is, ekphrasis), even theory becomes performative and reflects back on the subject as theorizer'.[9] In Minghella's film, instead, self-reflexivity is promoted by the 'visual rhythms of the camera movements' (Kennedy, p. 152) echoing those of the painter's brush stroke (ibid.), which we see in the opening scene. However, before proceeding with further reflections on theoretical, technical, or structural issues, I would like to concentrate on the most obvious feature these works have in common, the presence of a character called David Caravaggio.

David Caravaggio: an artist in disguise

David Caravaggio first appears in *In the Skin of a Lion*,[10] a novel about Finnish, Macedonian, and Italian immigrants who, in the early twentieth century, contributed to the building of Toronto, but whose efforts were never fully acknowledged by official history. Ondaatje pays homage to their investment of labour in the construction of some of the city's landmarks, including the Prince Edward Viaduct and the R. C. Harris Water Treatment Plant. The novel includes a series of true stories of the time such as the fall of a nun from a bridge, the disappearance of the millionaire and theatre owner Ambrose Small and the murder of two labour union organizers. Its key themes are: the exploration of the relationship between fiction and reality; memory, (hi)story, and imagination; micro and macro history; the role of narration and narrative as tools of social and historical integration;[11] the use of violence as a means of implementing social change and a 'critique of the ongoing racial stratification in contemporary Canadian society'.[12] In typical Ondaatje style, the novel contains several intertextual references, some of which are fully acknowledged by the author while others are left for the reader to discover. Some of the most significant are: *The Epic of Gilgamesh*, one of the oldest examples of literary fiction, from which the title comes;[13] the photographs of Lewis Heine, one of the first photographers to document social situations in the hope of promoting some change; the letters of Joseph Conrad; the New Orleans Jazz musician Buddy Bolden; and last, but certainly not least, the Baroque painter Michelangelo Merisi da Caravaggio.

By naming one of the characters David Caravaggio, Ondaatje suggests a two-tier intertextuality by referring to the painter and his legacy on a more general level and, more specifically, to one of his most famous and controversial pictures, *David with the Head of Goliath*. David Caravaggio is mentioned for the first time in book one, in the chapter entitled 'The Bridge',[14] where he features amongst a group of 'bitumiers' or tarrers who when 'the tar is spread [...] get on to their knees and lean their weight over the wooden block irons, which arc and sweep' (*SL*, p. 29), crawling backwards towards the bridge in an activity that cripples their bodies and dulls their minds due to the poisonous fumes they are forced to inhale. All we know is his name when it gets called out by the foreman. Whilst he initially appears to play a minor role, his significance increases progressively, and book three has a chapter devoted entirely to him. From the start, there are noticeable similarities between this young Canadian immigrant and the Baroque painter. Like the original Caravaggio, David suffers from outbursts of temper. His face is scarred as a result of the various fights he gets involved in and he owns a dog.[15] His second appearance is equally fleeting. Once again he is just a name. This time he is mentioned by the main character (Patrick) who tells us he is a thief: 'a man with a carpet draped over his shoulder accompanied by a red dog. It was the neighbourhood thief, Caravaggio, returning from work. He passed calmly under me absorbed in the eating of Sicilian ice cream' (*SL*, p. 88). His ethnic origin is reinforced by the reference to the rather stereotypical image of the Sicilian ice cream. His status as an outsider is also stressed by the fact that he is no longer a construction worker providing a useful service to the community in which he lives, but makes a living out of stealing. The fact that what he does is regarded by Patrick as work seems to suggest the extreme poverty of some of the immigrants, who were forced to resort to all sort of tricks to survive. As Lundgren reminds us, of all the immigrant groups the Italians were those who held 'the lowest position in the class system' (p. 21). His stealing, however, is also a political act. He robs only the houses of rich people in a kind of protest against those capitalist forces that make people like him invisible. The issue of visibility is extremely important, as the entire novel is dominated by chiaroscuro images of light and shade and by frequent references to blindness. They are used to interconnect 'skin, colour, nationality and ethnicity' (Lundgren, p. 18), as one of the most-quoted passages about the tannery workers demonstrates:

> For the dyers the one moment of superiority came in the showers at the end of the day. They stood under the hot pipes, not noticeably changing for two or three minutes as if [...] they would be for ever contained in that livid colour [...]. And then the blue suddenly dropped off, the colour disrobed itself from the body, fell in one piece to their ankles, and they stepped out, in the erotica of being made free. (*SL*, p. 138)

Since the colours of the dyes had been previously 'associated with the labourers' various non-British countries of origin', Lundgren argues, their loss suggests loss of heritage and rebirth as generic English-speaking Canadians (p. 20) in a metaphor that racializes the moment of emancipation as white (ibid.). Similar images recur in the chapter devoted to Caravaggio where we learn how in order to escape from prison he paints his clothes and body with the same blue varnish he and other inmates were using to paint the prison's roof. In this way he makes himself invisible by blending with the environment. Like the workers in the tannery, however, once out, he has to shed his colour by washing with turpentine (*SL*, p. 188). By showing how, like a Deleuzian fold, this acquisition and stripping of colours could continue to infinity or at least, in the case of the dyers, until they died of consumption, poisoned by the acid of the solutions they had been stepping into and out of every day (*SL*, p. 137), Ondaatje deconstructs the idea of assimilation and a notion of social integration based on whiteness which would inevitably exclude non-European minorities, as the story of Kip in *The English Patient* partially illustrates.[16] Ironically, in the aforementioned scene in which, following his escape from prison, David Caravaggio seeks refuge in a factory in the hope of finding water and turpentine, he introduces himself to the boy who helps him as 'Caravaggio, the painter' (*SL*, p. 190). Just before 'eradicating' (*SL*, p.187) himself again, he identifies with an artist constantly torn between the need for acceptance and recognition and his rebellious nature, in a gesture that can be seen as the equivalent of what Jacobs calls postcolonial impatience: 'the tension between, on the one hand, recognition by postcolonial subjects of the imperial narratives by which they are constrained, and, on the other, their impulse to repossess their own stories', aware of the 'cognitive maps they have inherited' and irritated 'at being blueprinted by these dominant discourses' (p. 102). Significantly, as Caravaggio washes the colour off his skin, he sees the horrific scar on his neck, which was the result of the nearly fatal prison attack three months earlier (*SL*, p. 190). This scene in which the colour white and the mirror are combined in a single image seems to illustrate what Bal says regarding the Baroque point of view, a point of view that challenges the power of the subject: 'microscopically decomposed in innumerable tiny convex mirrors, white ceases to be "just" a colour and becomes a motif or figure of baroque engagement' (*Quoting Caravaggio*, p. 30). White is also the site of the flipping of scale that threatens the stability of the object, reminding us that 'perception is always microscopic and macroscopic' (p. 46). The sudden visibility of the scar on David's clean (and, therefore, white) neck 'serves to emphasize the inextricable mixture that any culture [...] is' (*Quoting Caravaggio*, p. 71), thus reinforcing the previously explored notion of 'postcolonial impatience'. Caravaggio, the Italian immigrant, after all owes his life to Patrick who, despite being also an outsider, is a white Canadian (*SL*, pp. 193 and 197). Interestingly, when from his cell Patrick notices that three men have approached Caravaggio and are about to beat him, he starts singing at the top of his voice: 'As they raise their hands over Caravaggio, Patrick breaks into a square dance call — "*Allemande left your corners all*" — screaming it absurdly as warning up into the stone darkness' (*SL*, p. 193). Since colour and sound and movement affect the brain in similar ways (Kennedy, p. 160), it could be argued that this adds an element of similarity to our 'painter'/tarrer/thief and his Canadian fellow prisoner.

The sense of entanglement increases further towards the end of the novel when Caravaggio helps Patrick to carry out his plan to blow up the water purification plant on which the whole city of Toronto depends for drinking water. In trying to reach the plant, which he had helped build, Patrick cuts his own throat and a rather 'caravaggiesque' description of his wound makes us see the two characters almost as a mirror image of each other (*SL*, pp. 194 and 253).[17] Patrick's gesture is partially a sort of personal vendetta for the loss of his girlfriend Alice Gull, who had been accidentally killed by an explosive device, and partially an act of rebellion against the city officials who were getting richer at the expenses of labourers like Patrick. The city officials never acknowledged all those victims who died in horrific accidents whilst working for the community (*SL*, pp. 247–48), thus reiterating the importance of both the microscopic and macroscopic levels of perception. Commissioner Harris, the man in charge of the water purification plant, however, 'refuses to be constructed as Patrick's opposite' (Lundgren, p. 21). From the start he dismisses the class difference between himself and his former employee by stressing what they have in common, such as their humble origins and their love for City Hall: 'I was practically *born* in City Hall. My mother was a caretaker. I worked up' (*SL*, p. 247). At the end of their confrontation, Harris is not bitter, even though Patrick could have easily killed both of them and destroyed the waterworks which Harris had built for himself, following 'a stray dream he'd always had about water' (*SL*, p. 114), and whose interior, like a Deleuzian monad, was constructed as an image of the ideal city (*SL*, pp. 13–14). Instead of hatred, Harris shows compassion. When the security officer arrives at six o'clock, he tells him to defuse the blasting box but let Patrick sleep and asks him to come back with a nurse and some medical supplies to treat Patrick's wound (*SL*, p. 254). The whole scene prior to the arrival of the guard is played out as a battle between light and shade:

> Patrick moved in shadow now, the blasting-box still under his right arm. [...] He had been drowning in Harris' eyes and sleepy hand-movements, felt hypnotised by that calm voice, the solitary focus of the lamp. Without light he felt more awake [...].
> [...]
> Harris knew he had to survive until early morning. Then a column of sunlight would fall directly onto his large desk [...]. He had to survive until the first hint of morning colour came through the oculus above him [...]. (*SL*, pp. 248–49)

As in Caravaggio's paintings, light and the colour white challenge preconceived notions of scale (*Quoting Caravaggio*, p. 57). Ironically, what appears clear and straightforward in the shelter of darkness becomes fuzzier and complicated in the light. At daybreak, Patrick will no longer be able to escape his opponent's gaze and will lose his autonomy as subject (*Quoting Caravaggio*, p. 39). Eyes are traditionally associated with mirrors. By staring at a reflective surface, Patrick, like Narcissus, 'drowns' as he is unable to distinguish between self and other and, as a result, loses his sense of self.[18] Through this novel, Ondaatje seems to stress the inevitable failure of a politics based on difference, and suggests the need to move towards a 'pragmatics of becoming' (Kennedy, p. 6). As Kennedy explains, pragmatism is to be understood as 'a process of thinking contingently and relationally' (p. 11), and in some respects it is synonymous with micro-politics (p. 29). By contrast, 'becoming' refers to

> an autonomous, autopoietic level of existence through which life is lived and experienced at a molecular level, outside the exigencies of self to other relations, a purely viral and genetic evolution of life, in a truly biological or germinal way: mind and body becoming with the world, in true autopoiesis. A vital sense of who and what we are. (p. 149)

According to Kennedy/Ondaatje, we need to follow Deleuze's teachings and recover that essential core, 'an essential autopoiesis, or becoming, which is eradicated out of us' through a social process that orders the singularities of the proto-subjective state into fixed entities such as gender (Kennedy, p. 160). 'Becoming', in other words, is what allows 'hegemonic formations' to be resisted in a move away from subjectivity. It, in turn, gets retheorized through a more complex relationship between the concept of *affect* and *sensation* (Kennedy, p. 29), which, as we shall later see, allows us to 'bring back the political through the aesthetic' (Kennedy, p. 83).

This link between 'the political' and 'the aesthetic' is another feature that brings us back to Caravaggio. If, on the one hand, Caravaggio created through his paintings a 'visual version of the Barthesian equivalent of the *plaisir du text*' (*Quoting Caravaggio*, p. 20), on the other, by making ordinary people, including beggars and prostitutes, visible in a highly hypocritical society where poverty had turned into 'the condition of the devil himself',[19] his works represented a political statement.[20] Ondaatje, however, is also aware of the difficulties and potential dangers of reintroducing the political through the aesthetic and it is Patrick, Caravaggio's alter-ego in *In the Skin of a Lion*, who voices such concerns. When talking about the tannery workers the narrator says:

> This is how Patrick would remember them. Their bodies standing there tired, only the heads white. If he were an artist he would have painted them but that was false celebration. [...] What would the painting tell? [...] That during the day they ate standing up. That they had consumed that most evil smell in history, they were consuming it now [...]. That they would die of consumption and at present they did not know it. [...] Nobody could last in the job more than six months and only the desperate took it. (*SL*, pp. 136–37)

As Lundgren points out, 'Patrick's awareness of representation as a process [...] motivates the reader to reflect on the function of aesthetics and on the politics

DELEUZIAN FOLDS 181

of representation' (p. 18), alerting us to the risks of making certain events appear 'aesthetically plumaged' (*SL*, p. 136). In Ondaatje's case, though, 'the practice of aestheticizing labour does not idealize it but honours those who perform it and commits their suffering to memory' (Lundgren, p. 25). The act of remembering is in itself political as, by generating a sense of empathy with those who suffer, it can promote the conquest of suffering. Only if in the process of aestheticization the need for eliminating oppressive social conditions becomes lost, then the outcome of such a process is reactionary, as Patrick suggests with his idea of 'false celebration' mentioned above (*SL*, p. 136). However, we must also point out that it is after his experience in 'The Garden of the Blind', which, according to Sarris, represents the aesthetic experience par excellence (p. 200), that Patrick comes to terms with the idea of taking responsibility for one's own actions. Despite the strong temptation of withdrawing from the world, of 'never emerging out of the shadows' and confining himself to the realm of the 'Unhistorical' (*SL*, p. 181), once he is on board the Cherokee steamer he no longer tries to hide. Patrick is ready to be punished for his attack on the Muskoka Hotel: 'he knows he will be caught, probably imprisoned' (*SL*, p. 182). Significantly, the chapter ends with a reference to the key image of the novel's title that symbolizes the assuming of responsibility (Sarris, p. 199). Like a lion, Patrick is shown eating raw meet, 'licking the juice that dribbles down his arm' (*SL*, p. 182). The novel concludes with a very similar image. When Patrick wakes up from sleep[21] and sits in the car, ready to drive to Marmora and tell Hana the story of Clara, her mother's best friend, he climbs in 'pretending to luxuriate in the passenger seat, making animal-like noises of satisfaction' (*SL*, p. 256).

As previously mentioned, the lion of the novel's title is taken from *The Epic of Gilgamesh*, a story which, like many of Caravaggio's paintings, celebrates the human element ('what makes us human'),[22] the need for compassion, the meaning of loss, ageing and mortality, and the duality of man. If Caravaggio humanizes religion by making it relevant to ordinary people, Ondaatje humanizes history (Sarris, pp. 186 and 200) by giving a voice to all those who had been traditionally excluded; he does so through the characters of Patrick and his alter ego Caravaggio. In other words, Ondaatje betrays official history 'by making it, in Patrick's terms, "private"' (Sarris, p. 200) or, as the French philosopher Jacques Rancière would put it, by providing 'a public stage for the private principle of work'.[23] In so doing Ondaatje turns his novel into a political act. The fact that it is David Caravaggio who enables Patrick to try to carry out his attack on the water purification plant reiterates the idea of art as a possible tool for changing the world.

The character Caravaggio reappears in *The English Patient*.[24] Set in Italy in 1944, this novel follows a group of four people — Hana, Caravaggio, Kirpal (known as Kip), and the English patient — whose shattered lives briefly intertwine in a Tuscan ruined villa where the Canadian nurse Hana decides to stop in order to look after one of her terminally ill patients, a man who had been burnt beyond recognition and had lost his memory and identity when his plane crashed in the Egyptian desert. The story of the main character, the English patient, is based on a historical figure, the Hungarian desert researcher Ladislaus Eduard Almásy (1895–1951). The novel consists of various flashbacks representing the efforts of the mysterious English patient and of those surrounding him in helping him to try to piece together various fragments from his past. Its key themes are love, friendship, and human relationships in wartime, the overlapping of private and public spaces, micro and macro history, and the deconstruction of clear-cut notions of national identity.[25] In this novel David Caravaggio acquires an additional function, that of illustrating the concept of art as 'inauguration' or emergence: in other words, a form of truth that transcends the metaphysical notion of a stable structure and 'offers a model of the experience of freedom in a pluralistic, postmodern culture "as continual oscillation between belonging and disorientation"',[26] as it is only through the constant challenging of certainties that new meanings can be produced. It is mainly thanks to David Caravaggio that we are able to reconstruct the story of Count Ladislaus de Almásy, the English patient. David spends hours trying to jog the English patient's memory. Almásy, however, is able to speak only when under the effect of morphine. Every time he reminisces we get a slightly different version of the events concerning his stay in Egypt and his affair with Katherine Clifton. As in the previous novel, we encounter an explicit mistrust of grand narratives and a reiteration of the idea that art can be a vehicle for the 'retrieval of ontological beginnings' provided we accept the impossibility of returning to 'any absolute origin' (Gibson, p. 88). The novel's insistence on memory, like Patrick's statement about the need to humanize history and ideology (*SL*, p. 141) in *In the Skin of a Lion*, illustrates the importance of privileging cultural memory as an alternative to traditional history (*Quoting Caravaggio*, p. 66). As Bal points out, memory is a function of subjectivity. Cultural memory is both collective and subjective by definition. Subjectivity is central to it but does not lead to an individualist subjectivism. Unlike history, whose main function is recuperation and reconstruction, the operational mode of cultural memory is 'recherche'. Its focus is the present (p. 66) and, being infused with feelings, cultural memory is what allows us to humanize/privatize history.[27] Also, this process alters the meaning of realism, which is no longer 'being deployed to capture or document reality' (p. 66) but to 'dignify the past through a "feeling" commemorating what is real' (pp. 66–67) in a discourse that inevitably involves nostalgia as 'the subjective sentiment that substantiates cultural memory as collective yet subjective' (p. 67).[28] Whilst traditionally perceived in negative terms, according to Bal, nostalgia can become a tool to unify the fragmented past (p. 74) and provide 'guidelines for a critical utopianism in the present, for a struggle towards a better future' (p. 72). Similar comments can be made about Caravaggio's working methods as he also used empathy and identification as tools to make the old Bible stories relevant to his contemporaries (Warwick, p. 19). These features are particularly visible in paintings such as the aforementioned *The Calling of St Matthew* and *The Martyrdom of St Matthew*.[29]

But let us return to David Caravaggio. What immediately strikes us in this novel is the fact that the first time we meet him he is referred to as 'the man with bandaged hands' (*EP*, p. 27). This act of maiming one of the greatest Western artists can be interpreted in different ways. First of all, it can be considered to be an example of the postcolonial tension between master narratives and alternative stories (Jacobs, p. 102): depriving a painter (or a thief, for that matter) of the use of his hands means denying him the possibility to express himself. Significantly, in order to piece together the various fragments of the English patient's story, David Caravaggio also needs the help of morphine (*EP*, pp. 176 and 267). Likewise, the demise of the Englishman can also be read as representing 'the end of the great imperial narratives of Western Europe' (Jacobs, p. 103). Another plausible interpretation is that it was intended as a statement about the nearly impossible task of being an artist in a post-Holocaust world, of trying to come to terms with a scenario of chaos that 'metonymically represents the destruction of a civilization' (Jacobs, p. 102).[30] The novel's obsession with fragments and mutilation[31] seems to suggest that the only way of dealing with the sense of disintegration of the postwar or postcolonial period is to focus on the fragmented nature of consciousness: 'immersing himself in the debris of the Other is Caravaggio's method of attempting to heal his own wounds'.[32] Finally, Caravaggio's bandaged hands can also be seen as an example of narcissism.[33] According to Hilger, Caravaggio's

> pain is tinted with the pleasure associated with the focus on fragments. At the same time that the bandages act as protective 'gloves', they also highlight Caravaggio's fetishized parts and thereby provide him with the narcissistic focus on the fact that he is not 'whole' anymore. (p. 45)

By directing our attention to 'an absence', Hilger concludes, 'the subject defends itself against the lack of identity by establishing this "hole" as his individuality' (ibid.). In other words, we see what Bal, in her comment on Merisi's *Narcissus* (1598), calls 'the collapse of narcissism' (*Looking in*, p. 249). David Caravaggio's bandaged hands function in the same way as the knee in Merisi's painting: looking detached from the rest of the body, the knee 'makes present an absence' and 'presents the prosthetic illusion of wholeness that props up the self into existence as a fiction' (ibid.).[34] As we have already pointed out regarding Patrick's falling asleep during his final confrontation with Commissioner Harris in *In the Skin of a Lion*, the illusion of wholeness can only be sustained through lack of consciousness (*Quoting Caravaggio*, p. 259). The total dependence of David Caravaggio and the English patient on morphine can also be interpreted as the expression of their need to move into a fictional dimension capable of giving them a sense of wholeness and an insight into the most traumatic events in their lives, particularly since both novels contain several references to blindness and to the inability to see.[35]

David Caravaggio's profession in *The English Patient* is also worthy of attention. We are told that because of his former skills as a thief during the war he had been selected to work as a spy: the war had simply made his skills official (*EP*, p. 37). Both activities involve secrecy and raise questions about voyeurism in art. What is more, as a spy, David Caravaggio

> had trained to invent double agents or phantoms who would take on flesh. He had been in charge of a mythical agent named 'Cheese' and he spent weeks clothing him with facts, giving him qualities of character — such as greed and a weakness for drink when he would spill false rumours to the enemy. (*EP*, p. 124)

Like the painter's realism, which was always staged and involved models who had to pose for hours in very uncomfortable positions in his studio, David Caravaggio's double agents are the result of a lengthy study and piecing together of details capable of producing an illusionistic effect. As Bal teaches us, illusionism is 'an excess of representation that undoes representation' (*Quoting Caravaggio*, p. 42) and raises questions about 'the ontology and accessibility of reality' (ibid.), questions we are constantly facing when reading *The English Patient*, particularly since, as we have already seen, the English patient's morphine addiction makes his reliability questionable: 'he rides the boat of morphine. It races in him, imploding time and geography the way maps compress the world onto a two-dimensional sheet of paper' (*EP*, p. 171).

Another interesting detail in the previously quoted passage about David Caravaggio's double agents is the reference to 'clothing', which bring us back to Deleuze and to his concept of secondary or clothed matter. Secondary matter, or *massa*, is what fills primary or naked matter (*mole*), that is to say the abstract structure of a body: it consists of several substances and does 'not go from one instant to another without being reconstituted' (*The Fold*, p. 134). Deleuze uses the term 'clothed' to indicate two things: first, the idea of matter as a lively/floating surface, a surface endowed with an organic fabric, and second, that matter is 'the very fabric or clothing, the texture enveloping the abstract structure' (*The Fold*, p. 131). As Bal would put it, Ondaatje's text, like Caravaggio's paintings 'participate in the production of matter in surface, in the production of flesh as skin' (*Quoting Caravaggio*, p. 52).[36] Interestingly, it is precisely this aspect that is explored at length in Minghella's cinematic adaptation. The film opens with an image of a painter's brush drawing abstract figures on a textured surface, which we later discover to be the notebook Katherine painted in the Cave of Swimmers just before she died, but which could be either the wall of a cave, a porous sheet of paper, or skin.[37] The image of the painter's brush and of the textured skin-like surface could also be seen as a comment on what Michel de Certeau calls 'scriptural economy', on how writing turns 'a *flesh*' into 'a *body*', thus creating 'paving stones and paths, networks of rationality through the incoherence of the universe' (p. 144). These remarks are very similar to those we find in *In the Skin of a Lion* about the function of art: 'only the best art can order the chaotic tumble of events. Only the best can realign chaos to suggest both the chaos and order it will become' (*SL*, p. 152). The story of Katherine and Almásy, however, illustrates on the one hand the desire to find 'in a discourse the means of turning themselves into a unit of meaning, into an identity' (de Certeau, p. 149). On the other hand, it illustrates the need to resist such temptation, to challenge the power of the law that can only support itself 'on the obscure desire to exchange one's flesh for a glorious body, to be written, even if it means dying, and to be transformed into a recognized word' (de Certeau, p. 149). Unlike Almásy, who despite being fluent in several languages was often 'wordless' (*EP*, p. 185), Katherine loved being called by her name: 'she had always wanted words, she loved them, grew up on them. Words gave her clarity, brought reason, shape. Whereas I thought words bent emotions like sticks in water' (*EP*, p. 253).

Owing to its strong visual impact, the Cave of Swimmers plays a much more central role in the film than in the book. The importance of caves becomes even more striking if we consider Deleuze, for whom caves symbolize matter: 'matter offers an infinitely porous, spongy, or cavernous texture without emptiness, caverns endlessly contained in other caverns' (*The Fold*, p. 5). Matter, in turn, brings us back to the concept of fold that we introduced at the beginning of this chapter. For Deleuze, 'the smallest unit of matter, the smallest element of the labyrinth is the fold' (p. 6); this is visually explored in the film through the various desert shots focusing on sand dunes, ripples, and wind.[38] The desert is also compared to the body of a woman, and the film's images are extremely sensual and aesthetically pleasing. As we learned from Bal, illusionism and excessive perfection are features that challenge all boundaries, 'including that between self and other', by initiating a 'dazzling game of mirroring' (*Quoting Caravaggio*, p. 43). Both novel and film contain countless references to mirrors. We are repeatedly told that the stories of various characters are mirror-images of each other: those of Caravaggio and the English patient and the English patient and Kip, but also that of the English patient and Katherine, can all be considered in these terms. In the film, the theme of mirroring is also explored through the use of white, the colour which, as we have already seen, symbolizes the Baroque point of view and which Deleuze conceives as 'consisting in a great number of small reflecting mirrors' (*The Fold*, p. 35). Significantly, throughout the film Katherine is mainly dressed in white but so is Almásy (particularly in the scenes when he is with Katherine), and Caravaggio also frequently wears white items of clothing. Even more significantly, when Almásy walks out of the Cave of Swimmers holding Katherine in his arms, her dead body is wrapped in a copious amount of white fabric, which is seen flapping in the wind. Here the folds of the shroud-like cloth (an obvious quotation of Baroque draperies) appear to connect some of the film's key motifs, such as death, violence, pleasure, eroticism, and the body (*Quoting Caravaggio*, p. 51). The white of the fabric symbolizes the interior of the tomb. As such, on the one hand, it monumentalizes the dead[39] and the past, whilst at the same time celebrating life through its memory in the present. On the other hand, it promotes cultural memory as the only tool capable of bridging the gap between past and present, of creating a 'connection between the subject and the object of historical knowledge' (*Quoting Caravaggio*, pp. 53 and 70), as the case of Kip also shows. Despite having returned to India, become a doctor, and being married with two children (a boy and a girl), Kip keeps the 'stone of history' alive through his memory, never letting it plunge too deep into the water. Thanks to this limited but very useful gift he can see Hana, as if in a film, in front of his eyes whilst watching his own daughter (also called Hana) struggle with her cutlery (*EP*, pp. 318–21). White also features prominently at the end of the film. In the final scene, the classic Tuscan country road flanked by cypresses, and with sunshine filtering through them, seen from the perspective of Hana, who is sitting on a moving vehicle, becomes a sequence of black and bright white stripes as if to signify that clarity is always a matter of perception and therefore destined to change with time.[40]

But let us return to David Caravaggio's activity as a spy (or as a thief) and the question of voyeurism in art that Ondaatje addresses through it. As previously mentioned, both 'professions' involve secrecy and prying into people's private spheres. In *In the Skin of a Lion*, for instance, the sight of a woman's bare feet on the wooden floor of the boat house, of the desk and the mattress on the floor of her bedroom, prompt David to reflect on his intrusion: 'he knew there was such an intimacy in what he was seeing that not even a husband could get closer than him, a thief who saw this rich woman trying to discover what she was or what she was capable of making' (*SL*, p. 207). Voyeurism, of course, is also a key theme in 'The Wife of Candaules', from Herodotus' *The Histories*, which is one of Katherine's favourite stories and one of the novel's major intertexts. Candaules, the king of Lydia, was so infatuated with the perfection and beauty of his wife's body that he persuaded one of his bodyguards, Gyges, to hide in his master's bedroom just before his wife went to bed so that he would get a chance to admire the queen naked. Candaules reassured Gyges that he had nothing to fear as he would be so well hidden that the queen would not notice his presence. Unfortunately, as Gyges is leaving the royal bedroom, the queen catches a glimpse of him and the following day calls him in and confronts him with two choices:

> Either you must slay Candaules and possess both me and the kingdom of Lydia, or you must yourself here on the spot be slain, so that you mayest not in future, by obeying Candaules in all things, see that which you should not. (*EP*, p. 248)

This story problematizes the act of looking as 'something that affects the looker more than the subject being looked at' (*Looking in*, p. 148) and can be read as an explicit criticism of the gaze, that is to say the colonizing act of looking (p. 143) involved in voyeurism. As Bal explains through references to Bryson, Lacan, and Silverman, this colonialist variety of looking is often encouraged in the social gaze, that is to say the 'internalized social construction of vision', a construction mainly dominated by a masculine, aggressive perspective (ibid.). In contrast to the 'predatory' gaze, the glance is a mode of looking 'as desire, but not appropriation' (ibid.), which emphasizes the viewer's position as a viewer (p. 142). These two modes of looking are not exclusive and the English patient, that is, Count Ladislaus de Almásy, a cartographer, epitomizes the tension between the two. His profession, by definition, inserts him in the Western imperialist tradition. However, as an individual, he is full of contradictions. Whilst telling Katherine that what he hates the most is ownership and begging her to forget him once she leaves (*EP*, p. 162), he starts following her at a distance when she is going through the market in Cairo, a gesture which, as Katherine reminds him during their first dance in the film, is essentially voyeuristic and thus predatory (37:10–37:30). His attitudes towards the desert are equally ambiguous. On the one hand, he loves it as he sees in it a symbol of the other, of a possible alternative to a world shaped by financial and military despots where the only things that mattered were money, trade, and power (*EP*, p. 265), on the other, he is aware of having contributed to turning the desert into 'a theatre of war'.[41] As we have already seen, the desert can also be considered a symbol of the Deleuzian/Leibnizian monad, that is to say, a model of self-sufficiency to which Almásy aspired: 'here, apart from the sun compass and the odometer mileage and the book, he was alone, his own invention. He knew during these times how the mirage worked, the fata morgana, for he was within it' (*EP*, p. 262).[42] The thing he admired the most in the desert was a plant that even when cut out could regenerate itself for up to a year before dying from 'some lack or other'

(*EP*, p. 165). As Katherine suggests, the Leibnizian model, whilst in some respects desirable as a possible alternative to the traditional identity model, particularly in a fragmented and shattered world where nothing makes sense anymore, can have its dangers and deprive us of what makes us human. Self-sufficiency can lead to moral indifference:[43]

> I don't think that you care — that this has happened among us. You slide past everything with your fear and hate of ownership, of owning, of being owned, of being named. You think this is a virtue. I think this is inhuman. (*EP*, p. 253)

Ironically, it is Katherine who understands the true meaning of mapping, in Deleuzian terms, as experience. Her last letter to Almásy, in the film, is particularly revealing:

> We die, we die rich with lovers and tribes, tastes we have swallowed, bodies we have entered and swum up like rivers, fears we have hidden in, like this wretched cave. I want all this marked on my body where the real country is, not the boundaries drawn on maps, the names of powerful men. I know you'll come and carry me out into the palace of winds. That's all I wanted … to walk in such a place with you. With friends. An earth without maps. (2:25:16–2:26:26)

In the novel we gain access to Katherine's last words through Almásy's final account of her death. He appears to have internalized them to the point that it is not immediately obvious whether they are his or her thoughts and, although very similar to what we hear in the film, there are some small but important differences. The last few lines are particularly interesting:

> I wish for all this to be marked on my body when I am dead. I believe in such cartography — to be marked by nature, not just to label ourselves on a map like names of rich men and women on buildings. We are communal histories, communal books. We are not owned or monogamous in our taste or experience. All I desired was to walk upon such an earth that had no maps. (*EP*, p. 277)

Both versions highlight some fundamental points. The first one, in line with Baroque aesthetics, represents a celebration of the body, whilst the second stresses the importance of nature, or better, of 'an unseverable relationship between identity, body, and land' (*Quoting Caravaggio*, p. 41). By directing our attention to the link between 'the body and the earth on which the person treads' (ibid.) both the novel and the film make a comment on mortality, on the transience of all things, and emphasize the idea of process (all themes dear to Caravaggio).

Before proceeding to a more detailed analysis of various paintings that constitute the key intertexts to Ondaatje's and Minghella's works, I would like to return briefly to 'The Wife of Candaules', pointing out that Herodotus' story is also about the issue of responsibility, another theme previously explored in *In the Skin of a Lion*.[44] The queen forces Gyges to accept the consequences of his actions because looking is never an innocent act. This is also what Caravaggio's paintings demonstrate, starting from his early depictions of male nudes, which are obviously meant to encourage a voyeuristic pleasure in the viewer,[45] to his later self-portraits as a witness to violent scenes, such as the *Martyrdom of St Matthew* (1599–1600) or

The Burial of St Lucy (1608), *The Resurrection of Lazarus* (1609) and *The Martyrdom of St Ursula* (1610), where the artist reflects on mortality and on his own attraction to sin. By including himself as an observer of acts of violence he turns into an accomplice and thus is responsible for what he is witnessing, and, in so doing, he illustrates the dual nature of man.

Key pictorial intertextual references

As previously mentioned, both Ondaatje's *In the Skin of a Lion* and *The English Patient*, and Minghella's cinematic adaptation of the latter, are rich in intertextual references which, in true Baroque style, fold and unfold in various directions and are used to reiterate, reinforce, or present from slightly different angles those themes which are central to both the novels and the film. We have already seen that from the point of view of Caravaggio the major intertextual reference common to all three works is *David with the Head of Goliath* (c. 1605–06). Considered by many to be one of Caravaggio's last paintings, it was probably completed during his late Roman period, between 1605 and 1606. Interestingly, this is often believed to be the work that Caravaggio intended to donate to Scipione Borghese as a plea for pardon when, after his flight from Malta and his stay in Sicily, he was desperately trying to return to Rome (Sgarbi; Langdon). Whilst it is universally accepted that Goliath represents a self-portrait of the painter, some scholars (e.g. Hunt) maintain that David is also a self-portrait of the artist when he was younger. This scene, Hunt maintains, 'vicariously fulfils the threat of "serving" his own head to present it to a judge for the capital punishment awarded Caravaggio over the murder of Tomassoni' (pp. 132–34). The fact that Ondaatje combined the names David and Caravaggio in a single character could be already seen as an indication that he supports the double portrait theory; indeed, this is confirmed in *The English Patient* when Almásy explicitly refers to *David with the Head of Goliath* as containing two portraits of Caravaggio (*EP*, p. 123). In this way, Ondaatje re-emphasizes the issue of taking responsibility for one's actions and stories which is always central to his writing.

However, regardless of whether the two figures are self-portraits of the artist, what is clear is that the relationship between the model and the painter (as Goliath) suggests 'sexual intimacy' (Puglisi, p. 363). Both Langdon and Puglisi see in the 'phallic sword' an 'erotic resonance' (Langdon, pp. 384–86; Puglisi, p. 363). Langdon also points out that already in the biblical story the relationship between David and Goliath is homoerotic and that David means 'beloved'. Significantly, the eroticization of death is omnipresent in *The English Patient* (both novel and film), as the scene in which Hana feeds her patient 'a very plum, plum' demonstrates (*EP*, pp. 4 and 47–48). Through Hana and the English patient, who is often referred to as her 'despairing saint' (*EP*, pp. 3 and 47), Ondaatje and Minghella explore another key theme of the *David with the Head of Goliath* painting: the need for expiation or atonement. Hana feels responsible for the deaths of the people who are closest to her, particularly her father and the baby she had aborted when she discovered the father of the baby was dead and she was in a country devastated by war (*EP*,

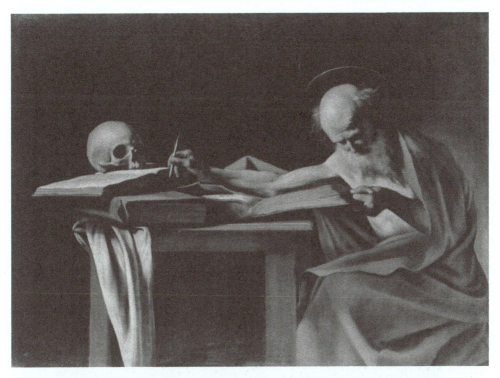

FIG. 5.1. Caravaggio, *St Jerome Writing* (c. 1605–06), Rome: Galleria Borghese

FIG. 5.2. Caravaggio, *Narcissus* (1597–98), Rome: Galleria Nazionale d'Arte Antica

p. 87).[46] Hana's feelings for the English patient are more than just love: she adores him (*EP*, p. 47). It is as if, in looking after him, she were looking for an 'ecstasy', for something capable of transcending 'the dynamic that leads living beings to become signs' (de Certeau, p. 149), since in a shattered world traditional signs have become meaningless. As de Certeau explains, an ecstasy is like a cry, a revolt or a flight, the only force capable of opposing 'the law of the named' (ibid.).

As suggested by Jover, another interesting aspect of Caravaggio's *David with the Head of Goliath* is the fact that 'this prodigiously visual painting includes the spectacle of the destruction of sight, of the gaze of the painter' (p. 242). Also, the colour white plays a fundamental role in this work: even if we disregard the double portrait theory, white links the two figures through the shirt, the light on the sword, the white of the eyes of Goliath and the teeth in his open mouth, forcing us to look closely at even the most repulsive details (*Quoting Caravaggio*, p. 47). Since, as we have already seen, white functions like a mirror, we can conclude that the two figures are mirror images of each other and that, like the Medusa (another 'severed-head' portrait) or Narcissus, Goliath 'meets with death in a mirror' (Jover, p. 96). Interestingly, in *In the Skin of a Lion*, Ondaatje presents us with the conflation of the *David with the Head of Goliath* and *Narcissus* paintings. When Patrick prevents the murder of Caravaggio by shouting from his prison cell, we are told:

> Caravaggio finds the bed. He gets to his knees on the mattress — head and elbows propping up his bruised body so nothing touches the pain. The blood flows along his chin into his mouth. He feels as if he has eaten the animal that attacked him and he spits out everything he can, old saliva, blood, spits again and again. Everything is escaping. His left hand touches his neck and it is not there. (*SL*, p. 194)

The reference to the knee and to Caravaggio's bodily position inevitably evoke the figure of Narcissus kneeling by the pond whilst the severed head of a character called David Caravaggio cannot but be an explicit quotation of *David with the Head of Goliath*. The conflation of the two paintings becomes even more obvious if we consider another passage in which, this time, Patrick during his final confrontation with Commissioner Harris is depicted as the 'beheaded' victim: 'Patrick lay strangely — the lower half of his body crouched, knees drawn up, and at the top half sprawled out, head back. The blood across his neck and shirt. He had cut his throat in the darkness' (*SL*, p. 253). If we look closely at these two passages the positions of Caravaggio and Patrick appear as mirror images of each other. As we have already seen, in this novel, this device is used to explore the notions of cultural entanglement and postcolonial impatience.[47]

As for *The English Patient*, references to Narcissus and narcissism are everywhere, both in the novel and in the film, whether we think of them in terms of reflections, actual mirrors, ponds, or water. In the film, for instance, we often see Hana's image reflected either in the washing bowl or in the garden pond of Villa San Girolamo. Even her improvised scarecrow consists of various strings with splinters of mirrors attached to them and hanging from the arms of a six-foot crucifix which she had taken from the chapel's cemetery. Katherine is described as 'a woman who misses moisture' (*EP*, p. 163) and even the Cave of Swimmers indicates that what is now sand used to be water. As previously argued, these references are used to explore issues of identity and of how to develop a clear sense of who we are in a world consisting of ruins. They are also used to analyse different ways of looking, such as the gaze and the glance;[48] and the idea of writing as a tool capable of transgressing the boundaries of fiction and reality, of story and history, of self and other. Significantly, when analysing Caravaggio's *Narcissus* (*Quoting Caravaggio*, p. 242; *Looking in*, p. 246), Bal focuses on the dotted line separating the boy from his reflection and calls it Narcissus's act of writing: a permeable line indicating the surface of the mirror and signifying the lack of limits. The power of writing can be extended to the power of the artistic imagination; Langdon compares *David with the Head of Goliath* to the *Medusa*, reminding us of its power to entrap the spectator: 'it plays on the idea of life and death, on the power of the artist to make the dead live and to petrify the living' (pp. 384–86). According to this interpretation the severed head is a symbol of immortality (ibid.).

Interestingly, the other intertextual reference linking both the novels and the film is *Judith with the Head of Holophernes*, yet again a decapitation scene. This time, however, the 'executioner' is a woman. As Bal points out, this is 'one of the popular mythical stories in which the power struggle between men and women ends in favour of the weak(er) sex'.[49] As such, it can be easily adapted to express the demise of grand narratives, the fact that 'never again will a single story be told as though it were the only one', as these words from John Berger on the opening page of *In the Skin of a Lion* demonstrate.[50] In this novel, Patrick appears to feel threatened by Clara and Alice, the two women he loves:

> Later he will think of the seconds when he was almost asleep and they entered the dark room with candles [...] Patrick and the two women. A study for the New World. Judith and Holophernes. Patrick and the Two Women. He loves the tableau, even though being asleep he had not witnessed the ceremony. (*SL*, p. 82)

Apart from stressing the idea that 'uncertainty and vulnerability always influence relationships' (*Mieke Bal Reader*, p. 410), this scene comes across as a classic example of the Freudian fear of castration, which is further explored in *The English Patient* (both novel and film) through the image of the nurse amputating Caravaggio's thumbs. In the film, as in the painting, we see the actual 'castrating' action, with emphasis on the knife/sword used to carry out this 'task' and the blood gushing out of the severed body parts. In the novel, instead, we see more obviously how Ondaatje combined this reference to *Judith Beheading Holofernes* to a detail in Michelangelo Merisi's life which possibly led to his unfortunate confrontation with Ranuccio Tomassoni in via della Scrofa in Rome on 28 May 1606:

> They found a woman to do it. They thought it was more trenchant. They brought in one of their nurses. My wrists handcuffed to the table legs. When they cut off my thumbs my hands slipped out of them without any power. Like a wish in a dream. But the man who called her in, he was really in charge — he was the one. Ranuccio Tomassoni. She was an innocent, knew nothing about me, my name or what I may have done. (*EP*, pp. 58–59)

The link between the painting and the fight with Tomassoni is made possible by the fact that the woman posing as Judith is sometimes believed to be Fillide Melandroni (Hunt, p. 57), an upper-class courtesan who had as one of her protectors Ranuccio Tomassoni. Fillide is also believed to have been one of the possible sources of disagreement between Tomassoni and the painter which led to their final duel during which Tomassoni was killed. As we know, Caravaggio was sentenced to death and forced into exile as a result. By depicting Caravaggio rather than Tomassoni as the victim, Ondaatje subverts the official narrative of those events, highlighting how the painter never recovered from that experience, which haunted him for the rest of his life and which he must have perceived as a form of castration since Rome was *the* place to be for an artist in search of success. It could also be argued that since both in *In the Skin of a Lion* and in *The English Patient* Ondaatje identifies in some ways with the character of David Caravaggio, the subversion of the official perception of one of the most tragic incidents in Merisi's life represents a further example of postcolonial impatience. On the one hand, it makes us reflect on the tensions between colonizer and colonized; on the other, it encourages us to look at Caravaggio in a new light. As we have already pointed out at the beginning of this book, the world in which Caravaggio lived was extremely violent. Incidents like that of Via della Scrofa were extremely common and the perpetrators often walked away unpunished. The severity of Caravaggio's sentence should not be read just as the direct expression of the seriousness of the crime, but more as a reflection of the social status of the Tomassoni family and of their powerful connections. If Caravaggio's victim had been an ordinary man, his fate might have been very different and, interestingly, as we mentioned in Chapter 1, members of the Tomassoni family had got away 'scot-free' in similar incidents on previous occasions (Langdon, p. 314). By drawing our attention to the violence and abuses of power that characterized the Renaissance society, Ondaatje is also forcing us to engage with similar issues in our contemporary Western world, particularly with regard to the process of constructing national identities. Ondaatje seems to suggest that in order to create a multicultural society capable of offering real possibilities of cross-cultural encounters and exchange we must move beyond clear-cut notions of victim and victimizer, acknowledge that no community is immune from racism and that national myths are just empty constructs.[51]

Finally, before moving to some of the other less obvious intertextual references, I would like to point out the textual nature of *Judith Beheading Holophernes*. As Bal suggests, this painting 'is emphatically a "text": a structured, complex, meaningful surface' (*Quoting Caravaggio*, p. 102), consisting of rhymes, rhythms, echoes, and alliterations, features that are extremely important in Ondaatje's novels but also in the film where, for instance, as we have already suggested, in the opening shot the movement of the camera echoes that of the brush stroke on Katherine's notebook. According to Bal, what Narcissus's knee, Holophernes's blood and Judith's petrification have in common is not just the fact that they are visual signs but that they cannot be integrated 'within a totalizing meaning' and are 'structurally identical to "words" — but to words which, for that matter, are structurally identical to such visual signs' and therefore highlight the need to read (*Quoting Caravaggio*, p. 102) even if we are dealing with exclusively visual images (ibid.). More importantly, they also challenge causality and in so doing promote a self-critical move (pp. 104–05). In the context of Ondaatje's work, the textual nature of *Judith Beheading Holophernes* reiterates the notion of entanglement, whether we think of it in terms of race, culture, history or language/writing, which is one of the most dominant features of both novels. Like Caravaggio's paintings, Ondaatje's works have a profound rhetorical construction that draws attention to their semantic multiplicity, their ambiguity, and the importance of irony and self-irony.[52]

Before concluding, I would like to look at some other, less dominant intertextual references to Caravaggio's opus such as *St Jerome*, *Doubting Thomas*, and, as far as Minghella's adaptation of *The English Patient* is concerned, *The Resurrection of Lazarus*. St Jerome is mainly referred to in *In the Skin of a Lion* (pp. 82 and 249), possibly because of the saint's frequent association with a lion, but we could argue that Villa San Girolamo in *The English Patient* can also be seen as an indirect reference to the saint that Caravaggio painted three times, even though never with the lion.[53] Jerome is mainly famous for his scholarly activities, hence the insistence on writing, and his translation of the Bible into Latin which, to date, is the only version accepted by the Catholic Church. Even the least experienced of readers cannot but notice the constant references to translation in *The English Patient*. We are told, for instance, that the aeroplane crash which killed Clifton had 'translated' Katherine into 'leaves and twigs' (*EP*, p. 187), that Almásy had translated Katherine into his text of the desert (*EP*, p. 250), or that Katherine was 'a woman who translated her face when she put on makeup' (*EP*, p. 264). As for Kirpal's nickname Kip, we are informed that 'the name had attached itself curiously' and that when one day he had stained a document with butter his officer had teasingly remarked: '"What's this? Kipper grease?" and laughter surrounded him. He had no idea what a kipper was, but the young Sikh had been thereby translated into a salty English fish' (*EP*, pp. 93–94). Also, we find references to Poliziano, the first translator of Homer (*EP*, p. 60) and someone Almásy admires for his fluency in several languages and for having lived, like Michelangelo, Lorenzo de Medici, or Pico della Mirandola, in a time of transition, literally across two worlds: 'they held in each hand the new and the old world' (*EP*, p. 60). Through 'translation', Ondaatje stresses the idea of process: he 'applies translation to narrative in the novel so that, at the story's heart there is deferment, for a translation is never definitive'.[54] In this way he also shows how an activity traditionally 'linked to colonialism and national identity, "used in all kinds of ways to perpetuate the superiority of some culture over another"',[55] can be used to challenge those very notions of hegemony and identity. Curran reminds us that Girolamo (Jerome) was also the name of Savonarola (Curran, p. 23), the Dominican friar who is probably best known for his Bonfire of the Vanities of 1497, thus providing through the image of the transience of all things a further link between Ondaatje, Minghella, and Caravaggio.

As for *Doubting Thomas*, the omnipresence of wounds in Ondaatje's texts and Minghella's film seems inevitably to evoke this painting. The significance of this reference is more important than one might initially think. *Doubting Thomas* raises many of the issues present in the works we are studying, such as the bond between subjectivity and suffering, the connection between eroticism/desire and vision, death and the body, the suspension of the distinction between abject and holy, and the notion of Baroque point of view, but above all it is what Bal calls a navel picture, 'one whose subject is overruled by an odd detail that takes over the representation, abducting it in different directions, resisting coherence, and thereby provoking resistance' (*Quoting Caravaggio*, p. 31). This idea of a detail expressing or inviting resistance is clearly explored in the film through the image of the play of light on the English patient's head, when lying in his bed in Villa San Girolamo, which forces the viewer to focus on the growth of his hair. This use of light makes us notice almost every single hair, which, as Bal would say, becomes a symbol of fighting back (p. 61). The minimal growth of his hair reintroduces temporality (or the notion of change) and prevents us from dismissing the badly disfigured Almásy as already dead, forcing us to engage with him and reflect on the very nature of looking, an act that in our societies has almost ceased to be an act and has turned into 'an unreflected reflex' (*Quoting Caravaggio*, p. 61). The use of light in this image, which from the point of view of colour is mainly dominated by white and grey, brings to mind another painting by Caravaggio, *The Resurrection of Lazarus*. This is another highly theoretical work where 'light is the "discourse" of representation and white is its primary tool' (*Quoting Caravaggio*, pp. 49–50) and where, as in *The English Patient*, 'details with mirroring meanings begin to emerge and narrativize the still body/work into an ambiguous event of perception of both life and death' (ibid.).

As we have seen, both Ondaatje's novels and Minghella's film perform Caravaggio's lesson by employing different, but equally effective, medium-specific devices. Ondaatje, for instance, makes ample use of ekphrasis, not in the modern and narrower sense of a 'verbal representation of visual representation',[56] but in the ancient sense of 'a speech which leads around, bringing the subject matter vividly before the eyes'.[57] According to Elsner, another key feature of ancient ekphrasis is its ability to generate desire.'[58] Looking at this rhetorical device from a psychoanalytical perspective, combining Lacanian and Freudian theories, Elsner is able to demonstrate how ekphrasis can be used to problematize the process of gazing and the process of speaking (p. 178); and, we could add, the concept of mimesis and the accessibility of reality. Ekphrasis operates always according to two simultaneous axes: a 'Lacanian' visual axis of a viewer (a silent object and a speech generated by the viewing) and a Freudian verbal axis of a speaker (an audience and the speech that creates some form of communication between the two), bridging the gap between self and other (p. 157). What is particularly interesting for our analysis is the fact that for Lacan, as for Caravaggio, light is central to our perception of the world and to our sense of identity. Quoting Lacan, Elsner says: 'that which is light looks at me, and by means of that light, in the depths of my eye, something is painted [...] It is through the gaze that I enter into light and it is from the gaze that I receive its effects' (p. 165). If ekphrasis can turn into an object that causes desire it is because language, according to Lacan/Elsner, is 'driven by an excess of *jouissance*' (p. 175). This link between eroticism and language is typical of Ondaatje's style, but it becomes particularly obvious in *The English Patient*, where we are told not only that desire is what 'makes the story errant, flickering like a compass needle' (*EP*,

p. 263), but also that even ordinary words can acquire sexual connotations: 'Libya. A sexual, drawn-out word, a coaxed well. The *b* and the *y*. Madox said it was one of the few words in which you heard the tongue turn a corner' (*EP*, p. 273). For David Caravaggio, the eroticism of language can be more rewarding than physical intercourse: 'Sometimes I really do like to talk more than fuck [...] The trouble with words is that you can really talk yourself into a corner. Whereas you can't fuck yourself into a corner' (*EP*, p. 127). As for the act of looking, all the characters in *The English Patient* keep looking at each other. We are repeatedly told that Caravaggio watches Hana and vice versa, that Hana watches the English patient and he watches her, but, as Lacan would say, what they look at is never what they wish to see (Elsner, p. 166), because the object of our gaze opposes a resistance and refuses to be confined to a clear and single interpretation (p. 167). As a result, in ekphrasis, 'the gaze becomes itself the subject of the description' (ibid.). We also experience a 'loss of authorial (or viewing) autonomy' as the viewer feels threatened by the gaze of the other (p. 171), which is what we saw when we discussed the Baroque point of view. As in the concept of narcissism discussed above, 'the ekphrases keep the dynamic of desire flowing and yet simultaneously demonstrate its failure and lack' (p. 175). Significantly none of the love stories described in *The English Patient* has a happy ending.

Regarding Minghella's cinematic adaptation of *The English Patient*, I argue that it performs Caravaggio's lesson by offering, as Hsuan Hsu demonstrates, 'a cinema of radical movement and heteropathic contact' that challenges the voyeuristic model of the apparatus 'composed of flames and silhouettes in Plato's allegorical cave', whose illusory images transfixed the prisoners and dissuaded them from pursuing the truth.[59] Minghella, instead, demands the active involvement of the spectator, turning him/her into half witness and half assistant, who by watching the film helps it to be born (p. 59). Hana, who already in *In the Skin of a Lion* plays the role of the listener, can be seen as the model spectator. The scene which best captures this concept of cinema is the one in which we see her swinging up and down from one wall to another of the ruined convent near Villa San Girolamo looking at Renaissance frescos 'on a rope counterweighted by Kip' (p. 59). Her moving from one picture to the next, selecting which detail to illuminate with the torch Kip lit for her, and in so doing adding her flare to it, contributes to the spectacle and creates a strong erotic atmosphere in what is one of the most powerful love scenes in the whole film. By combining images, light, shade, music, and movement, this scene turns the film experience into an event. As Kennedy explains, '*The English Patient* offers an example of film explored as experience, as sensation, as a perception-consciousness formation' (p. 5), where perception is to be understood not just in visual terms but 'through the synaesthetics of sensation' (ibid.). Kennedy's views are clearly influenced by Deleuzian philosophy, that is to say, by a concept of art having as its aim the production of sensation. For Deleuze, sensation is always connected to the concept of 'affect' as theorized by Spinoza. Affect, which differs from emotion as it operates beyond subjectivity, has a bodily nature: 'by affect I understand affections of the body by which the body's power of acting is increased or diminished, aided or restrained, and at the same time the ideas of these affections'.[60] But let us return to the issue of sensation. In cinema, it is through style that sensation is manifested: colour, light, tone, music, sound, and movement interact and create a rhythm which constitutes the essence of sensation. In this way, as Kennedy points out:

> We can think of the experience of the cinematic not only as a representation of something with a meaning, but also as aesthetic assemblage, which moves, modulates and resonates with its audience or spectator through the process of molecularity. It connects. It works through affect, intensity and becoming — and ultimately through sensation, not necessarily through subjectivity, identity and representation. (p. 114)

Finally, I would like to conclude by stressing that the 'erotic embodied look' described in Hsu's seminal article is another feature which, like in Caravaggio's paintings, 'effectively dissolves the boundaries between self and other' (Hsu, p. 60). The breaking of boundaries is particularly obvious towards the end of the film when 'Hana's voice blends with Katherine's as they read the letter, Hana's piano theme blends with Almásy's song in Hungarian' (ibid.). Hsu makes us also notice that in the last sequence Hana's eyes, as she leaves Villa San Girolamo on a truck, are full of tears and so are the eyes of most spectators: 'the film produces a physical and more or less collective and collaborative trace and its images cross the boundary between the screen and the viewers' eyes' (p. 60). These remarks bring us back to Bal's notion of nostalgia discussed earlier in this chapter; or Marcuse's idea of sensuousness as a tool capable of subverting 'the tyranny of reason' (Lundgren, p. 19) and of subversive art as appealing to the spirit rather than to the intellect (ibid.).

Notes to Chapter 5

1. Mimicry here is understood in the sense proposed by Homi Bhabha, 'Of Mimicry and Man', in *The Location of Culture* (London: Routledge, 1994), pp. 85–92.
2. For an overview of some key critical responses to the concept of mimicry see *The Post-Colonial Studies Reader*, ed. by Bill Ashcroft, Gareth Griffiths, and Helen Tiffin, (London: Routledge, 1995), pp. 7–11.
3. J. U. Jacobs, 'Michael Ondaatje's *The English Patient* (1992) and Postcolonial Impatience', *Journal of Literary Studies*, 13 (1997), 92–112 (p. 106).
4. Raphael Ingelbien, 'A Novelist's Caravaggism: Michael Ondaatje's *In the Skin of a Lion*', in *The Guises of Canadian Diversity: New European Perspectives*, ed. by Serge Jaumain and Marc Maufort (Amsterdam: Rodopi, 1995), pp. 27–37 (p. 28).
5. Bal, *Quoting Caravaggio*, p. 20.
6. Gilles Deleuze, *The Fold: Leibniz and the Baroque*, trans. by Tom Conley (London: Continuum, 2006), pp. 38–39.
7. Helen Tiffin, 'Post-colonial Literatures and Counter-discourse', in *The Post-Colonial Studies Reader*, ed. by Ashcroft, Bill, Gareth Griffiths, and Helen Tiffin (London: Routledge, 1995), pp. 95–98 (p. 95).
8. Barbara M. Kennedy, *Deleuze and Cinema: The Aesthetics of Sensation* (Edinburgh: Edinburgh University Press, 2000), p. 6.
9. Shadi Bartsch and Jaś Elsner, 'Ekphrasis through the Ages. Introduction: Eight Ways of Looking at Ekphrasis' <http://humanities.uchicago.edu/depts/classics/people/PDF.Files/Ekphrasis.briefintro.final.pdf> [accessed 12 March 2008].
10. Michael Ondaatje, *In the Skin of a Lion* (Oxford: Picador, 1988; first published 1987); abbreviated as *SL*.
11. Fotois Sarris, '*In the Skin of a Lion*: Michael Ondaatje's Tenebristic Narrative', *Essays on Canadian Writing*, 44 (1991), 183–201 (p. 194).

12. Jodi Lundgren, '"Colour Disrobed Itself from the Body": The Racialized Aesthetics of Liberation in Michael Ondaatje's *In the Skin of a Lion*', *Canadian Literature*, 190 (2006), 15–29 (p. 17).
13. The first of the two epigraphs to the novel is a quote from *The Epic of Gilgamesh*: 'the joyful will stoop with sorrow, and when you have gone to the earth I will let my hair grow long for your sake, I will wander through the wilderness in the skin of a lion'. This ancient Mesopotamian narrative tells the story of a great friendship between Gilgamesh, the king of Uruk, and Enkidu, a wild man created by the gods as Gilgamesh's equal in order to prevent him from oppressing his people. When Enkidu dies, Gilgamesh feels so lost that he starts wandering through the wilderness in search of purpose. As Srikanth points out, this story becomes the metaphor through which Ondaatje expresses his ideal vision of Canada as a nation that without the presence of immigrants from other countries would lose its identity. Rajini Srikanth, *The World Next Door: South Asian American Literature and the Idea of America* (Philadelphia: Temple University Press, 2004), p. 193.
14. According to de Certeau, the bridge signifies 'the "betrayal" of an order', a transgression but also 'something that allows or causes the re-emergence beyond the frontiers of the alien element that was controlled in the interior, and gives ob-jectivity (that is, expression and re-presentation) to the alterity which was hidden inside the limits' (Michel de Certeau, *The Practice of Everyday Life* (Berkeley and Los Angeles: University of California Press, 1988), p. 128).
15. According to his early biographers, Caravaggio was often seen playing with his black dog named Cornacchia (crow). See Roberto Longhi, *Caravaggio*, with an introduction by G. Previtali (Rome: Editori Riuniti, 2006; first published in 1952), p. 51.
16. As Don Randall points out, Kip's invisibility is more prominent in the film:

> Kip does not challenge or 'interrupt' (to use Chamber's figure) the experience of selfhood and culture that the European principals represent. Indeed, in being presented as a spectacle, 'a sexy Sikh', he effectively recedes into cultural invisibility, the very invisibility the novel presents as a problem [...]

(Don Randall, 'Ondaatje Goes to Hollywood: The Costs of Mainstream Arrival for the Representation of Cultural Difference', in *Adjacencies: Minority Writing in Canada*, ed. by Dominic A. Beneventi, Licia Canton, and Lianne Moyes (Toronto: Guernica, 2004), pp. 128–42 (p. 140))
17. See p. 191.
18. Mieke Bal, *Looking in: The Art of Viewing* (Amsterdam: G + B Arts International Imprint, 2001), p. 246.
19. Alberto Manguel, *Reading Pictures: A History of Love and Hate* (London: Bloomsbury, 2001), pp. 270–73.
20. We must also remember that Caravaggio's frequent use of apocryphal sources for his religious subjects was also highly political in the climate of the Counter-Reformation. On this topic see Dario Fo, *Caravaggio al tempo di Caravaggio* (Modena: Franco Cosimo Panini, 2005), p. 142. Fo also makes a very interesting observation regarding the political significance of Caravaggio's paintings in his analysis of *The Calling of St Matthew* and *The Martyrdom of St Matthew*, in which, by showing a striking resemblance between the face of Matthew and that of a well-known portrait of Henry IV of Bourbon, he claims that the two Caravaggio paintings are more about one of the most significant episodes in the history of the Counter-Reformation, the conversion of the French King to Catholicism, than about the life of one of the apostles (pp. 84–100).
21. According to Sarris, sleep, like darkness or blindness, symbolizes the 'forfeit of moral responsibility' (p. 200).
22. Arthur A. Brown, 'Storytelling, the Meaning of Life and *The Epic of Gilgamesh*', <http://eawc.evansville.edu/essays/brown.htm> [accessed 20 March 2008].
23. Jacques Rancière, *The Politics of Aesthetics* (London: Continuum, 2007), p. 43.
24. Michael Ondaatje, *The English Patient* (London: Bloomsbury, 1992); abbreviated as *EP*.
25. Graham Huggan, *The Post-colonial Exotic: Marketing the Margins* (London: Routledge, 2001), p. 116.
26. Andrew Gibson, *Towards a Postmodern Theory of Narrative* (Edinburgh: Edinburgh University Press, 1996), p. 90.

27. Significantly, one of the chapters in *SL* is entitled 'The Searcher'. It narrates the story of Patrick's search for Ambrose Small, a millionaire and compulsive gambler who owned ninety-six theatres in Toronto at the beginning of the twentieth century. He suddenly disappeared on 16 December 1919 and was never found. Unlike the police who were in charge of the initial investigation, Patrick begins his search by trying to bridge Ambrose's private and public images, focusing on Small's private correspondence:

   > What held most interest for Patrick was the collection of letters the police had handed over to the family. Gradually he came into contact with Small's two sisters who until then had found no one to take the letters seriously. Cranks, mediums, blackmail threats, the claims of kidnappers — the police and Small's wife had scorned them all. (*SL*, p. 62)

   As Lowry points out, it is Patrick's activity as 'the searcher' that allows him 'to knit together the characters and plot of the novel'. Glen Lowry, 'The Representations of "Race" in Ondaatje's *In the Skin of a Lion*', *CLCWeb: Comparative Literature and Culture*, 6 (2004), <http://docs.lib.purdue.edu/clcweb/vol6/iss3/7> [accessed 10 April 2012].
28. If we apply Bal's theory to Ondaatje's novels and Minghella's film, it could be argued that these works constitute *acts of memory* because, although they do not represent our memories, they work on our memory and by 'suturing collectivity and subjectivity through fiction' make us complicit in the stories they narrate (*Quoting Caravaggio*, p. 68). As Bal would put it, they present us with 'a memory that we can no longer disavow' (p. 68). It is also worth noting that the dimension of nostalgia is more prominent in Minghella's adaptation of *The English Patient* where, starting with the opening shots which present 'the desert landscape as an expanse of grainy, golden, flesh-evoking contours', we are encouraged to indulge 'in a delicious, nostalgic yearning for forms of erotic experience that seem almost constitutively incompatible with our late-twentieth-century lives in urban space' (Randall, p. 131). According to Randall, however, in this case the nostalgic element contributes to the de-politicization of Ondaatje's text.
29. See n. 20.
30. It is worth remembering that David Caravaggio claims he has lost his skills in stealing (*EP*, p. 36).
31. One of the most frequently used terms in the book is 'gap': there are gaps in time, people's lives, places and in the plot (*EP*, pp. 7, 38, 45, 97, 100, 102, 116, 181 and 189).
32. Stephanie M. Hilger, 'Ondaatje's *The English Patient* and Rewriting History', in *Comparative Cultural Studies and Michael Ondaatje's Writing*, ed. by Steven Tötösy de Zepetnek (West Lafayette: Purdue University Press, 2005), pp. 38–48 (p. 45). In this essay Hilger takes up some of the ideas presented by Theodor Adorno in his 1951 *Minima Moralia*.
33. Significantly, when in the novel Hana removes the bandages from his hands to inspect Caravaggio's wounds, the position of his hands resembles a basin: 'his hands held together like a human bowl' (*EP*, p. 57).
34. It is perhaps worth remembering that while in the novel the relationship between David and Hana appears to be a continuation of the relationship they had in *In the Skin of a Lion* where David Caravaggio, being Patrick's best friend, was a kind of uncle to young Hana, in the film, they are strangers, thus increasing the sense of fragmentation.
35. For some examples see: *SL*, pp. 82–83, 86, 98–99, 166, 176–82, 248; *EP*, pp. 22, 116, 125, 166, 231, 237, and 287. Metaphors of blindness or limited vision are extremely common in Ondaatje's works; they are used to stress the notions of vulnerability, transience, the limited nature of knowledge, and questions of class and identity.
36. Interestingly, when the English patient returns to the Cave of Swimmers hoping to rescue Katherine, he remembers a story about demon lovers and how demons and witches could be easily identified by asking them to turn around as they had no back, 'only what they wish to present to you' (*EP*, p. 276).
37. Regarding the significance of the film's opening shot see also Kennedy's book, in which the critic argues that the opening sequence illustrates a 'Deleuzian sense of collusion [...] between the material and the sensation' as '"the material is so varied that it is difficult to say where in fact the material ends and the sensation begins"' (p. 152).

38. According to Deleuze, the fold is inseparable from wind (*The Fold*, p. 34).
39. Significantly Katherine's dying words link dying to the idea of 'communal history' implicit in the notion of monumentalization (*EP*, p. 277). For a more detailed analysis of Katherine's last words both in the novel and in the film see: pp. 313–14.
40. See also Deleuze on 'chiaroscuro' (*The Fold*, pp. 102–03).
41. 'This country — had I chartered it and turned it into a place of war?' (*EP*, p. 276).
42. In line with Deleuzian philosophy, the last sentence can also be seen as a statement on the hallucinatory nature of perception. For Deleuze what we commonly call perception is always the product of two kinds of perception: tiny, confused, or unconscious perceptions which eventually unfold into macro, clear, or conscious perceptions in an endless movement of folding and unfolding through which a new series of micro perceptions destabilizes the previous conscious/macro perception. Perception is hallucinatory, Deleuze argues, because perceiving in folds means that we are 'grasping figures without objects, but through the haze of dust without objects that the figures themselves raise up from the depths, and that falls back again, but with time enough to be seen for an instant' (*The Fold*, p. 107).
43. For references to the issue of moral indifference in *In the Skin of a Lion* see the analysis of the passage devoted to the tannery workers on p. 293. Also, concerning the issue of 'being' or 'becoming' human in *SL*, we must remember that this was an important theme in *The Epic of Gilgamesh*, the novel's most prominent intertext.
44. See p. 181.
45. A classic example is *The Musicians* (1595), which Caravaggio painted for Cardinal Del Monte and which was highly sensual and meant to arouse erotic desire as a statement on the power of looking (Langdon, p. 111). Other relevant examples are the *Victorious Cupid* (1602) and *St John the Baptist* (1602), which, as Langdon suggests, are both about 'the dangerous power of love' (p. 213), a theme that features prominently in *The English Patient* where Katherine repeatedly accuses Almásy of having killed everything in her (*EP*, pp. 185 and 273).
46. Like a Deleuzian fold which in principle continues to infinity, this theme is reinforced through the image of Hana as modern Mary Magdalene (another of Caravaggio's favourite subjects), washing her Jesus' feet at the very beginning of the novel (*EP*, p. 3).
47. See pp. 178–79.
48. Jover suggests that we can read this painting as a criticism of the voyeuristic and predatory gaze: Caravaggio, who was 'the painter of seen things' and whose desire as a painter 'found its primary fulfilment in a finely honed exercise of the gaze', by cutting off his head kills the gaze and even more drastically 'the power to see — and to show — via painting' (pp. 96–97).
49. Mieke Bal, *A Mieke Bal Reader* (Chicago: University of Chicago Press, 2006), p. 409.
50. It is worth noting that *Judith Beheading Holofernes* can also be read as Caravaggio's homage to Beatrice Cenci, the girl who had been publicly executed for having killed her violent and abusive father in his sleep. Although the general public and many members of the nobility had been in favour of granting a pardon to Beatrice, the pope had decided to punish her and turn this case into an example of Counter-Reformation morality. By depicting the murder of her father, Caravaggio was violating Clement VIII's ban issued on 11 September 1600 with which he prohibited any form of writing concerned with Beatrice's story. For a detailed account of this topic see Bassani and Bellini, pp. 80 and 95–97.
51. Regarding questions of race and multiculturalism in *In the Skin of a Lion* see Glen Lowry, 'The Representation of "Race" in Ondaatje's *In the Skin of a Lion*', *CLCWeb: Comparative Literature and Culture*, 6 (2004), <http://docs.lib.purdue.edu/clcweb/vol6/iss3/7> [accessed 10 April 2012] and Kit Dobson, 'Multicultural Postmodernities in Michael's Ondaatje's *In the Skin of a Lion*', in Kit Dobson, *Transnational Canadas: Anglo-Canadian Literature and Globalization* (Waterloo, ON: Wilfrid Laurier University Press, 2009), pp. 105–11.
52. For a detailed analysis of the rhetorical construction of some of Caravaggio's paintings see Rudolf Preimesberger, 'Golia e Davide', in *Docere, Delectare, Movere: Affetti, devozione e retorica nel linguaggio artistico del primo barocco romano*, ed. by Anna Gramiccia and others (Rome: De Luca, 1998), pp. 63–69.
53. *St Jerome in Meditation* (Monserrat, Barcelona), probably painted in 1606; *St Jerome Writing* (Rome, Galleria Borghese), also painted in 1606; *St Jerome Writing* (Malta), painted in 1607.

54. Steven Tötösy de Zepetnek (ed.), 'Introduction', in *Comparative Cultural Studies*, p. 2.
55. Beverley Curran, 'Ondaatje's *The English Patient* and Altered States of Narrative', in *Comparative Cultural studies*, ed. by Steven Tötösy de Zepetnek (West Lafayette: Purdue University Press, 2005), pp. 16–26 (p. 18). Curran quotes Steiner to remind us how St Jerome used the image of 'meaning brought home captive by the translator' to describe translation. He also points out that former European colonies have often been seen as 'translations of a distant and idealized original whose standards have been reduced to imperfect copies, characterized by absence or imitation' (p. 16). See also George Steiner, *After Babel: Aspects of Language and Translation* (Oxford: Oxford University Press, 1998), p. 314.
56. James A. W. Heffernan, *Museum of Words: The Poetics of Ekphrasis from Homer to Ashbery* (Chicago: University of Chicago Press, 1993), p. 3.
57. Ruth Webb, '*Ekphrasis* Ancient and Modern: The Invention of a Genre', *Word & Image*, 15 (1999), 7–18 (p. 11).
58. Jaś Elsner, 'Seeing and Saying: A Psychoanalytic Account of Ekphrasis', *Helios*, 31 (2004), 157–85 (p. 158).
59. Hsuan Hsu, 'Post-nationalism and the Cinematic Apparatus in Minghella's Adaptation of Ondaatje's *The English Patient*', in *Comparative Cultural Studies*, ed. by Tötösy de Zepetnek, pp. 49–61 (pp. 58 and 49).
60. Benedict de Spinoza, *Ethics* (London: Penguin Books, 1996), p. 70: D3. Interestingly, the second postulate of the third part of the *Ethics* devoted to the nature and origin of affects cannot but make us think of Katherine's last words before she dies in the Cave of Swimmers: 'the human body can undergo many changes, and nevertheless retain impressions, *or* traces, of the objects, and consequently the same images of things (p. 70: P2).

CONCLUSION

Caravaggio and the Neo-Baroque: Some Final Considerations

e allora sconvolto presi uno
specchio e mi vidi anch'io riflesso
dietro davanti dritto a traverso
riflesso e catapultato
incollato parola e
immagine
show

[and then shattered I took a | mirror and saw myself reflected too | back front straight through | reflected and catapulted | glued word and | image | show]

CLAUDIO BRANCALEONI, 'Visioni'[1]

This monograph has shown that the myth of Caravaggio can be traced through a variety of texts and genres. However, despite the extremely diverse nature of the works studied, contemporary responses to the life and works of the Lombard painter address common themes. *Self and identity* feature prominently in all our case studies, whether we think of the fictional biographies of Chapter 2; the crime fiction works of Chapter 3; Jarman's *Caravaggio*, Gunn's poetry, and Fernandez's *Dans la main de l'ange* in Chapter 4; or Ondaatje's novels and Minghella's adaptation of *The English Patient* in Chapter 5. The *tension between micro and macro history* and the *violence of history* are also widely explored, particularly in Chapters 3 and 5. Stemming from these more general concerns with history, most of the texts and films we have analysed show an interest in *social and political criticism* that manifests itself in the desire to draw attention to the problems caused by organized crime, greed, and the myth of happiness, or the use of drugs, particularly among young people. All the authors studied in the various chapters seem keen to emphasize the grotesque, gruesome, and traumatic aspects of reality (particularly in Chapters 3 and 4) and the relationship between sex and death. Other important themes are those of the nature of the aesthetic experience, the function of art in our contemporary world, questions of value, and the idea of art as fetish. As for the relationship between painting and literature we have seen the importance of the *canvas as an emblem of the novel* (particularly of the way a novel is constructed) and, in some cases, of life.

More broadly, however, the aforementioned themes are part of a wider fascination with the Baroque that has transcended the sphere of art, spreading to all aspects of life. According to Ndalianis, we have developed a true 'Baroque mentality', and this has become so engrained in contemporary culture that it can no longer be dismissed as a fashion or style ('Neo-Baroques', p. 268). Ndalianis and Perniola remind us that this reassessment of the Baroque began at the beginning of the twentieth century in all major European cultures and in South America, particularly in the works of the Cuban writer Severo Sarduy, who, as Ndalianis explains, consciously embraced the Baroque as a revolutionary form capable of countering the dominance of capitalism and socialism' (*Neo-Baroque Aesthetics*, p. 12). According to Perniola, within Europe Baudelaire can be considered as the precursor of this renewed interest in the Baroque but 'it was above all German Expressionism that provided a platform for a neo-Baroque poetics'.[2] Although we should refrain from conflating the seventeenth-century Baroque with its modern/postmodern counterpart, there are commonalities between these two 'movements', which include a sense of performativity and theatricality, a love of spectacle, a self-reflexive attitude to its methods of construction, a desire to play with the borders that separate illusion and reality and, above all, a virtuosity of exuberance that requires the audience to revel in the artistry and skill of the artist. ('Neo-Baroques, p. 277)

However, in order to highlight the significance of Caravaggio for neo-Baroque aesthetics, we also need to focus on other features of the Baroque that are relevant to our contemporary world or, more specifically, to postmodernism since most of the texts/films used in the case studies are the product of postmodern culture. As pointed out by Maravall, Baroque culture develops as a response to a deep social and economic state of crisis[3] and the same can be said of postmodernism. Hassan, for instance, defines postmodernism as the manifestation of 'a global crisis of identity'[4] and identifies a 'reflexive affinity between postmodernism and autobiography'.[5] The self, he argues, 'remains a vital existential category, an organizing, pragmatic, if not ontological principle keenly relevant to us all to the degree that the postmodern condition appears, unstable conflictual, dispersive' ('Postmodernism Revisited', p. 144). As we have seen in Chapter 2, the 'author/painter as character' genre seems to prove Hassan's point: in the age of weak thought, authors who are at the beginning of their creative career and/or are interested in talking about themselves often feel the need to speak through the voice of a more famous and authoritative personality. Significantly, the popularity of biographies began to develop during the Baroque when the pedagogical value of the genre was discovered (Maravall, p. 164). Although the exemplary value of biographies, in terms of the moral and political education of an individual, was much stronger during the Baroque, a certain pedagogical intent has survived in the postmodern era, as revealed by most of the texts analysed in Chapter 2. The Baroque interest in biography was also related to the discovery of psychology and studies in physiognomy, and to the fact that the seventeenth-century individual was fundamentally in conflict with himself (Maravall, pp. 113–14 and 262). In this respect, with his various self-portraits, Caravaggio was a child of his age. As art historians have shown (e.g. Stone; Cropper), these self-portraits played a vital role in the construction of one the most popular myths about his persona, that of the *pittore maledetto*, a myth that also furthered the notion of the painter's gender-confused personality, which appeals to contemporary gay artists (Chapter 4).

The image of the *pittore maledetto* is linked to another aspect of the Baroque, that is the violence of its society which is depicted in many works of art and develops into an 'aesthetics of cruelty' and a taste for horror (Maravall, p. 267). According to Maravall, the Baroque is marked by a morbid fascination with death. The corpse as death loses its impersonal medieval character and becomes 'un'esperienza che tocca ogni singolo individuo e causa una dolorosa ripulsa' [an experience that affects every single individual and causes a painful repulsion] (Maravall, p. 270). As mentioned above, these themes are also present in contemporary responses to Caravaggio where, significantly, one of the most quoted paintings is his *David with the Head of Goliath*, by far the most gruesome of Caravaggio's works. According to Perniola, a focus on 'the most violent and the most raw aspects of reality' and an interest in the topics of sex and death are the key features of contemporary forms of realism.[6] As mentioned in the introduction to this volume and as demonstrated by the various case studies, realism represents the red thread that joins Caravaggio, the Baroque, neo-Baroque/postmodernism, and the various reappropriations of Caravaggio by popular culture. This book has confirmed that, as Mario Perniola highlights, 'in the artistic adventure of the West one can single out two opposite trends, one oriented toward the celebration of appearance, the other toward the experience of reality' (*Art and its Shadow*, p. 3). Although, at times (the period varies slightly from country to country), the realist trend seemed to be dying out, by the 1990s we see a return to 'more or less "realistic"' storytelling on an international scale.[7] Reality, however, can no longer be represented unproblematically; so, already during the 1980s (particularly in America), but more so since the 1990s, representations of reality are marked by 'sudden disruptions of continuity that take the form of a mystery' (Grabes, p. 15), hence the interest in crime fiction.[8] According to Grabes, 'the revival of realistic narration [...] meant also a reintroduction of social problems and social criticism' (ibid.). Not surprisingly, many of the debates on crime fiction today and most of the textual examples analysed in Chapter 3 highlight the role of this genre in addressing (more or less successfully) burning social issues.[9] This 'ethical turn' (Grabes, p. 20) is not just confined to crime fiction/the noir (e.g. Ondaatje's works in Chapter 5). It extends beyond the literary world into the spheres of critical theory and philosophy as reflected, for instance, in Hassan's desire to return to '"soft" universals' and to develop an ethic of trust ('Beyond Postmodernism', pp. 6–12). It can also be seen many of the debates about postmodernism and engagement which flourished towards the end of the last millennium and the beginning of the new one.[10]

Such debates bring us back to Perniola's statements about the key currents in the cultural history of the West, as they seem to confirm his view that whenever we encounter the realist trend a special emphasis is put 'on the idea of participation, involvement, compromise' and art is conceived as '*perturbation, electrocution, shock*' (*Art and its Shadow*, p. 3; emphasis in the original).[11] However, since both the Baroque and neo-Baroque/Postmodernism are mass cultures, parallel to the more engaged/ethical trend in art we also find a more escapist one. As Perniola explains, the proponents of this trend focus their attention on 'the notions of separation, distance, suspension' and consider the 'aesthetic attitude as a process of catharsis and de-realization' (ibid.). In Chapter 2, for instance, we have seen how people with an amateur interest in art are hungry for fictional works that acknowledge the sense of wonder they experience when looking at a painting or a sculpture. This resulted in the habit of commissioning fictional works devoted to a particular artist to mark the opening of a new exhibition and feed such 'hunger'. The other key feature of mass culture is the tendency to develop a fetishistic attachment to objects and works of art (Perniola, *Art and its Shadow*, p. xvi), as seen in most of our case studies. What makes Caravaggio particularly interesting in terms of the cultural trends identified by Perniola is that although his paintings were aimed at ordinary people, as they portrayed the privileged position beggars and sinners occupied according to the Gospel, they also contained an elitist discourse, a theological allegory, a learned disquisition (see Calvesi, *Le realtà del Caravaggio*, p. 59). Despite the use of simple realistic images, his paintings are skilled rhetorical constructions, which is why, today, they appeal to artists and audiences of all kinds. However, according to Perniola, contemporary appreciations of art are characterized by a certain naivety, as people tend either to place too much emphasis on the work itself as an 'entity endowed with cultural, symbolic or economic value' or to attribute to the artistic operation 'the characteristics of immediate and direct communication' (*Art and its Shadow*, p. xv). Both attitudes lead to the trivialization of art as they ignore 'the shadow that inevitably accompanies the works and the artistic operation' (p. xvi). As Silverman explains in his preface to the English translation of Perniola's book, for Perniola the shadow is linked to Derrida's notion of *remainder*, to be understood as a 'super-addition of sense' or 'a frame, an edge, but also a trace of what it remains from' (p. xi). In Perniola's view, shadows 'accompany art and give it meaning [...], accompany each and every experience of art — as trauma, as disgust, as splendor, as grandeur, as exceptional' (p. xiii). Paradoxically, although they give art meaning they represent that element which cannot be fully explained:

> The more violent is the light which one pretends to shed on the work and the artistic operation, the higher is the shadow they project. The more diurnal and banal is the approach to artistic experience, the more what is essential withdraws and takes refuge in the shadow. (p. xvi)

Most of the case studies included in this book address the theme of the shadow of art by drawing our attention to the gap between the work of art and the place it occupies. As for Caravaggio, there is no doubt that the shadow of his art is rather large because 'the more art grows, the bigger its shadow becomes, the greater the spaces that it is unable to illuminate become' (p. xviii). However, it is precisely in this shadow that the self-perpetuating nature of Caravaggio's myth lies, because we could argue that the more elusive something becomes the more one feels the need to provide new interpretations. What is more, for centuries Caravaggio's elusiveness was accentuated by lack of concrete evidence about certain periods of his life and by the fact that he did not leave any form of written testimony. Finally, given the neo-Baroque love of spectacle, it is no surprise that Caravaggio's myth keeps thriving as his life and works are truly spectacular in the sense of stunning, dramatic, sensational, and magnificent.

Notes to the Conclusion

1. Claudio Brancaleoni, *Apocalissi di inizio millennio: Frammenti a più voci 2001–2011* (Perugia: Morlacchi Editore, 2011), p. 14.
2. Mario Perniola, *Enigmas: The Egyptian Moment in Society and Art*, trans. by Christopher Woodall (London Verso: 1995), pp. 91–92.
3. José Antonio Maravall, *La cultura del Barroco: Análisis de una estructura histórica* (Barcelona: Ariel, 1975). All references in this book are from the 1985 Italian translation. José Antonio Maravall, *La cultura del Barocco: Analisi di una struttura storica*, trans. by Christian Paez (Bologna: Il Mulino, 1985), pp. 39 and 44.
4. Ihab Hassan, 'Beyond Postmodernism: Toward an Aesthetic of Trust', in *Beyond Postmodernism: Reassessments in Literature, Theory, and Culture*, ed. by Klaus Stierstorfer (Berlin: Walter de Gruyter, 2003), pp. 199–212 (p. 201).
5. Ihab Hassan, 'Postmodernism Revisited: A Personal Account', *American Studies*, 43 (1998), 143–53 (p. 144). According to Hal Foster, the 'return of the subject' in Postmodernism is a characteristic of the 1990s: Hal Foster, *The Return of the Real* (Cambridge, MA: MIT Press, 1996), p. 212.
6. Mario Perniola, *Art and its Shadow*, trans. by Massimo Verdicchio (New York: Continuum, 2004), p. 4. All references are from this English edition. For other interesting assessments of the role of realism in Western culture, see Foster (*The Return of the Real*) and Hassan ('Beyond Postmodernism').
7. Herbert Grabes, 'From the Post-Modern to the Pre-Modern: More Recent Changes in Literature, Art and Theory', in *Postmodernism and After: Visions and Revisions*, ed. by Regina Rudaityté (New Castle: Cambridge Scholars Publishing, 2008), pp. 11–27 (p. 14).
8. It is worth noting that, according to Maravall, the modern notion of suspense originates in the Baroque, as testified by the frequency with which the term *sospensione* [suspension] is used. During the seventeenth century the technique of 'suspense' became widespread in various forms of art, including painting, and it was used to force the reader/spectator/viewer to fill in the gap in his own way. Maravall uses Shakespeare as an example of an artist whose late plays have often been dismissed as lacking a finishing touch. Considering the undisputed quality of most of Shakespeare's works, Maravall argues that the so-called defects of some of his late plays should be seen as reflection of the Baroque taste for suspension and the incomplete rather than as a sign of his artistic exhaustion (pp. 356 and 360–61). Interestingly, in commenting on Caravaggio's style of painting during the final years of his life, Stone says: 'the brushstrokes in the late works have a kind of autonomy. Rather than defining form, they simply construct a mass with general highlights in a place where the spectator understands by context which form should reside' (in Stone (ed.), p. 23).
9. Debates on crime as a tool for social criticism are particularly strong in the field of Italian studies. See: Marco Sangiorini, *Il giallo come nuovo romanzo sociale* (Ravenna: Longo, 2004); *Differences, Deceits and Desires: Murder and Mayhem in Italian Crime Fiction*, ed. by Mirna Cicioni and Nicoletta Di Ciolla (Newark: University of Delaware Press, 2008); *Postmodern Impegno: Ethics and Commitment in Contemporary Italian Culture*, ed. by Pierpaolo Antonello and Florian Mussgnug (Berne: Peter Lang, 2009); *Noir de noir: Un'indagine pluridisciplinare*, ed. by Dieter Vermandere, Monica Jansen, and Inge Lanslots (Berne: Peter Lang, 2010).
10. See Gary Brent Madison and Marty Fairbairn, *The Ethics of Postmodernity: Current Trends in Continental Thought* (Evanston, IL: Northwestern University Press, 1999); Stefan Herbrechter, *Lawrence Durrell, Postmodernism and the Ethics of Alterity* (Amsterdam: Rodopi, 1999); Frederick Ferré, *Living and Value: Toward a Constructive Postmodern Ethics* (Albany: State University of New York Press, 2001); Andrew Gibson, *Postmodernity, Ethics and the Novel* (London: Routledge, 2002); *Post-modernism and the Ethical Subject*, ed. by Barbara Gabriel and Suzan Ilcan (Montreal: McGill-Queen's University Press, 2004), to mention just a few examples. For the Italian context, see Jennifer Burns, *Fragments of Impegno: Interpretation of Commitment in Contemporary Italian Narrative, 1980–2000* (Leeds: Northern Universities Press, 2001) and, more recently, the aforementioned volume *Postmodern Impegno*, ed. by Antonello and Mussgnug.
11. Regarding the term 'shock', it is worth noting that Hal Foster talks of 'traumatic realism',

arguing that the twentieth century is dominated by the 'tendency to redefine experience, individual and historical, in terms of trauma' (p. 168). Whilst, in art and critical theory, trauma discourses propose the critique of the subject (as in psychoanalytical terms the subject of trauma does not exist), in popular culture, by contrast, trauma is seen as 'an event that guarantees the subject' and gives it 'absolute authority, for one cannot challenge the trauma of another' (ibid.). The notions of shock and trauma are particularly relevant to Piersanti's novel (in Chapter 3) but also to the homoerotic works of Chapter 4.

BIBLIOGRAPHY

ACKROYD, PETER, *Poe: A Life Cut Short* (London: Chatto & Windus, 2008)
ALDRICH, ROBERT, *The Seduction of the Mediterranean* (London: Routledge, 1993)
——, and GARRY WOTHERSPOON, *Who's Who in Contemporary Gay and Lesbian History*, II: *From World War II to the Present Day* (London: Routledge, 2001)
ALLMER, PATRICIA, 'La Reproduction Interdite: René Magritte and Forgery', *Papers of Surrealism*, 5 (2007), 1–19
ANTONELLO, PIERPAOLO, and FLORIAN MUSSGNUG, eds, *Postmodern Impegno: Ethics and Commitment in Contemporary Italian Culture* (Berne: Peter Lang, 2009)
ARGAN, CARLO GIULIO, 'Un'ipotesi caravaggesca', *Parallelo*, 2 (1943), 40–43
ASHCROFT, BILL, GARETH GRIFFITHS, and HELEN TIFFIN, eds, *The Post-Colonial Studies Reader* (London: Routledge, 1995)
BACHELARD, GASTON, *The Poetics of Space* (Boston: Beacon Press, 1969)
BADIOU, ALAIN, *St Paul: The Founder of Universalism*, trans. by Ray Brassier (Palo Alto: Stanford University Press, 2003)
BAL, MIEKE, *Double Exposure: The Subject of Cultural Analysis* (London: Routledge, 1996)
—— *Looking in: The Art of Viewing* (Amsterdam: G + B Arts International Imprint, 2001)
—— *A Mieke Bal Reader* (Chicago: University of Chicago Press, 2006)
—— *Quoting Caravaggio: Contemporary Art, Preposterous History* (Chicago: University of Chicago Press, 1999)
—— *Reading Rembrandt: Beyond the Word–Image Opposition*, rev. edn (Amsterdam: Amsterdam University Press, 2006)
BALDASSARRI, FABIO, *Il Mistero del Caravaggio* (Milan: Il Ponte delle Grazie, 2003)
BANKS, OLIVER, *The Caravaggio Obsession* (New York: New American Library, 1984)
BARKER, JENNIFER M., *The Tactile Eye: Touch and the Cinematic Experience* (Berkeley and Los Angeles: University of California Press, 2009)
BAROLINI, HELEN, *The Other Side: Six American Women and the Lure of Italy* (New York: Fordham University Press, 2006)
BARTSCH, SHADI, and JAŚ ELSNER, 'Ekphrasis through the Ages. Introduction: Eight Ways of Looking at Ekphrasis' <http://humanities.uchicago.edu/depts/classics/people/PDF.Files/Ekphrasis.briefintro.final.pdf> [accessed 12 March 2008]
BASSANI, RICCARDO, and FIORA BELLINI, *Caravaggio Assassino: La carriera di un 'valentuomo' fazioso nella Roma della Controriforma* (Rome: Donzelli, 1994)
BELLORI, GIOVAN PIETRO, *Le vite de' pittori, scultori et architetti moderni* (Rome: [n. pub.], 1672)
BENFEY, CHRISTOPHER, '"Caravaggio": The Artist as Outlaw', *The New York Times*, 2 October 2005, <http://www.nytimes.com/2005/10/02/books/review/02benfy.html> [accessed 16 April 2008]
BERENSON, BERNARD, *Caravaggio: Delle sue incongruenze e della sua fama*, trans. by Luisa Vetrova (Milan: Abscondita, 2006)
BERG, KAJSA, 'Empathy and Movement in Caravaggio's Paintings'. *Communicare*, 1 (2009), 17–29
BERGMAN, DAVID, ed., *Gay American Autobiography: Writings from Whitman to Sedaris* (Madison: University of Wisconsin Press, 2009)

BERNE-JOFFROY, ANDRÉ, *Le dossier Caravage* (Paris: Editions de Minuit, 1959)
—— *Dossier Caravaggio*, trans. by Arturo Galansino (Milan: 5 Continents Editions, 2005)
BERNSTOCK, JUDITH E., *Under the Spell of Orpheus: The Persistence of a Myth in Twentieth-Century Art* (Carbondale, IL: SIU Press, 1991)
BERSANI, LEO, and ULYSSE DUTOIT, *Caravaggio* (London: BFI Publishing, 1999)
—— *Caravaggio's Secrets* (Cambridge, MA and London: MIT Press, 1998)
BHABHA, HOMI, *The Location of Culture* (London: Routledge, 1994)
BIGONZETTI, MAURO, *Caravaggio* (Berlin: ArtHaus Musik, NTSC 101 463, 2009)
BLANCHOT, MAURICE, 'Orpheus's Gaze', in *The Space of Literature*, by Maurice Blanchot, trans. by Ann Smock (Lincoln, NB: University of Nebraska Press, 1982), pp. 170–76
BOHLEN, CELESTINE, 'Mafia and a Lost Caravaggio Stun Andreotti Trial', *The New York Times*, 8 November 1996, <http://www.nytimes.com/1996/11/08/world/mafia-and-a-lost-caravaggio-stun-andreotti-trial.html?n=Top/Reference/Times%20Topics/People/A/Andreotti,%20Giulio> [accessed 12 January 2008]
BONACCORSO, MADDALENA, 'Ecco la verità su Caravaggio. Ho inventato tutte le prove. "Caravaggio sono"', *Stilos*, 20 February 2007, <http://www.vigata.org/rassegna_stampa/2007/stilos_200207_1.htm> [accessed 18 May 2008]
BORDIGON, ANTONIA, 'Caccia allo scheletro: Trovate le ossa di Caravaggio?', *Il Sole 24 Ore*, 16 June 2010, <http://www.ilsole24ore.com/art/cultura/2010-06-16/caccia-scheletro-trovate-ossa-192300.shtml?uuid=AYl5P7yB> [accessed 10 July 2010]
BRANCALEONI, CLAUDIO, *Apocalissi di inizio millennio: Frammenti a più voci 2001–2011* (Perugia: Morlacchi Editore, 2011)
BROWN, ARTHUR A., 'Storytelling, the Meaning of Life and *The Epic of Gilgamesh*', <http://eawc.evansville.edu/essays/brown.htm> [accessed 20 March 2008]
BUCHANAN, BRADLEY W., *Oedipus against Freud: Myth and the End(s) of Humanism in Twentieth-Century British Literature* (Toronto: University of Toronto Press, 2010)
BUONANNO, MILLY, *Leggere la fiction* (Naples: Liguori, 1996)
BURNS, JENNIFER, *Fragments of Impegno: Interpretation of Commitment in Contemporary Italian Narrative, 1980–2000* (Leeds: Northern Universities Press, 2001)
CAIRNS, LUCILLE, *Changing Conceptions of Male and Female Homosexuality: A (French Oriented) Theoretical Perspective*, <http://www.well.ac.uk/cfol/homosexuality.asp> [accessed 12 March 2011]
—— *Privileged Pariahdom: Homosexuality in the Novels of Dominique Fernandez* (Oxford: Peter Lang, 1996)
CALABRESE, OMAR, *Neo-Baroque: A Sign of Times* (Princeton: Princeton University Press, 1992)
CALVESI, MAURIZIO, *Caravaggio* (Florence: Giunti, 2009)
—— 'Caravaggio: The Excellent Art of a Slandered Painter'/'L'arte eccelsa di un pittore calunniato', in *Caravaggio Bacon*, ed. by Anna Coliva and Michael Peppiatt (Milan: Federico Motta, 2009), pp. 51–65
—— *Le realtà del Caravaggio* (Turin: Einaudi, 1990)
—— ed., *L'ultimo Caravaggio e la cultura artistica a Napoli, in Sicilia e a Malta* (Milan: Ediprint, 1987)
CAMILLERI, ANDREA, *Il colore del sole* (Milan: Mondadori, 2007)
—— *Maler Mörder Mythos: Geschichten zu Caravaggio* (Hatje Cantz: Ostfildern, 2006)
—— *Le pecore e il pastore* (Palermo: Sellerio, 2007)
CARRIER, DAVID, *Principles of Art History Writing* (University Park: Penn State University Press, 1993)
CERTEAU, MICHEL DE, *The Practice of Everyday Life* (Berkeley and Los Angeles: University of California Press, 1988)
CHARNEY, NOAH, *The Art Thief* (New York: Simon and Schuster, 2007)

——'Chasing Dr No: Art Crime Fact and Fiction-1', <http://www.noahcharney.com/pdf/ArtCrime-Fact&Fiction-1.pdf> [accessed 1 February 2009]
CHEVALIER, TRACY, *Girl with a Pearl Earring* (Hammersmith: HarperCollins, 1999)
CHINAGLIA, ANTONELLA, 'Camilleri A., *Il colore del sole*, 2007 — Fuga continua del Caravaggio in Sicilia?', <http://www.spigolature.org/mambo/index.php?option=com_content&task=view&id=574&Itemid=353> [accessed 27 April 2008]
CHRÉTIEN, JEAN-LOUIS, *Hand to Hand: Listening to the Work of Art* (New York: Fordham University Press, 2003)
CICIONI, MIRNA, and NICOLETTA DI CIOLLA, eds, *Differences, Deceits and Desires: Murder and Mayhem in Italian Crime Fiction* (Newark: University of Delaware Press, 2008)
CICIRELLI, FRANCA, *Camilla e il pirata Caravaggio: una fiaba di educazione alimentare* (Molfetta: Edizioni La Meridiana, 2006)
CLÉMENT, CATHERINE, *Syncope: The Philosophy of Rupture* (Minneapolis: University of Minnesota Press, 1994)
——, and JULIA KRISTEVA, *The Feminine and the Sacred* (New York: Columbia University Press, 2001)
COHEN, THOMAS V., and ELIZABETH S. COHEN, *Words and Deeds in Renaissance Rome* (Toronto: University of Toronto Press, 1993; repr. 2000)
COLANTUONO, ANTHONY, 'Caravaggio's Literary Culture', in *Caravaggio: Realism, Rebellion and Reception*, ed. by Genevieve Warwick (Newark: University of Delaware Press, 2006), pp. 57–68
COLIVA, ANNA, and MICHAEL PEPPIATT, eds, *Caravaggio Bacon* (Milan: Federico Motta, 2009)
CONGEDO, FIORELLA, *Caravaggio e il segreto del Tasso Barbasso* (Naples: Electa, 2004)
CORN, ALFRED, 'Existentialism and Homosexuality in Gunn's Early Poetry', in *At the Barriers*, ed. by Joshua Weiner (Chicago and London: University of Chicago Press, 2009), pp. 35–44
CROPPER, ELIZABETH, 'Caravaggio and the Matter of Lyric', in *Caravaggio: Realism, Rebellion and Reception*, ed. by Genevieve Warwick (Newark: University of Delaware Press, 2006), pp. 47–56
——, and CHARLES DEMPSEY, 'The State of Research in Italian Painting of the Seventeenth Century', *The Art Bulletin*, 69 (1987), 494–509
CURRAN, BEVERLEY, 'Ondaatje's *The English Patient* and Altered States of Narrative', in *Comparative Cultural studies and Michael Ondaatje's Writing*, ed. by Steven Tötösy de Zepetnek (West Lafayette: Purdue University Press, 2005), pp. 16–26
DAL BELLO, MARIO, *Caravaggio: Percorsi d'arte e cinema* (Turin: Effatà Editrice, 2007)
DELEUZE, GILLES, *The Fold: Leibniz and the Baroque*, trans. by Tom Conley (London: Continuum, 2006)
——*Masochism* (New York: Zone Books, 1971)
DELEUZE, GILLES, and FÉLIX GUATTARI, *What is Philosophy?*, trans. by Graham Burchell and Hugh Tomlinson (London: Verso, 1994)
DICKIE, JOHN, *Cosa Nostra* (London: Hodder & Stoughton, 2004)
DIPOLLINA, ANTONIO, 'Caravaggio, un grande artista bollito dalla tv', *La Repubblica*, 20 February 2008, p. 67
DOBSON, KIT, 'Multicultural Postmodernities in Michael's Ondaatje's *In the Skin of a Lion*', in Kit Dobson, *Transnational Canadas: Anglo-Canadian Literature and Globalization* (Waterloo, ON: Wilfrid Laurier University Press, 2009), pp. 105–11
ELIOT, T. S., 'The Waste Land', in *The Waste Land and Other Poems* (London: Faber and Faber, 1972), pp. 21–46
ELLIS, JIM, *Derek Jarman's Angelic Conversations* (Minneapolis: University of Minnesota Press, 2009)

ELSNER, JAŚ, 'Seeing and Saying: A Psychoanalytic Account of Ekphrasis', *Helios*, 31 (2004), 157–85
ESOLEN, ANTHONY M., *Jerusalem Delivered* (Baltimore: Johns Hopkins University Press, 2000)
FAGIOLO, ROBERTO, *L'ombra del Caravaggio* (Rome: Nutrimenti, 2007)
FARRUGIA RANDON, PHILIP, *Caravaggio, Knight of Malta* (Sliema: AVC, 2004)
FERNANDEZ, DOMINIQUE, *La Course à l'abîme* (Paris: Éditions Grasset & Fasquelle, 2002)
—— *Dans la main de l'ange* (Paris: Bernard Grasset, 1982)
—— *A Hidden Love: Art and Homosexuality* (London: Prestel Publishing, 2002)
FERRÉ, FREDERICK, *Living and Value: Toward a Constructive Postmodern Ethics* (Albany: State University of New York Press, 2001)
FO, DARIO, *Caravaggio al tempo di Caravaggio* (Modena: Franco Cosimo Panini, 2005)
FOKKEMA, ALEID, 'The Author: Postmodernism's Stock Character', in *The Author as Character: Representing Historical Writers in Western Literature*, ed. by Paul Franssen and Ton Hoenselaars (London: Associated University Presses, 1999), pp. 39–51
FOSTER, HAL, *The Return of the Real* (Cambridge, MA: MIT Press, 1996)
FOUCAULT, MICHEL, *The History of Sexuality*, 3 vols, trans. by Robert Hurley (London: Penguin Books, 1998)
—— *The Use of Pleasure* (London: Penguin, 1992)
FRANSSEN, PAUL, and TON HOENSELAARS, eds, *The Author as Character: Representing Historical Writers in Western Literature* (London: Associated University Presses, 1999)
FRASCHINI, PAOLA CRISTINA, *La metamorfosi del corpo: Il grottesco nell'arte e nella vita* (Milan: Mimesis, 2002)
FREEMAN, AUSTIN R., 'The Art of the Detective Story', in *The Art of the Mystery Story: A Collection of Critical Essays*, ed. by Howard Haycraft (New York: Carroll & Graf, 1992), pp. 7–17
FRIED, MICHAEL, *The Moment of Caravaggio* (Princeton: Princeton University Press, 2010)
FROMMEL, C. L., *Caravaggio und seine modelle* (Amsterdam: Stichting Castrum Peregrini, 1971)
FULLER, DAVID, *The Life in the Sonnets: Shakespeare Now* (London: Continuum, 2011)
GABRIEL, BARBARA, and SUZAN ILCAN, eds, *Post-modernism and the Ethical Subject* (Montreal: McGill-Queen's University Press, 2004)
GARBOLI, CESARE, 'Ricordo di Longhi', *Nuovi Argomenti*, 1 (1970), 39
GARCÍA-CARO, PEDRO, 'Behind the Canvas: The Role of Paintings in Peter Ackroyd's *Chatterton* and Arturo Pérez-Reverte's *The Flanders Panel*', in *Crime Scenes: Detective Narratives in European Culture since 1945*, ed. by Anne Mullen and Emer O'Beirne (Amsterdam: Rodopi, 2000), pp. 160–70
GARRETT, GEORGE, ed., *Botteghe Oscure Reader* (Middletown: Wesleyan University Press, 1974)
GASH, JOHN, *Caravaggio* (London: Chaucer, 2003)
GEARHEART, SUZANNE, 'Foucault's Response to Freud: Sado-masochism and the Aestheticization of Power', *Style*, 29 (1995), <http://findarticles.com/p/articles/mi_m2342/is_n3_v29/ai_18096757/> [accessed 6 December 2011]
GEISER, CHRISTOPH, *Das geheime Fieber* (Zurich und Frauenfeld: Verlag Nagel & Kinchel, 1987)
GIANOULIS, TINA, 'Fernandez, Dominique', in *glbtq: An Encyclopedia of Gay, Lesbian, Transgender, Bisexual and Queer Culture*, ed. by Calude J. Summers (2007), <http://www.glbtq.com/literature/fernandez_d.html> [accessed 28 April 2008]
GIBSON, ANDREW, *Postmodernity, Ethics and the Novel* (London: Routledge, 2002)
—— *Towards a Postmodern Theory of Narrative* (Edinburgh: Edinburgh University Press, 1996)
GILLS, COLIN, 'Rethinking Sexuality in Thom Gunn's *The Man with Night Sweats*', *Contemporary Literature*, 50 (2009), 156–82

GOLDBERG, JONATHAN, *The Seeds of Things: Theorizing Sexuality and Materiality in Renaissance* (New York: Fordham University Press, 2009)
GOVIER, LOUISE, 'The Fiction Phenomenon: Art in the Airport Lounge?', *The Art Book*, 10 (2003), 28–30
GRABES, HERBERT, 'From the Post-Modern to the Pre-Modern: More Recent Changes in Literature, Art and Theory', in *Postmodernism and After: Visions and Revisions*, ed. by Regina Rudaitytė (New Castle: Cambridge Scholars Publishing, 2008), pp. 11–27
GRAHAM-DIXON, ANDREW, *Caravaggio: A Life Sacred and Profane* (London: Allen Lane, 2010)
GRASSO, ALDO, '*Caravaggio*: Una fiction che fa 30 ma non 31', online video: <http://mediacenter.corriere.it/MediaCenter/action/player?uuid=93dcec0c-e131-11dc-b2e4-0003ba99c667> [accessed 14 May 2008]
GREGG, JOHN, *Maurice Blanchot and the Literature of Transgression* (Princeton: Princeton University Press, 1994)
GREGORI, MINA, 'Significato delle mostre Caravaggesche dal 1951 a oggi', in *Novità sul Caravaggio*, ed. by Mia Cinotti and Carlo Nitti (Milan: Regione Lombardia: 1975), pp. 27–60
GRIFFITHS, NEIL, *Saving Caravaggio*, 2nd edn (London: Penguin Books 2007)
GRIST, LEIGHTON, *The Films of Martin Scorsese, 1963–77: Authorship and Context* (London: Macmillan Press, 2000)
GUIDI, RITA, *Il gigante perduto* (Milan: Bevivino, 2004)
GUNN, THOM, *Collected Poems* (London: Faber and Faber, 1994)
—— *The Occasions of Poetry: Essays in Criticism and Autobiography* (Ann Arbor: University of Michigan Press, 1982)
HAMMILL, GRAHAM L., *Sexuality and Form: Caravaggio, Marlowe, and Bacon* (Chicago and London: University of Chicago Press, 2000)
HANDY, BRUCE, '*The Lost Painting*: The Caravaggio Trail', *The New York Times*, 13 November 2005, <http://www.nytimes.com/2005/11/13/books/review/13handy.html> [accessed 5 August 2007]
HARPHAM, GEOFFREY GALT, *On the Grotesque: Strategies of Contradiction in Art and Literature* (Princeton: Princeton University Press, 1982)
HARR, JONATHAN, *The Lost Painting* (New York: Random House, 2005)
HASSAN, IHAB, 'Beyond Postmodernism: Toward an Aesthetic of Trust', in *Beyond Postmodernism: Reassessments in Literature, Theory, and Culture*, ed. by Klaus Stierstorfer (Berlin: Walter de Gruyter, 2003), pp. 199–212
—— 'Postmodernism Revisited: A Personal Account', *American Studies*, 43 (1998), 143–53
HEATHCOTE, OWEN, ALEX HUGHES, and JAMES S. WILLIAMS, *Gay Signatures: Gay and Lesbian Theory, Fiction and Film in France, 1945–1995* (Oxford: Berg, 1998)
HEFFERNAN, JAMES A. W., *Museum of Words: The Poetics of Ekphrasis from Homer to Ashbery* (Chicago: University of Chicago Press, 1993)
HENRICKSON, PAUL, 'Caravaggio and Sexual Adjustment' (1961, repr. 2005), <http://www.glbtq.com/arts/caravaggio.html>, p. 6 [accessed 28 February 2009]
HERBRECHTER, STEFAN, *Lawrence Durrell, Postmodernism and the Ethics of Alterity* (Amsterdam: Rodopi, 1999)
HIBBARD, HOWARD, *Caravaggio* (Boulder, CO: Westview Press, 1985; first published 1983)
HILGER, STEPHANIE M., 'Ondaatje's *The English Patient* and Rewriting History', in *Comparative Cultural Studies and Michael Ondaatje's Writing*, ed. by Steven Tötösy de Zepetnek (West Lafayette: Purdue University Press, 2005), pp. 38–48
HILL, LESLIE, BRIAN NELSON, and DIMITRIS VARDOULAKIS, *After Blanchot: Literature, Criticism, Philosophy* (Newark: University of Delaware Press, 2005)
HUGGAN, GRAHAM, *The Post-colonial Exotic: Marketing the Margins* (London: Routledge, 2001)

Hunt, Patrick, *Caravaggio* (London: Haus Publishing, 2004)
Hsu, Hsuan, 'Post-nationalism and the Cinematic Apparatus in Minghella's Adaptation of Ondaatje's *The English Patient*', in *Comparative Cultural Studies and Michael Ondaatje's Writing*, ed. by Steven Tötösy de Zepetnek (West Lafayette: Purdue University Press, 2005), pp. 49–61
Iftikhar, Nazia, 'A Journey through "The Wasteland": A Masterpiece of T. S. Eliot', *Journal of Research (Faculty of Languages and Islamic Studies)*, 3 (2003), 57–65
Ingelbien, Raphael, 'A Novelist's Caravaggism: Michael Ondaatje's *In the Skin of a Lion*', in *The Guises of Canadian Diversity: New European Perspectives*, ed. by Serge Jaumain and Marc Maufort (Amsterdam: Rodopi, 1995), pp. 27–37
Iovinelli, Alessandro, *L'autore e il personaggio: L'opera metabiografica nella narrative italiana* (Catanzaro: Rubettino Editore, 2004)
Jacobs, J. U., 'Michael Ondaatje's *The English Patient* (1992) and Postcolonial Impatience', *Journal of Literary Studies*, 13 (1997), 92–112
Jagodzinski, Jan, *Postmodern Dilemmas: Outrageous Essays in Art and Education* (Mahwah: Lawrence Earlbaum Associates, 1997)
Jop, Toni, 'Caravaggio, diglielo a questi politici', *L'Unità*, 20 February 2008, p. 19
Jover, Manuel, *Caravaggio* (Paris: Terrail, 2007)
Keltner, Stacy K., *Kristeva* (Cambridge: Polity Press, 2011)
Kennedy, Barbara M., *Deleuze and Cinema: The Aesthetics of Sensation* (Edinburgh: Edinburgh University Press, 2000)
Kesselman, Tod, 'The Abject, the Object and the Thing', *Styles of Communication*, 1 (2009), 1–5
Klawitter, George, 'Piety and the Agnostic Gay Poet: Thom Gunn's Biblical Homoerotics', *Journal of Homosexuality*, 33 (1997), 207–32
Kristeva, Julia, *Powers of Horror: An Essay on Abjection*, trans. by Leon S. Rudiez (New York: Columbia University Press, 1982)
Lacan, Jacques, *The Four Fundamental Concepts of Psycho-Analysis*, ed. by Jacques Alain Miller and trans. by Alan Sheridan (Harmondsworth: Penguin, 1987; first published 1977)
La Fauci, Giuseppe, and Gianna Anastasia, 'L'ultima verità sulla fine di Caravaggio', *Corriere della sera*, 21 December 2001, <http://archiviostorico.corriere.it/2001/dicembre/21/ultima_verita_sulla_fine_CARAVAGGIO_co_0_01122111249.shtml> [accessed 10 December 2007]
Lambert, Gregg, *The Return of the Baroque in Modern Culture* (London and New York: Continuum, 2004)
Langdon, Helen, *Caravaggio: A life* (London: Pimlico, 1999; first published by Chatto & Windus, 1998)
La Porta, Filippo, 'Ancora sul *neonoir*', in *Roma Noir 2008: 'Hannibal the Cannibal c'est moi?' Realismo e finzione nel romanzo noir italiano*, ed. by Elisabetta Mondello (Rome: Robin Edizioni, 2008), pp. 49–58
Leader, Darian, *What Art Stops Us from Seeing* (Washington: Shoemaker & Hoard, 2004)
Lindner, Christian, *The James Bond Phenomenon: A Critical Reader* (Manchester: Manchester University Press, 2005)
Lipkin, Steven N., *Television Docudrama as Persuasive Practice* (Carbondale: Southern Illinois University Press, 2002)
Loh, Maria H., 'New and Improved: Repetition as Originality in Italian Baroque practice and theory', *The Art Bulletin*, 86 (2004), 1–41
Longhi, Roberto, 'Battistello', *L'arte*, 9 (1915), 120–37
—— *Caravaggio*, with an introduction by G. Previtali (Rome: Editori Riuniti, 2006)
—— 'Gentileschi padre e figlia', *L'arte*, 32 (1916), 245–314
—— 'Novelletta del Caravaggio invertito', *Paragone*, 3 (1952), 62–64

―― 'Orazio Borgianni', *L'arte,* 17 (1914), 7–23
―― 'Precisioni nelle gallerie italiane I, R. Galleria Borghese, Michelangelo da Caravaggio', *Vita artistica,* 2 (1927), 28–31
―― 'Quesiti Caravaggeschi: I. Registro dei tempi', *Pinacotheca,* 5–6 (1928–29), 15–35
―― 'Quesiti Caravaggeschi: II. I precedenti', *Pinacotheca,* 5–6 (1929), 258–320
LOVE, HEATHER K., 'Emotional Rescue', in *Gay Shame,* ed. by David M. Halperin and Valerie Traub (Chicago: University of Chicago Press, 2009), pp. 256–76
LOWRY, GLEN, 'The Representations of "Race" in Ondaatje's *In the Skin of a Lion*', *CLCWeb: Comparative Literature and Culture,* 6 (2004), <http://docs.lib.purdue.edu/clcweb/vol6/iss3/7> [accessed 10 April 2012]
LUCA, ERRI DE, 'Agguati', in *Alzaia* (Milan: Feltrinelli, 1997)
LUNDGREN, JODI, '"Colour Disrobed Itself from the Body": The Racialized Aesthetics of Liberation in Michael Ondaatje's *In the Skin of a Lion*', *Canadian Literature,* 190 (2006), 15–29
LUPERINI, ROMANO, *La fine del postmoderno* (Naples: Alfredo Guida Editore, 2005)
MCCANCE, DAWNE, *Medusa's Ear: University Foundings from Kant to Chora L* (Albany: State University of New York Press, 2004)
MCGUINNESS, FRANK, *Innocence: The Life and Death of Michelangelo Merisi, Caravaggio* (London: Faber & Faber, 1987)
MCTIGUE, ANDREA, '"Resisting, by embracing, nothingness": Reflections of Caravaggio (1573–1610) and his Art in Contemporary Literature', in *Text into Image: Image into Text,* ed. by Jeff Morrison and Florian Krobb (Amsterdam: Rodopi, 1997), pp. 95–104
MCTIGHE, SHEILA, 'The End of Caravaggio', *The Art Bulletin,* 88 (2006), 583–89
MADISON, GARY BRENT, and MARTY FAIRBAIRN, *The Ethics of Postmodernity: Current Trends in Continental Thought* (Evanston, IL: Northwestern University Press, 1999)
MAGEE, AUDREY, 'Beetles show Excellent Taste by selecting £30m painting for Snack', <http://www.museum-security.org/97/artcrime7.html> [accessed on 6 August 2007]
MAGGI, ARMANDO, *The Resurrection of the Body* (Chicago: University of Chicago Press, 2009)
MANCINI, GIULIO, GIOVANNI BAGLIONE, and GIOVANNI PIETRO BELLORI, *The Lives of Caravaggio* (London: Pallas Athene, 2005)
MANGUEL, ALBERTO, *Reading Pictures: A History of Love and Hate* (London: Bloomsbury, 2001)
MARAVALL, JOSÉ ANTONIO, *La cultura del Barroco: Análisis de una estructura histórica* (Barcelona: Ariel, 1975)
―― *La cultura del Barocco: Analisi di una struttura storica,* trans. by Christian Paez (Bologna: Il Mulino, 1985)
MARCUS, MILLICENT, 'Cross-Fertilization: Folklore and Literature in *Decameron* 4,5', *Italica,* 66 (1989), 383–98
MARCUS, STEVEN, 'Dashiell Hammett', in *The Poetics of Murder: Detective Fiction and Literary Theory,* ed. by Glenn W. Most and William W. Stowe (New York: Harcourt Brace, 1983), pp. 197–209
MARIANI, LUCA, PARISELLA, AGATA, and TRAPANI, GIOVANNA, *La pittura in cucina* (Palermo: Sellerio, 2003)
MARINELLI, PETER, 'Narrative Poetry', in *The Cambridge History of Italian Literature,* ed. by Peter Brand and Lino Pertile (Cambridge: Cambridge University Press, 1996), pp. 248–49
MARLING, WILLIAM, 'Erle Stanley Gardner', <http://www.detnovel.com/Gardner.html> [accessed 10 January 2008]
MARKOWITZ, JUDITH A., *The Gay Detective Novel: Lesbian and Gay Main Characters in Mystery Fiction* (Jefferson: McFarland, 2004)
MARKS, LAURA U., *The Skin of the Film: Intercultural Cinema, Embodiment and the Senses* (Durham, NC: Duke University Press, 2000)

MARTEL, FRÉDÉRIC, *The Pink and the Black: Homosexuals in France since 1968* (Palo Alto: Stanford University Press, 2000)
MARTIN, JOHN RUPERT, *Baroque* (New York: Harper & Row, 1977)
MATTIA, LUISA, *Caravaggio e l'incanto della strega* (Rome: Lapis, 2009)
MAZZUCCO, MELANIA, *Un giorno perfetto* (Milan: Rizzoli, 2005)
MECKEL, CHRISTOPH, 'Wissen Sie wie Caravaggio gestorben ist?', in Christoph Meckel, *Ein roter Faden* (Munich: Hanser Verlag, 1983)
MEYERS, JEFFREY, 'Thom Gunn and Caravaggio's *Conversion of St Paul*', *Style*, 44 (2010), 586–90
MICHELUCCI, STEFANIA, *The Poetry of Thom Gunn*, trans. by Jill Franks (Jefferson, NC: McFarland, 2009)
MITCHINSON, PAUL, 'Bristling with Life', *National Post*, 26 February 2000, <http://paulmitchinson.com/reviews/bristling-with-life> [accessed 16 April 2008]
MOCCIA, FEDERICO, *Tre metri sopra il cielo* (Rome: Il Ventaglio, 1992)
MONDELLO, ELISABETTA, 'Finzione narrativa ed "effetto realtà"', in *Roma Noir 2008: 'Hannibal the Cannibal c'est moi?' Realismo e finzione nel romanzo noir italiano*, ed. by Elisabetta Mondello (Rome: Robin Edizioni 2008), pp. 13–48
—— 'Introduzione', in *Roma Noir 2008*, pp. 23–24
—— ED., *Luoghi e nonluoghi nel romanzo nero contemporaneo* (Rome: Robin Edizioni 2007)
MORRISON, JEFF, and FLORIAN KROBB, eds, *Text into Image: Image into Text* (Amsterdam: Rodopi, 1997)
MOSS, MARISSA, *Mira's Diary: Home Sweet Rome* (Brainerd, MN: Bang Printing, 2013)
MUELLER, TOM, 'To Sketch a Thief', *The New York Times Magazine*, 17 December 2006, <http://www.nytimes.com/2006/12/17/magazine/17art.t.html?fta=y> [accessed 6 February 2009]
MURRAY, TIMOTHY, *Like a Film* (London: Routledge, 1993)
NÆSS, ATLE, *Den tvilende Thomas: Roman* (Oslo: Gyldendal Norsk Forlag, 1997)
—— *Doubting Thomas: A Novel about Caravaggio*, trans. by Anne Borne (London: Peter Owen, 2000)
NARDIZZI, VINCENT JOSEPH, STEPHEN GUY-BRAY, and WILL STOCKTON, eds, *Queer Renaissance Historiography* (Farnham: Ashgate, 2009)
NDALIANIS, ANGELA, 'From Neo-Baroque to Neo-Baroques', *Revista Canadiense de Estudios Hispánicos*, 33 (2008), 265–80
—— *Neo-Baroque Aesthetics and Contemporary Entertainment* (Cambridge, MA: MIT Press, 2004)
NICOLETTI, GIANLUCA, 'Il Caravaggio RAI fa arrabbiare i gay: "La vera fiction? Farlo diventare etero"', *La Stampa*, 14 February 2008, p. 62
NOISET, MARIE THÉRÈSE, 'Dominique Fernandez', in *The Contemporary Novel in France*, ed. by William Thompson (Gainesville: University Press of Florida, 1995), pp. 313–30
ONDAATJE, MICHAEL, *The English Patient* (London: Bloomsbury, 1992)
—— *In the Skin of a Lion* (Oxford: Picador, 1988; first published 1987)
ONEGA, SUSANA, *Myth in Peter Ackroyd's Novels* (New York: Camden House, 1999)
OSSORIO, ANTONELLA, *L'angelo della luce: Il giovane Caravaggio sogna il suo destino* (Naples: Electa, 2004)
PACELLI, VINCENZO, *L'ultimo Caravaggio, dalla Maddalena a mezza figura ai due san Giovanni (1606–1610)* (Todi: Ediart, 1994)
PAGET, DEREK, *No Other Way to Tell It: Dramadoc/Docudrama on Television* (Manchester: Manchester University Press, 1998)
PANAGIA, DAVIDE, 'The Effects of Viewing: Caravaggio, Bacon and *The Ring*', *Theory & Event* (Baltimore), 10 (2007), 1, par. 25: <http://proquest.umi.com/pqdweb?did=000000156193371&Fml=3&clientId=43168&RQT=309&VName=PQD> [accessed 16 October 2011]

PANZA, PIERLUIGI, 'Caravaggio Milanese', *Il Corriere della sera*, 26 February 2007, <http://www.corriere.it> [accessed 12 October 2008]
PASCALE, ANTONIO, 'Il responsabile dello stile', in *Il corpo e il snague d'Italia*, ed. by Christian Raimo (Rome: Minimum Fax, 2008), pp. 52–95
PASOLINI, PIER PAOLO, *Empirismo eretico* (Milan: Garzanti, 1972)
—— 'Gennariello', in *Lettere Luterane: Il progresso come falso progresso* (Turin: Einaudi, 1976 and 2003), pp. 15–67
—— 'Appunti per un film sull'india', documentary short (34 minutes), transmitted on Italian television in August 1968, <http://vimeo.com/31957336> (accessed 17 June 2014)
PENCAK, WILLIAM, *The Films of Derek Jarman*, trans. by Stephen E. Lewis (Jefferson: McFarland, 2002)
PERNIOLA, MARIO, *Art and its Shadow*, trans. by Massimo Verdicchio (New York: Continuum, 2004)
—— *Enigmas: The Egyptian Moment in Society and Art*, trans. by Christopher Woodall (London: Verso, 1995)
PETRONIO, GIUSEPPE, *Sulle trace del giallo* (Rome: Gamberetti Editore, 2000)
PICONE, MICHELANGELO, 'La "ballata" di Lisabetta (*Decameron* IV, 5)', *Cuadernos de filología italiana*, special issue (2001), pp. 177–91
PIERSANTI, GILDA, *Jaune Caravage* (Paris and New York: Le Passage, 2008)
POSNER, DONALD, 'Caravaggio's Homo-erotic Early Works', *The Art Quarterly*, 34 (1971), 301–24
POWELL, NEIL, *Carpenters of Light: Some Contemporary English Poets* (Lanham: Rowman & Littlefield Publishers, 1980)
PREIMESBERGER, RUDOLF, 'Golia e Davide', in *Docere, Delectare, Movere: Affetti, devozione e retorica nel linguaggio artistico del primo barocco romano*, ed. by Anna Gramiccia and others (Rome: De Luca, 1998), pp. 63–69
PROSE, FRANCINE, *Caravaggio: Painter of Miracles* (Hammersmith: Harper Press, 2007; first published in 2005)
PUGLISI, CATHERINE, *Caravaggio* (London: Phaidon Press, 1998)
RANCIÈRE, JACQUES, *The Politics of Aesthetics* (London: Continuum, 2007)
RANDALL, DON, 'Ondaatje Goes to Hollywood: The Costs of Mainstream Arrival for the Representation of Cultural Difference', in *Adjacencies: Minority Writing in Canada*, ed. by Dominic A. Beneventi, Licia Canton, and Lianne Moyes (Toronto: Guernica, 2004), pp. 128–42
RANIERI, POLESE, 'In Giappone tutti pazzi per Caravaggio, da maledetto a mito pop', *Corriere della sera*, 30 September 2001, p. 31
RESCA, GIUSEPPE, *La spada e la misericordia: Caravaggio e il demone della violenza* (Rome: Armando Editore, 2001)
RICHARDSON, NIALL, *The Queer Cinema of Derek Jarman* (London and New York: Tauris, 2009)
ROBB, PETER, *M: The Man Who Became Caravaggio* (New York: Picador, 2001)
—— 'Will we ever see it again?', *The Daily Telegraph*, 4 February 2005, <http://www.telegraph.co.uk/culture/art/3636386/Will-we-ever-see-it-again.html> [accessed 12 January 2008]
ROHDIE, SAM, *The Passion of Pier Paolo Pasolini* (Bloomington: Indiana University Press, 1995)
RORATO, LAURA, '"The Colour of Light": Caravaggio's *The Burial of St Lucy* Revisited by Pino Di Silvestro in *La fuga, la sosta*', *Romance Studies*, 23 (2005), 131–41
RYAN, ELLEN, '*Murder at the Opera* by Margaret Truman', *The Washingtonian.com*, <http://www.washingtonian.com/bookreviews/187.html> [accessed 12 January 2008]
SANGIORINI, MARCO, *Il giallo come nuovo romanzo sociale* (Ravenna: Longo, 2004)

SARRIS, FOTOIS, 'In the Skin of a Lion: Michael Ondaatje's Tenebristic Narrative', Essays on Canadian Writing, 44 (1991), 183–201

SAVRAN, DAVID Take it like a Man: White Masculinity, Masochism, and Contemporary American Culture (Princeton: Princeton University Press, 1998)

SCRIVANO, FABRIZIO, Lo spazio e le forme: Basi teoriche del vedere contemporaneo (Florence: Alinea Editrice, 1996)

SCHEHR, LAWRENCE R., Parts of an Andrology: On Representations of Men's Bodies (Palo Alto: Stanford University Press, 1997)

SCHELER, MAX, The Nature of Sympathy (Piscataway: Transaction Publishers, 2010)

SCHUDT, LUDWIG, Caravaggio (Vienna: Anton Schroll, 1942)

SCIBERRAS, KEITH, and DAVID M., STONE, Caravaggio: Art, Knighthood and Malta (Valletta: Midsea Books, 2006)

SCRAGGS, JOHN, Crime Fiction (London: Routledge, 2005)

SGARBI, VITTORIO, Caravaggio (Milan: Skira, 2005)

SHOHAM, SHLOMO GIORA, Art, Crime and Madness: Gesualdo, Caravaggio, Genet, Van Gogh, Artaud (Brighton: Sussex Academic Press, 2002)

SICILIANO, ENZO, 'Morte di Caravaggio', in Cuore e fantasmi (Milan: Mondadori, 1990)

SILVERMAN, KAJA, Male Subjectivity at the Margins (London: Routledge, 1992)

SILVESTRI, GOFFREDO, 'Quel record sprecato alle Scuderie: Troppo breve la mostra del Caravaggio', Repubblica, 17 June 2010, <www.repubblica.it/speciali/arte/classifiche/2010/06/17/news> [accessed 20 October 2011]

SOHM, PHILIP, 'Caravaggio's Deaths', The Art Bulletin, 84 (2002), 449–68 (online 1–22), <http://www.collegeart.org/artbulletin> [accessed 20 January 2008]

SORICE, MICHELE, 'La fiction televisiva nella prospettiva italiana', Studies in Communication Sciences, 4 (2004), 49–67

SPAGNOLETTI, GIOVANNI, 'Fiction Italia — Caravaggio ovvero The Dark Side of TV', online resource: <http://www.Close-Up.it> [accessed 18 May 2008]

SPEAR, RICHARD, Caravaggio and his Followers (London: Harper & Row, 1975)

SPIKE, JOHN T., Caravaggio (New York: Abbeville Press, 2001)

SPINOZA, BENEDICT DE, Ethics (London: Penguin Books, 1996)

SPRING, JUSTIN, Secret Historian: The Life and Times of Samuel Steward, Professor, Tattoo Artist and Sexual Renegade (New York: Farrar, Straus and Giroux, 2010)

SRIKANTH, RAJINI, The World Next Door: South Asian American Literature and the Idea of America (Philadelphia: Temple University Press, 2004)

STEDMAN, DAVID, That Terrible Shadowing (Leicester: Matador, 2009)

STEINER, GEORGE, After Babel: Aspects of Language and Translation (Oxford: Oxford University Press, 1998)

STEINER, WENDY, Pictures of Romance Form against Context in Painting and Literature (Chicago: University of Chicago Press, 1998)

STEWARD, SAMUEL M., The Caravaggio Shawl (Boston: Alyson Publications, 1989)

STONE, DAVID M., 'In Figura Diaboli: Self and Myth in Caravaggio's David and Goliath', in From Rome to Eternity: Catholicism and the Arts in Italy, ca. 1550–1650, ed. by Pamela M. Jones and Thomas Worcester (Leiden: Brill, 2002), pp. 19–42

STORCHI, SIMONA, Valori Plastici 1918–1922: Le inquietudini del nuovo classico, supplement to The Italianist (2006)

STORINI, MONICA CRISTINA '"Antonio c'est moi?" Sul realismo di Un giorno perfetto di Melania Mazzucco', in Roma Noir 2008: 'Hannibal the Cannibal c'est moi?' Realismo e finzione nel romanzo noir italiano, ed. by Elisabetta Mondello (Rome: Robin Edizioni 2008), pp. 89–112

STRINATI, CLAUDIO, La [vera] vita di Caravaggio secondo Claudio Strinati (Naples: Arte'm, 2009)

SYMONS, JULIAN, *Bloody Murder: From the Detective Story to the Crime Novel*, 3rd rev. edn (New York: The Mysterious Press, 1993)

TAYLOR, JANE, '"Why do you tear me from myself?": Torture, Truth and the Arts of Counter-Reformation', in *The Rhetoric of Sincerity*, ed. by Ernst Van Alphen, Mieke Bal, and Carel E. Smith (Stanford: Stanford University Press, 2009), pp. 19–43

TERRONE, PATRICE, 'Portraits d'un inconnu illustre: Biographies fictives du Caravage', *Recherches et Travaux*, 68 (2006), 57–69

TERZOLI, ANTONIETTA, 'La testa di Lorenzo: Lettura di *Decameron* IV, 5', *Cuadernos de filología italiana*, special issue (2001), 193–211

TIFFIN, HELEN, 'Post-colonial Literatures and Counter-discourse', in *The Post-Colonial Studies Reader*, ed. by Bill Ashcroft, Gareth Griffiths and Helen Tiffin, (London: Routledge, 1995), pp. 95–98

TORLASCO, DOMIETTA, *The Time of Crime: Phenomenology, Psychoanalysis, Italian Film* (Stanford: Stanford University Press, 2008)

TREHERNE, MATTHEW, 'Pictorial Space and Sacred Time in Tasso', *Italian Studies*, 62 (2007), 5–25

TRIGILIA, LUCIA, 'Premessa', in *L'ultimo Caravaggio e la cultura artistic a Napoli, in Sicilia e a Malta*, ed. by Maurizio Calvesi, pp. 7–11 (p. 7)

TROGAL, ENRIQUE, *Il Caravaggio: Fábula escénica con música de Monteverdi* (Cuenca: Carboneras de Guadazaoń, 1983)

TRUMAN, MARGARET, *Murder at the National Gallery* (New York: Random House, 1996)

TURNATURI, GABRIELLA, 'Mediterraneo: Rappresentazioni in nero', in *Roma Noir 2007: Luoghi e nonluoghi nel romanzo nero contemporaneo*, ed. by Elisabetta Mondello (Rome: Robin Edizioni, 2007), pp. 47–68

TURATI, PAOLO, *Notturno Barocco* (Turin: Ananke, 2005)

TYMIENIECKA, ANNA-TERESA, *Phenomenology of Life and the Human Creative Condition* (New York: Springer 1998)

VARRIANO, JOHN, *Caravaggio: The Art of Realism* (University Park: Penn State University Press, 2006)

——'Caravaggio and the Decorative Arts in the Two Suppers at Emmaus', *The Art Bulletin*, 68 (1986), 218–24

VENTURI, LIONELLO, *Il Caravaggio: Quaranta riproduzioni con testo e catalogo* (Rome: Società Editrice d'Arte Illustrata, 1925)

——'Note sulla Galleria Borghese', *L'Arte*, 12 (1909), 31–50

VERMANDERE, DIETER, MONICA JANSEN, and INGE LANSLOTS, eds, *Noir de noir: Un'indagine pluridisciplinare* (Berne: Peter Lang, 2010)

VIA, DAN O., and ROBERT A. J. GAGNON, *Homosexuality and the Bible: Two Views* (Minneapolis: Fortress Press, 2003)

VIGHI, FABIO, *Traumatic Encounters in Italian Film: Locating the Cinematic Unconscious* (Bristol: Intellect, 2006)

VITOUX, FRÉDÉRIC, 'Dominique Fernandez parle de l'homosexualité, du sida et du roman', *Nouvel Observateur*, 1165, 6 March 1987, p. 55

WARREN, ROGER, 'Troilus and Cressida (1976)', in *Aspects of Shakespeare's 'Problem Plays'*, ed. by Kenneth Muir and Stanley W. Wells (New York: Cambridge University Press, 1982), pp. 152–53

WARWICK, GENEVIEVE, 'Allegories of Eros: Caravaggio's Masque', in *Caravaggio: Realism, Rebellion, Reception*, ed. by Genevieve Warwick (Newark: University of Delaware Press, 2006), pp. 82–90

——ed., *Caravaggio. Realism, Rebellion, Reception* (Newark: University of Delaware Press, 2006)

WEBB, RUTH, '*Ekphrasis* Ancient and Modern: The Invention of a Genre', *Word & Image*, 15 (1999), 7–18

Webber, F. R., and Ralph Adams Cram, *Church Symbolism*, 2nd edn (Cleveland: The Central Lithograph, 2003)

Werness, Hope B., *The Continuum Encyclopaedia of Animal Symbolism in Art* (New York: Continuum, 2003)

Wilmer, Clive, 'Gunn, Shakespeare, and the Elizabethans', in *At the Barriers*, ed. by Joshua Weiner (Chicago and London: University of Chicago Press, 2009), pp. 45–67

Whitfield, Clovis, *Caravaggio's Eye* (Washington: University of Washington Press, 2011)

Whitfield, Sarah, *René Magritte* (London: South Bank Centre, 1992)

Wood, Mary P., 'Italian Film Noir', in *European Film Noir*, ed. by Andrew Spicer (Manchester: Manchester University Press, 2007), pp. 236–72

Wrobel, Arthur, 'The Origin of Chandler's "Mean Streets"', *American Notes and Queries*, 7 (1994), 225–30

Wymer, Rowland, *Derek Jarman* (Manchester: Manchester University Press, 2005)

Wyschogrod, Edith, *Saints and Postmodernism: Revisioning Moral Philosophy* (Chicago: University of Chicago Press, 1990)

Zepetnek, Steven Tötösy de, ed., 'Introduction', in *Comparative Cultural Studies and Michael Ondaatje's Writing* (West Lafayette: Purdue University Press, 2005), pp. 1–5

Žižek, Slavoj, *The Puppet and the Dwarf: The Perverse Core of Christianity* (Cambridge, MA: MIT Press, 2003)

INDEX

Ackroyd, Peter 73, 112, 117, 209, 212, 216
affect 175, 180, 196–97, 201 n. 60
AIDS 103, 121, 169 n. 39
Aldrich, Robert 166, 167, 168, 209
Aldobrandini, family 17, 22
Allmer, Patricia 94, 95, 116, 209
Almásy, Ladislaus Eduard 181
  as fictional character 181–200
Annarumma, Antonio 91–92
Antonello, Pierpaolo, and Florian Mussgnug 207 nn.
  9 & 10, 209
Antonietti, Maddalena 28, 77
  see also Lena
Aratori, Lucia 18
Arciprete, Caterina 61
Argan, Carlo Giulio, 34, 209
Ariosto, Ludovico 55, 67 n. 42
Ashcroft, Bill 197, 209, 219

Bachelard, Gaston 36, 209
Badiou, Alain 122–26, 137, 140, 144, 167, 209
Baglione, Giovanni 5, 12 n. 14, 21–22, 27, 38 n. 27, 42, 146–47, 155, 215
Bal Mieke, 1–2, 10–12, 49, 51, 54, 66, 78, 80, 113, 150, 151, 170–72, 176, 178, 182–86, 192–93, 197–200, 209, 219
Baldassarri, Fabio 9, 64 n. 2, 70, 90–93, 95–97, 104, 109, 115 n. 48, 116 nn. 53, 54 & 55, 168 n. 33, 209
Banks, Oliver 12, 209
Barker, Jennifer 153, 172, 209
Baroque 1–7, 10–11, 12 nn. 8 & 13, 13 nn. 221, 22, 28, 32–34, 37 n. 3, 51, 61, 64 n. 1, 67 n. 45, 69, 77, 80, 82, 85, 90, 92, 97, 103, 108, 113 n. 17, 122, 130, 134–36, 158, 166, 167 n. 18, 170 n. 48, 175–77, 185, 187–88, 195–96, 197 n. 6, 203–05, 207 n. 8, 211, 214, 216
  and neo-Baroque 2–3, 5–7, 10–11, 12 nn. 8 & 19, 203–06, 210, 216
  see also fold, matter, mirror(s) and monad
Barthes, Roland 47
  and plaisir du text 180
Bassani, Riccardo 53, 65 n. 16, 200 n. 50, 209
  and Bellini, Fiora 53, 65 n. 16, 200 n. 50, 209
Bellori, Giovan Pietro 6, 12, 18, 31, 37, 42, 209, 215
Benedetti, Sergio 97, 99–101
Benfey, Christopher 47, 66, 209
Berenson, Bernard 4, 34–35, 39, 119, 166, 209
Berg, Kajsa 173, 209

Bergman, David 160–61, 174, 209
Berne-Joffroy, André 33–36, 38, 210
Bernstock, Judith 163, 174, 210
Bersni, Leo 28, 152, 155–57, 166, 171–72, 174, 210
Bhabha, Homi 13, 195, 210
Bianchini, Anna 28
Blanchot, Maurice 164, 174, 210, 213
Boccaccio, Giovanni 108–09, 117 n. 70, 118 nn. 87 & 89
Bonaccorso, Maddalena 53–55, 66–67, 210
Bordigon, Antonia 28 n. 23, 210
Borghese, Scipione 26, 130, 146, 158, 188
Borromeo, Carlo 16, 18–19, 46
Borromeo Federico 17, 19–20, 32
Botticelli 33
Bruno, Giordano 15, 68 n. 59, 130
Buonanno, Milly 63–64, 68, 210

Cairns, Lucille 59–60, 67, 167, 210
Calabrese, Omar 5–6, 12, 210
Calvesi, Maurizio 4, 12, 17–18, 20, 22, 25, 28, 32, 37–38, 53, 99, 168–69, 206, 210, 219
Camilleri, Andrea, 7–8, 40–41, 46, 53–58, 66–67, 210–11
Campanella, Tommaso 130
canvas 21, 72–73, 82, 94, 100–01, 112 n. 13, 113 n. 15, 140, 146, 149–50, 156, 203, 212
Cappelletti, Francesca 99, 101
Carrier, David, 2, 11, 210
Caravaggio, Michelangelo Merisi da:
  pittore maledetto 6, 8, 12 n. 20, 31, 40, 42, 46, 63–64, 89, 204
  self-portrait(s) 6, 26, 45–46, 51, 97, 150, 152, 155, 168 n. 30, 187–88, 204
  works:
    Amor Vincit Omnia x, 28, 29, 143; see also Victorious Cupid
    Bacchino Malato 28, 74; see also Sick Bacchus
    Bacchus x, 79, 83, 116 n. 61, 119, 146
    Basket of Fruit x, 107–08, 110
    The Beheading of St John the Baptist x, 24–25, 131, 133
    Boy Bitten by a Lizard x, 28, 30, 119
    Boy Peeling Fruit 28
    Boy with a Basket of Fruit 83, 108
    The Burial of St Lucy 1, 11 n. 1, 25, 188, 217
    The Calling of St Matthew x, 20, 83, 108, 111, 140, 182, 198 n. 20
    The Conversion of St Paul (Cerasi) x, 20, 123, 132, 134–36, 140, 167 n. 23, 171 n. 59

222 INDEX

The Conversion of St Paul (Odaleschi) x, 123, 131
The Crucifixion of St Peter 20
David with the Head of Goliath x, 6, 9–10, 43, 45–46, 51–52, 57, 59, 65 n. 13, 78, 82, 89, 92–93, 95–96, 112, 123, 127, 133, 147, 161, 166, 173 n. 92, 175, 177, 188, 191–92, 205
Death of the Virgin 5, 21, 113 n. 22, 156, 173 n. 98
Doubting Thomas 194; see also *The Incredulity of St Thomas*
The Entombment of Christ 148, 155
The Flagellation of Christ 161
The Gypsy Fortune Teller 83
The Incredulity of St Thomas x, 44
Judith Beheading Holofernes x, 31, 75, 151, 192, 200 n. 50
Lute Player x, 28–29, 51, 56, 83, 119, 160
Madonna dei Palafrenieri 21, 74, 113 n. 22
Madonna dei Pellegrini 76, 113 n. 22, 116 n. 61
Madonna of Loreto 5, 81
The Martyrdom of St Matthew x, 20–21, 59, 112 n. 15, 146, 148, 155, 158–59, 168 n. 30, 182, 187, 198 n. 20
The Martyrdom of St Ursula 188
Mary Magdalene 60; see also *Penitent Magdalene*
Medusa x, 6, 45, 51, 84, 114 n. 35, 145, 149, 151–54, 173 n. 90, 191
The Musicians 83, 200 n. 45
Narcissus x, 10, 74, 175, 183, 190–92
Nativity with the Saints Francis and Lawrence 86, 89–90
Penitent Magdalene 74
Profane Love 156–58
The Raising of Lazarus x, 137–39, 148
The Resurrection of Christ 5
St Catherine of Alexandria 31
St Jerome Writing x, 74, 173 n. 90, 175, 189, 194, 200 n. 53
St John the Baptist 99, 119, 146, 200 n. 45
St Matthew and the Angel 5, 20
The Sacrifice of Isaac x, 143, 145, 161, 171 n. 67
Salome with the Head of John the Baptist 74
The Seven Works of Mercy 23
Sick Bacchus 45
Supper at Emmaus 3, 60, 114 n. 32
The Taking of Christ x, 97–100
Victorious Cupid 143, 200 n. 45
Youth with Ram 119
Carracci, Annibale 22, 31
castration 151, 192–93
Cavalier D'Arpino 19
Cenci, Beatrice 15, 63, 200 n. 50
Certeau, Michel de 184, 191, 198, 210
Cesari, Giuseppe 19, 22; see also Cavalier d'Arpino
Charles V 16
Charney, Noah 9, 64, 70–72, 81, 86–88, 90–95, 97, 101, 112, 114–15, 210

chiaroscuro 20, 49, 52, 56, 61, 74, 80, 82, 89, 103, 106, 113 n. 17, 122, 127, 134, 149, 166, 169 n. 44, 177, 200 n. 40; see also tenebrism
Chinaglia, Antonella 55, 67, 211
Christie, Agatha 70
Cinotti, Mia 4, 6, 39 n. 36, 53, 213
Clément, Catherine, 143–44, 169, 171, 211
Clement VIII, Pope 15–17, 48, 200
Cocteau, Jean 144, 163
Cohen, Thomas and Elizabeth 15, 37, 211
Colantuono, Anthony 51, 66 n. 28, 211
Coliva, Anna 166, 169, 210, 211
Colonna, Costanza 17, 23, 63; see also Marchesa of Caravaggio
Colonna, family 23
Colonna, Marcantonio 17
Conan Doyle, Arthur 70
Corn, Alfred 170 n. 47, 211
Council of Trent 16
Counter-Reformation 17–18, 32–33, 46, 58, 170 n. 50, 198 n. 20, 200 n. 50, 219
Cropper, Elizabeth 51, 66 n. 27, 160, 174 n. 104, 204, 211
   and Charles Dempsey 4, 6, 12 nn. 12 & 15, 211
Curran Beverley 194, 201 n. 55, 211

Dal Bello, Mario 11 n. 5, 63, 68 n. 65, 211
David, Jacques Louis 31
De Chirico 33
Deleuze, Gilles 133, 169 n. 36, 176, 180, 184–85, 196, 197 nn. 6 & 8, 200 nn. 38, 40 & 42, 211, 214
   and Félix Guattari 175, 211
Deluzian 10, 78, 130, 175–76, 178–79, 186–87, 196, 199 n. 37, 200 nn. 42 & 46
Del Monte, Cardinal 19, 27, 83, 120, 144, 146–47, 149, 157–58, 200 n. 45
   and Del Monte, Francesco Maria 17, 19–22, 27, 56, 83, 120, 144, 146–47, 149, 157–58, 200 n. 45
Dickie, John 115 n. 47, 211
Dipollina, Antonio 63, 68 n. 66, 211
Di Silvestro Pino, 1, 11 n. 1, 217

ekphrasis 176, 195–96, 197 n. 9, 201 nn. 56, 57 & 58, 209, 212, 213, 219
Eliot, T. S. 108–09, 117 n. 70, 118 nn. 83 & 84, 211
Ellis, Jim 144, 146–48, 158, 171 n. 69, 211
Elsner, Jaś 195–96, 197 n. 9, 201 n.58, 212
Epic of Gilgamesh 177, 181, 198 nn. 13 & 22, 200 n. 43, 210
Esolen, Anthony 56, 67 n. 46, 212

Fantin Petrignani, Monsignor 19
Farnese, family 22
Farrugia, Randon 24–25, 37 nn. 16, 17, 19 & 20, 212
Fernandez, Dominique 8–9, 13 n. 22, 25, 38 n. 25, 40, 46, 49, 56–60, 67 nn. 50, 51, 52, 53, 54 & 55,

Index

120–26, 129–30, 133, 141, 144, 154, 166 n. 6, 167 nn. 14, 16 & 18, 168 nn. 31 & 34, 169 nn. 34 & 39, 203, 210, 212
Fo, Dario 7, 11 n. 6, 198 n. 20, 212
Fokkema, Aleid 47–48, 65 n. 18, 212
fold 10, 175–76, 78, 184–85, 197 n. 6, 200 nn. 38, 40, 42 & 46, 211
Foster, Hal 207 nn. 5, 6 & 11, 212
Foucault, Michel 158, 164, 166 n. 1, 173 n. 102, 174 n. 102, 212
Franssen, Paul, and Ton Hoenselaars 42, 47–50, 53, 65 nn. 10 & 18, 212
Fraschini, Paola Cristina 84, 114 n. 36, 212
Freeman, Austin R. 70, 112 n. 5, 212
Freud, Sigmund 72, 130, 173 n. 101, 174 n. 102, 210, 212
and Freudian 148, 172 n. 80, 192, 195
Fried, Michael 154, 173 n. 92, 212
Frommel, Christopher. L. 28, 120, 212
Fuller, David 174 n. 117, 212

Garboli, Cesare 166 n. 8, 167 n. 26, 212
García-Caro, Pedro 73, 112 n. 13, 212
Garret, George, 171 nn. 65 & 66, 212
Gash, John 73, 113 n. 23, 212
gay 2–3, 9, 57–60, 63, 67 nn. 51, 68 & 69, 120–21, 129, 140–41, 143, 147, 160, 164, 166, 167 nn. 13 & 19, 168 n. 31, 169 n. 40, 174 nn. 106, 114 & 116, 204, 209, 212–16
gaze 3, 78, 94–95, 151–53, 160, 164, 173 n. 91, 174 n. 115, 180, 186, 191–92, 195–96, 200 n. 48, 201
Gearheart, Suzsanne 173 n. 102, 174 n. 102, 212
Gentileschi, Ottavio 21, 34, 214
Gianoulis, Tina 56–59, 67 nn. 51 & 54, 212
Gibson, Andrew 11 n. 5, 182, 198 n. 26, 207 n. 10, 212
Giovanni da Udine 82
Giustiniani, Vincenzo 19–20, 56
Goldberg, Jonathan 170 n.54, 171 n. 59, 213
Govier, Louise 41–42, 65 n. 8, 212
Grabes, Herbert, 205, 207 n. 7, 213
Graham-Dixon, Andrew 37 n. 11, 213
Grammatica, Antiveduto 19
Grasso, Aldo 63, 68 n. 67, 213
Gregori, Mina 34–35, 39 n. 36, 59, 99, 213
Griffiths, Gareth 197 nn. 2 & 7, 209, 219
Griffiths, Neil 9, 41, 70, 86–89, 93, 113 n. 25, 114–15 n. 41, 115 n. 47, 197 n. 2, 213
Grist, Leighton 77–78, 80, 113 n. 19, 213
grottesca/ grottesche 81–83
grotesque 82, 84–85, 105, 114 nn. 31 & 33, 203, 213
Guidi, Rita 8, 40–41, 49, 52–53, 66 n. 31, 213
Gunn, Thom 2, 9, 120, 133–37, 139–44, 154, 169 nn. 39–44, 170 nn. 45–47 & 49, 171 nn. 60, 62, 65 & 68, 203, 211–14, 216, 220

Hamilton Nisbet, William 99
Hammil, Graham 140–41, 143–44, 170 n. 52, 213
Handy, Bruce 99, 116 n. 66, 213
haptic 149, 152–54, 157, 172 n. 77
Harpham, Geoffrey Galt 82–83, 114 n. 33, 213
Harr, Jonathan 9, 70, 97, 99–101, 112 n. 11, 113 n. 28, 116 n. 64, 213
Hassan, Ihab 12 n. 17, 204–05, 207 nn. 4, 5 & 6, 213
Henrickson, Paul 77, 113 n. 23, 213
Henry IV 16–17, 198 n. 20
Herodotus 186–87
Hibbard, Howard 3, 12 nn. 10 & 14, 17–19, 21, 28, 37 n. 9, 73, 78, 143–44, 146, 166 n. 3, 170 nn. 49, 55 & 57, 171 n. 67, 172 n. 72, 213
Hilger, Stephanie 183, 199 n. 32, 313
Hocquenghem, Guy 121, 169 n. 34
Homer 194, 201 n. 56, 213
homosexual(s) 9, 25, 27, 35, 57–58, 83, 103, 119–21, 123–24, 144, 147, 150, 152, 156, 161, 163–65, 166 n. 10
homosexuality 9, 27–28, 38 nn. 27 & 28, 57–58, 60, 63, 67 n. 52 & 55, 73, 119, 122–23, 129, 141, 144, 147, 157, 161, 167 n. 22, 168 n. 27, 169 n. 40, 170 n. 47, 171 n. 64, 210–12, 214, 219
Honthorst, Gerard van 97, 99
Hunt, Patrick 1, 8, 15–23, 25–27, 31, 36, 37 n. 14, 38 n. 20, 77, 83–84, 116 n. 52, 170 n. 57, 188, 193, 214
Hsu, Hsuan 196–97, 201 n. 59, 214

Iovinelli, Alessandro 64 n. 3, 66 n. 37, 133, 167 n. 14, 214

Jacobs, J. U. 178, 182–83, 197 n. 3, 214
Jagodzinski, Jan 95, 116 nn. 60 & 61, 214
Jarman, Derek 1, 9, 63, 120, 144, 146–48, 150–58, 162, 168 n. 32, 171 nn. 69 & 70, 172, nn. 74, 79, 81, 83 & 87, 173 nn. 90 & 97, 174 n. 117, 203, 211, 217, 220
Jop, Toni 62, 68 n. 64, 214
jouissance 122–23, 133, 143, 155, 195
Jover, Manuel 173 n. 98, 191, 200 n. 48, 214

Kallab, Wolfgang 33
Keltner, Stacy K. 126–27, 168 n. 28, 214
Kennedy, Barbara 176, 179–80, 196, 197 n. 8, 199 n. 37, 214
Klawitter, George 137, 140, 142–43, 169 n. 40, 214
Kristeva, Julia 126–27, 129, 168 nn. 28 & 29, 169 n. 35, 211, 214

Lacan, Jacques 72, 80, 94, 116 n. 58, 157, 186, 195–96, 214
and Lacanian 73, 122, 126, 140, 195
Lambert, Gregg 135–37, 170 nn. 48 & 52, 214
Langdon, Helen 16, 21–26, 37 nn. 5 & 18, 48, 86, 115 n. 42, 188, 192–93, 200 n. 45, 214

La Porta, Filippo 9, 13 n. 24, 90, 109, 115 n. 49, 116 n. 62, 118 n. 90, 214
Leader, Darian 72–74, 112 n. 12, 214
Leibniz, Gttfried Wilhelm von 197 n. 6, 211
  and Leibnizian 10, 78, 176, 186–87
Lena 146–48, 152–53, 156–58, 160
Leoni, Ottavio iv, x, 21
lesbian 67 n. 51, 160, 167 nn. 13 & 19, 168 n. 31, 174 n. 114, 209, 212–13
Lichtenstein, Roy 96–97
Lindner, Christian 95, 116 n. 62, 214
Longhi, Roberto 2, 4–5, 7, 11 n. 4, 12 n. 11, 31, 33–36, 39 n. 39, 46, 99, 116 n. 55, 119, 121, 166 n. 8, 198 n. 15, 212, 214
Longo, Luigi 129, 168 n. 33
Longoni, Angelo 8, 40, 62–63
Lowry, Glen 199 n. 27, 200 n. 51, 215
Lundgren, Jodi 177–81, 197, 198 n. 12, 215

McCance, Dawne 153, 157, 172 n. 88, 215
McTighe, Sheila 46, 65 n. 17, 215
McTigue, Andrea 120, 166 n. 4, 215
Maggi, Armando 123–24, 126, 167 nn. 18, 20 & 22, 171 n. 64, 215
Mahon, Denis 4, 6, 99–100
Malevich, Kazimir 73, 90–91, 95
Mancini, Giulio 12 n. 14, 18, 33, 215
Mannerism 3, 19
  and mannerist 3, 33
Marangoni, Matteo 4, 12 n. 11, 33
Maravall, José Antonio 11, 135, 204–205, 207 nn. 3 & 8, 215
Marchesa of Caravaggio 17, 23, 26
Marchese of Caravaggio 18–19
Marcus, Millicent 118 nn 87, 88 & 89
Marinelli, Peter 55, 67 n. 43, 215
Marini, Maurizio 26, 88
Marino, Giovan Battista 32, 51, 56, 63, 67 n. 45, 160, 163
Marks, Laura 153, 172 n. 77, 173 n. 91, 215
Martin, John Rupert 4, 12 n. 13, 216
Martone, Mario 64–65 n. 4
masochism 128, 130, 133, 148, 150, 153, 169 n. 36, 172 n. 81, 174 n. 110, 211, 218
  and sadomasochism 10, 120, 128, 143, 158, 161, 174 n. 102, 212
Mattei, Ciriaco 97, 99
  and Mattei family 99
matter 176, 184–85
Mazzucco, Melania 105, 117 n. 74, 216, 218
Medici, Lorenzo de 194
Melandroni, Fillide 28, 31, 193
Meyers, Jeffrey 134–35, 169 n. 42, 216
Michelangelo 93, 144, 147, 170 n. 57, 194
Michelucci, Stefania 135–37, 141, 169 nn. 41 & 44, 170 n. 53 & 56, 171 nn. 59, 60, 62, 63 & 65, 216
Minghella, Anthony 2, 10, 68 n. 71, 166, 175–76, 184, 187–88, 194–96, 199 n. 28, 201 n. 59, 203, 214

Minniti, Mario 19, 25, 54, 58–59, 83
Mirandola, Pico della 194
mirror(s) 27, 45, 52, 63, 78, 80, 128, 143, 152, 178, 180, 185, 191–92
  and mirroring 47, 51, 54, 151–52, 185, 195
mirror neurons 157
Moccia, Federico 105, 117 n. 73, 216
monad 179, 186
Mona Lisa 71–73, 112 n. 9, 164
Mondello, Elisabetta 84, 112 n. 7, 115 n. 49, 116 nn. 54 & 62, 117 nn. 74 & 75, 214, 216, 218–20
Monnikendam, Vincent 65 n. 4
Moro, Aldo 91–92, 129, 168 n. 33
Mueller, Tom 71, 112 n. 10, 216
Murray, Timothy 155–58, 172 n. 76, 216

Naess, Atle 8, 40, 49–53, 66 nn. 26 & 30, 216
narcissism 49, 51, 66 n. 29, 143, 148, 152, 183, 191, 196
Ndalianis, Angela 3, 7, 11, 12 n. 8, 203–04, 216
Nenni, Pietro 88
Neri, Filippo 60
Nicoletti, Gianluca 63, 68 n. 69, 216

Oedipus 60, 72, 157–58, 160, 173 n. 101, 210
Ondaatje, Michael 1–2, 10, 68 n. 71, 166, 175–78, 180–81, 184–85, 187–88, 191–95, 197 nn. 3, 4, 10 & 11, 198 nn. 12, 13, 16 & 24, 199 nn. 27, 28, 32 & 35, 200 n. 51, 201 nn. 55 & 59, 203, 205, 211, 213–18, 220
Orpheus 160, 162–64, 174 n. 111 & 115, 210
  and Eurydice 160, 162–64
Ossorio, Antonella 7–8, 40–41, 61–62, 67 n. 58, 68 nn. 59 & 60, 216

Pacelli, Vincenzo, 27, 32–33, 39 n. 32, 53, 216
Panagia, Davide 154, 173 n. 90, 216
Parrhasius 94–95
Pasolini, Pier Paolo 57, 120–24, 126–27, 129, 141, 144, 154, 157, 166 n. 9, 167 nn. 14, 15, 20 & 26, 168 n. 27, 171 n. 70, 217
Pasqualini, Mariano 28
Paul V 17–18, 22, 158
Pencak, William 156, 173 n. 97, 217
Perniola, Mario 7, 11, 12 n. 17, 204–06, 207 nn. 2 & 6, 217
Perry Mason 85
Peruggia, Vincenzo 71, 112 n. 9
Peterzano, Simone 18, 61
Petrarch 160 & 162
  and Petrarchan lyricism 51 & 160
Petronio, Giuseppe 42, 49, 65 n. 9, 217
Philip II, 16
Piero della Francesca 33
Piersanti, Gilda 9, 70, 73, 101, 103–09, 117 nn. 69, 70, 71, 74 & 78, 118 n. 85, 208, 217
Poe, Edgar Allan 82, 105–06, 117 nn. 70 & 76, 118 n. 85, 209

Poliziano 194
Pomarancio 22
Posner, Donald 28, 73, 120, 166 n. 3, 217
post-colonial impatience 178–79, 191, 193, 197 n. 3, 214
Postmodernism 2, 4–6, 12 n. 17, 47, 49, 65 n. 18, 67 n. 56, 204–05, 207 nn. 4–6, 7 & 10, 212–13, 20
and postmodern 3, 6, 12 n. 8, 42, 47–49, 56, 85, 108, 116 n. 60, 122, 182, 198 n. 26, 204–05, 207 nn. 9 & 10, 209, 212, 214
Preimesberger, Rudolf 45–46, 51, 65 n. 15, 200 n. 52, 217
Previtali, Giovanni 6, 11 n. 4, 12 nn. 11, 14 & 18, 198 n. 15, 214
Prose, Francine 18, 31, 36–37 n. 3, 38 n. 28, 42, 47–48, 50, 65 n. 11, 217
Pucci, Pndolfo 19
Puglisi, Catherine 17–18, 21, 25, 27, 37 n. 6, 38 nn. 20 & 21, 188, 217

queer 59, 67 n. 51, 144, 164, 166, 168 n. 32, 174, 212, 216–17

Rancière, Jacques 181, 198 n. 23, 217
Randall, Don 198 n. 16, 199 n. 28, 217
Ranieri, Polese 41, 65 n. 7, 217
Raphael 82
realism 3–5, 11, 12 nn. 14, 16 & 17, 22, 31–32, 36 n. 2, 48, 54, 59, 63–64, 66 nn. 27 & 28, 69, 71, 74, 76–77, 84, 89, 103, 107, 112 n. 7, 117 n. 75, 146, 166 n. 5, 182–83, 205, 207 nn. 6 & 11, 211, 214, 216, 218–19
and realist 4, 22, 33, 36, 90, 109, 146, 205
Renaissance 3–4, 6, 13 n. 22, 23, 32, 37 n. 4, 38 n. 28, 56, 82, 84, 144, 147, 170 n. 54, 174 n. 17, 193, 196, 211, 213, 216
Resca, Giuseppe 13 n. 21, 123, 128, 130, 167 nn. 20 & 23, 168 nn. 30 & 31, 217
Richardson, Niall 128, 130, 160, 168 n. 32, 172 nn. 71 & 87, 173 n. 93, 174 n. 103, 217
Robb, Peter 13 n. 21, 42, 47–48, 65 nn. 11 & 16, 115 n. 44, 217
Rubens 31, 34, 93–94
Ruskin, John 31

Sannesio, Giacomo 21
Saragat, Giuseppe 129, 168 n. 33
Sarris, Fotois 181, 197 n. 11, 198 n. 21, 218
Savall, Jordi 13 n. 22
Savonarola, Girolamo 194
Scrivano, Fabrizio 3, 12 n. 9, 218
Schehr, Lawrence R., 167 n. 12, 169 n. 34, 218
Schudt, Ludwig 34, 39 n. 37, 218
Sciberras, Keith 23–26, 28, 31, 37 nn. 15, 16 & 19, 218
Scorsese, Martin 1, 8, 69, 74, 76–78, 80, 101, 103, 113 n. 19, 144, 213
Scraggs, John 69–70, 74, 112 nn. 2 & 3, 218

Sedgwick, Eve 144
Sforza, Francesco I 18
see also Marchese of Caravaggio
Sforza Colonna, Fabrizio 37 n. 18, 38 n. 20
Sgarbi, Vittorio 31, 38 n. 29, 41, 65 n. 13, 188, 218
Shakespeare, William 108, 136, 147, 165, 170 nn. 45 & 51, 174 n. 117, 207 n. 8, 212, 219–20
Shoham, Shlomo Giora 13 n. 21, 65 n. 14, 174 n. 109, 218
Silverman, Kaja 150, 172 n. 81, 186, 206, 218
Siverio, Rodolfo 90
Sixtus V 17
Sohm, Philip 27, 38 nn. 25 & 26, 52, 74, 80, 82, 113 n. 6, 218
Sorice, Michele 63, 68 nn. 62 & 63, 218
Spagnoletti, Giovanni 63, 68 n. 68, 218
Spear, Richard 37 n. 10, 172 n. 72, 218
Spike, John 18–19, 37 n. 13, 83, 114 n. 34, 218
Spinoza, Benedict De 196, 201 n. 60, 218
Spring, Justin 161, 165, 174 n. 107, 218
Stein, Gertrude 161
and Alice Toklas 161
as fictional characters 161–66
Steiner, Wendy 97, 116 n. 63, 218
Steward, Samuel M. 9, 120, 160–65, 174 nn. 107, 108 & 114, 218
Stone, David 6, 23–26, 28, 31, 37 nn. 15, 16 & 19, 42, 45–46, 65 nn. 12, 13 & 16, 67 n. 44, 204, 207 n. 8, 218
Storaro, Vittorio 63, 115 n. 47
Storchi, Simona 33, 39 n. 34, 218
Storini, Monica Cristina 105, 117 n. 74, 218
Strinati, Claudio 115 n. 47, 218
Swynton, Tilda 156
Symons, Julian 71, 112 n. 6, 219

Tasso, Torquato 55–56, 67 nn. 42, 45 & 47, 219
tenebrism 20, 27, 74, 113 n. 16
Terrone, Patrice 49, 57, 66 nn. 23 & 30, 219
Terzoli, Antonietta 109, 118 n. 85, 219
Tiffin, Helen 176, 197 nn. 2 & 7, 209, 219
Tintoretto 33
Titian 18, 33
Tomasi, Mario 55–56, 67 n. 41
Tomasi di Lampedusa, Giuseppe 55–56
Tomassoni, Ranuccio 22, 25, 28, 49–50, 65 n. 13, 188, 192–93
Torlasco, Domietta 157, 173 n. 100, 219
Treherne, Matthew 56, 67 n. 47, 219
Trisegni, Filippo 21
Truman, Margaret 8, 69, 80, 82, 84–86, 89, 113–14 n. 28, 114 nn. 35 & 39, 217, 219
Turnaturi, Gabriella 96, 104, 116 n. 54, 219

Varriano, John 5, 12 n. 16, 22, 36 n. 2, 77, 114 n. 32, 165, 172 n. 72, 219
Velázquez 31, 93–94

Venturi, Adolfo 33
Venturi, Lionello 33–34, 39 nn. 33 & 35, 112 n. 15, 219
Vermeer 31, 49, 93–94
Veronese 33
Vighi, Fabio 133, 167 n. 17, 219
voyeurism 183, 185–86

Warwick, Genevieve 66 nn. 27 & 28, 120, 166 n. 5, 171 n. 58, 172 n. 72, 174 n. 104, 182, 211, 219
Wignacourt, Alof de 23–24
Wilmer, Clive 170 n. 45, 171 nn. 61 & 62, 220

Wood, Mary 113 n. 17, 115 n. 47, 220
Wright, Joseph 31
Wrobel, Arthur 74, 113 n. 18, 220
Wymar, Rowland 152, 156–57, 172 n. 83, 220

Zepetnek, Steven Tötösy De 199 n. 32, 201 nn. 54, 55 & 59, 211, 213–14, 220
Zeuxis 94
Žižek, Slavoj 139, 170 n. 53, 220
Zuccaro, Federico 22